day trips®
new england

day trips® series

day trips®
new england

third edition

getaway ideas for the local traveler

maria olia

Globe
Pequot

Guilford, Connecticut

All the information in this guidebook is subject to change. We recommend that you call ahead to obtain current information before traveling.

Globe Pequot

An imprint of Rowman & Littlefield

Day Trips is a registered trademark of Rowman & Littlefield.

Distributed by NATIONAL BOOK NETWORK

Copyright © 2017 by Rowman & Littlefield
Spot photography © iStock.com/ Sean Pavone
Maps: Trailhead Graphics Inc. © Rowman & Littlefield

British Library Cataloguing in Publication Information available

ISSN 2325-4327

ISBN 978-1-4930-3113-9
ISBN 978-1-4930-3114-7

∞™ The paper used in this publication meets the minimum requirements of American National Standard for Information Sciences—Permanence of Paper for Printed Library Materials, ANSI/NISO Z39.48-1992.

Printed in the United States of America

contents

introduction xi
using this guide xiv

boston

day trip 01
the hub of new england 3
boston, ma. 3

day trip 02
quirky intellectualism 27
cambridge, ma. 27

day trip 03
a tale of two revolutions 36
lexington, ma 36
concord, ma. 41
lowell, ma. 45

day trip 04
the dark arts & maritime
   heritage 49
salem, ma 49
gloucester, ma 54
ipswich, ma 58

day trip 05
presidents, pilgrims & whales 62
quincy, ma. 62
plymouth, ma. 65
new bedford, ma 68

day trip 06
the heart of the
   commonwealth 71
worcester, ma 71
sturbridge, ma 75

cape cod

day trip 07
quintessential new england
   summer. 80
hyannis, ma 80

day trip 08
family vacation playground 84
brewster, ma 84
orleans, ma 88
chatham, ma 90

day trip 09
ye old cape cod. 95
sandwich, ma. 95
falmouth, ma 98

day trip 10
beautiful beaches 101
eastham, ma 101
wellfleet, ma. 104
provincetown, ma. 105

day trip 11
the vineyard 110
martha's vineyard, ma 110

day trip 12

romance of the sea 116

nantucket, ma 116

providence

day trip 13

the creative capital 125

providence, ri 125

day trip 14

legendary seaside mansions 134

newport, ri 134

day trip 15

island serenity 143

block island, ri 143

new haven

day trip 16

the elm city 151

new haven, ct. 151

day trip 17

authors' homes, art & roses 158

hartford, ct 158

day trip 18

along the river & shore 164

madison, ct 164

essex, ct. 167

old lyme, ct 169

mystic, ct 170

day trip 19

so very town & country 175

woodbury, ct 175

litchfield, ct. 178

kent, ct. 180

burlington

day trip 20

made--in--vermont 185

burlington, vt 185

day trip 21

down on the farm 190

shelburne, vt. 190

middlebury, vt. 193

day trip 22

powered by ice cream—
  from foothills to
    mountain peaks 195

waterbury, vt 195

montpelier, vt 198

stowe, vt 199

day trip 23

mountain hamlets 203

norwich, vt 203

quechee, vt 206

woodstock, vt. 207

killington, vt 209

manchester

day trip 24

the queen city 213

manchester, nh 213

day trip 25

historically charming & hip. 216

portsmouth, nh. 216

day trip 26

lakeside pleasures 222

wolfeboro, nh. 222

meredith, nh. 225

weirs beach, nh 227

portland

day trip 27

maine's cultural capital. 233

portland, me. 233

day trip 28

coastal maine quaint. 238

the kennebunks, me. 238

wells, me 243

ogunquit, me 244

the yorks, me. 246

day trip 29

the craggy coast 250

freeport, me 250

bath, me. 253

rockland, me 254

camden, me. 256

day trip 30

moose in the woods 258

poland spring, me 258

bethel, me 261

sebago lake, me. 262

historic trips

day trip 31

colonial history 266

boston, ma. 266

cambridge, ma. 268

lexington, ma 269

concord, ma. 271

deerfield, ma 272

day trip 32

**southern new england
    colonial trail** 273

quincy, ma. 273

providence, ri 274

newport, ri 276

day trip 33

**northern new england
    colonial trail** 278

salem, ma 278

exeter, nh. 281

portsmouth, nh. 282

food & drink

day trip 34

new england food tour 286

providence, ri 286

boston, ma. 289

burlington, vt 291

day trip 35

new england seafood trail 294

chatham, ma 294

boston, ma. 295

mid--coast maine. 296

day trip 36

**new hampshire & massachusetts
    wine trail**. 298

lee, nh 298

south hampton, nh. 299

bolton, ma 299

new marlborough, ma 300

richmond, ma. 301

day trip 37

southern new england
   wine tour 302
north dartmouth, ma 302
westport, ma 303
little compton, ri 303
portsmouth, ri. 305
middletown, ri. 305

day trip 38

litchfield hills wine tour 306
brookfield, ct 306
new preston, ct 307
litchfield, ct 308

day trip 39

vermont brewery tour 309
windsor, vt 309
bridgewater corners, vt. 310
burlington, vt 310
morrisville, vt. 311

day trip 40

maine brewery tour 312
kennebunkport, me 312
portland, me. 313
bar harbor, me 314

scenic & seasonal

day trip 41

cape cod lighthouse tour 316
falmouth, ma 316
chatham, ma 317
nauset beach, ma 318
truro, ma 319
provincetown, ma. 319

day trip 42

maine lighthouse tour 320
york, me. 320
cape elizabeth, me 321
bath, me. 322
boothbay harbor, me 322
bristol, me 323
rockland, me 323

day trip 43

christmas in new england 325
boston, ma. 325
newport, ri 327
stowe, vt 328

day trip 44

the mohawk trail 330
deerfield, ma 330
shelburne falls, ma 332
north adams, ma 334

day trip 45

unspoiled southern vermont 337
brattleboro, vt. 337
grafton, vt. 340
weston, vt 341
manchester, vt 342

day trip 46

down east nature walks
   & scenic drives 347
bar harbor, me. 347
acadia national park 351

day trip 47

fall foliage & mountain
   magnificence 354
north conway, nh 354
mount washington 358
bretton woods, nh 359
franconia, nh 360

day trip 48

trains, trains, trains 363

mid--coast maine 363

white mountains 364

essex, ct. 365

hyannis, ma 366

arts & culture

day trip 49

the berkshire hills are alive

   with music, dance & art 368

lenox, ma 368

stockbridge, ma 372

pittsfield, ma. 374

williamstown, ma 375

day trip 50

new england family fun 377

boston, ma. 377

cape cod, ma. 381

white mountains 382

appendix:

   festivals & celebrations 384

index 392

about the author

Maria Olia has called Massachusetts her home for the past three decades. She is a travel guidebook and freelance writer whose work has appeared in the *Boston Globe, Mobil Travel,* and *Working Mother* magazine, among many other publications. She is also the author of *Discovering Vintage Boston* and *New England's Colonial Inns & Taverns* (Globe Pequot). She lives in Newton, Massachusetts, with her husband and four children. When she isn't researching her next travel writing project, she spends her time frequenting her favorite Boston haunts. Catch up with Maria on her website mariaolia.com.

acknowledgments

Many thanks to my husband, Masoud, for your love and support. Thanks also to my children, Bijan, Kian, Cameron, and Leda—true New Englanders all—for inspiring me to do my best. Finally, with gratitude to my parents: my mother, Josephine Dascanio, Charlestown born and raised, who first brought me to Boston; and to my father, Robert Dascanio, who gave me the gift of travel.

introduction

The six-state New England region is an all-season vacation destination that offers an unrivaled landscape of forested mountain byways, wind-swept beaches, and sophisticated cities. Iconic New England scenes really do exist here, including covered bridges, blazing fall foliage, lighthouses perched above a granite shore, peaceful village greens, and cobblestone-paved streets.

New England's history is America's history. From the arrival of the Pilgrims to the American Revolution to the Industrial Revolution, New England is the country's historic heart—and said to be the only true province in America.

You'll find that New Englanders have a sense of history and pride (some would even say self-importance) in their roots. And while the region is viewed as a Democratic stronghold, New Englanders are actually more diverse than the "looney liberal" stereotype. Vermont and New Hampshire both have a tradition of principled independence. While even in overwhelmingly left-leaning Massachusetts, four of the last five elected governors have been Republican.

New Englanders also share an unwavering love of their professional sports teams—the Red Sox, Patriots, Celtics and Bruins. Surely, these are the glory years for New England sports fans. Since the start of the 21st century, the city has enjoyed an unprecedented 10 professional sports championships. Most recently, the Patriot's comeback win over Atlanta in the 2017 Superbowl was one for the ages—and vindication after Tom Brady's 4-game suspension for Deflate-gate. The year 2017 marks a new era for Boston sports. With the retirement of David Ortiz, everyone's asking how will the Red Sox fill the void?

There is both breathtaking beauty and tremendous variety in this corner of the US to explore. Since the earliest days of the colonies, events in **Massachusetts** have greatly influenced American history. From the Pilgrims' landing at Plymouth to Boston's role as the center for opposition to British rule, which led to the Revolutionary War, from Concord's literary greats like Emerson, Thoreau and Hawthorne, to those who crusaded for abolition and suffrage in the 18th century and more recently pioneering same-sex marriage and universal healthcare, Massachusetts has a historical and cultural importance that far surpasses its relative size. Boston is New England's largest city, steeped in both rich history and modern-day appeal. With its colonial-era architecture, world-renowned cultural and academic institutions, surprisingly chic hotels, and a locavore dining scene that is constantly evolving with restaurants of seemingly every ethnic and gastronomic stripe, Boston is an essential stop to any visit to the region. Within an easy drive of the city are several other historic towns—nearby Concord and Lexington, Salem to the north, and Plymouth to the south. In the far western part of the state, natural beauty and the arts converge in the Berkshires, a destination known for its summer festivals including Tanglewood, the summer home of the Boston Symphony.

Head south to **Cape Cod** where 300 miles of shoreline enchants with some of the best swimming beaches in New England including the seemingly endless sands and spectacular dunes of the Cape Cod National Seashore. At the very tip of the Cape, Provincetown, once a sleepy Portuguese fishing village, is a gay extravaganza where the people-watching on Commercial Street is always first class. Just a short ferry ride off the mainland, the islands of Martha's Vineyard and Nantucket are known for great natural beauty—and as enclaves for the very wealthy.

Rhode Island may be the country's smallest state, but it more than makes up for it with 400 miles of shoreline—attributable to the state's large bay, many harbors and some 30 islands. It's no small wonder that Rhode Island is known as the "Ocean State." Providence has both historic colonial charm and a college town's modern and creative spirit. In Newport see the glitzy Gilded Age mansions, then find quiet from the untamed seascape of Block Island's towering bluffs and grassy moors.

Away from the urban charms of New Haven and Hartford you'll find plenty of tranquil pockets in **Connecticut**. There are award-winning vineyards as well as antiquing in the Litchfield Hills, swimming along the quiet beaches of Long Island Sound, and picturesque small river and shoreline towns along the lower Connecticut River.

Cross into **Vermont** and northern New England. Vermont is named for the Green Mountains, *vert* (green) and *mont* (mountain), which form the heart of the state, running from north to south. Seasonal pursuits include some of the finest skiing in the east at Stowe, the discovery of spring wildflowers on the bare forest floor, and a drive along quiet country roads that lead to woods that in autumn erupt in a blaze of magnificent foliage.

To the east, **New Hampshire** is both authentic and down-to-earth. Along the Merrimack River, scrappy Manchester is the state's largest city and an ideal base from which to explore the rest of the state. Portsmouth is both historic and newly hip with a growing restaurant and gallery scene and is the jewel of the state's tiny 18-mile seacoast. In the center of the state, Lake Winnipesaukee boasts endless water fun. While the woods and waterfalls of the White Mountains challenge the intrepid with hiking, mountain biking, and rock climbing, there's also terrific skiing in the shadow of the cloud-piercing summit of Mount Washington.

Meander up to **Maine,** the country's most northeastern state. Maine's license plate motto is "Vacationland" for a reason. With a population of just over 65,000, once-sleepy Portland is garnering big-city buzz for its chefs, artists, and musicians. Summer visitors especially flock to mid-coast Maine, where life really is slower, to enjoy the state's famed rocky 3,500-mile coastline dotted with lighthouses and tranquil fishing villages. Deeper inland, find a vast wilderness of pine forest, rugged mountains, and remote lakes that lure skiers, hikers, boaters, and anglers to explore. And of course, one of the sea's greatest delicacies—Maine lobster—is without equal; a vacation spent eating lobster at least once a day is reason enough to visit.

New England is an endlessly fascinating region of cultural hot spots, unspoiled natural beauty, and some of America's most important historical monuments.

Whether you visit Connecticut or Maine, or somewhere—or everywhere—in between, *Day Trips New England* will guide you to discover the best that the region has to offer. Let's look around.

using this guide

This guide is organized around seven areas that include each of the New England states— Massachusetts, Rhode Island, Connecticut, Vermont, New Hampshire, and Maine—along with Cape Cod. Each destination focuses on attractions and activities, shopping, dining, and hotel choices for a main city that can serve as a home base for you to explore the rest of the area. These cities are:

Boston, MA

Hyannis, MA

Providence, RI

New Haven, CT

Burlington, VT

Manchester, NH

Portland, ME

Day trips, along with directions, distances, and a map, are then suggested for each city. Day trips range from excursions to nearby towns and villages to trips further afield to the countryside and coast. For most day trips you can be back to your hotel in time for dinner and the evening news. But if you choose to make an overnight of a day trip, we've provided options for that, too, with suggestions for places to eat and sleep.

We've also included 20 themed itineraries split into the following categories:

Historic Trips: Explore New England's rich colonial and revolutionary history with these three trips that span Massachusetts, Rhode Island, and New Hampshire.

Food & Drink: From lobster rolls along the shoreline to farm-to-table dining in beautiful Vermont, these trips will satisfy any food lover's appetite. Pair your meal with a winery or brewery tour and drink up some of New England's best homegrown beverages.

Scenic & Seasonal: You can experience Christmas in New England, savor the region's famous fall foliage, go lighthouse-hopping along the coast, travel to the summit of Mount Washington, and much more with these outdoor-centric trips.

Arts & Culture: Go museum-hopping in the Berkshires, check out a Cape Cod League baseball game, or spend the day at the amusement park—these trips feature some quintessential New England art attractions and fun activities for the whole family.

You can follow the themed itineraries on their own or mix things up entirely and just include those elements that fit your interests and schedule. Together, the main city and themed day trip itineraries allow you to customize your New England vacation, depending on the way that you want to travel.

hours of operation, prices & credit cards

Since hours of operation, attraction prices, and other facts are always subject to change, remember to confirm ahead before making final travel plans. You can assume all establishments listed accept major credit cards unless otherwise noted. If you have any questions, contact the establishment for specifics.

pricing key

accommodations

The price codes are for a double room per night during the peak-price period. Peak periods are generally June through October throughout the entire region, and from Christmas through President's week in the ski mountains. Room prices do not include state or local sales taxes or any other lodging fees that may be included in your final bill.

$	less than $150
$$	$151 to $300
$$$	$301 to $500
$$$$	more than $500

restaurants

The price code reflects an estimate of the average price of dinner entrees for two (excluding drinks, appetizers, tax, and tip) and is a benchmark only. Lunch and breakfast are usually 25–30 percent less.

$	less than $25
$$	$25 to $50
$$$	$51 to $100
$$$$	more than $100

driving tips

This corner of the country encompasses six states in a relatively small area. Boston is geographically the region's hub, with both Providence and Manchester an hour away, Portland and Hartford can each be reached in just 2 hours, and Montpelier is within a 4-hour drive.

No matter where you travel, it's always a good idea to plan out your route in advance. The itinerary maps in this guide are representative of the area; all distances are approximate. To get the most out of your travels, use GPS (from a stand-alone device or your smart phone) along with a conventional map so you won't be led astray.

Rotaries, or traffic circles, are common in New England and can confound even local drivers. The rules are simple, though: Vehicles already in the rotary have the right of way; those entering must yield. If you miss your exit, just go around the rotary again (and again, if necessary).

Whether through the winding roads of the Green Mountains or along the rocky shores of Penobscot Bay, most of New England is best explored by car. As well, outside of Boston, public transportation options in New England are fairly limited.

Boston is the exception; because of a lack of parking and heavy traffic, driving is not a good option. In Boston you will want to confine your driving to the bare minimum, which means arriving and parking. Besides, Boston is compact, and it's easy to get around by walking or by taking the subway, known as the T.

New England's winter weather varies widely across the region, but it deserves special mention. Vermont, New Hampshire, and Maine are especially well known for brutal weather conditions: heavy snow, extreme cold, and blizzard conditions. Winter driving can challenge even native New Englanders. In general, when there is snow and ice, slow down and keep a greater distance between you and the car ahead. And if it's not safe to travel, don't.

New England is a true four-season tourist destination, but traffic is heaviest from June through October throughout the entire region, and is also notably heavy in ski country from mid-December through late February.

Roads are well maintained, although some rural and mountain roads test even seasoned drivers—they are both narrow and winding. In comparison with other regions of the country, you will find that New England road crews know how to get rid of snow, and they have the equipment to move it fast!

Northern New England is moose country. Heed those "moose crossing" signs, especially at dusk. A collision with a 1,000-pound moose can be fatal.

highway designations

Interstates are prefaced by "I" and are generally multilane divided highways. New England is crossed by six interstates. I-95 links five of the New England states (the exception is Vermont) connecting with the New York metropolitan area. I-90 and I-84 come in from the west. I-91 links New Haven, Hartford, Springfield, and Vermont, while I-89 connects Burlington, Vermont, with Concord, New Hampshire. I-93 cuts through Boston, connecting the city with New Hampshire and the Northeast Kingdom of Vermont.

US highways are two- and three-lane undivided roads and prefaced by "US." For instance, US 1 links Connecticut, Rhode Island, Massachusetts, New Hampshire, and Maine.

State highways are paved and divided and are prefaced by the state's two-letter postal abbreviation. For example, a well-known New England route is New Hampshire's NH 112, also known as the Kancamagus Highway, and stretches 35 miles from Conway to Lincoln in the White Mountains.

where to get more information

Day Trips New England attempts to cover a variety of bases and interests, but those looking for additional material can contact the following agencies by phone, mail, or on the Web. Regarding the latter, when checking out the various destinations, be aware that online reviews may be contradictory and conflicting. Everyone's experience can be different, and the Web allows for a forum for these diverse opinions. Many of the areas have chain hotels and restaurants that are generally not included in the listings in each chapter. Within each chapter we provide contact information for chambers of commerce and/or convention and visitor bureaus, which are often valuable sources for information. Here are some additional general resources.

Discover New England (the region's international tourism representative)
100 International Dr.
Portsmouth, NH 03801
(603) 766-0606
discovernewengland.org

Connecticut Commission on Culture & Tourism
1 Constitution Plaza
Hartford, CT 06103
(860) 256-2800
ctvisit.com

Maine Office of Tourism
#59 State House Station
Augusta, ME 04333
(888) 624-6345
visitmaine.com

Massachusetts Office of Travel & Tourism
10 Park Plaza, Ste. 4510
Boston, MA 02116
(617) 973-8500 or (800) 227-MASS
massvacation.com

New Hampshire Division of Travel & Tourism
172 Pembroke Rd.
Concord, NH 03302
(603) 271-2665
visitnh.gov

Rhode Island Tourism Division
315 Iron Horse Way, Ste. 101
Providence, RI 02908
(800) 556-2484
visitrhodeisland.com

Vermont Department of Tourism & Marketing
National Life Building, 6th Floor
Montpelier, VT 05620
(802) 828-3237 or (800) VERMONT
vermontvacation.com

boston

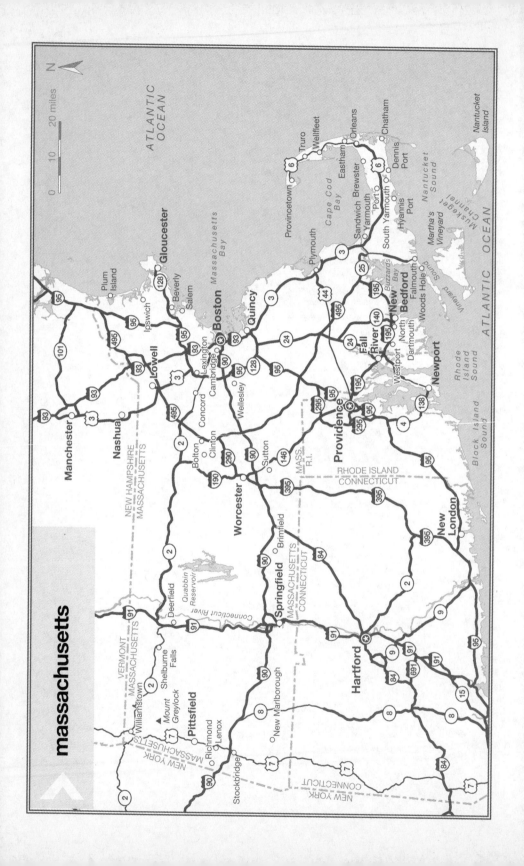

day trip 01

boston

the hub of new england:
boston, ma

boston, ma

Prim, white steepled churches, cobblestone streets, and lots of colonial-era redbrick buildings. The Puritans founded Boston in 1630. They discovered a deep harbor, and by the mid-1700s shipping was Boston's lifeblood, helping to make it the largest and one of the most prosperous cities in America.

Because of its traditional feel, Boston is often described as a European-like city, even as it was the first American settlement to urge the other colonies to fight for independence from the British.

But it wasn't until the 1800s that Boston's modern city began to take shape. Marshland was reclaimed, and landfill was used to expand the city and create the Back Bay. Today, those same Victorian-era brownstones house block after block of world-class retail shops, trendy art galleries, and chic cafes. It is this ability to repurpose its past that has allowed Boston to change with the times. It helps, too, that Boston has always had a love affair with learning and is home to a lively student population that attend the area's 50 colleges and universities.

But there is always that ever-present sense of history when you visit Boston. The shrines of America's past are all around, from the simple circle of stones that mark the location of the Boston Massacre, to the home of Paul Revere, to the fabled navy war frigate the USS *Constitution*. But there are also cutting-edge skyscrapers and big-city buzz,

3

with a jam-packed cultural calendar of music, theater, and art shows and a chef-driven food scene that has increasingly (thankfully) embraced the use of fresh, sustainable New England ingredients—all packed into a small and eminently walkable city.

To experience the best of what is new in the city, head to the Seaport District, Boston's "it" neighborhood. Until recently, this was an overlooked stretch of muddy wasteland and abandoned Boston Harbor warehouses. Now office buildings flourish—and the world head-quarters of General Electric will relocate here in 2018. Already the area is teeming with hotels and restaurants that appeal to a creative-minded and tech-savvy clientele.

getting there

Boston is both literally and figuratively "the hub." Oliver Wendell Holmes said as much in 1858 when he referred to the Massachusetts State House as the "hub of the solar system." A bit of satire, to be sure, but Boston is New England's largest city, its transportation center, and the gateway to the six-state region.

All roads in New England (at least the big ones) do lead to Boston. From the west, the Massachusetts Turnpike (I-90) runs directly into the city. From the south, take I-95 North to I-93 North to downtown. From Vermont and points northwest, take I-93 South to downtown. From Maine and points northeast, take I-95 South to I-93 South to downtown.

where to go

The Greater Boston Convention and Visitors Bureau. Boston Common, 139 Tremont St.; the Shops at the Prudential Center, 100 Boylston St.; (617) 536-4100 or (888) 733-2678; bostonusa.com. Boston has two visitor centers. The visitor center on Boston Common is located in a kiosk next to the Park Street subway or T station. There is also a visitor information desk in the mall at the Prudential Center. Both locations are fully staffed and have racks of Boston maps and brochures. They also have information about Massachusetts as well as helpful resources specific for international travelers. Open daily 9 a.m. to 5 p.m.

The Boston Children's Museum. 308 Congress St., Waterfront; (617) 426-6500; boston childrensmuseum.org. The Boston Children's Museum is an awesome place for young children and their families. The fun begins in the lobby: Kids can't get enough of the 3-story New Balance Climb structure. Next, head over to the exhibit halls where kids can investigate bubbles at Science Playground, explore race and ethnicity issues at Boston Black, and learn about fitness on the very cool light-box dance floor at Kid Power. Need a break? The giant Hood Milk Bottle outside the museum entrance sells hot dogs, ice cream and snacks during the warm weather months. Open Sun through Thurs 10 a.m. to 5 p.m., Fri 10 a.m. to 9 p.m., Sat 10 a.m. to 5 p.m. Admission $16 per person, ages 12 months and under free. Admission Fri 5 to 9 p.m. is $1 per person.

Boston Harbor Islands National Park. Long Wharf, Waterfront; (617) 223-8666; boston harborislands.org, bostonbestcruises.com. Hop on a Harbor Express ferry and you can experience an island getaway just 30 minutes from downtown Boston. There are sandy beaches, nature trails, and historic sites to discover. Georges Island features historic Fort Warren, a Civil War–era prison that is perfect for exploring. Walk along the ramparts, play a game of Frisbee on the parade grounds, and check out the dark (and very spooky) labyrinth-like corridors. Take a ranger-led tour and stroll the beach, and visit the small museum in the visitor center. Spectacle Island offers beaches and 5 miles of walking trails. Both Georges and Spectacle Islands have seasonal cafes, which sell grab-and-go lunch boxes, drinks, ice cream, and other summertime favorites.

Georges Island and Spectacle Island ferry service runs May through Oct; check website for departure times. Ferry tickets: $17 adults, $12 seniors, $10 children ages 4 to 11, free under age 4. The inter-island shuttle ferry between Georges Island and Lovell's and Spectacle Island is free.

Boston Public Library. 700 Boylston St., Back Bay; (617) 536-5400; bpl.org. Boston is a bookish city, and the Boston Public Library is a revered cultural institution. Although the Italianate Renaissance Revival building designed by McKim, Mead, and White dates from 1895, the Boston Public Library was established much earlier—in 1848—making it the country's first publicly supported municipal library.

Among the architectural treasures are the great bronze doors by Daniel Chester French and gorgeous ceiling murals depicting Judaism and Christianity by John Singer Sargent. For bibliophiles, the Bates Reading Room is a sight to behold, with a barrel-vaulted ceiling, soaring windows, and rows of timeworn wood tables illuminated by green library lamps. Enjoy the library's beautiful inner courtyard and arcade—it's one of the city's best-kept secrets and a wonderful place to sit and read. Tucked inside the library are not one, but three places to eat. The Map Room Cafe (open Mon through Sat 9 a.m. to 5 p.m.) offers a spot to recharge with coffee, muffins, sandwiches, and salads. The Courtyard (open Mon through Sat 11:30 a.m. to 3:30 p.m.) is charmingly intimate and proffers one of the city's best afternoon teas. The Boston Public Library has partnered with Boston's National Public Radio Station, WGBH, to open the Newsfeed Café (617-357-7333; open Mon through Thurs 9 a.m. to 9 p.m., Fri and Sat 9 a.m. to 5 p.m., Sun 1 p.m. to 5 p.m.), a satellite station that also offers gourmet coffee, soup, salads and sandwiches to nourish both the bodies and minds of visitors and scholars. Brilliant!

Library open Mon through Thurs 9 a.m. to 9 p.m., Fri and Sat 9 a.m. to 5 p.m., Sun 1 to 5 p.m. from mid-Oct through May; closed Sun June through mid-Oct. You can explore the library on your own or check the website for guided-tour times. Free.

Boston Symphony Hall. 301 Massachusetts Ave., Back Bay; (617) 262-1492; bso .org. Home to both the Boston Symphony and the Boston Pops, attending a concert at Boston Symphony Hall is a special experience. From October through April, the Boston Symphony presents a full concert season of classical music, often with a world-renowned guest artist or conductor. The city has recently welcomed Andris Nelsons, the young (just 38) Latvian conductor, as the BSO's new music director—ushering in a new era for the symphony and its audiences. In May and June, the Boston Pops, led by maestro Keith Lockhart, plays a mix of American musical show tunes, jazz standards, movie themes, light classical, and even contemporary music. In December, Holiday Pops concerts are perennially popular.

Huntington Theatre Company. 264 Huntington Ave., Back Bay; (617) 266-0800; hun tingtontheatre.org. The Huntington Theatre is Boston's most prominent resident theater company, the performance season runs from September through May and typically features a dynamic mix of classic dramas, acclaimed comedies, world premieres, and on occasion a musical.

Edward M. Kennedy Institute for the United State Senate. 210 Morrissey Blvd.; Dorchester; (617) 740-7000; emkinstitute.org. Boston's newest museum is dedicated to the late Edward (Ted) Kennedy. It is not hyperbole to suggest that every constituent in every city and town of the Commonwealth was helped in some way over the course of Kennedy's nearly 50-year career as the US Senator from Massachusetts. The centerpiece attraction of the museum is a full-scale replica of the Senate chamber. Visitors can participate in a simulation of Senate proceedings: attend hearings, debate the issues and vote on legislation. The institute also hopes to inspire the next generation of civic leaders by encouraging visitors to add their own promise of community service to the pledge wall. The museum is adjacent to the John F. Kennedy Library & Musuem and there is an admission discount if you visit both. Open Tues through Sun 10 a.m. to 5 p.m. Admission $16 for adults, $14 for seniors and students, $8 children for ages 6 to 17, and free for ages 5 and under.

Fenway Park. 4 Yawkey Way, Fenway; (617) 226-6666; redsox.mlb.com. Baseball history is thick here. To understand New Englanders, you must experience Fenway Park, home to the beloved Boston Red Sox. Fenway is the smallest (its seating capacity is just under 34,000) and oldest baseball stadium in the major leagues. Its first professional game took place on April 20, 1912, against the New York Highlanders, the precursor to the New York Yankees.

The park has several endearing quirks. There's the fabled 37-foot Green Monster left-field wall, a hand-operated scoreboard, and really uncomfortable seats—but Sox fans would not have it any other way. Regardless of the standings, Red Sox Nation is fiercely and unwaveringly loyal—scoring tickets can be tough. Your best bet to catch the Sox in action may be to line up for game-day tickets. A limited number of tickets—often standing room,

the fenway park sound track

Boston is a city of tradition and the songs played at Fenway Park are a huge part of the Fenway experience.

- *"Sweet Caroline." Played in the middle of the eighth inning since 2002, Neil Diamond's 1967 feel-good ditty is the tune most associated with Fenway. Forget the words? The lyrics are always projected on the big screen—hand motions optional.*

- *"Dirty Water." Red Sox fans really love their "Dirty Water." Referring to Boston's once notoriously polluted Charles River, the Standell's 1967 hit and its catchy refrain.*

- *"Tessie." The Red Sox second victory song is also a pub favorite. The Red Sox broke an 86-year World Series drought in 2004, the same year that local Irish punk band the Drop Kick Murphys recorded a modernized version of an old-timey 1902 Broadway tune with new lyrics telling the story of the Boston Royal Rooters fan club and the Red Sox 1903 World Series win. Coincidence? Not likely.*

- *"Joy to the World." Three Dog Night's version is the final song in Boston's victory trilogy with fans belting out "Jeremiah was a bullfrog, was a good friend of mine" and soaking in the win.*

obstructed view, or bleacher seats—are sold 2 hours before game time at Gate E, with a limit of one ticket per customer.

If you come up empty-handed for tickets or are visiting during the off-season, take a guided tour of Fenway. During the baseball season tours are offered on the hour daily from 9 a.m. to 4 p.m. (on home-game days, the last tour leaves 3.5 hours before game start). Off-season tours are offered daily Nov through early Apr from 10 a.m. to 5 p.m. Admission $20 adults, $17 military, $14 ages 3 to 15, children 2 and under are free.

The Franklin Park Zoo. 1 Franklin Park Zoo, Dorchester; (617) 541-LIONS; zoonew england.org. A just-the-right-size city zoo for kids with more than 200 species of animals. At the indoor, glass-enclosed Tropical Forest exhibit, the zoo's 7 lowland gorillas are real crowd-pleasers. And at Kalahari Kingdom, come face-to-face with an African lion; because of the clever placement of a jeep in the exhibit, you will almost feel part of the lion's world. Open Apr through Sep Mon through Fri 10 a.m. to 5 p.m.; Sat and Sun 10 a.m. to 6 p.m.,

Oct through Mar daily 10 a.m. to 4 p.m. Admission $19.95 adults, $16.95 seniors, $13.95 ages 2 to 12, free for children under age 2.

Freedom Trail. Follow the 2.5-mile redbrick (sometimes it's red-painted) line that wends its way through downtown, the North End, and Charlestown and be inspired by Boston's revolutionary past. The Freedom Trail links 16 historic sites that tell the story of America's struggle for independence.

The Freedom Trail is mostly free. Only three sites—the Old State House, the Old South Meeting House, and the Paul Revere House—charge a small admission fee.

The Freedom Trail was designed to be self-guided. The usual starting point is the visitor center on Boston Common, where you can pick up a free Freedom Trail map and/or rent an audio tour. Another high-tech option? Download the MP3 file from the **Freedom Trail Foundation**'s website (thefreedomtrail.org) onto your smart phone.

It takes a full day to complete the entire route. But if you are short on time, consider taking a guided Freedom Trail tour. The National Park Service offers a popular free hour-long guided walking tour (check website for times) that leaves from the **National Park Visitor Center** (Faneuil Hall, 1st floor; 617-242-5642; nps.gov/bost/index.htm). The Freedom Trail Foundation's Walk into History tour departs (check website for times) from the **Boston Common Visitor Center** (617-357-8300; thefreedomtrail.org) and is led by invariably enthusiastic guides in 18th-century costumes.

Follow the sites in order, and you will find that the restaurants and eateries at Quincy Market make a logical place to stop for lunch. Then press onward to Charlestown to check out the USS *Constitution.* To get there, you can walk across the Charlestown Bridge or better yet, take the **Inner Harbor Ferry** (mbta.com; $3.50 per person) from Long Wharf for a 10-minute cruise across the harbor to the Charlestown Navy Yard. This is a case where getting there really is half the fun!

Of course, if you're going to follow in the footsteps of our Founding Fathers, the best way to do the Freedom Trail is to walk it. But no one says you have to hike the entire route, and it's perfectly OK to see just some of the sites. Here is a rundown of the Freedom Trail highlights to help you choose what sites are of most interest to you.

> **Boston Common.** Bordered by Park, Tremont, Beacon, and Charles Streets, Downtown. Dating from 1634 and practically as old as Boston itself, the Boston Common has been in constant use ever since as a cow pasture, a place for public hangings, and the site of the British encampment during the Siege of Boston in 1775. Today, the Boston Common is mostly used for recreation and features walking paths among the towering trees, open ball fields, and lots of benches for people and pigeon watchers. Your first stop should be the visitor center on the Tremont Street side of the park to pick up a Freedom Trail map. On the Beacon Street side of the Common, across from the Massachusetts State House, is an impressive Augustus Saint-Gaudens bronze bas-relief sculpture, the Robert Gould Shaw and 54th Massachusetts Regiment

Memorial, which pays homage to the only Union Civil War unit made entirely of free African-American troops. Frog Pond is another Boston Common delight, which features a children's wading pool during the summer months, a refrigerated ice rink during the winter, and a carousel in the spring and fall.

Massachusetts State House. Corner of Beacon and Park Streets, Downtown; (617) 727-3676; malegislature.gov. The golden dome of the Massachusetts capitol building dominates the Boston skyline. Designed by Charles Bulfinch in 1798, it is a wonderful example of Federal-style architecture. The dome is copper and covered with gold leaf. The original dome was sheathed with copper from Paul Revere's foundry. Tours offered Mon through Fri, 10 a.m. to 3:30 p.m. Free.

Park Street Church. 1 Park St., Downtown; parkstreet.org. Pretty Park Street Church is an active Congregational Church, which was founded in 1809 and is notable for its many "firsts." America's oldest continuously performing professional arts organization, the Handel & Haydn Society, was founded here in 1815; abolitionist William Lloyd Garrison's first major public antislavery speech took place here in 1829, and Samuel Smith's hymn "America" (also known as "My Country 'Tis of Thee") was first sung by the children's choir on the steps of the church in 1831.

Granary Burying Ground. Park and Tremont Streets, Downtown. Established in 1660, there are lots of famous residents here. Among them are Paul Revere, the five victims of the Boston Massacre, Benjamin Franklin's parents, and three signers of the Declaration of Independence—John Hancock, Samuel Adams, and Robert Treat Paine. There are some fine examples of colonial funerary art as well—with some seriously scary headstones carved of skulls and crossbones, flying skeletons, and winged cherub heads. Open daily 9 a.m. to 5 p.m.

King's Chapel. School and Park Streets, Downtown; kings-chapel.org. Seen as a symbol of British rule in America, the austere granite building dates from 1749 and was designed by Newport architect Peter Harrison to replace the modest wooden Anglican chapel originally on the site. Its Loyalist parishioners were run out of town after the Revolutionary War, and by the 1780s it had become the country's first Unitarian church.

King's Chapel Burying Ground. Tremont Street, Downtown. Adjacent to King's Chapel, this is Boston's oldest cemetery, dating from 1630. William Dawes, the other "midnight rider" who rode with Paul Revere to warn of the advancing British troops, is buried here. Look for the grave of Elizabeth Pain, whose marker (note the large letter *A*) is said to have inspired the final paragraph of Nathanial Hawthorne's novel *The Scarlet Letter,* in which he describes the grave of the character Hester Prynne. Open daily 9 a.m. to 5 p.m.

Benjamin Franklin and Boston Latin. 45 School St., Downtown. Philadelphia may claim Benjamin Franklin as their most famous resident, but he was Boston born and bred. The colorful sidewalk mosaic marks the original site of Boston Latin, which was the first public school in America, established by the Puritans in 1635. Franklin attended Boston Latin for a short time—but did not graduate—making him the school's most famous dropout.

Old Corner Bookstore. 285 Washington St., Downtown. Dating from 1712, and originally an apothecary, this brick gambrel building is one of Boston's oldest. During the early to mid-1800s, it was the site of Ticknor and Fields, the publishing house that counted among its authors Nathaniel Hawthorne, Ralph Waldo Emerson, Henry David Thoreau, Louisa May Alcott, and Harriet Beecher Stowe. Today, the Old Corner Bookstore is occupied—by a Chipotle.

Old State House. 206 Washington St., Downtown; (617) 720-1713; bostonhistory .org. Adorned with a gilded lion and the unicorn, symbols of the British monarchy, this graceful 1713 brick building was built as the seat of the colonial government. It was here in 1761 that James Otis waged an impassioned argument against the British Writs of Assistance (general search warrants). John Adams later said of Otis's speech, "then and there the child independence was born." It was from this balcony, on July 18, 1776, that the Declaration of Independence was first read to the people of Boston, and it has been read to the people from this balcony every Fourth of July since. Today the Old State House is home to the Bostonian Society Museum. Open daily 9 a.m. to 5 p.m. Admission $10 adults, $8.50 seniors and students, free ages 18 and under.

Site of the Boston Massacre. At the intersection of State, Devonshire, and Court Streets, Downtown. The small circle of granite cobblestones in front of the Old State House marks the place of what was later known as the Boston Massacre. On March 5, 1770, after two years of occupation, an angry mob of Boston colonists taunted a group of British soldiers, who fired into the crowd, resulting in five civilian deaths.

Old South Meeting House. 310 Washington St., Downtown; oldsouthmeetinghouse .org. The voices of protest have always spoken loudly here. In colonial times, this 1729 Congregational Church was Boston's largest meeting space and was often used for public assemblies. In 1773, Samuel Adams's speech led to one of the Revolution's most storied moments: the Boston Tea Party and the dumping of 342 chests of tea into Boston Harbor. Open Apr through Oct 9:30 a.m. to 5 p.m.; Nov through Mar 10 a.m. to 4 p.m. Admission $6 adults, $5 seniors and students, $1 children ages 6 to 18, free ages 6 and under.

Faneuil Hall. Congress and North Streets, Downtown; (617) 242-5675; nps.gov/ bost. A gift to the city from wealthy colonial merchant Peter Faneuil, the building dates from 1742 and was to be used as both a meeting hall and a marketplace. Today,

Faneuil Hall still serves the very same function—there is shopping on the first floor, and the upper Great Hall is still used for political rallies. Known as the "Cradle of Liberty," it was here that a defiant Samuel Adams rallied against British taxation policies. There is a bronze statue of Samuel Adams, patriot and signer of the Declaration of Independence, in front of Faneuil Hall—although Sam Adams seems to be known these days mostly for the Boston beer brand that bears his name. Oh, and "Faneuil" is pronounced to rhyme with "Daniel." The first floor of Faneuil Hall is the new Boston National Park Service visitor center. Fully staffed and with all the usual brochures and maps, this state-of the art facility also boasts iPad kiosks to custom design your own Freedom Trail walking tour. Open daily 9 a.m. to 5 p.m., free admission. National Park Service rangers give short talks on this building's history on the hour and half hour.

Old North Church. 193 Salem St., North End; (617) 523-6676; oldnorth.com. Henry Wadsworth Longfellow's immortal words, "one if by land, two if by sea," forever captured Old North Church's pivotal role in Revolutionary history. On the eve of April 18, 1775, sexton Robert Newman, upon instruction from Paul Revere, climbed to the top of the church steeple—then the highest in Boston—and hung two lanterns to signal to the patriots that the British troops were leaving Boston by sea and advancing toward Lexington and Concord. Dating from 1723, this is the oldest church building in Boston. It's officially known as Christ Church and today is home to an active Episcopalian congregation. Short drop-in presentations are offered to the public. Open June through Oct daily, 10 a.m. to 6 p.m. (tours every half hour); check website for days and times the rest of the year. No admission fee, but a $3 per person donation is appreciated.

Paul Revere House. 19 North Sq., North End; (617) 523-2338; paulreverehouse.org. This small clapboard Tudor-style house dates from 1680, making it the oldest surviving house in Boston. Paul Revere bought the property in 1770, when it was already more than 100 years old, and lived here with his large family; he had 8 children from each of his 2 wives! Some of the furnishings are original, and the rooms are set up as if they are still inhabited. As was the custom at the time, the master bedchamber served double duty as a parlor to receive guests. Tour at your own pace; knowledgeable volunteers are on hand to provide fascinating insight. Open Apr 15 through Oct 31 daily 9:30 a.m. to 5:15 p.m.; Nov 1 through Apr 14 daily from 9:30 a.m. to 4:15 p.m. Closed Mon Jan through Mar. Admission $5 adults, $4.50 seniors and students, $1 children ages 5 to 17, free ages 4 and under.

Bunker Hill Monument. Monument Square, Charlestown; (617) 242-5641; nps.gov/bost/historyculture/bhm.htm. Just a 5-minute walk from the Charlestown Navy Yard, a 221-foot granite obelisk commemorates the June 17, 1775, conflict that was fought on this hill. It was one of the first major battles of the Revolutionary War, and although the British won the fight, they suffered heavy casualties, and the ragtag American troops proved themselves worthy. There is no elevator, so you will have to climb the 294 steps to reach the capstone, but the views of Boston, Charlestown, and Cambridge are worth it. Open daily Jan through May and Sept through Dec 9 a.m. to 5 p.m., July and Aug 9 a.m. to 6 p.m. Free admission.

USS Constitution. Charlestown Navy Yard, Charlestown; (617) 242-5670; nps.gov/bost/historyculture/ussconst.htm. This black-wood hull, 3-mast frigate is a beauty. Launched in 1797, during the age of sail, the USS *Constitution* is the world's oldest commissioned warship still afloat. She saw lots of action against the Barbary pirates off the coast of Africa from 1803 to 1805 but is most renowned for her role in the War of 1812 when she defeated the British warship HMS *Guerriere*. She earned her nickname "Old Ironsides" when cannonballs seemingly bounced off her, and a British seaman exclaimed, "Huzzah! Her sides are made of iron!" Active-duty young Navy sailors in period 1812 uniforms give 30-minute tours—and they take tremendous pride in telling *Constitution*'s story. **Note:** Give yourself time to go through security screening. Open Apr through Sep Tues through Sun 10 a.m. to 6 p.m.; Oct Tues through Sun 10 a.m. to 4 p.m.; Nov through Mar Thurs through Sun 10 a.m. to 4 p.m., closed Mon. Free admission.

Haymarket. Along Blackstone Street, Downtown. It's a gritty place—definitely not for the timid—but if you enjoy food shopping as entertainment, step off the tourist trail and wander through Haymarket, Boston's open-air produce market. It's a raucous scene as pushcart vendors hawk fruit, vegetables, and flowers at rock-bottom prices, and it's a great place to mix with the locals. Open Fri and Sat dawn to mid-afternoon, year-round.

Institute of Contemporary Art. 100 Northern Ave., Waterfront; (617) 478-3100; icaboston .org. It's nearly impossible not to be awestruck by the ICA's dramatic glass-and-steel building cantilevered over Boston Harbor. Inside, the museum's permanent collection showcases innovative works by contemporary artists. In recent years the ICA has hosted many blockbuster exhibitions including Shepard Fairey, Damian Ortega, Roni Horn, and Anish Kapoor. Open Sat, Sun, Tues, and Wed 10 a.m. to 5 p.m., Thurs and Fri 10 a.m. to 9 p.m., closed Mon. Admission $15 adults, $13 seniors, $10 students, free ages 17 and under. Admission free Thurs 5 to 9 p.m.

The Isabella Stewart Gardner Museum. 280 The Fenway, Back Bay; (617) 566-1401; gardnermuseum.org. The lighting is dim, the works of art are unlabeled and have a packed arrangement—it feels rather more like viewing someone's personal collection than a museum. Fenway Court, as it was originally named, was home to turn-of-the-20th-century Boston socialite Isabella Stewart Gardner. She modeled the design after a 15th-century Venetian palazzo complete with an enclosed courtyard that today blooms with flowers year-round. Three floors of galleries hold Gardner's collection of treasures: American and European paintings, ancient sculptures, and Asian artifacts. Among the masterpieces are

Titian's *The Rape of Europa*, Rembrandt's *Self-Portrait, Aged 23*, and John Singer Sargent's *Jaleo*. In 2012, the museum completed a Renzo Piano–designed renovation and expansion blending old and new. Cutting-edge Calderwood Hall is the Gardner's new performance space and hosts the museum's renowned Sunday afternoon concert series. The museum's restaurant, Cafe G, now has an expanded, sleekly modern space where visitors can enjoy an array of seasonal and museum-themed dishes complemented by wines and specialty cocktails. Open Wed 11 a.m. to 5 p.m., Thurs 11 a.m. to 9 p.m., Fri through Mon 11 a.m. to 5 p.m. Closed Tues. Admission $15 adults, $12 seniors, $5 students, free for children ages 18 and under.

John F. Kennedy Library and Museum. Columbia Point, Dorchester; (617) 514-1600; jfklibrary.org. The official presidential library of John F. Kennedy pays tribute to the life and legacy of Boston's favorite son. The striking I. M. Pei–designed building overlooks Boston Harbor and evokes the sail of a ship, a reminder of Kennedy's lifelong affection for the sea. Begin your visit with the 17-minute introductory film that's narrated by Kennedy himself as he describes growing up in Brookline, his college years at Harvard, and his time in the navy. The museum's permanent exhibits include memorabilia and videos relating to Kennedy's presidency, from the space race to civil rights to the Cuban Missile crisis, as well as footage of Kennedy's assassination and funeral. Open daily 9 a.m. to 5 p.m. Admission $14 adults, $12 seniors and students, $10 children ages 13 to 17, children 12 and under are free.

Museum of African American History. 46 Joy St., Beacon Hill; (617) 725-0022; maah .org. Beacon Hill is not just the bastion of blue bloods. Prior to the Civil War, and as far back as the Revolutionary War, this area was home to a thriving free black community. The Museum of African American History tells the story of Boston's role in the abolitionist movement and the history of African Americans in New England. The museum occupies the Abiel Smith School, the nation's first public school for African-American children. The next-door African Meeting House is one of America's oldest black churches. The museum also offers free guided tours daily (June through Sept) of the 14 sites of the Black Heritage Trail and provides maps for those interested in doing a self-guided walk of the trail on their own. Open Mon through Sat 10 a.m. to 4 p.m. Admission $5 adults, $3 seniors and students ages 13 to 17, free for children ages 12 and under.

Museum of Fine Arts. 465 Huntington Ave., Back Bay; (617) 267-9300; mfa.org. Boston's Museum of Fine Arts is a treasured Boston institution, a world-class art museum whose encyclopedic holdings include nearly 450,000 items that span an array of civilizations and cultures through the ages. Particular strengths of the MFA are its collection of ancient Egyptian sculpture and artifacts, Asian art, and French Impressionist masterpieces, including 38 works by Monet.

As you would expect, the MFA excels in 18th- and 19th-century American art. Don't miss the splendid Art of the Americas wing. From Paul Revere's silver Sons of Liberty bowl,

getting around: charlie is the way to go

New England may be best explored by car, and a car is almost a necessity if you want to take day trips and explore the coast and the mountains. But unless you absolutely have to, don't drive in Boston. Boston's streets are congested with traffic, parking is difficult to find (or nonexistent), and when it is available, it's expensive.

Boston is actually a very small city, and many of its major sites stand shoulder to shoulder, so walking is often the best way to go.

For traveling to those places that are not within walking distance, your best bet is to do as the locals do and take the T. The T is short for the MBTA, or Massachusetts Bay Transportation Authority, and its five lines—Green, Red, Blue, Orange, and Silver—can take you to most any place that you need to go. You can travel anywhere on the system for just one flat fare. Fares are paid with either a plastic CharlieCard for $2.25 per ride or a paper CharlieTicket (or cash-on-board) for $2.75 per ride. You can buy CharlieTickets from vending machines at any T station. CharlieCards are available at staffed T stations, and both CharlieCards and CharlieTickets are reusable and reloadable. So who is this Charlie? Charlie is the poor guy immortalized in the Kingston Trio's 1959 recording of the "M.T.A. Song" who was doomed to ride the train forever because he didn't have the five-cent exit fare. (617) 222-5000; mbta.com.

to John Singleton Copley's paintings of Boston revolutionaries John Hancock, Sam Adams, and Paul Revere, it's a terrific opportunity to tie together the history of the Freedom Trail. On the second floor of the wing, the delightful *Daughters of Edward Darley Boit* by John Singer Sargent is showcased, flanked by the very same vases that are depicted in the painting.

Strapped for time? The MFA offers docent-led tours throughout the day. Inquire at the Sharf Visitor Center when you arrive. And be sure to end your visit by browsing the MFA's superb bookstore and gift shops. Open Mon, Tues, Sat, and Sun 10 a.m. to 4:45 p.m., Wed through Fri 10 a.m. to 9:45 p.m. Admission $25 adults, $23 seniors and students, free for ages 7 to 17 after 3 p.m. and on weekends; otherwise $10, free children ages 6 and under. Admission by donation Wed after 4 p.m.

Museum of Science. 1 Science Park, West End; (617) 723-2500; mos.org. Where to begin? With scores of hands-on activities in the exhibit halls, an IMAX theater and plan-etarium, families can easily spend an entire day here. Swing by Science in the Park, an interactive exhibit that makes the principals of physics accessible to school-age children and up. Technology whizzes will likely take to Behind the Scenes and help the museum test new exhibits. The Discovery Center is the place for the youngest scientists, with fossils to touch and live animal encounters. Visitors of all ages will enjoy the out-of-this-world journey at the Hayden Planetarium. Renovated in 2011, it incorporates the latest HD video projection and digital acoustic technologies. Open from the day after Labor Day through July 4 Sat through Thurs 9 a.m. to 5 p.m., Fri 9 a.m. to 9 p.m.; July 5 through Labor Day open Sat through Thurs 9 a.m. to 7 p.m., Fri 9 a.m. to 9 p.m. Admission $25 adults, $21 seniors, $20 ages 3 to 11, free ages 2 and under.

New England Aquarium and New England Aquarium Whale Watch Excursions. Central Wharf, Downtown; (617) 973-5200; neaq.org. Enter the New England Aquarium and you can't miss the museum's centerpiece attraction: the recently renovated 4-story Giant Ocean Tank, which re-creates an underwater Caribbean coral reef. Other highlights are the informative penguin feedings and harbor seal training sessions. You can also see breathtaking 3D ocean-related films that are shown several times a day on the aquarium's 6-story IMAX screen.

While in Boston, you can let the New England Aquarium introduce you to some really big animals. Among local whale-watch excursions, the New England Aquarium's is among the very best. The 4-hour, naturalist-led adventures aboard a high-speed catamaran leave from the New England Aquarium dock for the Stellwagen Bank National Marine Sanctuary, a feeding ground for humpback, minke, and pilot whales.

Museum hours from the day after Labor Day through June are Mon through Fri 9 a.m. to 5 p.m., Sat and Sun 9 a.m. to 6 p.m. From July 1 to Labor Day open Sun through Thurs 9 a.m. to 6 p.m., Fri and Sat 9 a.m. to 7 p.m. Aquarium tickets $26.95 adults, $24.95 seniors, $18.95 children ages 3 to 11, free for children ages 2 and under. Whale Watch Excursions take place April through October; check website for exact departure times. Whale watch tickets $53 adults, $45 seniors, $33 children ages 3 to 11, $16 children ages 2 and under. Also check website for good value aquarium/whale watch and aquarium/IMAX ticket packages.

New England Holocaust Memorial. Union and Congress Streets, Downtown; nehm .com. Just steps from the Freedom Trail, New England's Holocaust Memorial is a sobering reminder of the victims of the Nazi horror. Walk along the black granite path among the six glass and steel towers, each representing one of the principal Nazi death camps. One million numbers are etched in random, yet orderly, sequence on each of the towers, representing the 6 million who died, and smoke rises from grates in each base. The towers are illuminated from within, making this memorial especially dramatic in the evening. Open daily 24 hours.

Prudential Center Skywalk. 800 Boylston St., Back Bay; (617) 859-0648; skywalkboston .com. Ride the lobby elevator up, up, up and away to the 50th floor enclosed observation deck of the Prudential Center for spectacular 360-degree views of downtown Boston and beyond. It's a good introduction to the layout of the city, and your ticket includes a handheld audio tour that explains all. Open daily Nov 1 through Mar 10 a.m. to 8 p.m.; Apr 1 through Oct 10 a.m. to 10 p.m. Admission $18 adults, $15 seniors and students, $13 ages 12 and under.

The Public Garden. Bordered by Arlington, Beacon, Charles, and Boylston Streets, Back Bay; cityofboston.gov/parks. Stroll the winding paths among formally planted flower beds and along the weeping willow–edged lagoon. You may be familiar with the Public Garden as the setting for *Make Way for Ducklings*, Robert McCloskey's 1941 Caldecott Award–winning picture book. It is as charming today as it was back then. The Public Garden actually dates from 1837 and is America's first public botanical garden.

The Public Garden is a lovely backdrop for the Swan Boats, a most delightful Boston tradition, created (and still operated) by the Paget family more than 130 years ago. The fleet of elegant Swan Boats each seat 20 passengers and are pedaled by a college kid on a 15-minute figure-eight lap around the tranquil lagoon. If you are traveling with kids, be sure to visit Nancy Schön's brass sculptures of Mrs. Mallard and her ducklings (Jack, Kack, Lack, et al.) at the corner of Charles and Beacon Streets for a great family photo op. The Public Garden is open year-round from dawn to dusk. The Swan Boats (617-522-1966; swanboats .com) are open mid-Apr to mid-Sept daily; spring and fall hours 10 a.m. to 4 p.m., summer (June 21 to Labor Day) 10 a.m. to 5 p.m.; adults $3.50, $3 seniors, $2.50 children ages 2 to 15.

Trinity Church. 206 Clarendon St., Back Bay; (617) 536-0944; trinitychurchboston.org. Located on Copley Plaza, across from the Boston Public Library, Trinity Church is Henry Hobson Richardson's masterwork. Dedicated in 1877, the Romanesque Revival design incorporates massive blocks of granite with red sandstone, a low center tower, and red-tile roof. The interior has a distinct Arts and Crafts aesthetic with ornately carved interior wood-work and brightly colored murals and stained glass windows created by John La Farge. Trinity Church also represents quite an engineering feat. Because the building was built on landfill and marshland, more than 4,500 pilings had to be driven into the ground before con-struction could even begin. Take a moment to contemplate the reflection of Trinity Church in the glass of the John Hancock Tower next door, designed in 1976 by I. M. Pei—it's a wonderful juxtaposition of Boston old and new. Guided and self-guided art and architecture tours are offered throughout the week. Public visiting hours Mon, Fri, and Sat 9 a.m. to 5 p.m.; Tues, Wed, and Thurs 9 a.m. to 6 p.m.; Sun 1 to 5 p.m. Admission $7 adults, $5 seniors and students, free for children ages 16 and under.

where to shop

For the most part, Boston's shopping is concentrated in a few specific neighborhoods that often have dozens of great stores. Here's a list by area of some favorites.

The Back Bay & Newbury Street. The Back Bay is truly Boston's main shopping district. This area includes famed Newbury Street, an 8-block, tree-lined stretch that boasts an eclectic mix of upscale clothing boutiques, galleries, and funky gift shops in 19th-century brownstone buildings. Nearby Boylston Street features large retail stores like Apple and the flagship stores of several Massachusetts-based retailers including Frye, Ball and Buck, and Talbots. Here, too, you will find Boston's best indoor malls. Both the Prudential Center and Copley Place offer some pretty fabulous shopping options among more than 150 stores, and they are connected to each other by a glass pedestrian bridge. If you have money, lots of money, then the international salons along Newbury Street, close to the Public Garden—Chanel, Gucci, and Armani—are for you. As you stroll down Newbury Street toward Massachusetts Avenue (known locally as Mass Ave) the stores give way to mass-market chain stores (Zara, H&M, and Ann Taylor) and more locally based stores and boutiques.

Copley Place. 100 Huntington Ave., Back Bay; (617) 262-6600; simon.com. This very swish multilevel complex attracts both browsers and buyers with its sky-lit interior, fountain, and plantings. There's a Neiman Marcus, Barney's New York, and dozens of other high-end international boutiques like Louis Vuitton, Jimmy Choo, Tiffany & Company, and L.K. Bennett. Open Mon through Sat 10 a.m. to 8 p.m., Sun noon to 6 p.m.

Fresh. 121 Newbury St., Back Bay; (617) 421-1212; fresh.com. The Boston-based beauty brand has a (deservedly) cultlike following for its organic and natural products, including a divine brown-sugar body polish and beautifully packaged artisanal soaps that smells fantastic. Open Mon through Sat 10 a.m. to 7 p.m., Sun noon to 6 p.m.

Johnny Cupcakes. 279 Newbury St., Back Bay; (617) 375-0100; johnnycupcakes .com. This is a bakery-themed store with nary a cupcake in sight. Johnny Cupcakes is a Boston-based, high-end street wear (now global with stores in LA and London) that's a coveted brand for the young hipster crowd. Open Mon through Sat 11 a.m. to 8 p.m., Sun 11 a.m. to 7 p.m.

Newbury Comics. 332 Newbury St., Back Bay; (617) 236-4930; newburycomics .com. This is the original store of the regional chain and a local institution for CDs, DVDs, and even vinyl. Find hip kitsch like political bobble-head dolls and *Star Wars* toy figures, along with must-have items that you never knew existed, like flamingo cocktail stirrers and a 2-foot plastic penguin. Open Mon through Sat 10 a.m. to 10 p.m., Sun 11 a.m. to 8 p.m.

Serenella. 134 Newbury St., Back Bay; (617) 262-5568; serenella-boston.com. Serenella has been a fixture on Newbury Street for decades, and for good reason. It still embraces the hip in fashion, from the up-and-coming like Stella McCartney as well as established designers like Emilio Pucci and Balmain. Open Mon through Sat 10 a.m. to 6 p.m.

The Shops at the Prudential Center. 800 Boylston St., Back Bay; (617) 236-3100; prudentialcenter.com. Anchored by Lord & Taylor and Saks Fifth Avenue, this bright glass and light-filled mall is a pleasant place to shop and contains nearly 75 stores, including Sephora, Lacoste, and Free People as well as several restaurants and a food court. Eataly Boston is here as well (see page 21). Open Mon through Sat 10 a.m. to 9 p.m., Sun 11 a.m. to 6 p.m.

Shreve, Crump & Low. 39 Newbury St., Back Bay; (617) 267-9100; shrevecrump andlow.com. Boston's high-society jeweler since 1796, Shreve's carries a distinctive line of Boston-themed gifts including sterling silver pins, charms, and ornaments; bone china boxes; and framed prints. The store's most recognizable product is its Gurgling Cod ceramic pitcher; the iconic fish-shaped jug makes a unique *glug-glug* sound when it is poured. Open Mon through Wed 10 a.m. to 6 p.m., Thurs and Fri 10 a.m. to 7 p.m., Sat 10 a.m. to 5 p.m., closed Sun.

Simon Pearce. 103 Newbury St., Back Bay; (617) 450-8388; simonpearce.com. Find an excellent selection of original handblown glass pieces and handmade pottery from the famed Vermont-based manufacturer. Open Mon through Sat 10 a.m. to 6 p.m., Sun noon to 5 p.m.

Beacon Hill. Pretty Charles Street begs a stroll. It's a terrific shopping street, tightly packed with several high-end gift and housewares stores.

Beacon Hill Chocolates. 91 Charles St., Beacon Hill; (617) 725-1900; beaconhill chocolates.com. A keepsake box illustrated with scenes of historic Boston and filled with handmade chocolates and truffles makes a tasty souvenir. Open Mon through Sat 11 a.m. to 7 p.m., Sun noon to 5:30 p.m.

Blackstone's of Beacon Hill. 46 Charles St., Beacon Hill; (617) 227-4646; black stonesbeaconhill.com. This store offers lots of quality gift options including exclusive Boston-themed items, artisan-made pottery, and collectibles. Open Mon through Wed 10 a.m. to 6:30 p.m., Thurs 10 a.m. to 7 p.m., Fri and Sat 10 a.m. to 6:30 p.m., and Sun 11 a.m. to 5 p.m.

Flat of the Hill. 60 Charles St., Beacon Hill; (617) 619-9977; flatofthehill.com. This shop will satisfy any woman's girly girl. Find cute purses, handmade jewelry, and delicious-smelling candles. Open Tues through Fri 11 a.m. to 6 p.m., Sat 10 a.m. to 5 p.m., Sun noon to 5 p.m.

Good. 133 Charles St., Beacon Hill; (617) 722-9200; shopatgood.com. Good is just that. Explore the wonders of this lovely (and recently expanded) shop offering home accessories like hand-blocked pillows, decoupage wall hangings, and artisanal vases by Farmhouse Pottery. Open Tues through Fri 10 a.m. to 7 p.m., Sat 10 a.m. to 6 p.m., closed Sun and Mon.

insider tip: affordable boston parking

Parking in Boston is problematic. Lucky you if you score a metered parking space downtown! If you must drive in Boston, here are two inexpensive and convenient parking garages worth knowing about.

Boston Common Garage. Zero Charles St.; (617) 954-2098; massconvention. com. Located between the Public Garden and the Boston Common, this parking lot is handy to Beacon Hill and the Theater District. The lot is owned by the city, open 24/7—and it's huge—with 1,300 spots. This lot also has prime dedicated spots for hybrid vehicles. The weekend rates—over 3 hours for $18—are among the cheapest in the city.

Parcel 7 (Haymarket) Garage. 136 Blackstone St.; (617) 973-6954. Just two blocks from Faneuil Hall, this garage offers validated parking for visitors to the North End. Parking rates are $1 for up to 2 hours and $3 for up to 3 hours—enough time to have a leisurely dinner in the North End. Most North End restaurants and shops can validate your ticket. The entrance is at the corner of Congress and Sudbury Streets.

Faneuil Hall Marketplace. Between Congress and Commercial Streets; (617) 523-1300; faneuilhallmarketplace.com. In the 1970s historic Faneuil Hall and the adjacent wholesale food distribution warehouse buildings were repurposed to become one of the country's first urban marketplace developments. It does seem that there are always a zillion people here, but it really is one of the best spots in the city for people watching.

The **Quincy Market Colonnade** (it's pronounced QUIN-zy) is primarily a food hall that draws visitors and financial district office workers with its wide array of American and ethnic fast food. Recommendations include Steve's for Greek, Megumi for Japanese, El Paso Enchiladas for Mexican, and the Monkey Bar for smoothies.

Shoppers head for the **North and South Market** buildings, filled with big-name retailers like Harley Davidson, Ann Taylor, and Build-a-Bear. Stores with local ties include Boston Pewter, Geoclassics, Yankee Candle, and the Kilvert & Forbes Bakeshop. The carnival-like atmosphere is further enhanced by dozens of pushcart vendors that sell everything from Irish sweaters to boxers-to-go. In warm weather, be sure to spend some time enjoying the musicians, artists, and jugglers that roll out their crowd-pleasing acts in front of the Quincy Market Colonnade. Open Mon through Sat 10 a.m. to 9 p.m., Sun noon to 6 p.m.

Located across from Faneuil Hall, the **Boston Public Market**. 100 Hanover St.; (617) 973-4909; bostonpublicmarket.org, has been a resounding success since opening in July 2015. Boston's newest public market is already a community hub, featuring local eateries along with regional food vendors and artisan shops. Among the notable stalls on the premises are Bon Me for Vietnamese pho (noodle soup) and Beantown Pastrami for carvery sandwiches. Check out Union Square Doughnuts and George Howell Coffee to sweeten (and caffeinate) your visit. The market offers possibilities for local souvenirs as well, including Boston Honey Company for beeswax candles and honey and American Stonecraft for trivets, coasters and cheese boards manufactured from fieldstone gathered from New England farms. Open Mon through Sat 8 a.m. to 8 p.m., Sun 10 a.m. to 8 p.m.

where to eat

Aquitaine Boston. 569 Tremont St.; (617) 424-8577; aquitaineboston.com. A regular haunt of practically everyone who has ever lived in the South End over the past two decades, Aquitaine has a lively ambience, a strong cocktail program and a kitchen that specializes in upscale French comfort food; the duck a l'orange and braised rabbit with baby turnips that will transport you back to Paris. Aquitaine's fixed price $11.95 weekend brunch is hugely popular with the under-30 student-loan paying set. Open Mon through Thurs 11:30 a.m. to 3 p.m., 5:30 to 10 p.m.; Fri 11 a.m. to 3 p.m., 5:30 p.m. to 11 p.m.; Sat 9 a.m. to 3 p.m., 5:30 to 11 p.m.; Sun 9 a.m. to 3 p.m., 5:30 to 10 p.m. $$$.

Antico Forno. 93 Salem St., North End; (617) 723-6733; anticofornoboston.com. This homey trattoria draws crowds for its highly satisfying, mostly southern Italian cuisine. The smoldering wood-burning brick oven turns out exquisite pizzas and baked pastas (the baked rigatoni with sausage and ricotta is a standout) as well as simple grills that are well seasoned with big flavor. And it is all very easy on the wallet too. Sun through Thurs 11:30 a.m. to 10 p.m., Fri and Sat 11:30 a.m. to 10:30 p.m. $$.

Beehive. 541 Tremont St., South End; (617) 423-0069; beehiveboston.com. Boston can do sexy boîte, too. Beehive has live music nightly—mostly jazz but also blues and world music—in a cavernous subterranean space that is equal parts 1920s boho Paris and present-day South End. And if you come to drink and mingle, you won't be disappointed by the food either, which mixes a variety of local, European, and Middle Eastern influences. Reservations recommended on weekends. Open Sun 10 a.m. to 1 a.m., Mon through Wed 5 p.m. to 1 a.m., Thurs through Fri 5 p.m. to 2 a.m., Sat 10 a.m. to 2 a.m. $–$$.

Doretta Tavern and Raw Bar. 79 Park Plaza; Back Bay; (617) 422-0008; dorettaboston. com. The sun-baked flavors of the Mediterranean shine through at this high-end Greece-meets-New England restaurant from star-chef Michael Schlow. Schlow is Greek by association; his wife Adrienne's family is from Sparta. Branzino with fennel is a popular choice, but look for the 15-hour lamb shoulder—it is extraordinary. The ever-busy massive central bar is a lively spot. In two short years, Doretta has become a regular haunt of Boston's local celebrities and sports stars as well as the place for theater-goers to stop in for a cocktail and a few *mezze* like beets with whipped feta, grilled octopus or zucchini chips before a show.

Open Mon through Thurs 11:30 a.m. to 2:30 p.m., 5 to 10 p.m.; Fri 11:30 a.m. to 2:30 p.m., 5-11 p.m., Sat. 5 to 11 p.m., closed Sun, bar open later. $$–$$$.

Eataly Boston. Prudential Center; 800 Boylston St.; (617) 807-7300. Markets open daily 9 a.m. to 11 p.m. Close your eyes as you enter Mario Batali's Boston Eataly, a temple to *la dolce vita.* The smells are many—a sweet cloud of fresh baked bread, flame-roasted chickens, warm wood-fired pizza, and espresso. Wander through *La Piazza,* designed to evoke an Italian village square with wine glass in hand sampling *formaggi* and *salumi* along the way. The 3-story space, a 45,000 square foot mega-emporium, is a playground for foodies, with 4 restaurants, 10 casual food court–like options, two caffes, 2 bars, a cooking school and a grocery store where you can buy *tutto* you need for an Italian feast. Eataly Boston is committed to working with local resources and distributors. For example, at *Il Pesce,* you'll find that the mainly Italian seafood preparations are made with New England seafood: lobster salad is made with fennel and lemon and there's a mackerel crudo. *Bravo* to that. Restaurants and caffes open Mon through Fri 7 a.m. to 11 p.m., Sat and Sun 9 a.m. to 11 p.m. $–$$$.

Flour Bakery + Cafe. 12 Farnsworth St., Seaport; (617) 338-4333; 1595 Washington St., South End; (617) 267-4300; and 131 Clarendon St., Back Bay, and other locations throughout the city; (617) 437-7700; flourbakery.com. Everything at Flour is sublime, from the buttery *pain aux raisins* at breakfast to the roast chicken, avocado, and jicama sandwich at lunch to a mid-afternoon snack of an oversized cappuccino with a slice of rhubarb-raspberry pound cake. Chef-owner Joanne Chang's sticky buns are widely considered amazing and are a must-order. Open daily; hours vary by location. $.

Gourmet Dumpling House. 52 Beach St., Chinatown; (617) 338-6223. It is little more than a Chinatown storefront, but when the food is this tasty, it is hard to criticize the decor. The menu specializes in all manner of soup dumplings, plump tender pouches filled with ground pork, vegetables, and broth. The scallion pancakes are incredibly good too. There is a wide selection of Chinese-American standards aimed at the "General Gao"–craving masses, but you'll also find pickled greens with intestinal blood pudding and simmered three-essence frog hot pot, so you know this place is authentic. Open daily 11 a.m. to 1 a.m. $$.

Legal Sea Foods. 255 State St., Waterfront, and other locations throughout the region; (617) 227-3115; legalseafoods.com. Legal's has never been better. In today's era of obsessive food sourcing, Legal Sea Foods still stands out from the rest after more than 60 years. They offer regional seafood classics like their famed New England clam chowder and baked stuffed whole lobsters, and terrific updated wood-grilled seafood choices. Open Sun through Thurs 11 a.m. to 10 p.m., Fri and Sat 11 a.m. to 11 p.m. $$–$$$.

Modern Pastry. 257 Hanover St., North End; (617) 523-3783; modernpastry.com. You'll brave a fearsome line, but the scrumptious cannolis are worth it. Linger over your espresso at one of the highly coveted tables in the front of the shop. Tip: Modern has recently expanded downstairs with table service. Modern Underground has a small menu of wings, nachos, beer, wine and pastries—and sometimes it's faster than the line upstairs! Open Sun through Thurs 8 a.m. to 10 p.m., Fri 8 a.m. to 11 p.m., Sat 8 a.m. to midnight. Still cash only though. $.

Neptune Oyster. 63 Salem St., North End; (617) 742-3474; neptuneoyster.com. Upscale, comfortable raw bars are in surprisingly short supply in Boston, but this polished restaurant fills the void with a vast selection of fantastically fresh oysters. It's a cozy space that attracts food lovers who like to share, and for whom everything is a discovery. This is the place for some of the best lobster rolls in the city, available either hot with butter or traditional-style with mayonnaise. They don't take reservations, so be prepared to wait. Mon through Fri 11:30 a.m. to 10 p.m., Sat and Sun 11:30 a.m. to 11 p.m. $$–$$$.

Picco. 513 Tremont St., South End; (617) 927-0066; piccorestaurant.com. This charming South End neighborhood pizza parlor offers a wind-ranging menu of pizza, pastas, salads, and homemade ice cream (Picco stands for "pizza and ice cream company"). The Alsatian has become their signature pie: gooey gruyère, crispy bits of bacon, and a scattering of sautéed onions is finished with a drizzle of tangy crème fraîche. Open daily 5 to 10 p.m. $–$$.

Pier 6. 1 Eighth St., Charlestown; (617) 337-0054; pier6boston.com. Located at the dock next to the USS *Constitution*, Pier 6 attracts both visitors and locals for glorious views of the Boston skyline. The menu features traditional seafood (lightly fried clams) and pub fare (burgers) at prices more reasonable than one might expect from a waterfront restaurant. Outdoor summer seating and an expansive specialty cocktail menu make for a lively atmosphere. Open Sun through Thurs 11 a.m. to 10 p.m., Fri and Sat 11 a.m. to 11 p.m., Sun 11 a.m. to 10 p.m. $$.

Rami's. 324 Harvard St., Brookline; (617) 325-2335; ramisboston.com. This no-frills cafe serves Israeli kosher cuisine and is on many diners' list of not-to-be-missed cheap eats in Boston. Rely on this place for over-stuffed falafel sandwiches accompanied by creamy hummus, purple cabbage, pickles and a killer homemade hot sauce. Open Sun through Thurs 10 a.m. to 10 p.m., Fri 10 a.m. to 2 p.m., closed Sat. $.

Stephanie's on Newbury. 190 Newbury St., Back Bay; (617) 236-0990; stephanieson newbury.com. On a warm summer day, Stephanie's expansive sidewalk patio is the best perch for watching the Newbury Street parade of beautiful people. Nibble on a pizzetta topped with duck confit and arugula and roasted pears, or give in to comfort food cravings and have the three-cheese macaroni that is made even more amazing with truffle oil and prosciutto. Open Mon through Fri 7:30 a.m. to 11 p.m., Sat 9 a.m. to 11 p.m., Sun 9 a.m. to 10 p.m. $$.

Stoddard's. 48 Temple Place, Downtown; (617) 426-0048; stoddardsfoodandale.com. Located in a historic 1868 building, Stoddard's has a wonderful speakeasy quality with its dark wood walls, massive carved oak and mahogany bar, and replica 19th-century gas street lamps. Some of the bar's decor even hints at its original incarnation as Chandler's Corset Store. The bar specializes in hard-to-find cask ales, with several always on tap, and features a well-thought-out gastropub menu. Find aged Gouda fondue, deviled eggs, and a house-made charcuterie plate as appetizer choices. Dinner selections include chicken potpie, a ballotine of rabbit, or ale-battered cod. Open Tues and Wed 11:30 a.m. to 1 a.m., Thurs through Sat 11:30 a.m. to 2 a.m., Sun 11:30 a.m. to midnight. Closed Mon. $$.

Top of the Hub. 800 Boylston St., Prudential Center; (617) 536-1775; topofthehub.net. End your evening with a nightcap and live jazz at this glamorous 52nd-floor aerie with glass windows that reveal killer Boston city views. The setting, along with a winning wine list and potent cocktails, makes this a smart spot to impress. No cover, but they do enforce a minimum purchase after 8 p.m. Open daily 11:30 a.m. to 1 a.m. $–$$.

U-Burger. 636 Beacon St., Kenmore; (617) 536-0448; 1022 Commonwealth Ave., Boston University; (617) 487-4855; uburgerboston.com. There's no better place to satisfy your burger craving than this duo of burger joints. The menu offers traditional, build-your-own options as well as specialty creations like the intense Boom Burger with chipotle sauce, cheddar cheese, and fried jalapeños. Hand-cut fries and a frappe (ice cream, milk, and syrup) are the perfect go-withs. Open daily for lunch, dinner, and late night; check website for exact times. $.

Union Oyster House. 41 Union St., Faneuil Hall; (617) 227-2750; unionoysterhouse .com. Generally, restaurants in New England with "ye olde" as part of their name should be avoided. The Union Oyster House is an exception, though, if only because the restaurant can claim several historic distinctions. Dating from 1826, this is the oldest continually operating restaurant in America. John F. Kennedy ate frequently in the upstairs dining room; his favorite booth has a plaque in his honor. And the semicircular raw bar in the front window is legendary—19th-century statesman Daniel Webster was a daily customer—and these are still the best seats in the house to slurp back a plate of just-shucked specimens. Open Sun through Thurs 11 a.m. to 9:30 p.m., Fri and Sat 11 a.m. to 10 p.m., bar open daily until midnight. $$.

where to stay

The Charlesmark Hotel. 655 Boylston St., Back Bay; (617) 247-1212; charlesmarkhotel .com. Yes, it is possible to stay in a centrally located boutique hotel in Boston from just $199 per night. The Charlesmark is famously known as the hotel at the finish line of the Boston Marathon. Rooms are smallish with a modern sensibility. Think uberchic for cheap. $$.

Hotel Commonwealth. 500 Commonwealth Ave., Kenmore; (617) 933-5000; hotelcommon wealth.com. The building is classic French Second Empire and boasts gorgeous interior spaces with sizable rooms that are luxuriously appointed with down comforters, Italian linens, and fresh toiletries. Practically in the shadow of Fenway Park, the hotel is a popular choice for Red Sox fans. The two in-house restaurants, Eastern Standard and Island Creek Oyster Bar, are both excellent and popular with both locals and out-of-towners. Very family friendly and pet friendly, too. $$$.

boston's irish pubs

Boston bleeds green, and there are practically as many Irish pubs in the city as there are Sullivans. The following pubs, all centrally located in Boston, Cambridge and Somerville, are great places to raise a pint of Guinness and should do you right. All of them serve food; many offer live music and a place to stop for a chat.

The Black Rose. *160 State St., Downtown; (617) 742-2286; blackroseboston.com. An Irish bar in Boston is not at all hard to find, but this is a good bet in the Faneuil Hall area. The two floors of this large pub and restaurant are usually busy, but you'll find perfect pints, live Celtic music, better-than-decent pub grub, and an amiable crowd. Open Mon through Fri 11 to 2 a.m., Sat and Sun 9 to 2 a.m. $–$$.*

Bull McCabe's*. 366 Somerville Ave., Somerville, (617) 440-6045; bullmccabesboston .com. This hidden gem in Union Square is a laid-back single room pub and restaurant with bare floorboards, wood walls, and shelves lined with books. Bull McCabe's is also known for its live music and its tasty food. Popular dishes include fish and chips, burgers and marinated steak tips. This pub is also well known for its nightly live music (except Mon). Open Mon through Fri 3 p.m. to 12:30 a.m., Sat and Sun 11 to 1 a.m. $*

Doyle's Café*. 3484 Washington St., Jamaica Plain, (617) 524-2345; doylescafe boston.com. Established in 1918 in Boston's Jamaica Plain neighborhood, Doyle's is deservedly considered a local landmark. It's one of the city's largest Irish pubs, popular*

Envoy. 70 Sleeper St., Seaport District; (617) 338-3030; theenvoyhotel.com. With its great aesthetics, prime Seaport District location and thrumming atmosphere, Envoy is one of Boston's most exciting recent hotel openings. Each of the 130 rooms is cushy where it counts with well-dressed beds and sleek modern bathrooms. All rooms feature large swaths of glass windows that are flooded with light and have at least a partial water view. The Lookout Rooftop Bar is packed (even midweek) and is just an elevator ride away. $$$.

The Inn at St. Botolph. 99 St. Botolph St., Back Bay; (617) 236-8099; innatstbotolph.com. This boutique hotel choice is located in a historic Back Bay brownstone. The rooms were designed by Celeste Cooper and are comfortable, elegant, and modern, each done up in shades of black, cream, and cinnamon. Each room is decorated differently, but all have kitchenettes and all the high-tech extras. Some rooms even feature a gas fireplace. All rates include continental breakfast and in-room Wi-Fi. $$–$$$.

with locals and tourists visiting the nearby Sam Adams Brewery. Doyle's pays homage to Boston's rich Irish history with an extensive collection of photographic and memorabilia of local politicians. Owner Jerry Burke Sr. still gets emotional when he talks about John F. Kennedy becoming the first Irish American president. If you want food, try the excellent clam chowder—although they do burgers and fish and chips too. Open Mon through Fri 11 to 12:30 a.m., Fri through Sun 9 to 12:30 a.m. $

J.J. Foley's Café*. 117 E. Berkeley St., South End, (617) 728-9101, jjfoleyscafe.com. Opened in 1909, this is unquestionably the oldest family-run bar in Boston. Once a working class pub, these days Foley's attracts a mixed bag of neighborhood folks, who are allowed to hang out in peace, as well as new faces. Foley's also has a reputation as a haunt for inebriated journalists from the* Boston Herald. *It's a large space with dark woodwork, a polished mahogany bar and stained glass details. Its excellent menu represents both New England classics like baked haddock and short rib pot roast as well as Irish cuisine like bangers and mash and a smoked pork shoulder boiled dinner. Open Mon 11 a.m. to 10 p.m., Tues through Thurs 11 a.m. to 11 p.m., Fri and Sat 11 to 12:30 a.m., Sun 10:30 a.m. to 10 p.m. $*

The Druid*. 1357 Cambridge St., Cambridge, (617) 497-0965; druidpub.com. Admittedly more dive-y than cozy, this is an exemplary watering hole to catch traditional Gaelic music. Sessions are held Saturday afternoon and Tuesday evening. A full Irish breakfast is ideal Sunday brunch food, and the Druid serves one of the best fry-ups in town. Open Mon through Fri noon to 2 a.m., Sat and Sun 11 to 2 a.m. $*

The Langham. 250 Franklin St., Downtown; (617) 451-1900; langhamhotels.com. Originally Boston's Federal Reserve Bank building, this 1920s Renaissance Revival beauty is a favorite hotel with both business execs and leisure travelers. The guest rooms are spacious and extravagantly comfortable with rich brocades, antique-style furniture, and Italian marble bathrooms. There is no need to go anywhere else with Cafe Fleuri, Bond Restaurant, an indoor pool (a favorite for families), state-of-the-art fitness center, and the full-service Chuan Body + Soul Spa, all on-site. If your stay includes the weekend, be sure to indulge in the Langham's weekly Saturday Chocolate Bar and Sunday brunch (both Sept through June). A super-convenient downtown location makes for an easy walk to Faneuil Hall and the Waterfront. $$$.

Omni Parker House. 60 School St., Downtown; (617) 227-8600; omniparkerhouse.com. You can't do better than staying at the Omni Parker House for a sense of place. There's lots of history here, the heart of the Freedom Trail is just outside the door. Open since 1855, this is the longest continuously operating luxury hotel in the US. The hotel's restaurant, Parker's, hosted the 19th-century literary Saturday Club; members included Emerson, Longfellow, Thoreau, and Hawthorne. The Boston cream pie (which is actually a cake) was invented here. So, too, were Parker House rolls. Both are still on the menu. Vietnamese leader Ho Chi Minh worked as a baker here from 1911 to 1913, activist Malcolm X bused tables during the early 1940s, and Emeril Lagasse did one of his early kitchen stints here. The hotel is superbly maintained. The wood-paneled lobby is traditionally genteel, featuring huge crystal chandeliers and a bank of elaborate bronze-sculpted elevator doors. The rooms have lots of character and have been recently spiffed up with modern comfort touches like triple-sheeting and fluffy duvets. $$–$$$.

The Taj. 15 Arlington St., Back Bay; (617) 536-5700; tajhotels.com/boston. If classic Boston luxury is high on your list, then choose the venerable Taj, located across from the Public Garden in a landmark 1927 building. The hotel features original art and lots of fresh flowers in the lobby; the rooms are splendid in ivory and celadon, and some have working fireplaces. The Taj is especially known for its impeccable service. A sweet perk here? Complimentary overnight shoeshine service. On weekends, afternoon tea is offered in the lounge, and one of the city's best Sunday brunches takes place on the enclosed rooftop from Apr through Nov. $$$.

day trip 02

boston

quirky intellectualism:
cambridge, ma

cambridge, ma

Famously liberal and free-thinking, Cambridge is known as Boston's Left Bank. Located just across the Charles River from Boston, the city was founded by the Puritans in 1630 as Newtowne and was later renamed Cambridge after the university town in England. Cambridge is home to Harvard University and the Massachusetts Institution of Technology (MIT). Both campuses are home to an impressive collection of museums, while the city's student population supports a slew of independent book stores and cheap eats.

getting there

The easiest way to get to Cambridge from Boston is to take the T (Red Line) to the Harvard Square station. To drive, travel west on Storrow Drive, which becomes Soldiers Field Road. Take the Harvard Square/Cambridge ramp, crossing the Charles River at the Anderson Bridge and continuing along JFK Street into the heart of Harvard Square. The distance from Boston to Cambridge is only about 4 miles, but it will take about 12 minutes to drive.

where to go

Cambridge Office of Tourism. Harvard Square; (617) 441-2884; cambridge-usa.org. Look for the kiosk located on the brick plaza just outside the Harvard Square T station. It is staffed by volunteer senior citizens (experts all) who are happy to give directions and

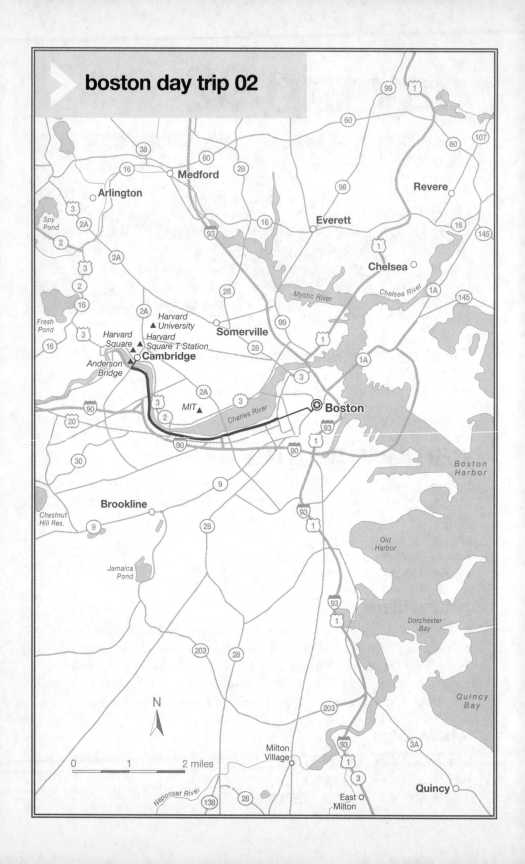

boston day trip 02

answer your questions. Open Mon through Fri 9 a.m. to 5 p.m., Sat 9 a.m. to 4 p.m., and Sun 9 a.m. to 1 p.m.

Harvard Art Museums. 32 Quincy St.; (617) 495-9400; harvardartmuseums.org. After a lengthy six-year renovation and expansion project that incorporates a dazzling Renzo Piano design blending the old with the new, Harvard's three art museums, the **Fogg** (European Masters), the **Arthur M. Sackler** (Asian, Islamic and Ancient art) and the **Busch-Reisinger** (Germanic art), are united under one roof. The heart of the museum remains beloved Calderwood Courtyard, modeled after the façade of a 15th-century Tuscan church, which gives way to expanded, light-filled galleries along with a new café and museum shop. Harvard's art holdings are extensive with more than 250,000 objects; only a small fraction, some 2,000 objects, are on display at any one time. Collection highlights include works by Fra Angelico, a Van Gogh self-portrait, a Blue Period Picasso, magnificent Chinese jades and superb illustrated Persian manuscripts. Cool fact: current Harvard students can rent prints from the museum to hang in their dorm rooms. Open daily 10 a.m. to 5 p.m. Admission $15 adults, $13 seniors, $10 students, free children under age 18.

Harvard Museum of Natural History. 26 Oxford St.; (617) 495-3045; hmnh.harvard.edu. Taxidermy and skeletons illustrate the natural world at this Harvard institution founded in 1872 by Harvard professor Louis Agassiz. The Ware Collection of Glass Flowers is world renowned for its meticulously crafted lifelike models of almost 4,000 plants and flowers. If you are traveling with kids, you know that bigger is definitely better. In Romer Hall little ones can get up close and personal with the skeleton of a triceratops, or view a dazzling 1,600-pound amethyst in the Mineral Hall. The museum's dramatic 2-story Great Mammal Hall displays mounted stuffed animals (most acquired during the 19th century) that are sure to intrigue both young and old. Open daily 9 a.m. to 5 p.m. Admission $12 adults, $10 seniors and students, $8 children ages 3 to 18.

Harvard Square. Intersection of Massachusetts Avenue, Brattle and JFK Streets; harvard square.com. Just beyond the Harvard University gates, tides of students, tourists, and local characters converge at Harvard Square. The sunken brick-paved area just outside the T station is referred to as "the Pit" and attracts protesters, street musicians, and skateboarding teens—and always makes for an interesting scene. Smack dab in the middle of the square is **Out of Town News,** which stocks newspapers and magazines from around the world. Fans of National Public Radio's now (sadly) defunct *Car Talk* should note the sign on the third floor of the office building at Brattle and JFK Streets that reads Dewey, Cheetham & Howe, which was in fact the business office for the show.

Harvard University. The Harvard Information Center, 30 Dunster St.; (617) 495-1573; harvard .edu/visitors. America's oldest and most prestigious university has been cultivating great minds since 1636. Harvard Yard is the oldest part of the university, an expanse of green lawn crossed with paths and shaded by majestic trees. The 1884 *John Harvard* statue by

Daniel Chester French is easily the most popular stop for visitors. It's inscribed JOHN HARVARD, FOUNDER, 1638 and is also known as the Statue of Three Lies. Why? There are no known portraits of Harvard, the statue's likeness is probably that of a student model; John Harvard didn't found the university, it was named after him; and the college was actually chartered in 1636. The university offers student-led guided historical tours of Harvard geared to the general public. (Prospective students and families should take the tour offered by the Harvard Admissions Office.) Tours are offered Mon through Sat 10 a.m. to 4 p.m., on the hour. Free.

Longfellow House–Washington Headquarters National Historic Site. 105 Brattle St.; (617) 876-4491; nps.gov/long. Writers, readers, and fans of history are all drawn to visit this pretty yellow clapboard mansion. Henry Wadsworth Longfellow lived in this Georgian home with his family for more than 40 years and penned "Paul Revere's Ride" and "Hiawatha" here. However, he was not the home's first famous resident; George Washington used this house from July 1775 to March 1776 as his headquarters during the Siege of Boston. On display are the furnishings, artwork, and books of the poet and his descendants. The grounds are open year-round daily dawn to dusk. The home is open seasonally June through Oct, Wed through Sun by guided tour only. Check website for exact times. Admission free.

Mount Auburn Cemetery. 580 Mount Auburn St.; (617) 547-7105; mountauburn.org. America's first garden cemetery, Mount Auburn features wide paths, stately trees, and ornamental plantings that make it a wonderful place for a stroll. Inspired by Paris's Père Lachaise, Mount Auburn was established in 1831. Among those buried here are Charles Bulfinch, Henry Wadsworth Longfellow, Winslow Homer, and Isabella Stewart Gardner. Climb the 95 steps to the top of Washington Tower for one of the best skyline views of Boston. In the spring, the cemetery is a mecca for birders. In the fall, leaf peepers come to see the autumnal show. Brochures and maps are available at the cemetery's entrance for a small fee. Open May through Aug 8 a.m. to 7 p.m., Sept through Apr 8 a.m. to 5 p.m.

The MIT Museum. 265 Massachusetts Ave.; (617) 253-5927; mit.edu/museum. Get in touch with your inner geek. Say hello to Kismet at Robots and Beyond. Arthur Ganson's whimsical kinetic sculptures mix art with mechanical engineering—very Rube Goldberg. And be sure to check out the museum's holography collection, said to be the world's largest, where what you see really does depend on how you look at it. Open daily 10 a.m. to 5 p.m. Admission $10 adults, $5 seniors, students and children ages 6 to 18.

where to shop

Black Ink. 5 Brattle St.; (617) 497-1221; blackinkboston.com. Discover covetable gifts and home accessories for every aesthetic; scattered alongside wood cheese boards and cookbooks you'll spot artfully decorated bicycle bells, red and white bakers twine and other small necessary gadgets. Open Mon through Sat 10 a.m. to 8 p.m., Sun 11 a.m. to 7 p.m.

Bob Slate Stationer. 30 Brattle St.; (617) 547-1230; bobslatestationer.com. Paper lovers are bound to find something special to take home from here. Find exquisite stationery from Crane and refined greeting cards from Smudge Ink. Aside from paper products the store also stocks leather-bound journals and diaries from Charring Cross and fine writing instruments from Waterman and Staedler. Open Mon through Sat 9:30 a.m. to 6:30 p.m., Sun noon to 5 p.m.

Cambridge Artists Cooperative. 59 A Church St.; (617) 868-4434; cambridgeartistscoop .com. This artist owned-and-operated two floor showroom is packed with the work of more than 200 contemporary craftspeople and artists and includes one-of-a-kind and limited edition pieces in basketry, pottery, jewelry, sculpture, glass, and mixed media. This is a wonderful opportunity to connect with the artist community, too. The craftspeople on hand are often eager to share information about the creative process. Open Mon through Sat 10 a.m. to 6 p.m., Sun noon to 6 p.m.

Grolier Poetry Bookshop. 6 Plympton St.; (617) 547-4648; grolierpoetrybookshop.org. A renowned Cambridge literary hangout, this is the oldest (since 1927) and said to be the only remaining bookstore dedicated exclusively to poetry in the country. A place to pore over obscure volumes available nowhere else. Open Tues and Wed 11 a.m. to 7 p.m., Thurs through Sat 11 a.m. to 6 p.m., closed Sun and Mon.

The Harvard Coop. 1400 Massachusetts Ave.; (617) 499-2000; thecoop.com. In the heart of Harvard Square, the Coop (rhymes with "scoop") is your one-stop shop for Harvard swag. Originally founded as a cooperative by a group of Harvard students in 1885 to buy text books and coal, today's Coop is open to the public and stocks a dizzying array of official Harvard apparel and gifts. Open Mon through Sat 9 a.m. to 10 p.m., Sun 10 a.m. to 9 p.m.

World's Only Curious George Store. 1 JFK St.; (617) 547-4500; thecuriousgeorgestore. com. Dedicated to everyone's favorite mischievous monkey, this red and yellow storefront is a Harvard Square mainstay. The store is stacked to the rafters with a generation-spanning selection of Curious George–themed books, toys and clothing. The shop's namesake has strong local roots. H.A. (Hans Augusto) and Margret Rey—the husband and wife illustrator/writer team that created the *Curious George* series—lived just a few blocks from Harvard Square during the 1960s and '70s. Open Sun through Thurs 10 a.m. to 6 p.m., Fri and Sat 10 a.m. to 8 p.m.

where to eat

Puritan & Company. 1166 Cambridge St.; (617) 615-6195; puritancambridge.com. Open since 2012 this hip Inman Square spot's progressive menu of market-driven mostly-American fare has drawn a devoted Boston/Cambridge following. Chef Will Gilson's moxie-glazed lamb belly is already considered an iconic dish of the Boston food scene. Open Sun

10:30 a.m. to 2 p.m., 5:30 to 9 p.m.; Mon through Thur 5:30 to 10 p.m., Fri and Sat 5:30 to 11 p.m. $$–$$$

Cafe Sushi. 1105 Massachusetts Ave.; (617) 492-0434; cafesushicambridge.com. What sets this tiny Harvard Square sushi bar apart from others is the high quality of fish and wide array of high-end sushi available (no crab stick here!), from luscious *ikura* (salmon roe) to three kinds of eel at very reasonable prices. On the cooked side of the menu (it's small) go for the whole fish steamed in sake and soy. Open Sun 5:30 to 10 p.m.; Mon through Thurs noon to 2:30 p.m., 5:30 to 10 p.m.; Fri and Sat noon to 2:30 p.m., 5:30 to 10:30 p.m. $$.

Craigie on Main. 853 Main St.; (617) 497-5511; craigieonmain.com. Chef-owner Tony Maws has created a menu that features honest, seasonal preparations of regional foods. The red chile–marinated skirt steak with oxtail pastrami is frequently on the menu, and the whole roasted chicken for two is a culinary event. It's a comfortable, lively dining room with an open kitchen, a bit like dining at the home of a friend—a friend who can really cook. Service is equally low-key but always impeccable. Reservations are strongly encouraged. Open Tues through Thurs 5:30 to 10 p.m., Fri and Sat 5:30 to 10:30 p.m., Sun 10:30 a.m. to 1:30 p.m. $$$.

Harvest. 44 Brattle St.; (617) 868-2255; harvestcambridge.com. A Harvard Square mainstay for stellar, seasonal New American cuisine where New England ingredients have pride of place. For lunch, order a lobster BLT or the Harvest burger with house-made pickles. For dinner, order duck—something divine made with duck is always on the menu. The pretty patio shaded with linden trees is the place to be in the summer and fall. And if the weather's foul, fear not: The interior with its linen-draped tables and flickering candlelight isn't bad either. Open Sun through Thurs 11:30 a.m. to 2:30 p.m. and 5:30 to 10 p.m., Fri and Sat 11:30 a.m. to 11 p.m. $$–$$$.

L. A. Burdick. 52 Brattle St.; (617) 491-4340; burdickchocolate.com. Feeling peckish? A slice of linzer torte, a kirsch-flavored tea cake, or a plate of homemade pastel macaroons and a cup of tea may just be the thing to tide you over. Burdick's is also well known for their delightful hand-piped mice and penguin chocolates—nothing makes a better souvenir! Open Sun through Thurs 8 a.m. to 9 p.m., Fri and Sat 8 a.m. to 10 p.m. $.

Little Donkey. 505 Massachusetts Ave.; (617) 945-1008; littledonkeybos.com. The new global small plates restaurant in Cambridge's Central Square was deemed "the best new restaurant of 2016" by the *Boston Globe* and is the latest collaboration of James Beard award-winning chefs Ken Oringer and Jamie Bissonnette. By Cambridge standards, this is an industrial-size operation, with seating for nearly 110 between its busy front-of-the house bar and main dining room. The white-washed bare brick walls and soaring ceilings give the space a loft-like feel while in the back of the room there's a view of the open kitchen and its line of young chefs. It's a high-energy atmosphere that attracts Harvard liberals and Boston-area food cognoscenti. The dishes here are dazzling, and the vibrant flavors are complex—like the snail fried rice with kimchi and the Istanbul meat ravioli with red pepper butter—yet are reasonably priced. The tuna poke bowl incorporates quinoa instead of rice to go along with a garnish of lightly pickled vegetables. The burger here has been given an upgrade with dry-age beef topped with fois gras and enhanced with an onion soup mayonnaise. Other menu highlights include the cocktails, which are not just delicious, but eye-catching too, like the signature "the one in the grapefruit" drink of tequila, agave, cassis, and lime. Fun. Open Sun 10 a.m. to 3 p.m. and 5 p.m. to 12:30 a.m., bar until 1 a.m. Mon through Wed 11:30 a.m. to 12:30 a.m., bar until 1 a.m. Thurs and Fri 11:30 a.m. to 1:30 a.m., bar until 2 a.m. Sat 5 p.m. to 1:30 a.m., bar until 2 a.m. $$.

Moona. 234 Hampshire St.; (617) 945-7448; moonsarestaurant.com. The word "moona" means "pantry" in Arabic. The restaurant is cozy and welcoming, the décor an elegant mash-up of copper trays from Turkey, ceramic plates from Morocco and shelves stocked with glass jars filled with provisions like pickled garlic and mandarins in rosemary syrup. The food takes inspiration from Turkey and its neighbors with flatbreads and various mezze. Start with the artful plate of dips, pickles and olives and perhaps the house-made merguez sausage. Among the enticing main dish options are a whole roasted fish and a luscious beef, saffron, prune and almond tagine. Open Sun through Thurs 5 to 10 p.m., Fri and Sat 5 to 11 p.m. $$.

Mr. Bartley's Burger. 1246 Massachusetts Ave.; (617) 354-6559; mrbartley.com. This funky Harvard Square burger joint flips seriously good 7-ounce hamburgers with creative toppings and satirical, Cambridge-related names like the "Facebook" and the "People's Republic of Cambridge." Pair with either the fried onion rings or sweet potato fries and a frappe or lime rickey. There are often lifelong waits, and it's cash only, but you are experiencing a Cambridge original. Open Mon through Sat 11 a.m. to 9 p.m. $.

Oleana. 134 Hampshire St.; (617) 661-0505; oleanarestaurant.com. Regularly a critic's choice as one of the Boston area's best restaurants, chef-owner Ana Sortun combines elements of Turkish cuisine with other flavors of the Mediterranean, and you get to experience all of the amazing tastes of the region with none of the jet lag. Try the Vermont lamb with Turkish spices and "everything green," or the pork saganaki with leeks, chanterelles, wild herbs, and kasseri cheese. And don't skip the wildly adventurous desserts like the baked Alaska with coconut ice cream and passion-fruit caramel or date terrine with rose petal jam—both are magnificent. In warm weather, the patio with a fountain, fig tree, and herb garden is one of the most romantic dinner à deux destinations around. Open Sun through Thurs 5:30 to 10 p.m., Fri and Sat 5:30 to 11 p.m. Reservations are an absolute must. $$$.

Punjabi Dhaba. 225 Hampshire St.; (617) 547-8272; royalbharatinc.com. The only downside at this non-descript Inman Square storefront is that they don't offer a lunch buffet. But don't hold that against this Cambridge grad student favorite—the prices are still ridiculously low for the creamy curries, tandoori cooked meats and hearty potato-stuffed naan. Open daily 12 p.m. to midnight. $.

Russell House Tavern. 14 John F. Kennedy St.; (617) 500-3055; russellhousecambridge .com. Located in the heart of Harvard Square, Russell Tavern is big, dark, and buzzing. There are two levels: ground and subterranean. You'll find a range of inspired American tavern food, from an 8-ounce burger with cheddar and caramelized onions served on a grilled English muffin to a leek and mushroom pizza, as well as small plates, a raw bar, and appetizers for the crowds that wander in late night. Open Mon through Wed 11 a.m. to 1 a.m., Thurs and Fri 11 a.m. to 2 a.m., Sat 10 a.m. to 2 a.m., Sun 10 a.m. to 1 a.m. $$.

Tatte Bakery & Café. 1288 Massachusetts Ave.; (617) 441-4011; tattebakery.com. Since opening in October 2016, this sixth and newest outpost of beloved local bakery Tatte has become the busiest place in Harvard Square. The look of the 2-floor light-filled space is nostalgic and hip with marble-topped communal and bistro tables, a hand-written menu on the wall and a glassed-in counter display with an impressive array of pastry that ranges from flaky croissants and custard bread puddings to elegant pear tarts. At lunch and dinner, Harvard students and tourists alike queue up for soups, salads and sandwiches that skew light Mediterranean—grilled halloumi salad with mint and pine nuts, roasted eggplant and feta on ciabatta bread and minestrone soup. Tip: The 2nd floor space is quieter, and you can order coffee drinks here from a bar. Open Mon through Fri 7 a.m. to 9 p.m., Sat 8 a.m. to 9 p.m., Sun 8 a.m. to 7 p.m. $

Toscanini's. 899 Main St.; (617) 491-5877; tosci.com. Located on the edge of the MIT campus, Tosci's, as it's affectionately known, is famed for its ultra-creamy homemade ice cream. The ice cream comes in a variety of eclectic "this is Cambridge" flavors like mango chile and cardamom coffee, but they also do a terrific job with the standards—especially that Belgian chocolate. Open Mon through Fri 8 a.m. to 11 p.m., Sat and Sun 10 a.m. to 11 p.m. $.

where to stay

The Charles Hotel. 1 Bennett St.; (617) 864-1200; charleshotel.com. Located in the heart of Harvard Square, the graciously tweedy Charles Hotel is an excellent choice for business or pleasure with perks for both, including "Web cubes" on each guest floor and access to the impressively huge Wellbridge Health Club next door. The decor is comfortably modern country with custom down quilts and Shaker-inspired furniture, flat-panel TVs, and complimentary Wi-Fi. The hotel's on-site restaurants, Henrietta's Table (New England) and Benedetto (regional Italian) are perennially popular dining spots for the campus glitterati. $$$.

Hotel Kendall. 350 Main St.; (866) 566-1300; kendallhotel.com. Housed in a renovated former fire-engine house, this 77-room hotel has lots of character. Extra touches, like American folk art on the walls, personalize the comfortably cozy rooms at this modern boutique hotel on the edge of the MIT campus. Rates include a buffet breakfast each morning and free high-speed Internet. Lots of visiting academics make for interesting conversation at the hosted wine hour held Monday through Thursday evenings at the indoor rooftop lounge. $$.

Hotel Veritas. 1 Remington St.; (617) 520-5000; thehotelveritas.com. Tucked away in a leafy neighborhood off Harvard Square, the Victorian exterior of this 31-room boutique hotel belies its superbly stylish interior. The rooms are compact but stunning, featuring an Art Deco–inspired design scheme of monochromatic shades of turquoise or toffee with accents of mirror and silver throughout. Beds are opulently dressed in Italian linens with coverlets and bolster pillows. No on-site restaurants, but the hotel's glam Simple Truth lounge and, in season, the intimate outdoor patio are both delightful places to unwind with a glass of wine and a cheese plate. $$$.

day trip 03

boston

a tale of two revolutions:
lexington, ma; concord, ma;
lowell, ma

Lexington and Concord are inextricably linked; together they witnessed the first major battle of the American Revolution. Concord is known, too, for its literary legacy and as the home of several important 19th-century writers, among them Ralph Waldo Emerson, Henry David Thoreau, Nathaniel Hawthorne, and Louisa May Alcott. Just a few miles to the north, Lowell's textile-mill buildings chronicle the beginning of the American Industrial Revolution.

lexington, ma

Just a short drive outside of Boston, Lexington is where a small band of farmers took up arms against their own government. It was Paul Revere's ride to Lexington on the eve of April 18, 1775, that alerted the townspeople of the British advance toward Concord. Today Lexington preserves and honors its rich history. Lexington's picture-perfect town common is dotted with several sites related to the first skirmish between the colonists and redcoats.

getting there

From downtown Boston, take Storrow Drive to MA 2. Follow MA 2 through Cambridge and Belmont. Exit at MA 4 and follow signs to Lexington Center. An alternative is to take MA 128 (I-95) to exit 31A and follow the signs to Lexington Center. Driving time from Boston is approximately 30 minutes.

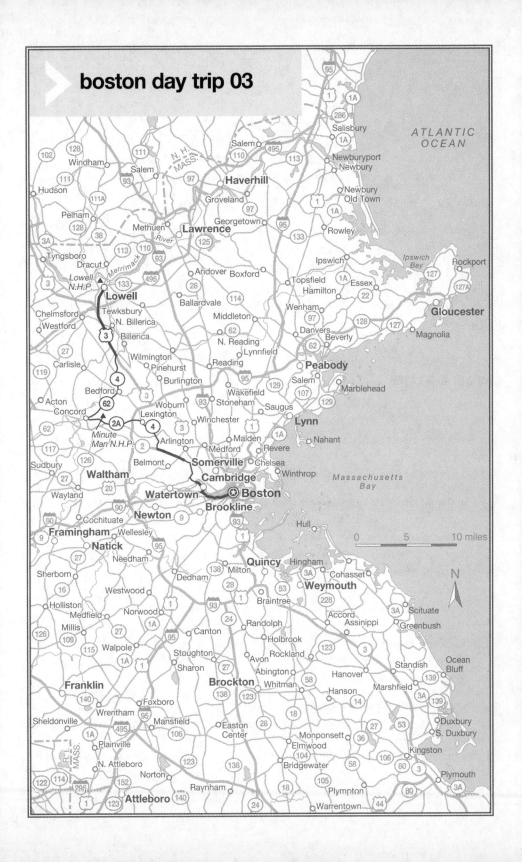

reenactment on the battle green

Every year on the third Monday of April, an army of patriots and redcoats gather on Lexington Green to participate in a reenactment of the Battle of Lexington. It is a stirring sight, but get up early: The Old Belfry sounds the alarm for the battle to begin at 5:30 a.m. Typically as many as 8,000–10,000 spectators begin arriving in town as early as 4 a.m. to claim a prime viewing spot. To get a sense of the battle without having to get up before dawn, you can attend a full dress rehearsal on the first Sunday in April at a more reasonable 2 p.m. The dress rehearsal is with muskets, but without powder, so there isn't any shooting, but there will be a lot fewer crowds. Check the Lexington Minute Men website (lexingtonminutemen .com) for details.

where to go

Lexington Visitor Center. 1875 Massachusetts Ave.; (781) 862-1450; lexingtonma.gov. The friendly staff is ready to assist with maps and walking directions to the Lexington Battle Green sites and is extremely well versed in giving directions to send you on your way to Concord. Be sure to check out the delightfully old-school diorama of the Battle of Lexington. Open daily Apr through Nov 9 a.m. to 5 p.m., Dec through Mar 10 a.m. to 4 p.m.

Battle Green. Massachusetts Avenue and Bedford Street. It was here, on the Lexington Common, that British soldiers first encountered an organized resistance by American colonial militia. At sunrise on April 19, 1775, some 77 militia men, led by Capt. John Parker, assembled to stand against an advancing army of some 700 British troops. Parker told his men, "Don't fire unless fired upon, but if they mean to have a war, let it begin here." A shot rang out, fire was exchanged, and eight colonists were killed. The British column then marched on toward Concord. In the warm weather months, you may see Lexington's costumed guides milling about; they are a great resource to answer your questions, so don't be shy—ask away! At the edge of the Battle Green, the *Lexington Minuteman* statue (erected in 1900) by Henry Hudson Kitson commemorates Captain Parker.

Lexington Historical Society. Lexington Depot, 13 Depot Sq.; (781) 862-1703; lexington history.org. The Lexington Historical Society manages the town's three historic home sites. Admission for all three properties is $15 adults, $8 ages 6 to 16, free for children under age 6. Admission for any one property is $8 adults, $5 ages 6 to 16, free for children under age 6.

Buckman Tavern. 1 Bedford St., (781) 862-5598. Prior to the impending arrival of British troops, Captain Parker's men fortified their courage with a night of drinking at this 1690 taproom. With its massive 7-foot fireplace, the property looks much as it did at the time of the battle on Lexington Green. Tours of the tavern recount the history of the building and the importance of taverns in colonial life. Open Apr through Oct, daily 10 a.m. to 4 p.m., tours on the half hour.

Hancock-Clarke House. 36 Hancock St., (781) 861-0928. On April 18, 1775, Paul Revere and William Dawes arrived here on their "midnight ride" to warn patriots John Hancock and Sam Adams (who were staying here to attend the Concord Provincial Congress) that British troops were approaching. Drop-in guided tours include a short orientation film about Lexington's role in the Revolution. Open Apr and May Sat and Sun 10 a.m. to 4 p.m.; June through Oct daily 10 a.m. to 4 p.m.

Munroe Tavern. 1332 Massachusetts Ave., (781) 862-0295. Just about a mile out of town, this 1695 tavern is where British troops regrouped for a few hours after the battle at Concord's North Bridge. Drop-in 30-minute guided tours (on the hour) tell the story of the British troop's return march to Boston. Open Apr through Nov, daily noon to 4 p.m.

Minute Man National Historical Park. Minute Man Visitor Center, 250 N. Great Rd., Lincoln; (978) 369-6993; nps.gov/mima. This nearly 1,000-acre park extends from Lexington through the town of Lincoln and into Concord. The Minute Man Visitor Center shows the excellent 25-minute film, *Road to Revolution,* which provides an introduction to the April 1775 events at Lexington and Concord. From the visitor center, a walk along part or all of the Battle Road Trail ties it all together. The 5-mile Battle Road Trail approximates a portion of the route followed by the British march to Concord through wooded forests, marshland, and open fields. The landscape then would have looked much as it does now. After a half mile, you will come upon a plaque that marks where Paul Revere was captured by a British patrol. Walk another half mile and you can visit the 1732 Hartwell Tavern, where costumed park rangers offer a short program (check website for schedule) on the Minute Men and demonstrate musket firing (cover your ears!). The Minute Man Visitor Center is open daily Apr through Oct 9 a.m. to 5 p.m. Grounds open dawn to dusk. Free.

where to eat

Artistry on the Green. 2027 Massachusetts Ave.; (781) 301-6665; innathastingspark.com. White wainscoting, simple Shaker-style wood furnishings and elegant chandeliers create a refined backdrop for New England cuisine at the acclaimed restaurant inside the Inn at Hastings Park. Seasonal ingredients sourced from nearby farms find their way into such dishes as duck breast with baby turnips and compressed apple walnut-black truffle jus or trout with leeks and fingerling potatoes at dinner. After a morning spent exploring the Revolutionary sites in Concord and Lexington enjoy a late lunch of pumpkin soup with persimmon and a bacon, lettuce and heirloom tomato sandwich. Open Sun 7 a.m. to 2 p.m. and 5 to 9 p.m.; Mon 7 to 10:30 a.m., Tues through Thurs 7 to 10:30 a.m., 11:30 a.m. to 2:30 p.m., 5:30 to 9 p.m.; Fri and Sat 7 to 10:30 a.m., 11:30 a.m. to 2:30 p.m., 5 to 9:30 p.m. $$–$$$.

Lexx. 1666 Massachusetts Ave.; (781) 674-2990; lexxrestaurant.com. Take a break from history. Just across from the post office, Lexx offers sit-down dining and a choice menu of high-end American pub grub: a grilled burger on a brioche roll, a chopped cobb salad, or baby back ribs in a pomegranate glaze. Thumbs up for the kids' menu choices, which include chicken tacos and burger sliders. Open Mon through Thurs 11:30 a.m. to 9 p.m., Fri and Sat 11:30 a.m. to 10 p.m., Sun 10 a.m. to 9 p.m. $$.

Neillio's Gourmet Kitchen. 53 Bedford St.; (781) 861-8466; neillioscatering.com. Locals swear by Neillio's. The must order? The Turkey Terrific, hand-carved roasted turkey with cranberry sauce and traditional stuffing. It's Thanksgiving in a sandwich and not like leftovers at all. There's a small stand-up counter where you can eat, but a better idea is to take it to go and enjoy your lunch on pretty Lexington Green. Open Mon through Fri 8 a.m. to 6:30 p.m., Sat 8 a.m. to 4 p.m., closed Sun. $.

Via Lago. 1845 Massachusetts Ave.; (781) 861-6174; vialagocatering.com. Regulars pack this local favorite for casual breakfasts of fresh-baked muffins and coffee; sandwiches and wraps, soups, and salads at lunch. At night the cafe transforms into a restaurant offering candle-lit waitress service that features apple-glazed chicken breast with sweet potatoes and a side salad that offers diners an especially good value. Open Mon through Wed 7 a.m. to 9 p.m., Thurs through Sat 7 a.m. to 9:30 p.m., closed Sun. $–$$.

where to stay

The Inn at Hastings Park. 2027 Massachusetts Ave.; (781) 301-6660; innathastingspark. com. This modern boutique inn of three historic 1800-era buildings has only operated as an inn since 2014. Owners Michael and Trisha Perez Kennealy have created a well-thought-out vision of New England hospitality. You feel as much at ease as if you were spending the weekend at the home of a good friend with a nicely appointed house. The inn has a creative colonial aesthetic with wide planked wood floors, high ceilings and multi-paned windows. Throughout the inn, trend meets tradition with wallpaper that offers a modern take on colonial design elements. Pops of bright color keeps everything fresh. Each of the 22 design-centric rooms is unique, complete with smartly sourced or custom furniture, original folk art and marble bathrooms; some have gas fireplaces. Count on niceties like beds with Frette linens and cozy Brahms Mount throws, flat-screen TVs and free Wi-Fi. The included, cooked-to-order breakfast at the inn's on-site casual fine dining restaurant Artistry on the Green may just be the highlight of your stay. $$$.

concord, ma

There are reminders of Concord's past on every corner, where historic colonial-era homes line the broad maple- and oak-shaded streets. The first official battle of the Revolution took place on Concord's North Bridge on April 19, 1775. In the late 1800s, Concord was the center of American literary life. Not only were writers Ralph Waldo Emerson, Nathaniel Hawthorne, Henry David Thoreau, and Louisa May Alcott contemporaries, they were friends and neighbors. The homes where they lived in Concord are extremely well preserved and are well worth a visit.

getting there

Concord is marching distance from Lexington—just 7 miles, or a 10-minute drive. Massachusetts Avenue parallels the Battle Road Trail. Bear right at Lexington Road and follow the signs to Concord Center.

where to go

Concord Visitor Center. 58 Main St.; (978) 371-0830; concordchamberofcommerce.org. Located in the center of town just a block from Monument Square, start here and pick up maps and brochures. The visitor center also offers a variety of themed historic walking tours. Check the website for schedules and pricing. Open Apr through Oct daily 10 a.m. to 4 p.m.

The Concord Museum. 53 Cambridge Tpke.; (978) 369-9763; concordmuseum.org. This is a great place to begin your visit to Concord. The two floors are packed with exhibits of Americana, including one of the Old North Church lanterns from the night of Paul Revere's ride, a doll belonging to Louisa May Alcott, the contents of Emerson's study, and Thoreau's bed and the desk where he wrote *Walden,* among his other artifacts. The museum's gift shop has a particularly good selection of American history-related items: tricornered hats and mob caps for the kids, replicas of Thoreau's walking stick, and a selection of Concord's literary best sellers that you may want to read or reread after your visit. Open Apr through May and Sept through Dec Mon through Sat 9 a.m. to 5 p.m., Sun noon to 5 p.m.; June through Aug Mon through Sat 9 a.m. to 5 p.m., Sun 9 a.m. to 5 p.m.; Jan through Mar Mon through Sat 11 a.m. to 4 p.m., Sun 1 to 4 p.m. Admission $10 adults, $8 seniors and students, $5 children ages 6 to 17, children under age 6 are free.

Minute Man National Historical Park. North Bridge Visitor Center, 174 Liberty St.; (978) 369-6993; nps.gov/mima. The western edge of the Minute Man National Historical Park that stretches into Concord includes the Old North Bridge, the town's most famous Revolutionary War site. It was here on April 19, 1775, that 400 minutemen successfully routed 700 British troops in what would become the first major battle of the Revolutionary War. Visit Daniel Chester French's iconic 1875 *Minute Man* statue; you may recognize it as the symbol of the US Army National Guard. The base is inscribed with words from the 1837 "Concord Hymn" by Ralph Waldo Emerson: "By the rude bridge that arched the flood,/ Their flag to April breeze unfurled,/Here once the embattled farmers stood,/And fired the shot heard round the world." Grounds open year-round, dawn to dusk. Visitor center open daily Apr through Oct 9:30 a.m. to 5 p.m., check website for off-season hours. Free.

The Old Manse. 269 Monument St.; (978) 369-3909; oldmanse.org. Lots of Revolutionary and literary connections here. The Old Manse, within sight of the North Bridge, was built in 1770 for the Reverend William Emerson, who witnessed the battle between the minutemen and the redcoats from his yard. His grandson Ralph Waldo Emerson lived here for a short time, as did Nathaniel Hawthorne, who rented the house as a newlywed. Tour highlights include the study used by both Emerson and Hawthorne, two window panes etched with terms of endearment between Hawthorne and his bride Sophia, and a restoration of the vegetable garden that Henry David Thoreau created as a wedding gift to the Hawthornes. Open mid-Apr through Oct, Tues through Sun, noon to 5 p.m.; Nov and Dec and mid-Mar through mid-Apr Sat and Sun noon to 5 p.m.; closed Jan through mid-Mar; also by appointment. Admission $10 adults, $9 seniors, $5 children ages 6 to 12.

Orchard House. 399 Lexington Rd.; (978) 369-5778; louisamayalcott.org. A must-visit for fans of Louisa May Alcott's beloved novel, *Little Women*. Orchard House is the setting for the book, and Alcott lived here while writing the story. A short video and guided tour of the house provides an intimate glimpse of Alcott's life here with her parents and three sisters— the models for *Little Women*'s March family. Of special interest is the (very small) shelf desk where Alcott wrote. Open Nov through Mar Mon through Fri 11 a.m. to 3 p.m., Sat 10 a.m. to 4:30 p.m., Sun 1 to 4:30 p.m.; Apr through Oct Mon through Sat 10 a.m. to 4:30 p.m., Sun 1 to 4:30 p.m. Admission $10 adults, $8 seniors and students, $5 ages 6 to 17, under age 6 are free, $25 family rate.

Sleepy Hollow Cemetery. 34 Bedford Street; (978) 318-3233. In the naturalized garden cemetery tradition of Cambridge's Mount Auburn Cemetery (see Day Trip 02), Concord's Sleepy Hollow Cemetery is as restful and peaceful as it sounds. Louisa May Alcott, Ralph Waldo Emerson, Henry David Thoreau, and Nathaniel Hawthorne are buried in the area known as Author's Ridge. The grave of sculptor David Chester French is here, too. Open daily dawn to dusk.

South Bridge Boathouse. 496 Main St.; (978) 369-9438; southbridgeboathouse.com. Rent a canoe or kayak for an idyllic paddle along the Concord River and gain a Thoreau-like perspective of Concord's pastoral beauty. From the boathouse, it is an easy 1.5-mile stretch to Concord's Old North Bridge. Open seasonally Mon through Fri 10 a.m. until 1 hour before dusk, Sat and Sun 9 a.m. until 1 hour before dusk. Rental rates from $16 per hour.

Walden Pond. 915 Walden St.; (978) 369-3254; mass.gov/dcr/parks/walden. A sort of shrine for both American-literature lovers and environmentalists, this is where Henry David

Thoreau "lived alone, in the woods, a mile from any neighbor in a house I had built myself, on the shores of Walden Pond." Thoreau's two-year experiment in solitude was the basis for his book *Walden,* published in 1854. You can visit a replica of his one-room cabin next to the parking lot. Today, much of the park's 460 acres of forest is still pristine and "Walden-like," and there are miles of well-marked nature trails to explore. Walden Pond is also one of the Boston area's most popular summertime swimming holes. Come early if you plan a weekend visit; the park closes when capacity is reached, usually by midmorning on a hot summer day. Open daily dawn to dusk. Free admission, $8 parking fee in summer.

where to shop

Concord Book Shop. 65 Main St.; (978) 369-2405; concordbookshop.com. In business since 1940, this wonderfully comfortable village shop keeps the focus on books and the people who love them with a balanced mix of best sellers and classics along with a bountiful selection of children's books. The shop also boasts a robust program of high-profile literary events. Open Mon through Wed 9:30 a.m. to 6 p.m., Thurs 9:30 a.m. to 9 p.m., Fri 9:30 a.m. to 6 p.m., Sat 9:30 a.m. to 5 p.m., Sun noon to 5 p.m.

Nesting. 44 Main St.; (978) 369-4133; nestingonmain.com. This shop is full of fanciful home accents and quirky gifts that you never knew existed. Find a mix of new and vintage pieces including antique sterling bracelets and handmade charms, flour-sack tea towels, white Ironstone, and an ever-changing selection of restored tables, cabinets, and clocks. Open Mon through Sat 10 a.m. to 5 p.m., Sun noon to 5 p.m.

West Concord Five & Ten. 106 Commonwealth Ave., (978) 369-9011; mainstreethub. com/westconcordfiveandten. The prices may have changed a bit from the days when a nickel or a dime had real purchasing power, but the vintage charm of this neighborhood store is very much intact. Originally opened in 1934, the product assortment offers a little bit of everything including light bulbs, finger puppets, wire egg whips and mason jars. Open Mon through Fri 8 a.m. to 6:30 p.m., Sat 9 a.m. to 6 p.m., closed Sun.

where to eat

Bedford Farms Ice Cream. 68 Thoreau St.; (978) 341-0000; bedfordfarmsicecream .com. A must-stop, especially after a visit to Walden Pond. This is homemade, small-batch, premium ice cream. If vanilla is the standard by which ice cream is judged, then Bedford Farms's vanilla is great. They do excellent gourmet flavors, too, like the cherry bomb—vanilla ice cream with black cherries and chocolate chips—as well as a true coffee ice cream. Open Mar through Nov, Mon through Sat 11 a.m. to 9 p.m., Sun noon to 9 p.m.; open rest of the year daily noon to 6 p.m.

Concord Cheese Shop. 29 Walden St., (978) 369-5778; concordcheeseshop.com. Minute Man National Park, Walden Pond and the grounds of the DeCordova Museum offer unique green spaces for an impromptu picnic. You can pull together the perfect eats for an outdoor lunch at this legendary cheese shop including made-to-order sandwiches like the French Picnic made of ham, brie, apples and champagne mustard on a baguette or the Black Stallion made of roast beef, Swiss, lettuce, roasted red peppers, sprouts and horseradish on wheat. Or you can pull together your own spread from the cheese case which brims with runny Robiolas and marbled blues along with salumi, charcuterie and a full array of exquisite picnic foodstuffs from around the world including small production wines and artisan chocolates. Note that the shop does have a few tables and chairs set up in the front of the store for customers' use. Open Tues through Thurs 10:30 a.m. to 5:30 p.m., Sat 9 a.m. to 5:30 p.m., closed Sun and Mon. $.

Main Streets Market & Cafe. 42 Main St.; (978) 369-9948; mainstreetsmarketandcafe .com. In a historic renovated brick gristmill in the center of Concord, this easy-going family-style New England eatery reigns for all-day dining. Breakfast dishes include eggs, toast, and home fries or waffles. Lunch caters to sightseers and locals with soups, chowders, and chili; grilled panini, wraps, and salads. At dinner, find sturdy fare like the Yankee pot roast dinner, baked haddock, or shrimp and scallop risotto. There's live music Monday through Saturday nights and a full bar. Open Tues through Sat 6:30 a.m. to 11 p.m., Sun and Mon 6:30 a.m. to 6 p.m. $–$$.

Woods Hill Table. 24 Commonwealth Ave.; (978) 369-6300; woodshilltable.com With its cream colored walls, iron chandeliers, enormous stone fireplace and reclaimed wood beams Woods Hill Table brings New England farmhouse chic to the village of West Concord. This is a destination restaurant that lures locals and tourists alike with the promise of a memorable meal of thoughtful, ingredient-driven fare. This is comfort food with just a bit of edge: wood grilled broccoli with cheddar and smoked garlic aioli, beef tartare with quail egg and toast, roast pork (with a proper fat cap) and apple fritters. And someone in the kitchen knows how to make gnocchi: pan seared with brown butter and wild mushrooms—sublime! Much of the meat and produce that is served is supplied from proprietor Kirstin Canty's Bath, New Hampshire farm. Naturally the menu changes with the season. Open Tues through Thurs 5 to 9:30 p.m.; Fri 5 to 10 p.m.; Sat 11 a.m. to 1:45 p.m., 5 to 10 p.m. Bar open Tues through Sat 5 to 9 p.m. Closed Sun. $$$.

where to stay

Concord's Colonial Inn. 48 Monument Sq.; (978) 369-9200 or (800) 370-9200; concords colonialinn.com. This 56-room country inn sits in the heart of Concord and just exudes antique charm. Some of the rooms in the original building, with wide-plank floors and post-beam ceilings, date from 1716. Rooms in the adjacent wing are of more recent vintage, but all are tastefully decorated in American Colonial Revival style. In fine weather, the inn's Liberty Restaurant serves meals on the front porch overlooking Monument Square. The Valley

Forge Tavern features live entertainment Tuesday through Sunday night. All rooms have private bathrooms and free Wi-Fi. Breakfast is extra. $$–$$$.

Hawthorne Inn. 462 Lexington Rd.; (978) 369-5610; hawthorneinnconcord.com. The longtime couple that ran the 7-room Hawthorne Inn found a buyer. New husband and wife owners Mark Vell and Toni Vincente bought the bed and breakfast in 2016 and gave it a chic overhaul for a new generation. Located across the street from Orchard House, the iconic clapboard still retains the architectural elements of the 1860s house but now with a playful, eye-catching design that includes such details as cream-colored linen settee, hummingbird print pillows, a mirror finish side table alongside antiques like a free-standing claw tub plus plenty of high-end linens to keep it feeling cozy. Mark and Toni are sociable hosts; each morning they put out a formidable breakfast spread of granola, pastries, jams, coffee and more on the long common table, all homemade or from local purveyors. $$.

lowell, ma

Founded on the banks of the Merrimack River in the 1820s, which provided the hydropower to run large-scale textile mills, Lowell was the country's first planned industrial city and is the historic center of the American textile industry. The mills flourished here until World War I and the migration of the textile industry to southern states. Today, Lowell is home to a large number of Cambodian and Latin American immigrants as well as a growing student population from the University of Massachusetts Lowell campus. But Lowell still holds tight to its mill-town roots and is home to several lesser-known but nonetheless fascinating museums on the textile arts. And although not totally "revitalized," it can be said that Lowell is well on its way.

getting there

From Concord, follow MA 62 East to MA 4 North to US 3. Take exit 30B, pick up the Lowell Connector to Thorndike Street, and follow the signs to the Lowell National Park Visitor Center parking lot on Dutton Street. Your total driving distance is only 17 miles, but total drive time will take about 30 minutes.

where to go

Boott Cotton Mills Museum. 115 John St.; (978) 970-5000. This is the principal exhibit of the Lowell National Historic Park. The focus here is the history of the Industrial Revolution, as the country's economy shifted from farm to factory. You can also experience the thunderous clatter of 88 operating power looms. Ear plugs are provided! Open daily 9:30 a.m. to 5 p.m. Admission $6 adults, $4 seniors and students, $3 children ages 6 to 16, free for children ages 5 and under.

Lowell National Historical Park. 304 Dutton St.; (978) 970-5000; nps.gov/lowe. An urban park that has a lot to offer the day-tripper with self-guided exhibits, guided walking tours, canal boat cruises (see next paragraph), and trolley rides. Start at the National Park Visitor Center to pick up a schedule of the day's activities and a walking map. The visitor center also serves as the de facto visitor information center for the city and has brochures and such for other places in town. Be sure to see the short introductory film *Lowell: The Continuing Revolution* before you set out. If canal tours are offered on the day of your visit, sign up if you haven't already done so in advance, and plan your activities accordingly. A free trolley transports visitors the short distance from the visitor center to the Boott Cotton Mills Museum. Open daily 9 a.m. to 5 p.m. Admission is free.

> **Canal Boat Tours.** Park Service guides will regale you with canal lore as your boat makes its way slowly through the locks and gates along the historic Merrimack River. The 2-hour tours are offered daily several times a day from late June to late August. Check website for exact times; reservations are required. Admission $12 adults, $10 seniors and students, $8 ages 6 to 16, free ages 5 and under.

New England Quilt Museum. 18 Shattuck St.; (978) 452-4207; nequiltmuseum.org. A haven for quilters, the museum showcases a collection of traditional and contemporary quilts. It is a stunning permanent collection, from simple patchwork and appliqué quilts to fine pictorial and botanical pieces to contemporary art hangings. Special themed quilt shows have included Civil War Quilts and Art Quilts from Haiti. Find all things quilting—books, fabric, thread, and gift items—at the museum's shop. Open May through Oct Tues through Sat 10 a.m. to 4 p.m., Sun noon to 4 p.m.; Nov through Apr Wed through Sat 10 a.m. to 4 p.m. Admission $8 adults, $5 seniors and students.

Patrick J. Mogan Cultural Center. 40 French St.; (978) 970-5000. Another NPS site, the exhibits here chronicle the lives of Lowell citizens. Learn the history of the "mill girls," the young women who came from area farms to work in the factories and lived in the company-run boardinghouses. Later, the worker pool transitioned to new immigrant groups, especially Irish and Canadians. Although not much appreciated in Lowell in his lifetime, the city has since come around to honoring native son, author Jack Kerouac, who often wrote about his hometown. See his typewriter and *On the Road* artifacts here. Open daily 1:30 to 5 p.m. Admission is free.

Whistler House Museum of Art. 243 Worthen St., (978) 452-7641; whistlerhouse.org. New England excels at small quirky art museums. Case in point is this unassuming 1823 clapboard house located in downtown Lowell. It is the birthplace of mid-19th-century American painter James McNeil Whistler. Whistler's most famous painting, *Grey and Black No.1*, known popularly as *Whistler's Mother*, hangs at the Musee D'Orsay in Paris. Along with a fine copy of *Whistler's Mother*, the museum is in possession of several of Whistler's etchings. The museum's permanent collection also includes works by Whistler's contemporaries

lowell folk festival: keeping the traditional arts alive

The Lowell Folk Festival is one of the best-attended festivals in New England and the largest free folk festival in the country. Whatever your musical taste—rockabilly, blues, gospel, zydeco, jazz, or world—there is something for everyone. Culinary offerings are just as wide-ranging and way better than your ordinary festival fare, with treats from Cambodia, Vietnam, Poland, Greece, Portugal, Jamaica, and more. The festival takes over most of downtown Lowell during the last weekend in July. Lowell Folk Festival; (978) 275-1764; lowellfolkfestival.org.

John Singer Sargent and William Morris Hunt. The museum attracts lots of visitors too for its splendid collection of 30 modern abstract paintings by mid-20th-century Armenian artist Arshile Gorky. Open Wed through Sat 11 a.m. to 4 p.m. Admission $10 adults, free under age 18.

where to eat

Brew'd Awakening Coffeehaus. 61 Market St.; (978) 454-2739; brewdawakening.com. This local favorite hangout attracts a colorful clientele and offers potent coffee drinks to please even purists and a good selection of pastries and light lunch salads and sandwiches. There's only one problem—it's way too popular on open-mic nights. If a table empties, you need to move in fast. Open Mon through Fri 6:30 a.m. to 9 p.m., Sat and Sun 7 a.m. to 9 p.m. $.

Cobblestones. 91 Dutton St.; (978) 970-2282; cobblestonesoflowell.com. Located in a former mill boardinghouse and within the Lowell National Historical Park, Cobblestones is American through and through. The menu of traditional fare features sandwiches, salads, and burgers for lunch, while dinner has comfort-food entrees like braised beef short ribs and baked haddock. Open Mon through Sat 11:30 a.m. to 11 p.m., Sun 11 a.m. to 9 p.m. $–$$.

Life Alive Organic Cafe. 194 Middle St.; (978) 453-1311; lifealive.com. Not only is everything on this cafe's creative globe-trotting menu either vegetarian or vegan, it is mouthwateringly good while nourishing your social conscience. Choose from a selection of salads, wraps, and grain-based entrees. You can't go wrong with their signature dish, the Goddess: smoked tofu and brown rice with steamed carrots, beets, broccoli, and a ginger dressing, available as a bowl or wrap. They sell fair-traded coffee and tea, too. Open Mon through Wed 10 a.m. to 8 p.m., Thurs and Fri 10 a.m. to 9 p.m., Sat 10 a.m. to 8 p.m., Sun noon to 6 p.m. $.

Simply Khmer. 26 Lincoln St.; (978) 454-6700; simplykhmerrestaurant.com. Lowell is home to the second largest Cambodian immigrant community in the country. Cambodian restaurants are to Lowell what Italian restaurants are to Boston's North End. The fried glazed chicken wings tend to get most of the attention from first time diners, but there is lots more to love here, including basil and chili loaded papaya salad and grilled cubes of *luk lak* beef served with sticky rice. Open Wed through Sun 10 a.m. to 9 p.m., closed Mon and Tues. $–$$.

day trip 04

boston

the dark arts & maritime heritage:
salem, ma; gloucester, ma;
ipswich, ma

Explore Salem's witch-kitsch attractions and its world-class art museum. Farther along the North Shore, discover Massachusetts's other Cape, Cape Ann. These are the quietly stunning rocky shores and the working class fishing villages that were depicted in the Matt Damon-produced 2016 movie Manchester-by-the-Sea starring Casey Affleck. The spit of land that juts out into the Atlantic Ocean is home to Gloucester, America's oldest working fishing port. Pretty Ipswich village boasts fine precolonial homes and one of Massachusetts' best sandy beaches. While in nearby Newburyport, the Parker National Wildlife Refuge on Plum Island attracts birders from all over.

salem, ma

Salem has never been shy to capitalize on its reputation as "Witch City." Halloween is serious business here, celebrated by the city for the entire month of October. Year-round, tourists come to pose in front of the *Bewitched* statue of Elizabeth Montgomery as Samantha Stevens at Essex and Washington Streets. And there are several witch-themed attractions and lots of stores that sell hokey witch paraphernalia. But Salem really has far more to offer visitors. Lovers of American literature will want to tour the House of the Seven Gables, made famous by Nathaniel Hawthorne's book of the same name. Salem is also a historic seaport. Salem merchants became extraordinarily wealthy in the years immediately following the Revolutionary War as their frigates sailed the world in search of international trade. You can

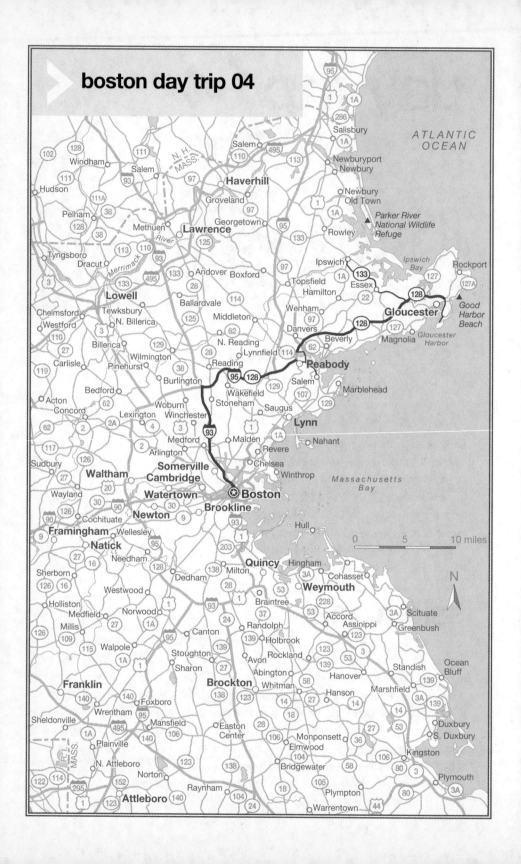

boston day trip 04

see the treasures from their voyages at the Peabody Essex Museum and hear tales of the "age of wooden ships and iron men" at the Salem Maritime Historic Site.

getting there

Take I-93 North to I-95 North to exit 45 and MA 128 North (Route 128). Take exit 25A to MA 114 East (North Street), which leads directly into town. The total driving distance is 25 miles, but depending on traffic on North Street, total drive time is 30–45 minutes. Salem is also accessible by high-speed ferry from Central Wharf in Boston. The *Nathaniel Bowditch* makes 5 round-trips daily from May through October, salemferry.com.

where to go

Cry Innocent: The People vs. Bridget Bishop. 32 Derby Sq.; (978) 867-4767; cryinnocent salem.com. Since 1992, this interactive historical stage performance offers an informative perspective to the witchcraft trials. Set in Salem in 1692, Bridget Bishop has been accused of witchcraft. Audience members can cross-examine the witnesses and ultimately decide Bridget's fate. Performances take place in a terrific venue for the subject matter—Salem's Old Town Hall. Season runs mid-June through Oct; check website for performance times. Tickets $14.50 adults, $13.50 seniors and students, $12.50 ages 6 to 12.

House of the Seven Gables. 115 Derby St.; (978) 744-0991; 7gables.org. Tour the mansion that inspired Nathaniel Hawthorne to write *The House of the Seven Gables.* Built in 1668, this is the oldest surviving 17th-century mansion in New England. Hands down, climbing up the secret staircase from the cellar to the attic is the highlight of the tour. The home is beautifully sited overlooking Salem Harbor, and the seaside garden offers a lovely stroll. Nathaniel Hawthorne's birthplace has been relocated to the property from its original site a few streets away. House visits are by guided tour, which run continuously throughout the day. Open Nov through June 10 a.m. to 5 p.m., July through Oct 10 a.m. to 7 p.m., closed the first 2 weeks of Jan. Admission $14 adults, $13 seniors and students, $11 ages 13 to 18, $9 children ages 5 to 12.

Peabody Essex Museum. 161 Essex St.; (978) 745-9500; pem.org. You don't run a seaport for 400 years without developing a few interests. Founded in 1799, the world-class Peabody Essex Museum is actually America's oldest continuously operating museum. The first thing you notice when entering is the building's architecture: The soaring glass ceiling over the central atrium space mimics a ship's sail, a nod to Salem's maritime heritage. The galleries are brimming with curios and treasures from around the world. Particular strengths are Asian export art, marine paintings, and American portraiture and furniture. Be sure to visit Yin Yu Tang, a reconstructed 200-year-old home of a Chinese merchant. Timed-entry tickets are an additional $6 and include a snazzy self-guided audio-wand. Open Tues through

salem's dark past: the witch trials

Salem's 1692 witchcraft hysteria began when two Salem-area girls began having unexplained "fits" and accused three local women of casting spells on them. A frenzy of accusations among the townspeople followed that year, and over 150 people—both men and women—were arrested and imprisoned for allegedly practicing witchcraft. Ultimately, 14 women and 5 men were executed by hanging, and a man was pressed to death by heavy stones placed on his chest. Today, Salem honors the victims of the tragedy by retelling their stories.

Sun and holidays falling on Mon 10 a.m. to 5 p.m. Admission $20 adults, $18 seniors, $12 students, free for children ages 16 and under.

When Salem was a humming seaport, there were dozens of shops like the **West India Goods Store.** Today it is operated on behalf of the National Park Service. Poke around for whole and ground spices, coffees, teas, and other curiosities like compasses and tortoise-shell combs.

Salem Witch Trials Memorial. 98 Liberty St., next to Salem's Burying Point (cemetery). Dedicated in 1992 to coincide with the 300th anniversary of Salem's witch trials, this solemn space commemorates the victims who were tried, convicted, and executed for practicing witchcraft. Under dappled shade, the low stone walls of the small park support 20 benches, each inscribed with the name of a victim and the date and cause of their death.

where to shop

Harbor Sweets. 85 Leavitt St.; (978) 745-7648; harborsweets.com. Just a short walk from Salem's downtown attractions you can visit the headquarters and working candy factory of Harbor Sweets. Their signature handmade Sweet Sloops chocolates were launched in 1973: a sailboat-shaped almond buttercrunch enrobed in white chocolate floating on a wave of dark chocolate and pecans. Free samples! The retail store is open Mon through Fri 8:30 a.m. to 5 p.m., Sat 9 a.m. to 5 p.m., closed Sun. Factory tours are offered most Tues and Thurs at 11 a.m.

where to eat

A & J King Artisan Bakers. 48 Central St.; (978) 744-4881; ajkingbakery.com. Using traditional craft methods and a locavore approach to bread baking, the faithful line up daily for just-out-of-the-oven loaves along with decadent pastries like seasonal fruit tarts and brown butter cakes. Their commitment extends to the made-to-order sandwiches including a wonderful smoked ham and brie on a baguette and for the kids, peanut butter, seasonal jam, and fluff. Open Mon through Fri 7 a.m. to 6 p.m., Sat through Sun 7 a.m. to 4 p.m. $.

Finz Seafood & Grill. 76 Wharf St.; (978) 744-8485; hipfinz.com. Overlooking lively Salem Harbor, patrons vie for spots on Finz's expansive patio. The menu specializes in creative takes on seafood like tuna tartare with mango, red onion, and avocado, and haddock with crab and a sherry cream sauce. Open Sun through Weds 11:30 a.m. to 9 p.m., Thurs 11:30 a.m. to 10 p.m., Fri and Sat 11:30 a.m. to 11 p.m. $$.

Flying Saucer Pizza. 118 Washington St., (978) 594-8189; livelongandpizza.com.Embrace your inner-nerd at this sci-fi themed pizza joint that serves seriously excellent upscale pizza. The décor is retro and funky—all action figures and movie posters—while the cheeky menu is full of Star Trek, Star Wars and Marvel Comics references like the Solaris (traditional cheese), the Admiral Akbar (clam chowder and bacon), and the Nick Fury (mac and cheese, buffalo chicken, scallion and siracha). Good crafts on tap here too. Open daily 11 a.m. to 11 p.m. $–$$.

Jaho Coffee & Tea. 197 Derby St.; (978) 744-4300; jaho.com. Relax and stay a while at this community-based coffeehouse/gathering place and watch the passing street parade of characters that Salem seems to attract. The baristas are artists and pull espresso with a perfect crema. Tea fans will be ecstatic because there are dozens of loose-leaf varieties here. Besides caffeine drinks, there are desserts, gelato, and sandwiches, too. Open Mon through Fri 7 a.m. to 11 p.m., Sat 8 a.m. to 11 p.m., and Sun 8 a.m. to 10 p.m. $.

where to stay

Hawthorne Hotel. 18 Washington Sq.; (978) 744-4080; hawthornehotel.com. Well located in the center of all that Salem has to offer, this historic 100-room hotel was built in 1925 and offers modern comforts with an old-fashioned New England feel. Note that some bathrooms have only a shower. $$–$$$.

Salem Waterfront Hotel & Suites. 225 Derby St.; (978) 740-8788; salemwaterfront hotel.com. This hotel is located right next to Salem Harbor and within convenient walking distance to Salem's attractions. Guest rooms are cheery, done up in neutrals and a subtle nautical theme. This modern hotel is well suited to leisure travelers with an indoor, heated pool and fitness center. Look for bargain packages that include breakfast and other amenities. This is a favorite choice for vacationing families. $$–$$$.

worth more time

Singing Beach. 119 Beach St., Manchester-by-the-Sea; (978) 526-2019; manchester. ma.us/facilities/facility/details/Singing-Beach-11. Locally famous for its "singing sand" which squeaks as you walk barefoot on it, Singing Beach is Manchester-by-the-Sea's most visited spot. The half-mile crescent is lifeguard supervised and features changing rooms and a snack shack. The beach has hard-packed flats ideal for play when the tide goes out. When sunning and swimming start to pale, it's just a short walk to town for ice cream. $5 walk-on beach fee and $25 parking fee from mid-June through Labor Day.

gloucester, ma

Just 20 miles northwest of Salem, Gloucester is America's oldest fishing port, first settled by Puritans from England in 1623. The heyday of the Gloucester fishing industry may have been in the mid-1800s, but Gloucester is still a working commercial fishing port and home to a trawler fleet that fish the waters of the Atlantic for cod, halibut, haddock, and lobster. You may remember the book and movie *The Perfect Storm,* which recounts the story of the Gloucester-based swordfishing boat, the *Andrea Gail,* that was lost during the Halloween storm of October 1991. Gloucester has it all for a seaside vacation, too, with miles of scenic sandy beaches and fine arts shopping at the galleries of the Rocky Neck summer art colony.

getting there

From Salem, pick up MA 128 North, which ends in Gloucester, and take exit 14 to reach the downtown harbor area or exit 13 for Good Harbor Beach.

where to go

Cape Ann Chamber of Commerce. 33 Commercial St.; (978) 283-1601; capeannvaca tions.com. The main information center on Commercial Street is open year-round. The small booth at the Harbor Loop and Rogers Street, close to the Gloucester Maritime Center and the day-trip docks, is open seasonally. Both are staffed by volunteers who can help with information and maps for Gloucester, and also for the Cape Ann region, including the towns of Rockport, Essex, and Manchester-by-the-Sea. Open Mon through Fri 9 a.m. to 5 p.m. in winter; Mon through Fri 9 a.m. to 5 p.m., Sat 10 a.m. to 5 p.m., and Sun 11 a.m. to 4 p.m. in summer.

Cape Ann Museum. 27 Pleasant St.; (978) 283-0455; capeannmusuem.org. Gloucester-born Fitz Henry Lane painted scenes of the coast of New England for his entire career. This small gem of a museum has the largest collection of the master luminist's paintings (40 paintings and more than 100 drawings) as well as works by Winslow Homer and Edward Hopper. The museum has recently completed a redesign of its galleries. This is no longer a white-wall museum—galleries now have subtle colors, and the entrance lobby is now open and light-filled. Open Tues through Sat 10 a.m. to 5 p.m., Sun 1 to 4 p.m. Admission $10 adults, $8 seniors and students. Free for children ages 18 and under.

The Gloucester Fisherman's Memorial. Stacy Boulevard. It's a pleasant walk from the docks along the seawall to the iconic *Gloucester Fisherman* statue, also known as the *Man at the Wheel.* It's sometimes referred to as the "Gorton's Fisherman's statue" because Gloucester-based Gorton's has used some form of the statue's image on its packaging since the 1960s. The larger-than-life 1925 bronze fisherman overlooks the harbor; its base is inscribed with THEY THAT GO DOWN TO THE SEA IN SHIPS 1623–1923, and it honors the more than 10,000 Gloucester fishermen who have lost their lives at sea since the city's founding.

Good Harbor Beach. MA 127A (Thatcher Road). A wide mile-long swath of windswept dunes, this is one of New England's premier beaches and hugely popular with both locals and tourists. At low tide you can walk across the tidal flats to explore nearby Salt Island. In season there are lifeguards, and there is a large bathhouse and concession stand that sells food, drinks, and boogie boards. Open daily summer 9 a.m. to 6 p.m.; off-season hours dawn to dusk. Admission charged from Memorial Day to Labor Day, $30 parking fee per vehicle weekends and summer holidays, $25 weekdays. Free admission off-season.

The *Thomas E. Lannon*. 63 Rogers St.; (978) 281-6634; schooner.org. Take to the high seas on a classic wooden two-mast fishing schooner. Built in 1996, the *Lannon* is a replica of a 1903 ship and makes daily 2-hour public sails of Gloucester Harbor from late June through early September, with weekend sails only in May and October. Tickets are $40 adults, $35 seniors, $27.50 for children to age 16.

Wingaersheek Beach. Access from Atlantic Street. A small picturesque ocean beach nestled at the mouth of the Annisquam River and Ipswich Bay. "Wing," as locals know it, is an especially good swimming beach for young children, with warm water, gentle waves, and hardly any undertow. Low tide encourages beachcombers of all ages to walk out along the sandbar as far as a quarter mile for one of the best views of Annisquam Lighthouse. The half-mile-long beach has lifeguards, a snack stand, and restrooms. Open daily in summer 9 a.m. to 6 p.m.; off-season hours dawn to dusk. Admission charged from Memorial Day to Labor Day, $30 parking fee per vehicle weekends and summer holidays, $25 weekdays. Free admission off-season.

where to shop

The Rocky Neck Art Colony. Along Rocky Neck Avenue; rockyneckartcolony.org. The scenic views and ramshackle waterfront buildings clustered along Smith Cove have attracted artists to Gloucester's Rocky Neck neighborhood since the mid-1850s, among them Fitz Henry Lane, Childe Hassam, Winslow Homer, and Edward Hopper. Rocky Neck is still a thriving art scene where contemporary craftspeople work and/or live in their studio galleries and put their modern-day spin on traditional seaside arts. The **John Nesta Gallery** (37 Rocky Neck Ave.; 978-283-4319; johnnesta.com) specializes in original oil paintings of Cape Ann seascapes. At **Gallery 53** (53 Rocky Neck Ave.; 978-282-0917) you'll find everything from pottery to photographs to oil paintings. And because the gallery represents 25 to 30 artists, you may just be able to afford to buy something here. **Hughes Bosca at the Side Street Gallery** (17 Rocky Neck Ave.; 978-283-3791; hugesbosca.com) specializes in delightfully and utterly original 18 k gold jewelry: hammered cuff bangles, lariats of Mediterranean coral and gold, cabochon rings of tourmaline all of which are shown to beautiful effect. Even if you are not buying, this is a fun store to visit. The Rocky Neck season runs from May through September, although some galleries are open year-round. Check individual websites for gallery hours.

where to eat

Cafe Sicillia. 40 Main St.; (978) 283-7345. It's a tiny space with only a few tables, but worth seeking out for delicious cappuccino and scrumptious baked-on-the-premises Italian pastries. Among them, the cannoli, tiramisu, and *sfogliatelle* (also known as "lobster tails" in New England) are all excellent. So, too, is the gelato. Open Mon through Sat 7 a.m. to 5 p.m., Sun 7 a.m. to 1 p.m. $.

Duckworth's Bistro. 197 E. Main St.; (978) 282-4426; duckworthsbistro.com. Considered one of the top culinary destinations on the North Shore (reservations are a must), Ken and Nicole Duckworth's welcoming restaurant offers the thoughtful composed salads, perfect duck leg confit, and classic crème caramel that you would expect from an elegant bistro. Diners love that many of the dishes—as well as 20 of the wines—are available in half portions. Open Tues through Thurs 5 to 9:30 p.m., Fri and Sat 4 to 9:30 p.m. $$$.

Franklin Cafe Cape Ann. 118 Main St.; (978) 283-7888; franklincafe.com. Always creative and sometimes sublime (lavender-honey–glazed salmon and the short ribs with roasted tomato risotto), this New American restaurant is also fairly easy on the wallet. On weekends especially, it's a buzzing place, but really friendly service (and strong drinks) make the room seem less noisy than it is. Open Sun through Thurs 5 to 10:30 p.m., Fri and Sat 5 p.m. to midnight. $$.

Jalapeños. 86 Main St.; (978) 283-8228; jalapenosgloucester.com. Find fine Mexican dining in Gloucester, where the well-executed seafood-centric menu includes dishes such as scallops ceviche, shrimp Veracruz, and lobster enchiladas. Their cantina standards are excellent, too, and the margaritas will knock you over. Open Mon through Thurs 4 p.m. to 9:30 p.m., Fri 3:30 p.m. to midnight, Sat 11:30 a.m. to midnight, Sun 3 to 9 p.m. $$.

Pleasant Street Tea Company. 7 Pleasant St.; (978) 283-3933. Lots of loyal local customers gravitate to this comfy cafe, and why not: they come for the laid-back vibe, tasty sandwich combos like the cheddar and ham with fig jam panini, and a long menu of coffee, tea, and fresh-pressed juices. Open Mon through Fri 7:30 a.m. to 8 p.m., Sat and Sun 8 a.m. to 8 p.m. $.

gloucester's greasy pole contest

Dating back to the 1930s, the Feast of Saint Peter honors the patron saint of fisherman and celebrates the Italian-American heritage of Gloucester's fishing fleet. Taking place during the last weekend in June, the highlight of the 5-day event is the greasy pole contest. Crowds gather to watch as the town's men and boys (women traditionally don't participate) run across a 45-foot telephone pole attached to a platform hanging 25 feet over Gloucester Harbor to capture a flag at its end. The pole is greased, making the task seem impossible, but every year, somehow, someway, several contestants manage the feat before splashing into the ocean to the cheers of enthusiastic crowds.

Short & Main. 36 Main St.; (978) 281-0444; shortandmain.com. You wouldn't know it necessarily from the name, but this is a pizza and seafood restaurant. It's also one of Gloucester's sleeker and buzzier establishments. Order oysters on the half shell and a glass of wine to start. Almost anything finished in chef-owner Nico's wood burning oven is a hit, including crackly Margherita pizza or the local haddock with cauliflower, oyster mushrooms and breadcrumb salsa. Open Fri and Sat 5 to 11 p.m.; Sun 11 a.m. to 2 p.m., 5 to 10 p.m., Mon, Wed and Thurs 5 to 10 p.m., closed Tues. $$.

Sugar Magnolias. 112 Main St.; (978) 281-5310; sugarmags.com. Well known on the North Shore for amazing breakfasts that include enough food for the whole day, Sugar Mags does out-of-this-world pancakes, specialty french toast, and a myriad of multi-ingredient omelets. It can be an excruciating wait, but those carrot-cake pancakes with maple cream cheese butter are worth it. Lunchtime choices include really big deli sandwiches and salads. Open Tues through Fri 7 a.m. to 2:30 p.m., Sat and Sun 7 a.m. to 1 p.m.; closed Mon Labor Day through Memorial Day. $.

where to stay

Bass Rocks Ocean Inn. 107 Atlantic Rd.; (978) 283-7600; bassrocksoceaninn.com. Every one of the 51 rooms of this pleasant hotel has a balcony or patio with ocean views. Rooms in the historic Stacy House mansion are suites and have a whirlpool tub, kitchenette, and a living room. The rooms in the modern block are spacious and smartly, but traditionally, furnished. The hotel has an outdoor heated pool, an old-fashioned billiards room, bikes to borrow, a firepit, lovely grounds, and a path to the beach. All rates include an expanded continental breakfast with homemade baked goods and fresh fruit, as well as afternoon tea and cookies. Open seasonally May through Oct. $$.

Beauport Hotel. 55 Commercial St.; (978) 282-0008; beauporthotel.com. Once a Birdseye flash freezing fish facility, this brand-new (2016) hotel has a rooftop pool with views of the Atlantic. The 94 rooms are decked out in a soothing coastal aesthetic with shades of navy and sandy white, framed sea bird prints and nautical striped rugs. The hotel's 1606 Tavern has both a casual and fine dining menu with outdoor seating on the deck in nice weather. And best of all, there's a dedicated shuttle to whisk guests to wherever they want to go within 3 miles of the hotel—avoiding the hassle of finding a parking spot. $$.

Sea Lion Motel & Cottages. 138 Eastern Ave.; (978) 283-7300; sealionmotel.com. Good Harbor Beach is just a short 2-minute drive from this family-friendly motel and cottage complex. Choose your accommodations from motel rooms, efficiencies with kitchenettes, or the 1- and 2-bedroom cottages. Some units have distant ocean views, and all are nicely but simply furnished. There is an outdoor heated pool set among the pretty grounds; rates include a basic continental breakfast, and the on-site owners couldn't be nicer. All in all, a great value for the money. Open seasonally mid-Apr through Oct. $–$$.

ipswich, ma

Summer vacationers enjoy Ipswich's Crane Beach, considered to be one of the best in the Northeast. On nearby Plum Island, nature lovers flock to the Parker River National Wildlife Refuge to watch migrating birds. And since Ipswich is also famous for its eponymous clams, be sure to sample some while you are here.

getting there

From Gloucester it's a quick 20-minute drive to Ipswich. Pick up MA 128 South and take exit 14 for MA 133 West, which joins MA 1A and becomes Main Street in Ipswich center.

where to go

Ipswich Visitor Center. 36 S. Main St.; (978) 356-8540; ipswichvisitorcenter.org. Known by locals as "the Little Red House," the current dwelling dates from 1819. Besides the usual maps and brochures, you can rent a handheld audio wand for a walking tour of Ipswich's many fine historic First Period homes dating from America's early colonial years. Open Memorial Day weekend through Oct daily 9 a.m. to 5 p.m.

Castle Hill on the Crane Estate. 290 Argilla Rd.; (978) 356-4351; thetrustees.org/places-to-visit/northeast-ma/castle-hill-on-the-crane. Once the summer home of the Chicago industrialist Crane family, this 1920s-era, 59-room English-style mansion is beautifully sited on acres of stunningly restored grounds on a promontory overlooking the Atlantic Ocean. Furnished with period antiques, the house is open for guided tours only. Great House is open end of May through early Oct Tues through Thurs 10 a.m. to 4 p.m., Fri and Sat 10 a.m. to 1 p.m. If you are a gardener, the landscape tour is a must. Also open for seasonal public programs; check website for details. House tours $15 adults, free for children ages 12 and under; landscape tours $20 adults.

Crane Beach. 310 Argilla Road; (978) 356-4354; thetrustees.org. This is a favorite northern Massachusetts beach with 2.5 miles of white, pristine sand. It's a shallow beach with a gradual drop, so when the tide goes out, the water is relatively warm. It has a number of beach amenities including lifeguards, plentiful parking, restrooms, and a snack bar. Crane Beach is a property of the nonprofit Trustees of Reservations and includes more than 1,200 acres of protected shoreline and pine forest. Although walking through beach dunes is generally prohibited at Massachusetts beaches, Crane Beach is a wonderful exception, with 5 miles of walking trails. Crane is an important nesting site for the tiny (and endangered) piping plover. Expect sections of the beach to be closed in summer to allow the chicks to hatch. And whether swimming or hiking, don't forget to bring bug spray; the greenhead flies here are wicked! Open daily 8 a.m. to sunset. Admission fee charged Memorial Day to Labor Day, $30 parking fee per vehicle weekends and summer holidays, $25 weekdays, half price after 4 p.m.

Wolf Hollow. 114 Essex Rd.; (978) 356-0216; wolfhollowipswich.org. Who's afraid of the big bad wolf? This sanctuary gives visitors the rare opportunity to see a pack of wolves interact with each other. There are scheduled presentations that explain the wolf's role in nature and man's history with wolves. At the conclusion of the talk, everyone is encouraged to howl! Check website for hours. Admission $8.50 adults, $6 seniors and children ages 3 to 17.

where to eat

Clam Box of Ipswich. 246 High St.; (978) 356-9707. ipswichma.com/clambox. An Ipswich landmark since 1935, this roadside clam shack resembles a giant take-out clam box. The ridiculously sweet, full belly fried clams are the must-order. This is strictly a paper-plate dining experience. Order at the counter, wait for your number to be called, and eat in the no-frills dining room. Check website for hours. $–$$.

Ithaki. 25 Hammatt St., Ipswich; (978) 356-0099; itahkicuisine.com. Located in Ipswich center, Ithaki aims to transport diners much further with a Mediterranean menu that celebrates the dishes of Greece while using ingredients found closer to home. There are pan-roasted cod cheeks with pickled fennel orange and harissa and pork medallions with roasted potatoes and zucchini. Or opt for Greek small plates classics like meatballs, stuffed grape leaves or the souvlaki, juicy and tender skewered lamb that sings with the simplicity of lemon and oregano. The space is chic-Greek with nary a Santorini poster in sight. There's a large bar and clever cocktail menu to match along with an impressive wine list and if you absolutely insist you can get retsina. Open Tues through Thurs 11:30 a.m. to 8:30 p.m., Fri and Sat 11:30 a.m. to 9:30 p.m., Sun 11 a.m. to 8 p.m. $$–$$$.

Salt Kitchen + Rum Bar. 1 Market St.; (978) 356-0002; saltkitchenandrumbar.com. Always packed, this cozy neighborhood pub is all about gutsy food and a well-crafted, rum-focused cocktail list. The often-changing seasonal menu might offer lamb ragout with house-made cavatelli or roasted scallops with vanilla brown butter and candied orange. The grilled oysters with herbed butter Parmesan and crispy prosciutto are always on the menu. They are a must-order. Open Mon through Thurs 11:30 a.m. to 11 p.m., Fri and Sat 11:30 a.m. to 11 p.m., Su 10 a.m. to 9 p.m., bar closes one hour after kitchen. $$.

1640 Hart House. 51 Linebrook Rd.; (978) 356-1640; 1640harthouse.com. Located in a 17th-century building—the original 1-room home traces its roots back to 1640—the Hart House is a fascinating place to dine and a quintessentially New England experience. Dine in the cozy tavern or elegant main dining room, which both have fireplaces. The separate menus feature contemporary twists on traditional New England cuisine; chicken potpie and burgers in the pub and baked scallops, rack of lamb, and praline bread pudding upstairs. Open Tues through Wed 4:30 to 9 p.m.; Thurs 11:30 a.m. to 2:30 p.m. and 4:30 to 9 p.m.; Fri 11:30 a.m. to 2:30 p.m. and 4:30 to 10 p.m.; Sat 4:30 to 10 p.m.; Sun 11 a.m. to 2 p.m. and 4:30 to 7:30 p.m. $$–$$$.

where to stay

Blue. 20 Fordham Way, Newbury; (978) 465-7171; blueinn.com. Located on Newbury's Plum Island Beach, Blue is a stylish boutique inn that borders on splendid isolation and is a modern castaway's dream. You'll find 13 white-washed rooms, suites and cottages with hues of blue, some with kitchenettes, decks and wood fireplaces. The beds are dressed in crisp white sheets with cozy throws, perfect for watching the sunrise from the ocean beyond. The wow factor here? A breakfast basket stocked with fruit, yogurt, muffins and fresh coffee shows up at your door each morning. $$–$$$.

The Inn at Castle Hill. 280 Argilla Rd.; (978) 412-2555; thetrustees.org/the-inn-at-castle-hill. The inn is set amid the conserved landscape of the spectacular Crane Estate. Stay here and pretend that this country retreat is all yours. A different local designer decorated each of the 10 elegantly appointed guest rooms. Enjoy dramatic views of the sea from your room. There's also easy access to Crane Beach and walking trails. Rates include full breakfast, admission to Crane Beach, and bikes for guests' use. Guests can also order from a nice selection of wine, spirits and cocktails to enjoy on the veranda overlooking the marsh. The inn has Wi-Fi throughout, but rooms do not have TVs, and children must be 12 years and older. The inn is closed Jan through Mar. $$–$$$.

Kaede Bed & Breakfast. 16 N. Main St.; (978) 356-8000; kaedebb.com. Pronounced *ka-eh-day*, which translates to "maple tree," Kaede combines the tradition of Japanese hospitality in a very New England setting. Located in the center of Ipswich in the 1845 Coburn House, each of the 10 guest rooms has a private bath and is decorated in charming New

England style with traditional Japanese flourishes like wood-block prints, tatami mats, and pottery lovingly crafted by the owner. For breakfast choose from an elaborate authentic Japanese breakfast, which can include scrambled eggs, rice, and miso soup, or a traditional American breakfast like stuffed french toast with apple butter. $$.

worth more time

Parker River National Wildlife Refuge. 6 Plum Island Tpke., Newburyport; (978) 465-5753; fws.gov/northeast/parkerriver. Plum Island is a natural barrier island located north of Cape Ann with miles of uncrowded sand beaches. The entire island is crisscrossed with walking trails that lead nature lovers along boardwalks from marshlands to thicket to wind-swept dunes. Plum Island is also an important stopover site for hundreds of thousands of birds on the Atlantic Flyway migration route; so pack your binoculars. You can access the island by car, crossing the causeway and bridge from the town of Newburyport. The refuge's one road runs the length of the 11-mile-long island with several parking lots and overlook turnouts. Open daily dawn to dusk, $5 parking fee per vehicle. *Note:* The main beach is closed from April through June so as not to disturb the nesting piping plovers.

day trip 05

boston

presidents, pilgrims & whales:
quincy, ma; plymouth, ma;
new bedford, ma

Boston's South Shore extends past the gritty docks of its Seaport District through working-class suburbs and coastal towns on the way to the Cape and islands. Learn about the first US presidential family dynasty at the Adams National Historical Park in Quincy. Relive the Pilgrim story at Plimoth Plantation and check out a museum dedicated to whaling in New Bedford.

quincy, ma

Dubbed the "City of Presidents," Quincy (pronounced KWIN-zee) is the birthplace of both John Adams and John Quincy Adams. Not as well known is that Quincy was also the birthplace of John Hancock, who as president of the Continental Congress was the first to put his signature on the Declaration of Independence (and sign it well he did!). Just 10 miles from Boston and en route to Plymouth and the Cape, Quincy is a worthwhile detour.

getting there

From Boston, take I-93 South, then take exit 7 to merge onto MA 3 South, bear left to take exit 19, and follow signs into Quincy Center. The total drive time is usually 20 minutes. Another option is to take the T Red Line train to Quincy Center.

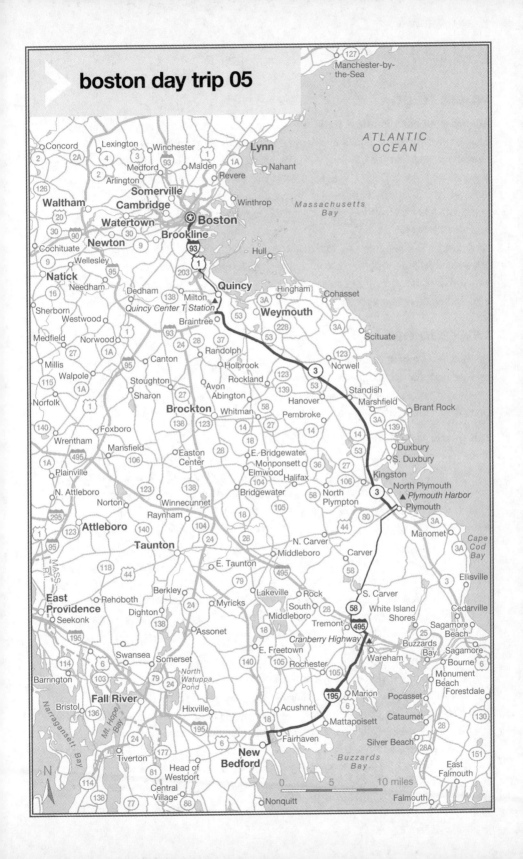

boston day trip 05

where to go

Adams National Historical Park. 1250 Hancock St.; (617) 770-1175; nps.gov/adam. Start your visit with the park's excellent new orientation film, *Enduring Legacy,* which features the voice talents of Tom Hanks, Laura Linney, and Paul Giamatti. Tours leave from the National Park Visitor Center where you will board a trolley bus with a guide to take you to the sites. You'll visit the birth houses (they are next door to each other) of the second US president, John Adams, and his son John Quincy Adams, the sixth US president. You will also tour the Old House at Peacefield, the small estate where four generations of the Adams family lived. It is truly a treasure, with many of the family's original artifacts. The period formal flower gardens are a delight. You can only see the site on a guided tour, which takes about 2 hours. Houses open mid-Apr through mid-Nov, daily 9 a.m. to 5 p.m. Admission $10 adults, free children age 16 and under.

where to eat

Fat Cat. 24 Chestnut St.; (617) 471-4363; fatcatrestaurant.com. There's an hour wait even on weeknights at this buzzy Quincy spot where the creative craft cocktails are excellent, as are the upscale pulled pork nachos and braised short ribs over garlic mashed potatoes. Open daily 11 a.m. to 1 a.m. $$.

The Quarry. 415 Whiting St., Hingham; (781) 340-7300; Quarryhingham.com. If you're up for a detour to the town of Hingham (do so, it's charming), you will find the Quarry. The 200-year-old stone block building is a local landmark and sits next to what was once an open pit quarry mine which has been reclaimed by nature creating a deep pond surrounded by woodlands. The local granite legacy is evident from the moment you walk through the restaurant's door with its cathedral ceiling, fireplace and a window wall overlooking the patio and pond. Young chef/owner Greg Jordan has created an innovative menu that runs the gamut from Asian and Mexican to New England and Italian. Start with his roasted house made sausage with pickled red onions and simple greens before tucking into entrees like wild boar pappardelle or chive and honey brick chicken. Frugal diners will be pleased with the Quarry burger or swordfish tacos. Open Tues through Thurs 4 to 9 p.m., Fri 4 to 11 p.m., Sat 1 to 11 p.m., Sun 10 a.m. to 9 p.m. $$–$$$.

The Townshend. 1250 Hancock St.; (617) 481-9694; www.thetownshend.com. This modern gastropub is tremendously convenient as it is located inside the President's Place complex which houses the National Park Service Welcome Center. The Townshend Acts were a series of British taxes dating from the 1760s on imported goods to the colonies. The Townshend honors the spirit of protest by the colonists who boycotted buying British goods. The restaurant caters to both tourists and office workers with its comfort-food-with-a-twist and excellent drinks. At lunch there is a grilled cheese and homemade soup combo and a marinated beet salad with whipped ricotta, walnut vinaigrette and grilled chicken. Even on a winter Monday night, the restaurant is full with locals enjoying a charcuterie board of cheese and meats along with glasses of rosé and dishes like hanger steak with roasted vegetables and duck fat butter and panko crusted haddock with potato puree. Open Mon through Wed 4 p.m. to 1 a.m., Thurs and Fri 11 a.m. to 1 a.m., Sat 4 p.m. to 1 a.m., Sun 11 a.m. to 9 p.m. $$.

plymouth, ma

The story of the first Thanksgiving comes alive in Plymouth, where a visit to Plymouth Rock, the *Mayflower II*, and Plimoth Plantation give an updated perspective of the Pilgrims arrival in the New World, the true story of the first Thanksgiving, and native Wampanoag culture.

getting there

Follow MA 3 South and take exit 4 to go directly to Plimoth Plantation, or take exit 6A into Plymouth Center and the harbor. The distance is about 40 miles from Boston and is normally a 45-minute drive, but it can take much longer on a warm summer afternoon since MA 3 South is also the main route between Boston and Cape Cod.

where to go

Plymouth Visitor Information Center. 130 Water St.; (508) 747-7525; seeplymouth.com. On Plymouth Harbor, the tidy shingle-style cottage that houses Plymouth's Visitor Center is always a busy place with information on Plymouth attractions. You can also save time by purchasing your Plimoth Plantation/*Mayflower II* tickets here. Open daily summer 8 a.m. to 8 p.m., open the rest of the year 9 a.m. to 5 p.m.

Mayflower II. The *Mayflower II* is a fully rigged seaworthy replica of the ship that brought the Pilgrims to Plymouth. Built in England in 1957, the 60-year-old ship is owned by Plimoth Plantation and is normally moored dockside at Plymouth State Pier. She is a local treasure—each year hundreds of thousands of tourists and school children on field trips come aboard to hear the stories of the hardships of that 1620 voyage. Currently, *Mayflower II* is undergoing an extensive restoration at the Mystic Seaport preservation shipyard (see page 171). The overhaul is scheduled to be completed in time for her to return to her home berth in Plymouth Harbor for the 400th anniversary of the Pilgrims' voyage to Plymouth in 2020.

Plimoth Plantation. 137 Warren Ave.; (508) 746-1622; plimoth.org. Travel back in time to 1620 and learn about the daily life of the English Separatists, who later became known as Pilgrims and settled in the land of the native Wampanoag people. This carefully researched living-history museum re-creates the English village with thatched-roof cottages, vegetable gardens, barns with heritage-breed livestock, and a church. As you wander through the

cranberries: the crimson harvest

It is one of Massachusetts's most iconic scenes: flooded bogs of crimson berries against a backdrop of blazing fall foliage. Southeastern Massachusetts is cranberry country; the low-growing vines are native to the region. The fruit was introduced by the native Wampanoags to the Pilgrims, who named it "craneberry" because the spring blossom of the vine resembles the head and beak of a crane. The majority of the Massachusetts cranberry harvest takes place during October, and several of the larger cranberry growers open their farms to the public for up-close tours of the bogs. MA 28 (Route 28), which runs through this area, is known as "The Cranberry Highway." Check with the Cranberry Growers Association (cranberries.org) for maps and information.

village, watch the townspeople as they go about everyday tasks: framing a house, mending clothes, and baling hay. The costumed interpreters stay in character and particularly like to interact with visitors. Walk along the wooded path to the adjacent re-created Wampanoag homesite where native people share information about Wampanoag culture. Here you can visit a *wetu* (home), turn a rabbit on a spit that is cooking over an open fire, and help scrape out the *mishoon* (canoe). In the Crafts Center, watch historic trades like cabinet-making and sail-making while native artisans create clothing from hides and make pottery. Open mid-Mar through Thanksgiving, daily 9 a.m. to 5 p.m. Admission $28 adults, $16 children ages 5 to 12, children under 5 are free. Prices may vary by season, so check online or call ahead with questions.

Plymouth Rock. Pilgrim Memorial State Park, Water Street. On the harbor, next to the *Mayflower II,* sits Plymouth Rock, protected by a granite portico. Every American schoolchild learns the story that this is the spot where the Pilgrims first set foot in the New World in 1620. It is perhaps a distortion, as it is well documented by Capt. William Bradford's ship journal that the Pilgrims first landed at the tip of Cape Cod, near present-day Provincetown, and explored the area for several weeks before settling in Plymouth. Still, the site is a huge tourist draw in Plymouth, and although it is really little more than a large stone, sometimes a rock is more than a rock. Open 24 hours daily. Admission free.

where to eat

The Lobster Hut. 25 Town Wharf; (508) 746-2270; lobsterhutplymouth.com. The very basic menu consists of fine fried and broiled fish—and all for a pittance. The setup is pure New England seacoast: counter service with plentiful indoor/outdoor seating and a harborfront view. Open Sun through Thurs 11 a.m. to 8 p.m., Fri and Sat 11 a.m. to 9 p.m. $–$$.

Rye Tavern. 517 Old Sandwich Rd.; (508) 591-7515; ryetavern.com. This is locally sourced, vegetable-driven cuisine with much of it from the garden right outside the back door. The bar opens an hour before the kitchen and features well made cocktails and a smart beer program. The intimate, historic dining room and patio spaces are a lovely spot to tuck into pesto baked cod and grilled garden squash, and apple tart with vanilla ice cream and salted caramel. It's well worth the short drive to the "country" from Plymouth Harbor. Open Mon through Wed 5 to 8 p.m., Thurs 5 to 9 p.m., Fri 5 to 10 p.m., Sat 11 a.m. to 10 p.m., Sun 11 a.m. to 8 p.m. $$–$$$.

Surfside Smokehouse. 14 Union St.; (508) 727-4111; surfsidesmokehouse.com. Located on Plymouth Harbor and overlooking Plymouth Rock and *Mayflower II* (when she is at her home berth). Score a seat on the deck for a water view, or sit inside to catch the live entertainment. Late afternoons are for the 60-seat bar where there are oysters aplenty and fun specialty cocktails. The menu is equal parts traditional Southern barbecue and classic New England seafood. The sweet chili sticky ribs and the smoked kielbasa and pineapple candy are among the favorite barbecue selections. For seafood purists there is a giant lobster roll, beer battered fish and chips or poached shrimp with a homemade cocktail sauce. Open seasonally St. Patrick's Day through Thanksgiving; Mon, Wed and Thurs 11:30 a.m. to 9 p.m., Fri and Sat 11:30 a.m. to 10 p.m., Sun 11 a.m. to 9 p.m., closed Tues. $–$$.

where to stay

The John Carver Inn. 25 Summer St.; (508) 746-7100 or (800) 774-1620; johncarverinn .com. Families with young kids adore this budget-friendly hotel. The American colonial-style rooms are modest but there's an indoor pool with a Mayflower-themed waterslide and the tried-and-rue pleasures of an on-site playground, and the hotel is within walking distance of the Plymouth waterfront. The inn is owned by the Catania family which also owns the local mini restaurant chain, the Hearth 'n Kettle. There's an outpost here, offering value and variety in a family-friendly setting. Their fried seafood is a specialty, as well as their turkey dinner—served year-round. New to the inn is Waterfire Tavern, which features a zesty menu of shareable dishes infused with flavors of the world: lemon grass pot stickers, craft beer battered cod sliders and artichoke and mushroom flatbreads. $$.

Mirbeau Inn & Spa. 35 Landmark Dr.; (508) 209-2626; plymouth.mirbeau.com. Opened in 2014, the South Shore has long needed an upscale destination resort. Just 7 miles from the hustle and bustle of the tourist hordes at Plymouth Harbor, Mirbeau's style can be best described as chateauesque. There's an enchanting lily pond and bridge, which evokes Monet's garden at Giverny, and the inn's 50 rooms are decorated with dueling floral upholstery motifs and have indulgent custom mattresses. Each room also has a gas fireplace and a soaking tub as well as a separate shower. The 14,000 square-foot spa offers 14 treatment rooms and a spa service menu that is short but luxe, with therapies like a crushed cabernet body scrub or a French clay detox. At night, guests congregate in the Library for a plate of local cheeses before heading to the resort's post and beam Wine Bar & Bistro for characteristic Gallic fare like chicken tagine with curried cous cous and steak frites with red onion jam. And be sure to pack your clubs. The resort features a pair of 18-hole, par 72–championship golf courses. $$$.

Pilgrim Sands on Long Beach. 150 Warren Ave.; (508) 747-0900; pilgrimsands.com. Popular with families and couples alike, the basic accommodations at this 64-room motel are an affordable choice for those who want a water view. Pilgrim Sands is just down the road from Plimoth Plantation and sits on an enviable stretch of private beach facing Plymouth Bay. Rates include a basic continental breakfast and free Wi-Fi. There is an indoor and outdoor pool as well. $$

new bedford, ma

In the 19th century, New Bedford was the epicenter of the whaling industry in America. In the classic seafaring tale *Moby Dick,* author Herman Melville describes New Bedford as "perhaps the dearest place to live in all New England." Today, New Bedford still charms with a bustling harbor that is one of the country's biggest commercial fishing ports. In New Bedford one-third of the city's population is of Portuguese descent; that, combined with the city's fishing traditions, makes for some terrific dining experiences.

getting there

From Plymouth head west on Federal Furnace Road and MA 58 South. Merge onto I-495. From I-495 South take exit 1 and pick up I-195 West. Take exit 15 and merge onto MA 18 toward downtown New Bedford.

where to go

New Bedford Visitor Information Center. Pier 3 Fisherman's Wharf; (508) 979-1745; destinationnewbedford.org. Located in the old wharfmaster's house, the city's visitor information center is pure New Bedford and provides maps and brochures. Open Memorial Day through Labor Day Mon through Fri 8 to 4 p.m., Sat and Sun 9 a.m. to 4 p.m.; day after Labor Day through May 30 Mon through Fri 8 a.m. to 4 p.m.

New Bedford Whaling Museum. 18 Johnny Cake Hill; (508) 997-0046; whalingmuseum .org. Wait till you get a glimpse of Kobo, the 66-foot blue whale skeleton suspended from the ceiling in the entrance gallery. This is the largest museum in America dedicated to the history of whaling. Walk the deck of the *Lagoda,* a half-scale model of a New Bedford whaling ship that dates from 1826. Rigged and with her sails set, she is impressively housed in her own dedicated gallery. Open Apr through Dec daily 9 a.m. to 5 p.m.; Jan through Mar Tues

> ## aha! new bedford
>
> *New Bedford's AHA! night is the city's must-see free monthly event. Taking place from 5 to 9 p.m. on the second Thursday of each month, AHA! (Art, History, Architecture) transforms the city's historic downtown into a vibrant arts district featuring dozens of visual artists, live musicians, street performers, and interactive children's activities. ahanewbedford.org.*

through Sat 9 a.m. to 4 p.m., Sun 11 a.m. to 4 p.m. Admission $16 adults, $14 seniors and students, $9 children ages 6 to 14, free for children ages 5 and under.

New Bedford Whaling National Park. 33 William St.; (508) 996-4095; nps.gov/nebe. Begin your visit to New Bedford with the 22-minute orientation film, *The City That Lit the World.* National Park Service rangers give free guided walking tours of the waterfront area in July and August and by appointment the rest of the year. Across the street, peek in at the Seamen's Bethel, the chapel described in *Moby Dick;* it's still used for services today. Open Apr through Dec daily 9 a.m. to 5 p.m., Jan through Mar Wed through Sun 9 a.m. to 5 p.m. Free admission.

where to eat

Antonio's. 267 Coggeshall St.; (508) 990-3636; antoniosnewbedford.com. Residents and visitors can't get enough of the authentic, reliable Portuguese dishes at this neighborhood standby. The seafood stew casserole is a stunner with lobster, scallops, shrimp, mussels, and clams in a bright tomato broth. Open Sun through Thurs 11:30 a.m. to 9:30 p.m., Fri and Sat 11:30 a.m. to 10 p.m. $$.

Cobblestone Restaurant. 7 S. 6th St.; (508) 999-5486; cobblestonerestaurant.net. Cobblestone is the go-to breakfast and lunch place in New Bedford for both locals and tourists. If you are lucky enough to get a seat, grab it and dig into the home-style staples you crave like stuffed french toast, hash browns, omelets, and burgers. Add some sparkle to your weekend morning brunch and order a Mismosa Sangria, to go along with the Portuguese egg Benedict—it's Cobblestone's specialty and features a poached egg on sweet bread with linguica sausage and hollandaise. Open 7 a.m. to 2 p.m. daily. $.

Moby Dick Brewing Company. 16 S. Water St.; (508) 542-1252; mobydickbrewing.com. New Bedford's downtown renaissance got a real boost when Moby Dick Brewing opened its 100-seat brewpub across from the New Bedford Whaling Museum in March 2017. This is a brewery where the beer—as well as the food—is worth a visit. Food-wise, you'll find a seafood centric menu which features skate pan roasted in a brown butter sauce, Atlantic cod fish and chips as well as a hanger steak with charred spring onion relish. Meanwhile, at the adjacent brewery operation, brew master Scott Brunelle crafts 7 to 8 German and American-style lagers, many with Moby Dick–inspired names like "stove boat" (a term for a dead whale) and Ishm-Ale. Open Sun through Thurs 11 a.m. to 10 p.m., Fri and Sat 11 a.m. to 11 p.m. $$.

Pizzeria Brick. 163 Union St.; (508) 999-4943; pizzeriabrick.com. It's a tiny hole-in-the-wall with just a few tables and counter service, but it serves stylish and authentic brick-oven pizzas. One to devour? The Pollo Rosto with oven-roasted chicken, caramelized onions, roasted wild mushrooms, and Gorgonzola. Open Mon through Sat 11 a.m. to 9 p.m., Sun noon to 8 p.m. $.

day trip 06

boston

Central Massachusetts offers an unbeatable blend of family fun and historic sites. Worcester claims a first-class art museum, or you can travel back in time at Old Sturbridge Village and visit the homes, shops, and mills of a re-created rural New England community. While Worcester offers cosmopolitan energy, you'll also find rustic serenity in the region's woodlands.

worcester, ma

Located at the crossroads of the state, Worcester (pronounced WUSS-ter) is the second largest city in New England according to 2010 census data. For 200 years, the city was a manufacturing giant. Today Worcester is home to 10 colleges and universities. Visitors will find that the city balances well its industrial and educational heritage with the excellent Worcester Art Museum, the not-dusty-at-all Worcester Historical Museum, and family favorite the Ecotarium.

getting there

From Boston, it's a straight shot west to Worcester. Pick up the Mass Turnpike (I-90 W) for 22 miles. Take exit 10A, Millbury/Worcester, follow Route 146 N and signs to downtown.

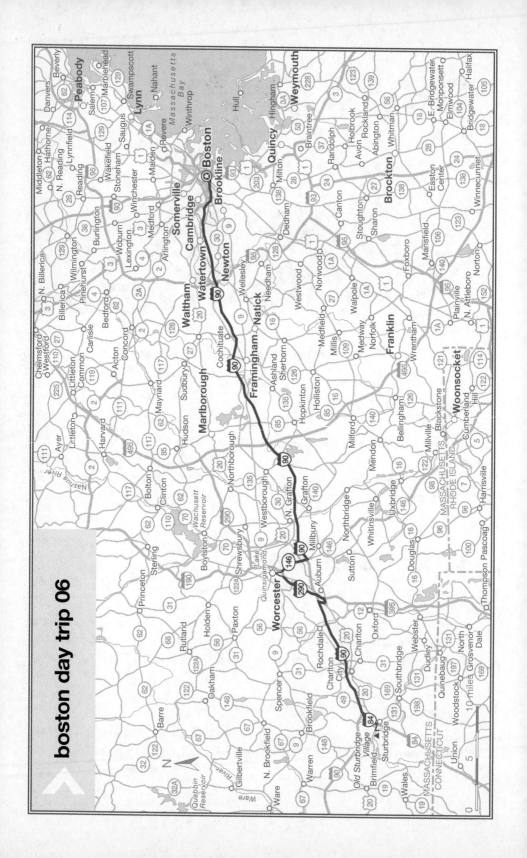

boston day trip 06

where to go

The Ecotarium. 222 Harrington Way; (508) 929-2700; ecotarium.org. This indoor and outdoor nature- and science-oriented museum is geared to families with young children. Inside, kids can visit their favorite creepy crawlies like turtles, salamanders, and snakes or see a planetarium show. Outside, walk along the path and visit the "big" animals: the bald eagles, the foxes, and the otters. The Tree Canopy Walkway offers quite a view from 40 feet above an ancient oak grove and is a terrific activity for energetic kids (summer only, additional fee). Open Tues through Sat 10 a.m. to 5 p.m., Sun noon to 5 p.m., closed Mon. Admission $18 adults, $14 seniors, $4 children ages 2 to 18, children under the age of 2 are free.

The Worcester Art Museum. 55 Salisbury St.; (508) 799-4406; worcesterart.org. Opened in 1898, this is the second largest art museum in New England. Highlights of this first-rate collection include floor mosaics from the ancient city of Antioch and major holdings of French Impressionist and American paintings, as well as Asian (especially Japanese) art. The museum's Old Master paintings from the 16th through 18th centuries, including its latest acquisition, Veronese's *Venus Disarming Cupid,* have recently been reinstalled in a less formal, more playful, "salon-style" (no labels) gallery arrangement. In 2014 the arms and armor collection of Worcester's beloved Higgins Armory Museum were integrated into the museum's Medieval Galleries. The WAM Cafe (open 11:30 a.m. to 2 p.m.) is a go-to local choice for lunch alfresco in the courtyard and features seasonal soups, salads, and sand- wiches including an excellent pulled pork wrap. Open Wed through Fri 11 a.m. to 5 p.m., Sat 10 a.m. to 5 p.m., Sun 11 a.m. to 5 p.m., closed Mon and Tues. Admission $14 adults, $12 seniors and students, $6 children ages 4 to 17, under age 4 are free.

Worcester Historical Museum. 30 Elm St.; (508) 753-8278; worcesterhistory.org. The museum's permanent exhibit, "In Their Shirtsleeves," tells the story of Worcester's tradition of innovation and technology. Among the items on display are barbed wire, corsets, and an anti-gravity space suit. Open Tues through Sat 10 a.m. to 4 p.m., closed Sun and Mon. Admission $5 adults, $4 seniors, free children ages 18 and under.

where to eat

Armsby Abbey. 144 Main St.; (508) 795-1012; armsbyabbey.com. Nothing precious. Nothing petite. It's all about local food and local suds at easy prices. The dimly lit room has exposed brick walls, a chalkboard menu, and mostly high-top tables. There's a showpiece bar with bartenders who will keep you happy with a selection of 22 craft beers always on tap. Order a selection of farmstead cheeses, the mac and cheese, or the jerk chicken sandwich. Open Mon through Thurs 11:30 a.m. to 12 a.m., Fri 11:30 a.m. to midnight, Sat and Sun 10 a.m. to midnight. $$.

Birch Tree Bread. 138 Green St.; (774) 243-6944; birchtreebreadcompany.com. The smell of fresh-baked bread, nutty and crusty, wafts through this light-filled neighborhood bakery with a pastry case that is bursting with peanut butter chunk cookies, almond croissants and red velvet cupcakes. Daily offerings scribbled on a chalkboard include a carrot ginger bisque and a sandwich made from house-made corned beef with braised red cabbage, gruyere and whole grain mustard on seeded rye and caraway. Wednesday night features pizza, beer and wine along with live music. There is some sort of live music most weekends too. This is a community-minded bakery that, in a very short time, has become a part of the Canal District neighborhood. The must-try item is whatever the daily toast special is—for example, the caramelized onion, bacon, cheddar and cream cheese topped with maple apple chutney on wheat bread elevates humble toast to new heights. Open Tues, Thurs and Fri 7 a.m. to 5 p.m., Wed 7 a.m. to 10 p.m., Sat 8 a.m. to 6 p.m., Sun 10 a.m. to 3 p.m. $.

Boulevard Diner. 155 Shrewbury St.; (508) 791-4535. Although the famed Worcester Lunch Car Company is long gone (manufacturing ceased in 1957), diner culture is still big here. The "Bully" is an iconic diner of 1936 vintage, with a long counter and stools and just a few booths. Order down-home breakfasts day and night and hefty blue-plate specials like franks and beans and meat loaf with mashed potatoes. Open daily 24 hours. $.

Pomir Grill. 119 Shrewsbury St.; (508) 755-7333; pomirgrill.com. Bored? Then eat at this modest Afghan establishment where the simple and satisfying fare is a pure delight. *Aushak*, the Afghan version of ravioli, is stuffed with leeks and spinach and topped with a minted garlic and yogurt sauce. The kebab dishes, whether lamb, beef, or chicken, are uniformly good and served along with rice, bread, salad, and grilled vegetables. And in true Shrewsbury Street tradition, Pomir Grill is BYOB. Open Mon 4 to 9 p.m.; Tues through Sat 4 to 10 p.m., closed Sun. $$.

Sole Proprietor. 118 Highland St.; (508) 798-3474; thesole.com. This is where native Worcesterites go for reliably excellent seafood in an upscale setting. You'll find well-prepared, classic dishes like baked stuffed lobster and maple-glazed scallops and more ambitious offerings like Sicilian swordfish and blackened tuna-steak sashimi. You'll also find excellent-value grilled, broiled, or fried fish lunch plates. Open Mon 11:30 a.m. to 9 p.m., Tues through Thurs 11:30 a.m. to 10 p.m., Fri and Sat 11:30 a.m. to 11 p.m., Sun 4 to 9 p.m. $$–$$$.

where to stay

Beechwood Hotel. 363 Plantation St.; (508) 754-5789; beechwoodhotel.com. Located adjacent to the UMass Medical Center campus, this pleasant hotel offers spacious, attractive rooms. The hotel caters to families of patients and business travelers and offers good weekend leisure deals. All rates include continental breakfast. $$–$$$.

worth more time

Tower Hill Botanical Garden. 11 French Dr., Boylston; (508) 869-6111; towerhillbg.org. No matter the season, Tower Hill always has something to see. This 132-acre property includes a large variety of distinct botanical environments, among them a cottage garden, an apple orchard, a vegetable garden, and a secret garden of perennials. If you are here in the winter, you can keep warm in the Orangerie, which shelters a rich collection of tropical as well as seasonal flower shows. Natural exhibits are augmented by year-round lectures, musical events, and educational programs for both adults and kids. Schedule your visit to include lunch at Twigs Cafe for delightful seasonal salads, soups, and sandwiches to enjoy on the terrace in warm weather or in the Great Room at other times of year. Open Tues through Sun 9 a.m. to 5 p.m. Admission $15 adults, $10 seniors, $5 children ages 6 to 18.

sturbridge, ma

Nestled in the heart of Massachusetts, Sturbridge is best known as the home of Old Sturbridge Village, a living-history museum that celebrates early 19th-century rural New England life. Nearby, the little town of Brimfield becomes the center of the antiques and collectibles world three times a year when it hosts its week-long Brimfield Antique and Collectibles Show in May, July, and September.

getting there

From Worcester take I-290 West for 6 miles and take exit 7 to I-90 West (also known as the Massachusetts Turnpike, or as it is locally called, "the Mass Pike"; note that it's a toll road). After 12 miles, take exit 9 to I-84 West. Take exit 3B toward Sturbridge, merge onto US 20 West, and follow signs to Old Sturbridge Village.

where to go

Old Sturbridge Village. 1 Old Sturbridge Village Rd.; (508) 347-3362 or (800) 733-1830; osv.org. Explore rural New England of the 1830s in this living-history museum. Here the past has been lovingly restored in more than 40 authentic buildings, while "villagers" (historic interpreters) in period dress go about their daily tasks and ply their trades. Tour the elegant townhome, step into a farmhouse kitchen, help in the garden or with the barn work, and inspect the handiwork of the shoemaker and tinsmith. **Note:** The village, countryside, and mill neighborhoods are connected by dirt roads, so be sure to dress appropriately and wear comfortable shoes. Find casual 21st-century dining options at the Village Cafe and at the Bullard Tavern Cafeteria, while the Oliver Wight Tavern is the museum's sit-down lunch restaurant. Open year-round, days and hours vary seasonally, check website for details. Admission $28 adults, $26 seniors, $14 children ages 3 to 17, free for children age 2 and under.

the thrill of the hunt at the brimfield antique shows

Three times a year, the otherwise quiet rural town of Brimfield is inundated with throngs of antiques dealers and collectors from around the world. An open-air market sprawls out along both sides of US 20 for nearly a mile with dealers in the fields selling, well, everything. From antiques to collectible nostalgia to artisan crafts to just plain junk, you will find it here.

Will you find a bargain? Will you get fleeced? It's all relative. Dealers do get first dibs and often have skimmed the best stuff, but shopping Brimfield is an experience. Expect a several-mile backup getting into town. And remember to bring cash, carry water, use sunscreen, and wear comfortable walking shoes; those fields are often muddy! Brimfield takes place in mid-May, mid-July, and early September. brimfieldshow.com.

where to eat

B.T.'s Smokehouse. 392 Main St.; (508) 347-3188; btsmokehouse.com. Got a hankering for dry-rub slow-smoked barbecue? On your way back from Old Sturbridge Village, head over to B.T.'s for some of the best Southern-style, falling-off-the-bone ribs and succulent brisket in New England. This is a totally no-frills setup and is BYOB, but people come from miles around—so you know it's good. Open Tues through Sat 11 a.m. to 9 p.m., Sun noon to 8 p.m., closed Mon. $–$$.

where to stay

Old Sturbridge Village Inn & Reeder Lodges. 369 Main St.; (508) 347-5056; osv.org/inn. Heritage travelers adore these budget-friendly lodgings next to Old Sturbridge Village. There are 29 restful country rooms spread among several buildings in a cul-de-sac setting. The Oliver Wight House adds ten more. Families appreciate the outdoor seasonal pool, the playground and the 19th-century toy- and game-lending basket. All rates include continental breakfast and discounted admission to the museum. $–$$.

worth more time

The Museum of Russian Icons. 203 Union St., Clinton; (978) 598-5000; museumofrussian icons.org. Russian icon art is the passion of Clinton industrialist Gordon Lankton, who built this state-of-the-art museum in 2006 to house his personal collection. He's living his dream, and you can share it, too. There are more than 400 pieces of Russian icons, dating from the 15th century to the present. The dazzling wood panels of saints and prophets are hand-painted with gold leaf and are rich in symbolism while offering a fascinating look at Russian culture, art, and history. Admission includes a complimentary audio tour of the permanent collection. Open Tues through Fri 11 a.m. to 4 p.m., Sat and Sun 11 a.m. to 5 p.m., closed Sun and Mon. Admission $10 adults, $7 seniors, $5 students and children ages 3 to 17.

Vaillancourt Folk Art Studios. 9 Main St., Sutton; (508) 476-3601; valfa.com. Vaillancourt specializes in whimsical, hand-painted chalkware figurines that are made from antique chocolate molds. The company's studios are located in a picturesque stone mill, and you can take a behind-the-scenes tour to observe the creative process up close. Afterward browse and shop the company store. Open Mon through Sat 9 a.m. to 5 p.m., Sun 10 a.m. to 5 p.m. Free.

cape cod

day trip 07

cape cod

quintessential new england summer:
hyannis, ma

Pristine sandy beaches, miles of bike and hiking trails, and clam shacks galore: Cape Cod offers the quintessential New England summer vacation experience.

Cape Cod, known simply as "the Cape," is a unique peninsula that is surrounded by the Atlantic Ocean and is often described as shaped like a "bended arm." The Cape is best explored by car, but as you travel, it is helpful to understand the lay of the land. There are three main roads on the Cape that run its length from west to east. Also known as the Old King's Highway, scenic MA 6A (Route 6A) is the northernmost road wending its way parallel to the Cape Cod shore. US 6 (Route 6) is known as the Mid-Cape Highway; it's the main route on and off the Cape and is generally the quickest way to get from one end to the other. MA 28 (Route 28) is the southernmost route along Nantucket Sound and is often the most congested.

hyannis, ma

Technically, Hyannis is a village, part of the town of Barnstable on Cape Cod. It's hardly a village-like place though. Hyannis is both the transportation and economic hub for the entire Cape region. The Cape's main airport, Barnstable Municipal Airport (HYA) is just a mile from Hyannis center, while Hyannis Harbor bustles with pleasure craft, fishing charters, and ferries bound for Martha's Vineyard and Nantucket. What Hyannis lacks in charm and attractions, it makes up with lots of accommodation and dining options. And its convenient location at the midpoint of the Cape makes it easy to take day trips throughout the region.

"old cape cod"

For many, Patti Page's evocative "Old Cape Cod" unforgettably captures the magic of the region. "If you're fond of sand dunes and salty air, quaint little villages here and there, you're sure to fall in love with old Cape Cod."

getting there

From Boston and points north, take I-93 South to MA 3 South. Take the Sagamore Bridge over the Cape Cod Canal where MA 3 becomes US 6. Take exit 6, MA 132, and follow signs to Hyannis.

From Springfield and points west, take I-90 East (the Mass Turnpike). Follow to exit 11A, I-495 South. Take the Bourne Bridge over the Cape Cod Canal. Go around the Bourne rotary and pick up US 6 East and follow along the canal. At the first set of lights, take a right onto US 6. Take exit 6, MA 132, and follow signs to Hyannis.

From New York, Connecticut, and points south, take I-95 to Providence. Take exit 20 to I-195 East. Follow to MA 25 South, exit 22, to the Bourne Bridge. Take the Bourne Bridge over the Cape Cod Canal. Go around the Bourne rotary and pick up US 6 East and follow along the canal. At the first set of lights, take a right onto US 6. Take exit 6, MA 132, and follow signs to Hyannis.

where to go

Cape Cod Visitor Center. 5 Patti Page Way, Centerville; (508) 362-3225; capecodcham ber.org. The Cape Cod Chamber Visitors Center is on the Hyannis/Centerville border. Fully staffed with volunteers, you can pick up maps, brochures, and travel guides. Memorial Day through Labor Day open Mon through Sat 10 a.m. to 5 p.m., closed Sun. Open 10 a.m. to 2 p.m. other times of the year.

Cape Cod Potato Chip Factory. 100 Breed's Hill Rd.; (888) 881-2447; capecodchips .com. What began as a small Hyannis mom-and-pop storefront business in 1980 has since become one of the nation's largest snack companies. Cape Cod Potato Chips are still kettle-cooked in small batches, and you can watch the process through the factory's picture windows. The best part of the tour is the free sample bag at the end (after you go through the gift shop of course!). Open Mon through Fri 9 a.m. to 5 p.m. Free.

John F. Kennedy Hyannis Museum. 397 Main St.; (508) 790-3077; jfkhyannismuseum .org. Hyannis and the Kennedy family are inextricably linked. The Kennedy Compound in Hyannis Port has been the summer home for the Kennedy clan for generations, and it was JFK's presidential retreat during his time at the White House. This museum captures the memories of JFK's years vacationing on Cape Cod (1934–1963) with family and friends through photographs, memorabilia, and videos. Open Memorial Day through Oct Mon through Sat 9 a.m. to 5 p.m., Sun noon to 5 p.m.; check website for days and times for spring and fall. Closed Dec and Jan. Admission $10 adults, $7 seniors, $5 ages 8 to 17, free for children under age 8.

where to shop

The Hyannis Mall. 769 Iyannough Rd.; (508) 771-0201; simon.com. Anchored by Macy's and Best Buy, this is the only real mall on the Cape. There are more than 100 stores, a food court, and a 12-screen movie theater with stadium seating. Expect crowds on a rainy day.

where to eat

Keltic Kitchen. 415 Rt. 28, West Yarmouth; (508) 771-4835; keltickitchen.com. On summer weekends the line snakes out the door with patrons waiting for authentic Irish hospitality at this family-owned breakfast and lunch spot. The specialty is a full Irish breakfast—2 eggs, Irish sausage, bacon, toast, mushrooms, tomatoes, and pudding (blood sausage). It is a massive affair and will set you up for the day. For a taste of the ould sod, head round the back to the market which offers a wide range of imported goods including tea, chocolate, biscuits (cookies) and crisps (potato chips). They even sell pudding for your own breakfast fry-up. Open year round, daily 7 a.m. to 2 p.m. $.

Naked Oyster. 410 Main St.; (508) 778-6500; nakedoyster.com. For those times when you want seafood but not another clam shack, this popular Hyannis place has an energetic vibe, urban decor, modern raw bar offerings, and high-quality seafood (they farm their own 2-acre oyster beds in Barnstable Harbor) that is simply but tastefully prepared. Open daily 11:30 a.m. to 11 p.m. $$–$$$.

Pain D'Avignon. 15 Hinckley Rd.; (508) 778-8588; paindavignon.com. One of the Cape's best bakeries/cafes serves gourmet croissants, pastries, soups, salads, and sandwiches to eat in or carry out by day, and morphs into a full-service French bistro at night. Enjoy unfussy, spot-on seasonal cuisine like pan-roasted sea scallops or an herb-roasted half chicken and chocolate mousse for dessert. The plates are stylish and a solid value and, along with live weekend music, make this a Cape Cod treasure. Open Mon and Tues 7 a.m. to 6 p.m., Wed, Thurs, and Sun 7 a.m. to 10 p.m., Fri and Sat 7 a.m. to 11 p.m. $–$$.

Spanky's Clam Shack. 138 Ocean St.; (508) 771-27770; spankysclamshack.com. Outdoor picnic tables overlooking Hyannis Harbor are best for ripping into a lobster and a bucket of clams. The inside saloon bar is perennially packed, serving raw bar oysters and fruit-infused cocktails. Just can't eat another fried clam? The garden or Caesar salad topped with the meat of an entire lobster is pure indulgence! Open Apr through mid-Oct daily 11 a.m. to 10 p.m. $$.

where to stay

Anchor In. 1 South St.; (508) 775-0357; anchorin.com. Just a minute's walk from the island ferries and blocks from Hyannis Center, this hotel is really in the center of it all. The rooms are done in a beach-cottage style with soft shades of linen and whitewashed furniture. Many of the rooms have ocean views and/or decks. The hotel's outdoor heated pool overlooks busy Hyannis Harbor. Rates include breakfast in the library or sun room. $$.

Sea Coast Inn. 33 Ocean St.; (508) 775-3828; seacoastcapecod.com. This modest 2-story motel has clean and neat no-frills rooms. The location is in Hyannis Center and within easy walking distance to the ferry terminals. Rates include a simple continental breakfast. $.

Simmons Homestead Inn. 288 Scudder Ave.; (508) 778-4999; simmonshomesteadinn .com. Offering a billiards room, a single malt scotch whiskey bar (with more than 600 types), and the on-site Toad Hall Sports Car Collection with almost 50 British red race cars, this is a bed-and-breakfast that a guy will love. Located in a manor house that dates from 1800, each of the inn's 12 rooms is decorated in traditional bed-and-breakfast style and comes with a private bath, Wi-Fi, and flat-screen TV. Rates include a home-cooked breakfast and afternoon hosted wine hour. This is also a pet-friendly inn with several rooms designed especially for their creature comforts. $$.

day trip 08

cape cod

family vacation playground:
brewster, ma; orleans, ma;
chatham, ma

Rent bikes or a canoe at Nickerson State Park in Brewster, swim at tot-friendly Ska-ket Beach in Orleans, and watch the basking seals at Monomoy Island. This day trip is a good opportunity to experience driving along a portion of MA 6A, also known as the Old King's Highway, one of the regions' most scenic byways, passing along the beaches of Cape Cod past windmills, lighthouses, and fine old sea captain's homes turned into B&Bs and antiques shops.

brewster, ma

Known as the "Sea Captain's Town," Brewster is rich with both historic homes and an eco-logical diversity that especially attracts outdoor enthusiasts. Explore the Cape Cod Natural History Museum, relax on the beach, or go for a bike ride along the Cape Cod Rail Trail.

getting there

It's a scenic drive from Orleans to Chatham along the windy inner shore. Pick up MA 28 South for 9 miles and turn right onto Main Street.

where to go

The Cape Cod Museum of Natural History. 869 Main St. (MA 6A); (508) 896-3867; ccmnh.org. Geared to families with young children, this museum stresses an appreciation of

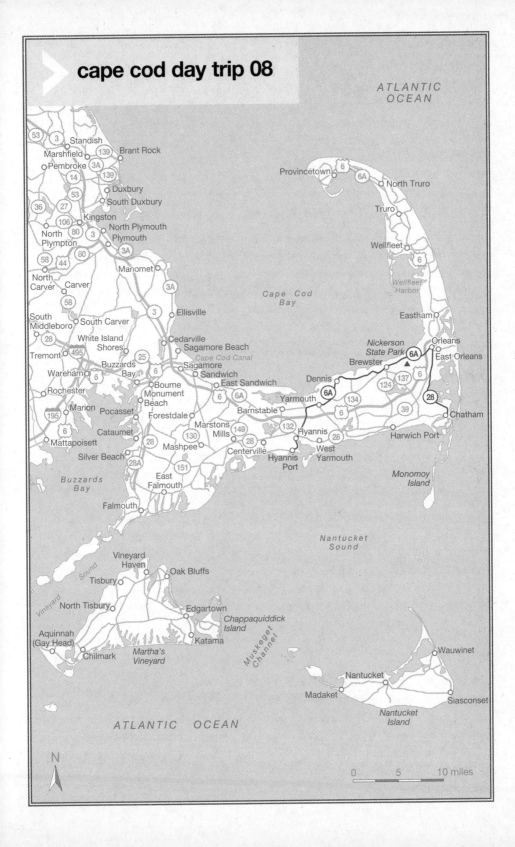

cape cod day trip 08

ATLANTIC OCEAN

ATLANTIC OCEAN

Cape Cod Bay

Nantucket Sound

Buzzards Bay

Vineyard Sound

Martha's Vineyard

Chappaquiddick Island

Muskeget Channel

Nantucket Island

Monomoy Island

Wellfleet Harbor

Cape Cod Canal

Provincetown
North Truro
Truro
Wellfleet
Eastham
Orleans
East Orleans
Nickerson State Park
Brewster
Chatham
Harwich Port
Dennis
Yarmouth
Barnstable
Hyannis
West Yarmouth
Hyannis Port
Centerville
Marstons Mills
Mashpee
East Falmouth
Falmouth
Cotuit
Forestdale
Sandwich
East Sandwich
Monument Beach
Bourne
Sagamore
Sagamore Beach
Cedarville
Pocasset
Cataumet
Silver Beach
Mattapoisett
Marion
Rochester
Wareham
Buzzards Bay
Tremont
White Island Shores
South Carver
South Middleboro
Ellisville
Carver
North Carver
Manomet
Plymouth
North Plympton
Kingston
North Plymouth
South Duxbury
Duxbury
Pembroke
Marshfield
Standish
Brant Rock
Vineyard Haven
Tisbury
Oak Bluffs
North Tisbury
Edgartown
Katama
Aquinnah (Gay Head)
Chilmark
Nantucket
Madaket
Wauwinet
Siasconset

N

0   5   10 miles

Cape Cod's coastal environment. Inside the 2-story nature center there are live animal presentations and interactive exhibits relating to beekeeping, birding, and several aquaria holding little critters. Adjacent to the museum, take a guided or self-guided hike along the easy walking trails (some parts have boardwalks) through piney woodlands, marshy wetlands, and along the shore of Cape Cod Bay. Stroll through the butterfly house, which is home to hundreds of free-flying butterflies and is included with admission. Open June through Sept daily 9:30 a.m. to 4 p.m.; rest of the year Wed through Sun 11 a.m. to 3 p.m. Admission $15 adults, $10 seniors, $6 children ages 3 to 12.

Nickerson State Park. MA 6A; (508) 896-3491; mass.gov/dcr. With a variety of landscapes, there is something to do and see for everyone at Nickerson. This 1,900-acre park offers swimming in crystal-clear glacial kettle ponds, miles of walking trails through heavily wooded oak and pine, and a bike path that is well connected to the Cape Cod Rail Trail. Other popular activities in the park include fishing, picnicking, and boating. Some of the park's amenities include a popular 400-site family campground, picnic tables, and canoe and paddleboat rentals. Free.

where to shop

The Brewster Store. 1935 Main St.; (508) 896-3744; brewsterstore.com. This is a real old-fashioned general store—in business since 1852—with 2 stories chock-full of a little bit of everything: groceries, housewares, buttons, toys, Cape Cod souvenirs, ice cream, and penny candy. The benches on the big front porch invite you to sit a spell. Open Memorial Day through Labor Day daily 6 a.m. to 10 p.m., Labor Day to Memorial Day Mon through Sat 6:30 a.m. to 5 p.m., Sun 6 a.m. to 4 p.m.

Claire Murray. 230 Main St.; (508) 694-5675; nantucketneedleworks.com. Claire Murray, the well-known designer of hand-hooked country-cottage area rugs, began her business from a small Nantucket storefront in 1986. This company store sells her latest rug designs, home decor accessories, and make-your-own needlework kits. Located in a Brewster colonial on 6A, its's a terrific way to visualize how her products will look in your home. Open Memorial Day through Labor Day Mon through Sat 10 a.m. to 9 p.m., Sun 10 a.m. to 6 p.m. Check website for hours during rest of the year.

where to eat

The Brewster Fish House. 2208 Main St.; (508) 896-7867; brewsterfish.com. Down-to-earth fare with enough edge to pique your interest, an intimate setting and a superb wine list, it's no wonder Cape Cod locals pick the Brewster Fish House for a big night out. Lunch could be a fried oyster po'boy with spicy red pepper aioli; for dinner, sesame-crusted flounder. No reservations. Open Tues through Sun 11:30 a.m. to 3 p.m. and 5 to 9:30 p.m., Mon 11:30 a.m. to 3 p.m. $$–$$$.

pedal power: the cape cod rail trail

One of the very best ways to enjoy the Cape's scenic beauty is on two wheels. The Cape Cod Rail Trail is a paved bike trail on the former railroad beds of the Old Colony Railroad and Penn Central Railroad. It meanders through woods and along salt marshes before allowing you to coast to the edge of the Atlantic Ocean.

The 25-mile trail begins in South Dennis at MA 134 and passes through the towns of Harwich, Brewster, Orleans, Eastham, and Wellfleet. The Cape Cod Rail Trail is a great choice even for occasional cyclists; the trail is mostly easy terrain and is well marked at road crossings. And with lots of access points along the route, you can pick the length of ride that's right for you.

Bike rental shops are located at several points along the way. For many, the part of the trail from Nickerson State Park in Brewster to Wellfleet is the most picturesque. Located at the halfway point (around mile 12), Nickerson offers convenient parking, restrooms, and bike rentals.

Guapo's Tortilla Shack. 239 Underpass Rd.; (508) 896-3338; guaposcapecod.com. For a little bit of Baja on Cape Cod. Find Mexican dishes lovingly prepared, like cod fish tacos, carne asada burritos, and grilled corn with cotija cheese and spices. Wash it down with some very nice sangria. Guapo's is an excellent place to refuel and replenish along the Cape Cod Rail Trail. Open seasonally daily 11 a.m. to 9 p.m. $–$$.

where to stay

Brewster by the Sea. 716 Main St.; (508) 896-3910 or (800) 892-3910; brewsterbythesea .com. This is a gracious B&B with 9 bright, quaint Cape Cod–style rooms. All have private baths, air-conditioning, TVs, and Wi-Fi; some rooms have fireplaces and whirlpools. Rates include a Cape Cod–style farm-to-table breakfast and afternoon tea. Walk among the flower beds and vegetable garden bloom or merely doze by the heated outdoor pool. No children under age 14. $$–$$$.

Ocean's Edge. 2907 Main St.; (508) 896-9000; oceanedge.com. With an amazing location directly on Cape Cod Bay, Ocean Edge has it all. This full-service resort has a private ocean beach, 6 pools, 4 restaurants, spa services, 11 tennis courts, and an 18-hole golf course. Choose your accommodations from the recently refreshed guest rooms in the mansion, or multi-bedroom beachside or golf course villas. Ocean Edge is an especially good choice for families, with an extensive supervised kids' program and a full slate of drop-in family activities such as beach bonfires and s'mores and movie nights under the stars. $$$.

orleans, ma

Located at the "elbow" of the Cape, Orleans is bordered by both the warm Cape Cod Bay and colder Atlantic Ocean. Enjoy miles of sandy beaches and take in the breathtaking sunset at Rock Harbor. It's not just pretty beaches, however. All three of the Cape's major roads (US 6, MA 6A, and MA 28) converge in Orleans, making the town a center of commerce packed with one-of-a-kind shops and cozy restaurants.

getting there

From Brewster, continue along MA 6A for 6 miles to Orleans.

where to go

French Cable Station Museum. Cove Road at Route 28; (508) 240-1735; frenchcable stationmuseum.org. This little museum is worth popping into to discover how the telegraph changed the world. The Cape became a hub for global communications in 1898 when pioneering engineers laid 3,200 miles of undersea cable between Orleans and Brest, France. Housed in Orleans's former telegraph facility, the museum has working telegraph equipment on display that enthusiastic and dedicated docents are eager to demonstrate. Open July and Aug Thurs through Sun 1 to 4 p.m.; June and Sept Fri through Sun 1 to 4 p.m. Free.

Nauset Beach. 299 Beach Rd. Break out the boogie boards! The water may be chilly, but the crashing waves and broad, sandy shore make Nauset a great all-around beach. Liam's Clam Shack is located directly on the beach and has picnic tables, too, so you won't get sand in your lunch! Bonus: Explore 2 beaches for the price of one; the Orleans parking fee is good for same-day entrance at both Nauset and Skaket Beach. Parking fee per vehicle $20. Beach open dawn to dusk, parking fees collected in season daily 9 a.m. to 4 p.m.

Skaket Beach. Rocky Harbor Road. A smaller beach—only a half mile long—but the water is warm and the waves are calm, perfect swimming conditions for the sand-pail set. Parents with small kids and lots of beach gear especially appreciate that it is a short walk from the parking lot to the beach. When the tide goes out here, it seems that you can walk out across the sandy flats forever. Same deal as Nauset above: The Orleans parking fee is good for entrance to both town beaches. Parking fee per vehicle $20. Beach open dawn to dusk, parking fees collected in season daily 9 a.m. to 4 p.m.

where to shop

Addison Art Gallery. 43 MA 28; (508) 255-6200; addisonartgallery.com. This small, personal gallery in a Cape-style home represents contemporary artists from across the country. Works that are for sale are affordable. Open year-round Mon through Sat 10 a.m. to 6 p.m., Sun 11 a.m. to 5 p.m.

The Birdwatchers General Store. 36 MA 6A; (508) 255-6974; birdwatchersgeneralstore .com. This is a haven for passionate or casual birders. Find every type of squirrel-proof bird feeder, barrels of birdseed, binoculars and other optics, books, and gifts for the birder in your life. Open Mon through Sat 9:30 a.m. to 5 p.m., Sun 10:30 a.m. to 5 p.m.

Christmas Tree Shops. MA 6A and MA 28; (508) 255-8494; christmastreeshops.com. A Cape Cod institution, now an expanding national chain, the Christmas Tree Shops feature a hodgepodge of seasonal goods. On the Cape, they are the go-to place to pick up everything you need (or have forgotten!) for a day at the beach—suntan lotion, beach umbrellas, beach towels, sand pails, and minnow nets—all priced "wicked" cheap. Stores also in Sagamore, Falmouth, Hyannis, West Yarmouth, and West Dennis. Open Mon through Sat 9 a.m. to 8 p.m., Sun 9 a.m. to 7 p.m.

Goose Hummock. 15 Route 6A; (508) 255-0455; goose.com. Started in 1946 as a humble sporting goods shop, Goose Hummock has since evolved into the Cape's largest outdoor outfitter. Stock up on everything you need to gear up for camping, hunting, fishing, paddle sports, and biking. The staff is incredibly knowledgeable and is keen to offer friendly advice. They also offer guided fishing trips and canoe and kayak excursions in season. Open Mon through Sat 8 a.m. to 6 p.m., Sun 8 a.m. to 4 p.m.

Weekend. 217 Main St., East Orleans; (508) 255-9300; capeweekend.com. At this welcoming boutique, stock up on of-the-minute summer frocks, stylishly cute casual tops, outfit-making accessories, and other fancy things. Open Mon, Tues, and Thurs through Sat 10 a.m. to 5 p.m., Sun noon to 5 p.m.; closed Wed.

where to eat

Abba. 89 Old Colony Way; (508) 255-8144; abbarestaurant.com. With its tucked-away location in a smallish Cape Cod–style home, this spot gets raves for its nuanced take on Mediterranean cuisine with a Thai twist. The mood is as relaxed and unpretentious as the food is serious. Order the grilled filet mignon with green coconut curry paste or the pan-seared halibut with basil and crispy garlic sauce. Always on the menu: the warm walnut date pudding cake with toffee sauce and ginger ice cream. Save room. Open summer Tues through Sun 5 to 10 p.m.; winter Wed through Sun 5 to 10 p.m. Reservations are a must. $$–$$$.

Cap't Cass. 117 Rock Harbor Rd. Part of the charm of Cap't Cass is knowing where to find it. Hint—it's the buoy-covered gray shanty at Rock Harbor. The menu is pure Cape Cod featuring clam chowder, fried fish plates, lobster dinners, and lobster rolls. Many try to time dinner for sunset over Rock Harbor and since there are just a few tables, you may have to wait. Cash only and BYOB, too. Open May through Oct Tues through Sun 11 a.m. to 2 p.m. and 5 to 8 p.m.; closed Mon. $.

Cooke's Seafood. 1 S. Orleans Rd.; (508) 255-5518; cookesorleans.com. Generations of families have forged summertime memories here. It's a fast-food atmosphere, but you do get plenty for your money. Platters of fried seafood—clams, scallops, shrimp, and haddock—with french fries or onion rings are the way to go. Open daily 11 a.m. to 8 p.m. $–$$.

Sundae School. 210 Main St., East Orleans; (508) 255-5473; sundaeschool.com. (Locations in Harwichport and Dennisport also.) Smooth and just sweet enough, Sundae School ice cream is old-school ice cream. This is homemade ice cream, made on the premises at the Dennisport shop. Their famous Sundae School sundae with hot fudge, hand-whipped cream, and a fresh Bing cherry is a great excuse to skip lunch! Open Memorial Day to mid-Sept. Call for hours. Cash only. $.

where to stay

The Governor Prence Inn. 66 MA 6A; (508) 255-1216 or (800) 342-4300; governorprence inn.com. This roadside motel has a retro motor-inn feel in the very best sort of way. Rooms are basic, and all rates include a continental breakfast. The inn has an outdoor pool and lovely grounds and is located just minutes from the Cape Cod National Seashore (see Day Trip 10). Open mid-May through mid-Oct. $.

A Little Inn on Pleasant Bay. 654 S. Orleans Rd.; (508) 255-0780 or (888) 332-3351; alittleinnonpleasantbay.com. Each of the 9 individual bedrooms (each with its own bath) embodies a style that is part New England coastal, part European cottage, with a view of either lush rose and hydrangea gardens or Pleasant Bay. The inn has its own small beach and dock. Rates include an exquisite European buffet breakfast and a 5 p.m. sherry hour—very civilized. Rooms do not have TVs, but there is free Wi-Fi throughout the property. Open May through Sept. $$$.

Orleans Waterfront Inn. 3 Old County Rd.; (508) 255-2222; orleansinn.com. Built in 1875, this sea captain's mansion fronts Orleans's Town Cove. You'll feel like a guest at a neighbor's cozy summer home at this 11-room inn. Each room has a private bathroom and is decorated in traditional Cape Cod style with a light blue color scheme. Wi-Fi is gratis, as is continental breakfast. There's an on-site dining room. Open year-round. $$–$$$.

chatham, ma

Also located at the "elbow" of Cape Cod, Chatham is one of the Cape's oldest and most picturesque seaside villages. Enjoy the wild natural beauty of the Monomoy National Wildlife Refuge, where 9 miles of barrier island beaches remain untouched and free from development. Visit Chatham Light, one of the Cape's most recognizable lighthouses. And Chatham's walkable Main Street charms with unique shops brimming with treasures yet to be discovered.

getting there

It's a scenic drive from Orleans to Chatham along the inner shore. Pick up MA 6A West. Turn onto MA 28 North for 9 miles and turn right onto Main Street.

where to go

Chatham Light. Shore Road; (508) 430-0628; lighthouse.cc/chatham. Perched high atop a cliff over the Atlantic, Chatham Light has been guiding the way for boaters since 1877. The lighthouse is located on Chatham Light Beach, which is a great beach for a walk, but is a non-lifeguarded beach for a reason: The currents are too strong for swimmers. The lighthouse is open for tours the first and third Wed of the month May through Oct, 1 to 3:30 p.m.

Monomoy National Wildlife Refuge. 30 Wikis Way, Morris Island; (508) 945-0594; fws .gov/northeast/monomoy. Seals and whitetail deer share space with thousands of birds at this 2,500-acre preserve just south of Chatham. Once connected to the mainland, Monomoy is a series of 3 natural and undeveloped barrier islands. The visitor center on Morris Island is accessible by car. Birders flock here during the spring and fall migratory seasons, and surf-casting (recreational anglers do not need a license) is also a popular activity. Herds of gray harbor seals (as many as 5,000!) thrive at both North and South Monomoy Islands, which are accessible only by boat. Monomoy Island Ferry (508-237-0420; monomoyisland ferry.com) and Monomoy Island Excursions (508-430-7772; monomoysealcruise.com) both run daily seal-watch cruises in season. The beach is open from sunrise to sunset. Visitor center is open daily 8 a.m. to 4 p.m.

where to shop

Chatham Candy Manor. 484 Main St.; (508) 945-0825; candymanor.com. There is just something about a summer beach vacation and homemade fudge. Chatham Candy Manor is an old-fashioned shop that makes more than a dozen varieties of fudge on the premises in small batches. Don't overlook the hand-dipped chocolates and nostalgic candy treats. Open June through Labor Day Mon through Sat 9 a.m. to 10 p.m., Sun 10 a.m. to 10 p.m.; rest of the year open Mon through Sat 9 a.m. to 5:30 p.m., Sun 10 a.m. to 5:30 p.m.

Maps of Antiquity. 1409 Main St.; (508) 945-1660; mapsofantiquity.com. Expand your horizons. This shop carries a wide-ranging selection of distinctive and finely detailed maps; many are attractively displayed like museum prints. Take your pick from more than 15,000 maps from all over the world, nautical charts, antique postcards, and prints. Open Mon through Sat 10 a.m. to 5 p.m., Sun noon to 5 p.m.

Yankee Ingenuity. 525 Main St.; (888) 945-9123; yankee-ingenuity.com. An affordable gift shop that stocks fun gifts and accessories, many manufactured locally or created by artisans. You'll find conch-shaped bowls, a gold dogwood flower bracelet, and Cape-themed photography. Open late June through Labor Day Mon through Sat 9 a.m. to 10 p.m., Sun 10 a.m. to 10 p.m.; rest of year Mon through Sat 9 a.m. to 5:30 p.m., Sun 10 a.m. to 5 p.m.

where to eat

Chatham Squire. 487 Main St.; (508) 945-0945; thesquire.com. Coming to the Chatham Squire is like visiting an old friend. The service is friendly and prompt, the drinks generous. You'll find ample and tasty sandwiches for lunch, and the baked codfish and center-cut sirloin have been pleasing locals and Cape visitors for more than 40 years. Open Mon through Sat 11:30 a.m. to 1 a.m., Sun noon to 1 a.m. $–$$.

Hanger B. 240 George Ryder Rd.; (508) 593-3655; hangarbcapecod.com. This cute breakfast/lunch spot is located at the Chatham airport, but it's not airport food at all. It's an organic chef-driven menu with specialties like lemon ricotta pancakes for breakfast and spicy pulled pork sandwiches for lunch. Open Wed through Mon 6 a.m. to 2 p.m., closed Tues. $.

Impudent Oyster. 15 Chatham Bars Ave.; (508) 945-3545. This classy Chatham restaurant feels worlds away from the noisy fish joints of the Cape and is a longtime favorite for its flawless, globally inspired coastal menu. The oysters Rockefeller, mussels in white wine, pasta fra diavolo, and sole piccata are all good bets. Reservations are a must at dinner, but it is fairly easy to get a table at lunch. Open daily 11:30 a.m. to 9 p.m. $$–$$$.

The Corner Store. 1403 Old Queen Anne Rd.; (508) 432-1077; chathamcornerstore.com. The crowds lining up outside what looks like a typical New England general store are not wrong: the soft and savory breakfast burritos with eggs and cheese and the build-your-own overstuffed burritos (chicken, pork, steak or grilled veggie) are great choices for a picnic at the beach. Open daily 6:30 a.m. to 6:30 p.m. $.

where to stay

Chatham Inn at 359 Main. 359 Main St.; (508) 945-9252; 359main.com. There are no floral ruffled bedspreads here. Each of the inn's 18 rooms has a chic beach vibe with crisp white duvets and restored wood floors, while some rooms have soaking tubs and fireplaces. Breakfast is included and takes place in the dining room or on the patio; patrons enjoy inspired options like the crab cake Benedict or cranberry nut French toast. This inn's location can't be beat—it's just a quick walk to both the beach and town. $$$.

Chatham Bars Inn. 297 Shore Rd.; (508) 945-0096; chathambarsinn.com. Set on 25 gorgeous landscaped acres overlooking the Atlantic Ocean at Pleasant Bay, there's an undeniable air of exclusivity at the Chatham Bars Inn. There are lots of choices among the resort's 200 rooms, which have an understated elegance done up in shades of cream and are enhanced with luxurious linens, marble bathrooms, and balcony ocean views. The resort has extensive facilities including 3 restaurants, a private beach, heated outdoor pool, and a luxe spa. Private boat service to Martha's Vineyard and Nantucket is available. On offer is a full slate of water and sports activities as well as supervised kids' programming (which keeps families returning summer after summer). $$$$.

worth more time

Located midway between Sandwich and Orleans, **Yarmouth** and its villages straddle both north and south sides of the Cape. Along MA 6A, Yarmouth and the village of **Yarmouth-port** offers antique homes on well-manicured gardens, while along MA 28, **South Yarmouth** and **West Yarmouth** are decidedly more honky-tonk and offer lots of family-friendly accommodation and dining choices.

Captain Parker's Pub. 668 MA 28, West Yarmouth; (508) 771-4266; captainparkers.com. For more than 30 years, this longtime seafood purveyor has been a tradition for vacationing families to the Cape serving solid New England fare at decent prices. At sunset, enjoy the view of the Parker River from the back deck. A cup of Captain Parker's multi-award-winning clam chowder is a must-order—the rich, creamy broth dense with clams and potatoes—is a perfect example of what the New England staple should be. Open Sun 11 a.m. to 10 p.m., Mon through Sat 11:30 a.m. to 10 p.m. $$.

Edward Gorey House. 8 Strawberry Ln., Yarmouthport; (508) 362-3909; edwardgorey house.org. There's a delightful incongruity in visiting this tidy 200-year-old, shingled Cape Cod, which was the home studio of Edward Gorey (1925–2000), the American writer and illustrator of the whimsically macabre. The richly imaginative vision of the artist is evident everywhere from the large number of his drawings on display to his collections of cheese

baseball by the beach

Watching amateur baseball on a soft summer night is a Cape Cod tradition. The Cape Cod Baseball League (CCBL) is the country's premier summer baseball pro-gram, attracting some of the best college ballplayers. One in seven current major league players has played Cape Cod summer league ball, including Tim Lincecum, Mark Teixeira, and Jackie Bradley Jr. It's a 10-team league that stretches from the town of Wareham in the west to Orleans in the east, and each team has its own history and passionate fan base. The season runs from mid-June through mid-August, and games are held almost nightly throughout the summer at town baseball fields throughout the Cape. Admission is free (although they do pass a baseball cap for donations). capecodbaseball.org.

graters and doorknobs. Open Apr through Dec: hours June through early Oct, Wed through Sat 11 a.m. to 4 p.m., Sun noon to 4 p.m.; check website for spring and fall hours. Admission $8 adults, $5 seniors and students, $2 children ages 6 to 12.

Green Harbor. 182 Baxter Ave., West Yarmouth; (508) 771-1126 or (800) 547-4733; red jacketresorts.com. Whether you rent a suite for two or a house for ten, you'll enjoy the best of both cottage and hotel living at this waterfront resort complex. All 53 units come with fully equipped kitchens, a charcoal grill, and many of the other comforts of home. Townhouse villas come with more bedrooms and baths. The resort has lovely grounds, a private beach, an outdoor pool, playground, and a dock with canoes for rent. The property is pet friendly, and you can book for as little as two nights. The on-site hotel manager couldn't be any nicer—no wonder some families return year after year! Rates include housekeeping. $$$.

day trip 09

cape cod

>>>

ye old cape cod:
sandwich, ma; falmouth, ma

The beginning of the Cape features quaint, old-timey villages with shop-lined streets, warm-water beaches, and several museums worth a look: the Sandwich Glass Museum, the Heritage Museum and Gardens, and the Woods Hole Oceanographic Institute. Sandwich and Falmouth are the towns that are closest to the Bourne and Sagamore Bridges and have larger year-round communities, so attractions and businesses here tend to be less seasonal than other places on the Cape.

sandwich, ma

Cape Cod's first town, established in 1637, Sandwich is a hideaway of pretty colonial homes, lush gardens, and several unique museums.

getting there

From Hyannis head north on Iyannough Road toward US 6 West and follow for 10 miles. Take exit 2 for MA 130 North and Sandwich.

where to go

Green Briar Nature Center and Jam Kitchen. 6 Discovery Hill Rd.; (508) 888-6870; thorntonburgess.org. Often overlooked by vacationers, this well-maintained wooded nature preserve in the heart of Sandwich Village is one of the Cape's most family-friendly

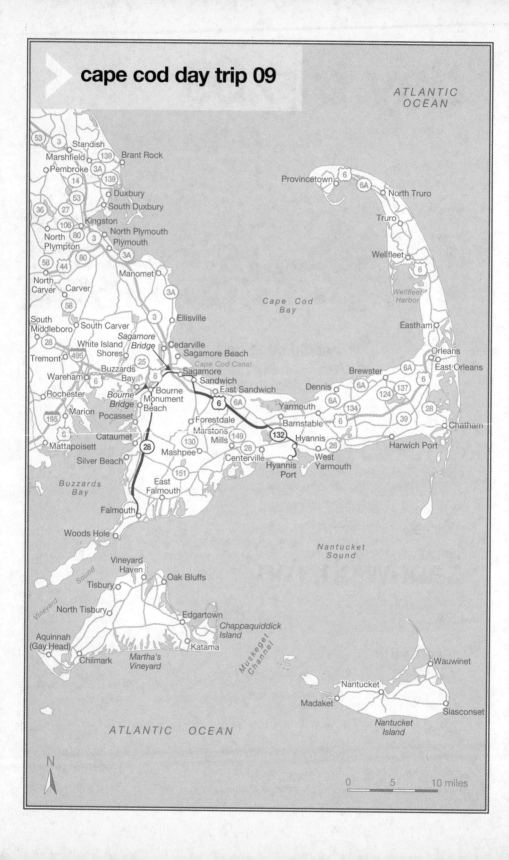

cape cod day trip 09

attractions. This nature center celebrates the life and the conservation legacy of Sandwich native Thornton Burgess, the renowned author of over 100 storybooks including *Peter Cottontail*. In the Nature Center, kids can visit the live animals (including bunnies and turtles) or participate in the regularly scheduled story times. Enjoy the walking trails and well-labeled award-winning wildflower botanical gardens. Sign up in advance for Green Briar's popular weekly jam-making workshops. Open mid-Apr through Dec Mon through Sat 10 a.m. to 4 p.m., Sun 1 to 4 p.m.; Jan through mid-Apr Tues through Sat 10 a.m. to 4 p.m. Admission by donation.

Heritage Garden Museums & Gardens. 67 Grove St.; (508) 888-3300; heritagemuseums andgardens.org. There is something for all ages here. The replica Shaker roundhouse barn displays a collection of 30 antique automobiles including a 1913 Ford Model T. The American History Museum has a collection of Native American artifacts and "military miniatures"—toy soldiers to the rest of us. The beautifully landscaped grounds are extensive and feature a dazzling display of azaleas and rhododendrons in the spring and annuals and daylilies in the summer. And the 100-year-old hand-carved carousel is a beauty. Carousel rides are included in the price of admission, and kids can ride it again and again and again! Open mid-Apr through Oct daily 10 a.m. to 5 p.m. Admission $18 adults, $8 ages 3 to 12, free children ages 2 and under.

Sandwich Glass Museum. 129 Main St.; (508) 888-0251; sandwichglassmuseum.org. From the 1820s to the1880s, glassmaking was Sandwich's main industry. The Boston and Sandwich Glass Works was mostly known for its mass-produced pressed glass in vivid hues of cobalt blue, canary yellow, and cranberry. This quaint museum tells the story of Sandwich and its glassmaking industry with displays of the company's highly collectible glass. Live glassblowing demonstrations take place every hour, and as you might expect, the museum has an exceptionally nice gift shop that features reproduction glass and contemporary artisan-made pieces. Open Apr through Dec daily 9:30 a.m. to 5 p.m.; Feb through Mar Wed through Sun 9:30 a.m. to 4 p.m., closed Jan. Admission $9 adults, $2 children ages 6 to 14, free children ages 5 and under.

where to eat

The Belfry Inne & Bistro. 8 Jarves St.; (508) 888-8550; belfryinn.com. The dining room at the Belfry Inne is open to the public and is known as one of the top restaurants on the Upper Cape. The food and the church setting are sufficiently romantic to cherish with your significant other. It's a well-executed menu of simple, elegant preparations—green apple and brie salad, five-spice Long Island duck breast with carrot cardamom puree—but don't overlook lunch, which features a casual menu that includes a very popular clam chowder with Portuguese chorizo and a grilled sirloin burger with Vermont cheddar. Open Tues through Sat 11:30 a.m. to 3 p.m. and 5 to 9 p.m., Sun 11 a.m. to 3 p.m. and 5 to 9 p.m. $$.

Beth's Bakery & Cafe. 16 Jarves St.; (508) 888-7716; bethsbakery.net. The lace curtains and decorative bric-a-brac are a little twee, but it is a lovely setting in which to enjoy a steaming pot of Earl Grey with scones and crumpets in the middle of the afternoon. Also offered are sandwiches, soups and salads, and other light fare. Open Mon through Sat 8 a.m. to 6 p.m., Sun 9 a.m. to 3 p.m. $.

Cafe Chew. 4 Merchant's Rd.; (508) 888-7717; cafechew.com. This sweet little spot serves hot and cold drinks, delicious bakery treats (try the peanut butter bars), homemade soups, and some of Sandwich's best sandwiches. The staff is friendly, and there's free Wi-Fi and a pretty outdoor patio too. Open daily 8 a.m. to 3 p.m. $.

where to stay

The Belfry Inne & Bistro. 8 Jarves St., Sandwich; (508) 888-8550; belfryinn.com. A distinctive B&B well located in the center of Sandwich Village. Guests can opt for rooms in either the turreted former Catholic rectory or the wood-framed 1872 Victorian next door. "Genesis-inspired Monday through Saturday" themed decor prevails in the 6 skillfully converted abbey rooms. All the rooms feature vaulted ceilings; some of the beds have headboards made from pews, and others have stained-glass windows. Rooms in the adjacent Victorian house are individually furnished in a more traditional B&B style. All rates include an inspired breakfast. $$–$$$.

falmouth, ma

The Falmouth village of Wood's Hole is a popular departure point for ferries to Martha's Vineyard. It is also a unique "company town" and scientific community, home to the internationally renowned Wood's Hole National Oceanographic Institute and several other auxiliary science-related agencies. Walk along the wharves and you just may catch a glimpse of one the great oceanographic research vessels being readied for its next important voyage.

getting there

From Sandwich head toward MA 6A West, pick up Sandwich Road for 4 miles until you reach the rotary. Take the fourth exit onto MA 28 South and continue for 13 miles to Falmouth.

where to go

Nobska Light. Church Street; lighthouse.cc/nobska. Built in 1876, Nobska is still an active lighthouse, standing guard between Buzzards Bay and Nantucket Sound. For the 10,000 runners of the annual 7-mile Falmouth Road Race, rounding Nobska Light offers an awe-inspiring view of the sound and the knowledge that you have 6 more miles to go! The lighthouse tower is open for tours; check website for dates and times.

Old Silver Beach. Quaker Road, North Falmouth. Located on Buzzards Bay, Falmouth is home to some of the warmest beaches in Massachusetts. Old Silver is especially popular with families because there is little current, the water is clear, and the fine white sand is perfect for making sand castles. A rock jetty divides this beach; one side is reserved for residents, the other is for visitors. Both are equally nice. Open dawn to dusk daily. $20 parking fee per vehicle collected Memorial Day through Labor Day.

Wood's Hole Science Aquarium. 166 Water St., Woods Hole; (508) 495-2001; aquarium .nefsc.noaa.gov. Need a rainy-day attraction tip? Part of the National Marine Fisheries Service agency and dating from 1887, this is actually the country's oldest public marine aquarium. Kids will gravitate to the touch tank where they can get their hands wet examining hermit crabs and sea stars. Open Tues through Sat 11 a.m. to 4 p.m. Admission free.

where to eat

Chapoquoit Grill. 410 W. Falmouth Hwy.; (508) 540-7794; chapoquoitgrill.com. Known locally as Chappy's, this place is always filled to capacity with both locals and visitors who come for the toothsome wood-fired artisan pizzas. John's pizza, with caramelized onions, fresh arugula, and goat cheese is a standout. They do quality homemade pastas and grilled entrees, too. Open Sun through Thurs 5 to 9 p.m., Fri and Sat 5 to 10 p.m. $$.

Bear in Boots Gastropub. 285 Main St.; (508) 444-8511; bearinboots.com. The restaurant is a passion project for husband and wife team Gates and Kate Rickard. It's evident in the repurposed tables from ancient Boston Harbor pilings, in the photos of the couple's three children throughout the restaurant, and most importantly in the restaurant's hospitality. The food is European by-way-of New England composed of refined versions of dishes like the *poutine* made of hand-cut French fries with chicken gravy, cheddar cheese curds and duck confit and an oven-roasted cod with house-cured bacon and cherry tomato and olive oil fondue. There are local beers on tap—and locals drinking them—especially on the evenings when there is often live music. Open Tues through Thurs 5 to 9 p.m., Fri and Sat 5 to 10 p.m., bar 5 p.m. to 1 a.m. $$.

Glass Onion. 37 N. Main St.; (508) 540-3730; theglassoniondining.com. One of the Cape's best special-occasion restaurants with a focus on clean, bright, seasonal flavors. Enjoy dishes that range from almond-dusted flounder to cider-brined pork chops, and green-apple bread pudding to honey poached pears with vanilla ice cream and caramel. Open Tues through Sat from 5 to 9 p.m. (sometimes later in summer), closed Sun and Mon, and mid-Feb through Mar. $$$.

Maison Villatte. 267 Main St.; (774) 255-1855. Opened in November 2012, Maison Villatte brings a bit of France to the Cape. Chef-owner Boris Villatte honed his considerable baking skills in the kitchens of France. Drawn in by the smell of freshly baked bread, there's a line out the door daily for the croissants and baguettes. The pastry cases are full of exquisite éclairs, fruit tarts, and mini–chocolate mousse cake. For lunch there are ready-made sandwiches, cheese and charcuterie, quiches, and soups. What could be more delicious? Open Tues through Sun 7 a.m. to 7 p.m. $.

Osteria La Civetta. 133 Main St.; (508) 540-1616; osterialacivetta. With its romantic/rustic feel, convenient Falmouth location and peerless pasta cabonara, *La Civetta*—it means "little owl" in Italian—has been a destination for occasion Italian dining on the Cape since it opened in 2007. The menu is inspired by the Emilia Romagna region. Dishes include artichoke hearts, poached quail eggs and speck and duck legs braised with wine and grapes. Cap off your evening with tiramisu or La Civetta's unrivaled *affogato* creamy vanilla gelato with espresso. Memorial Day through Columbus Day open Mon through Thurs 4:30 to 10 p.m., Fri through Sat noon to 2:30 p.m. and 4:30 to 10 p.m. After Columbus Day to Memorial Day weekend open Tues through Thurs 4:30 to 9:30 p.m., Fri and Sat noon to 2:30 p.m. and 4:30 to 9:30 p.m., Sun 4:30 to 9:30 p.m. $$–$$$.

where to stay

Inn on the Sound. 318 Grand Ave.; (508) 457-9666; innonthesound.com. With a prime location overlooking Vineyard Sound and just a few minutes' walk from both the beach and the village, this small inn features 10 attractive and sizeable rooms, and most have ocean views. A gourmet breakfast is included in the rates. Open year-round. $$–$$$.

day trip 10

cape cod

beautiful beaches:
eastham, ma; wellfleet, ma;
provincetown, ma

At the Cape Cod National Seashore, a protected 40-mile expanse of coastline that stretches from Eastham to Provincetown, you can enjoy the natural beauty of five separate white-sand beaches, visit a lighthouse, and find your own adventure among the walking trails. Added charms in these lower Cape towns include Eastham's excellent Salt Pond Visitor Center, Wellfleet's drive-in movie theater, and the exuberance that is Provincetown—one of the country's leading gay resort destinations.

eastham, ma

Known as Nauset by the Native Americans who once lived here, Eastham is where the outer Cape begins. Without a Main Street business center, Eastham doesn't have the seashore village vibe of other Cape Cod towns. Nonetheless, it is one of the Cape's most popular destinations as it is the gateway to the Cape Cod National Seashore.

getting there

From Hyannis, taking US 6 provides the quickest access to the outer Cape. Follow US 6 East for 22 miles (about 30 minutes).

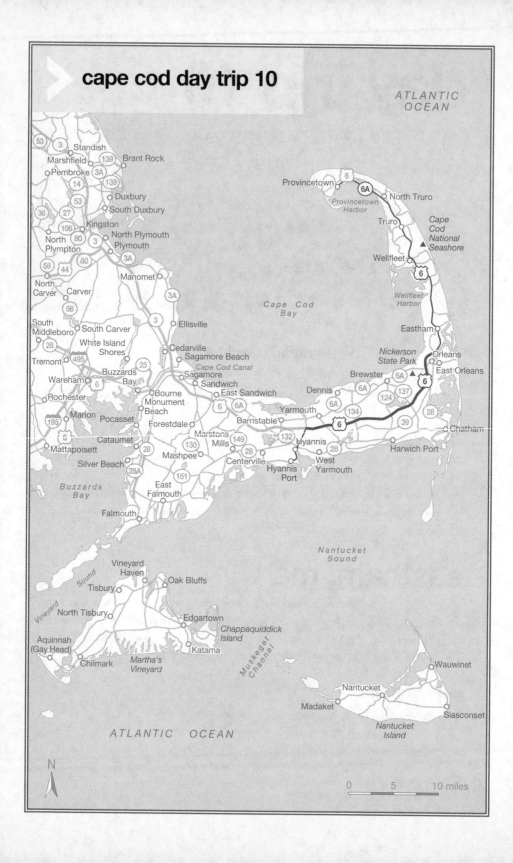

cape cod day trip 10

where to go

Salt Pond Visitor Center at the Cape Cod National Seashore. Nauset Road and US 6; (508) 255-3421; nps.gov/caco. This is no ordinary visitor center, and it should be your first stop when coming to visit the National Seashore. Here you will find exhibits pertaining to the Cape's natural history and wildlife. The indoor theater screens a rotating series of short, Cape Cod–themed films throughout the day. As this is the main visitor center for the National Seashore, many of the park's guided nature walks and self-guided trails (including the popular looping 1.5-mile Nauset Marsh Trail) begin and end here. There are also special activities and talks geared to all ages and interests including guided canoe paddles on Salt Pond, and evening beachside campfires. Open daily 9 a.m. to 4:30 p.m.

Nauset Light Beach. Ocean View Drive. This broad swath of sandy beach has a low surf zone and is a good all-around beach that is only moderately crowded even on the hottest of summer weekends. It's a lifeguarded beach with restrooms in season. Beach fee collected Memorial Day to Labor Day, daily 9 a.m. to 5 p.m. Vehicle parking fee $15.

You may recognize red and white **Nauset Light;** it's the lighthouse that is depicted on the Cape Cod Potato Chip bag, and it is one of the Cape's most popular and visited lighthouses. It's open for tours May through Oct on Sun from 1 to 4 p.m.; also on Wed in July and Aug from 4:30 to 7:30 p.m. Nauset Light itself dates from 1877; it was moved here in 1923 to replace the famed 19th-century wooden Three Sisters Lighthouses, which once stood in a row atop Nauset's cliffs. The Three Sisters are nearby, located in a pine clearing off of Cable Road.

where to eat

Arnold's Lobster & Clam Bar. 3580 US 6; (508) 255-2575; arnoldsrestaurant.com. Equal parts beer tent, lobster pound, and family-entertainment destination, this fish shanty is the kind of place that makes summer, summer in New England. You'll find a memorable hot-buttered lobster roll, huge mounds of deep-fried seafood, and a better-than-respectable raw bar. There's minigolf and ice cream here, too—a perfect way to end a perfect beach day. Open seasonally, daily 11:30 a.m. to 9:30 p.m. Cash only. $$.

Hole in One Donut Shop. 4295 US 6; (508) 255-9446; theholecapecod.com. Pop in early and grab a doughnut while it is still warm. A fiercely loyal local clientele crams around this tiny shop's diner countertop for coffee and massive, melt-in-your-mouth hand-cut donuts. The Boston cream is a delicious mess—glazed with chocolate and oozing vanilla filling. Open daily Memorial Day weekend to Labor Day weekend 5 a.m. to 4 p.m.; off-season open daily 5 a.m. to noon. $.

where to stay

Cottage Grove. 1975 US 6; (508) 255-0500; grovecape.com. A true getaway for those seeking a rustic (but not too rustic) cabin-in-the-woods experience. These 1930s-era cottages are vintage Cape Cod, adorably cozy and featuring knotty pine walls, wood floors, and cedar-beamed ceilings. There are 9 cottages in the pet-friendly complex, and all but one has a kitchenette/kitchen. Open seasonally late May through early Oct. $–$$.

wellfleet, ma

Just 2 miles wide and nearly surrounded by both the Atlantic Ocean and Cape Cod Bay, Wellfleet has miles of beaches and a tremendous landscape of natural beauty; between the Cape Cod National Seashore and the Wellfleet Bay Wildlife Sanctuary nearly 70 percent of the town's land is protected.

Of course, Wellfleet is synonymous for its oysters: Plump, mild, and sweet, they are regarded as some of the best in the world. You'll find plenty of opportunities to feast on the tasty delicacies; you'll see local oysters in some form on the menu of nearly every restaurant in town.

getting there

From Eastham, it's a short 10-mile drive along US 6 East to Wellfleet (about 15 minutes).

where to go

Marconi Beach. 99 Marconi Beach Rd.; (508) 771-2144; nps.gov/caco. Against the back-drop of a steep cliff, a white, sandy beach beckons. It's a spectacular setting and unusual among New England beaches because the 40-foot bluff creates a shadow across the sand. To access the beach, you need to walk down the stairs near the parking lot. Nearby, the Marconi Station site has an informational display that describes the work of Italian inventor Guglielmo Marconi, who sent the first wireless transatlantic telegraph message between the US and England in 1903 from this very spot. Check out the observation platform that offers breathtaking views of both Cape Cod Bay and the Atlantic. There is a wonderful hiking opportunity here as well; the 1.5-mile Atlantic White Cedar Swamp Trail is an easy looping trail, and one of the Cape's most scenic. Parking lots open daily 6 a.m. to midnight. Admission fee June through Sept $20 per vehicle.

Wellfleet Bay Wildlife Sanctuary. 291 US 6, South Wellfleet; (508) 349-2615; wellfleetbay .org. Bring your binoculars and a field guide. This 1,100-acre sanctuary features marshland and pine forests, as well as beach and attracts both song- and shorebirds. Nature lovers can walk the trails while observing salt-marsh wildlife in its natural habitat. Inside, a tidal-pool tank and a salt-marsh aquarium hold many common types of Cape Cod Bay's underwater creatures. Open Memorial Day through Columbus Day daily 8:30 a.m. to 5 p.m.; Columbus Day through Memorial Day, Tues through Sun 8:30 a.m. to 5 p.m. Admission $5 adults, $3 seniors and children ages 2 to 12.

Wellfleet Drive-In Theater. US 6; (508) 349-7176; wellfleetdrivein.com. Remember watching movies in the family car beneath the stars? Drive-in movies still thrill. First opened in 1957, this is the only drive-in theater on the Cape and one of the few remaining in Massachusetts. It shows only first-run movies (always a double feature), and the first show is usually appropriate for families. Other attractions include a snack bar, miniature golf, ice-cream stand, and a weekend open-air flea market. Open late May through Labor Day weekend; check website for times. Admission for drive-in $10 adults, $7.50 seniors and children ages 4 to 11, children ages 3 and under free. Cash only.

where to eat

The Beachcomber. 1120 Cahoon Hollow Rd.; (508) 349-6055; thebeachcomber.com. The Beachcomber sits high on the dunes of Cahoon Hollow Beach. During the day enjoy casual dining from a multifaceted menu that includes foot-long hot dogs, a Caesar salad with fresh grilled tuna, and even a kids' menu. Things heat up when the sun goes down; late night, the young and the beautiful chill out with a cold one and dance to live music into the early hours. Open Memorial Day through Labor Day daily 11:30 a.m. to 1 a.m. $$.

Mac's Shack. 91 Commercial St.; (508) 349-6333; macseafood.com. In an unassuming house by the road (look for the lobsterman and boat on the roof), Mac's is a pescavore paradise with stellar fare like pan-roasted halibut, lobster mashed potatoes, and seared coconut curry scallops, along with New England seafood standards. Mac's also does sushi—very good sushi. Straightforward sushi and sashimi choices are super-fresh and always masterfully prepared. Open seasonally Tues through Sun 5 to 9 p.m. Mac's at the Pier (508-349-9611) is a seasonal, takeout-only place located at the Wellfleet Town Pier selling lobster rolls, fried clams, and steamers. $$–$$$.

PB Boulangerie & Bistro. 15 Lecount Rd.; (508) 349-1600; pbboulangeriebistro.com. A *parfait* bistro on Cape Cod that evokes a classic bistro in the heart of Paris. Chef-owner Philippe Rispoli has created a chic, market-driven local menu that tempts with offerings like seared *foie gras* with seasonal fruit marmalade, steak frites, slow-poached cod with little-neck clams, and a tarte tatin studded with apples and drenched with Calvados, all served in a warmly contemporary dining room. Also stop by the boulangerie for phenomenal breads, cookies, and pastries to take to the beach. Bistro open Wed through Sun 5 to 10 p.m.; boulangerie open Wed through Sun 7 a.m. to 7 p.m. $–$$$.

provincetown, ma

Located at the very tip of Cape Cod, seemingly at the end of the world, Provincetown, or "P-town" as it is known, is a quirky fusion of a Portuguese fishing village and a world-renowned gay resort destination, all mixed with a good measure of early American history.

cruising (to) provincetown

*Hop a ferry from Boston to P-town and avoid the stress of being stuck in a Cape Cod–bound traffic nightmare. In the summer, daily high-speed ferry options make it entirely possible to do P-town as a day trip from Boston. The first ferries dock in P-town around 10 a.m.; the last ones leave at 7:30 and 8:30 p.m., which gives you almost 10 hours to enjoy the beaches of the Cape Cod National Seashore, gallery browse, and indulge in seaside epicurean dining. **Note:** If you are traveling holiday weekends or during the months of July and August, be sure to make ferry reservations in advance—March is not too early. All the ferry companies permit bicycles (extra charge).*

- *From Boston's World Trade Center, Bay State Cruise (617-748-3779; baystatecruisecompany.com) offers high-speed ferry service to MacMillan Wharf with 3 departures daily May through October (round-trip fares $88 adult, $78 seniors, $65 children ages 3–12). Popular with thrifty day-tripping families, Bay State also offers traditional 3-hour ferry service (round-trip $60 adults and free for children ages 3–12) on Saturdays during July.*

- *From mid-May through October Boston Harbor Cruises (617-227-4321; bostonharborcruises.com) makes several trips a day (round-trip $92 adults, $79 seniors, $72 children ages 3–11) from Long Wharf in Boston to MacMillan Pier in Provincetown in less than 90 minutes by high-speed catamaran.*

- *Another good option is to take the Plymouth to Provincetown Express Ferry (508-747-2400; p-townferry.com), which offers daily departures from late June through Labor Day weekend (round-trip fares $48 adults, $39 seniors, $30 children ages 3–12) leaving from the State Pier on Water Street and arriving 1.5 hours later in Provincetown.*

getting there

Provincetown is at the end of US 6 at the tip of Cape Cod, and it's an incredible landscape of barren sand dunes and crashing breakers all along the way. From Wellfleet, the drive is 13 miles and normally takes 25 minutes, but it can be much longer during peak-traffic congestion times. The last 3 miles can be especially slow going. Follow MA 6A to arrive at Commercial Street.

where to go

Provincetown Chamber of Commerce Visitor Center. 307 Commercial St., MacMillan Pier; (508) 487-3424; ptownchamber.com. Find event schedules, brochures on accommodations, dining, and area activities along with knowledgeable and friendly staff. Open Memorial Day to Labor Day, daily 9 a.m. to 7 p.m.; hours vary the rest of the year.

Art's Dune Tours. 4 Standish St.; (508) 487-1950; artsdunetours.com. Experience the exhilarating thrill of an off-road adventure on the Cape's sand dunes. Art's offers a popular 1-hour narrated tour of the outermost beaches of the Cape Cod National Seashore; see the dune shacks and lighthouses. Sunset, clambake, and Race Point Beach tours are available too. Open May through Oct, daily tours from $29 adults, $18 children ages 6 to 11.

Seashore Province Lands Visitor Center. Race Point Road; (508) 487-1256; nps.gov/caco. Here you are just 2 miles from the very tip of Cape Cod. The observation deck provides 360-degree views of the dunes and Atlantic Ocean, and whale sightings are common. The visitor center shows a rotating series of Cape Cod–themed orientation films and offers a variety of ranger-led walks and activities. Open daily May through Oct 9 a.m. to 5 p.m.

Dolphin Fleet. Depart from Macmillan Wharf; (508) 240-3636; whalewatch.com. Provincetown is a hot spot for whale-watching tours on Cape Cod, with close proximity to the Stellwagen Bank National Marine Sanctuary. Dolphin Fleet has run whale-watch tours since 1975. The trip, with a naturalist on board, lasts 3 to 4 hours, and with plentiful food supplies (seals) attracting whales in record numbers, you'll likely see several, if not dozens, on your trek. Daily April through Nov; check website for departure times. Tickets $47 adults, $31 children ages 5 to 12.

P-town Pedicabs. 377 Commercial St.; (508) 487-0660; ptownpedicabs.com. These bicycle rickshaws are a pedal-powered taxi service that offers an entertaining way to see P-town. Flag one down! Operates daily May through Oct. Pay is by tips.

Pilgrim Monument and Provincetown Museum. 1 High Pole Hill Rd.; (508) 487-1310; pilgrim-monument.org. Commemorating the first landing of the *Mayflower* in the New World, this is P-town's big-deal landmark. Completed in 1910, this slender Romanesque-style bell tower is—at 250 feet—the country's tallest all-granite structure. It's a healthy walk to climb the tower's 116 steps to the top, but your reward is an amazing view in all directions of lower Cape Cod. The next-door **Provincetown Museum** focuses on the town's *Mayflower* connection and the area's maritime heritage. Open Sept through Nov and Apr through May 9 a.m. to 5 p.m.; June through mid-Sept 9 a.m. to 7 p.m. Admission $10 adults, free for children 12 and under.

Race Point Beach. Off of US 6. A beach of sheer beauty, with windswept dunes and a long beach that is more than big enough to keep sunbathers and swimmers out of each other's

cape cod national seashore

"Magnificent" doesn't do the Cape Cod National Seashore justice. This 40-mile stretch of shoreline, where windswept sandy dunes meet pristine beach, was created in 1961 with legislation signed by President Kennedy, a longtime summer resident of the Cape. The Cape Cod National Seashore is a national treasure and one of President Kennedy's enduring legacies.

Stretching from the town of Chatham and ending in Provincetown, the Cape Cod National Seashore is managed by the National Park Service. Within the park there are a tremendous number of things to do and places to go, including 6 lifeguarded beaches, 11 walking trails, 3 bike trails, and several historical points of interest. The park's two principal visitor centers—Salt Pond in Eastham and Province Lands in Provincetown—not only offer orientation and visitor services but also operate as full-fledged nature centers and as a base for a host of ranger-led excursions and activities.

Cape Cod National Seashore; (508) 771-2144; nps.gov/caco. Parking lots open from 6 a.m. to midnight.

way. The beach faces north toward the Atlantic, so although it gets sun all day, the water is briskly cold and there is an undertow. It's a lifeguarded beach, and there are restrooms. ***Note:*** Nearby Herring Cove Beach is also a Cape Cod National Seashore Beach, with a very different beachy mood: it's known for welcoming *au naturel* bathers. Beach fee collected Memorial Day to Labor Day daily 9 a.m. to 5 p.m. Vehicle parking fee $20.

where to eat

Lobster Pot. 321 Commercial St.; (508) 487-0842; ptownlobsterpot.com. Considering its prime waterfront location and its reputation as a tourist magnet, the eclectic seafood cuisine here is actually quite a bit better than one would think. Savor the taste of Portuguese cuisine in the bouillabaisse Algarve or order lobster cooked in countless ways, both traditional and gourmet (think pan-roasted lobster with a brandy and herb butter sauce). The lobster, avocado, mango and tarragon aioli is their signature appetizer and a must order! Open daily 11:30 a.m. to 10 p.m. Closed Dec through Mar. $$.

Napi's. 7 Freeman St.; (508) 487-1145; napisptown.com. Locals and visitors gravitate to this funky restaurant to get their fix of world cuisine with dishes like Brazilian black beans and rice with banana fritters, a scallop stir-fry with bok choy, and chicken piccata. Open

May through Sept daily 11:30 a.m. to 2:30 p.m. and 5 to 10 p.m.; Oct through Apr daily 5 to 10 p.m. $$.

Nor'East Beer Garden. 206 Commercial St.; (508) 487-2337; noreastbeergarden.com. This modern, totally outdoor beer garden offers whimsical interpretations of the Cape's seasonal cuisine. You can graze on Wellfleet littlenecks with bacon and white beans, beer-braised veal cheeks, and doctored-up duck *poutine* (French fries with duck gravy). There are also 16 (always changing) American craft beers on tap, which positively ensures that the fun never stops. Open May through Oct, Thurs through Sun 11:30 a.m. to 1 a.m.; Tues and Wed 4:30 p.m. to 1 a.m. $$.

where to stay

Crowne Point Inn & Spa. 82 Bradford St.; (508) 487-6767; crownepointe.com. This 1870s-era sea captain's house turned 40-room inn combines the charm of a B&B with the reliability of a hotel. The rooms are pleasant and comfortably furnished; some have whirlpools and/or fireplaces. Amenities include complimentary buffet breakfast, evening wine and cheese hour, and free Wi-Fi and parking. There's an outdoor pool and full-service spa on-site as well. This is an adult-oriented hotel, no children under age 18. $$$.

Provincetown Hotel at Gabriel's. 102 Bradford St.; (508) 487-3232; gabriels.com. Located in the shadow of the Pilgrim Monument yet tucked away from Commercial Street, this property features 16 nicely decorated, renovated rooms and suites; some have fireplaces and Jacuzzi tubs. Guests are treated to exceptional hospitality from the longtime innkeepers. Extra touches include a beautifully landscaped garden courtyard with lots of seating and an outdoor fire pit. Rates include hot buffet breakfast and free Wi-Fi in rooms. A kid-friendly, pet-friendly, senior-friendly property. $$–$$$.

Salt House Inn. 6 Conwall St.; (508) 487-1911; salthouseinn.com. Opened as a hotel in 2013, this mid-1800s salt building is one of the Cape's newest lodging choices. The mid-1800s shingled building once housed P-town's salt-mine workers. Today this beautifully restored boutique property retains the character of the building with a breezy beach cottage feel that blends old and new. Each of the 15 guest rooms is individually decorated in a chic all-white palette with sea and sand accents and has a private en-suite spa-like bathroom with either a vintage cast-iron tub or walk-in shower. All rates include a gourmet breakfast— a bounty of fresh fruit, yogurt, granola, and a daily hot entree like spiced banana stuffed challah french toast or tomato and Parmesan tarts. Guests dine at a communal table in the dining room or at tables in the garden. Rates also include free Wi-Fi and parking. Open seasonally May through Oct. $$–$$$.

day trip 11

cape cod

the vineyard:
martha's vineyard, ma

martha's vineyard, ma

Just 7 miles off the coast of Massachusetts, hop a ferry (from Hyannis or Woods Hole) for a short 45-minute ride across Nantucket Sound to Martha's Vineyard. But best leave your car behind; biking is the preferred way to get around. Spend the day exploring the island's beaches and its distinctive villages. Leave time for upscale dining and shopping before taking the ferry back. Better yet, spend the night.

getting there

The *Island Queen* ferry (islandqueen.com) operates passenger-only service from Falmouth to Oak Bluffs. Alternatively, the **Steamship Authority ferry** (steamshipauthority.com) departs from Woods Hole to Vineyard Haven. The **Hy-Line ferry** (hy-linecruises.com) takes 95 minutes from Hyannis to Oak Bluffs. The Steamship Authority ferry is the only one that takes both passengers and cars (and is also the only year-round ferry service), but visitors to the Vineyard may want to forgo a car altogether; the Martha's Vineyard Transit Authority, or VTA (vineyardtransit.com, 508-693-9440) shuttle bus system connects all the towns and several of the public beaches, and the fare is just $1.25 per town (including town of origin).

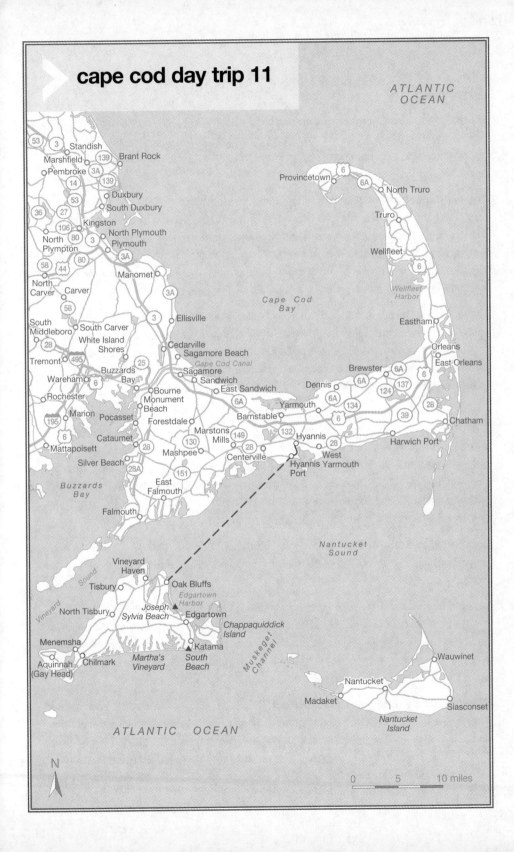

ATLANTIC
OCEAN

Provincetown
North Truro
Truro
Wellfleet

53 3 Standish
Marshfield 139 Brant Rock
Pembroke 3A
14 139
53 Duxbury
36 27 South Duxbury
106 Kingston
North 80 3 North Plymouth
Plympton Plymouth
58 44 80 3A
North
Carver Carver Manomet
58 3A
Cape Cod
Bay
South 3 Ellisville
Middleboro South Carver
28 White Island Cedarville
Shores Sagamore Beach
Tremont 495 Cape Cod Canal
Buzzards 25 Sagamore
Wareham Bay Sandwich
6 Bourne East Sandwich
Rochester Monument
Beach 6A
195 Marion Pocasset Forestdale Barnstable
6 Cataumet Marstons 149
Mattapoisett 28 Mills 132
Silver Beach Mashpee 28 Hyannis
28A Centerville West
East 151 Hyannis Yarmouth
Falmouth Port

Wellfleet
Harbor
Eastham
Orleans
Brewster 6A East Orleans
Dennis 6A 124 137
6A 134 28
Yarmouth 39
6 Chatham
Harwich Port

Buzzards
Bay

Falmouth

Nantucket
Sound

Vineyard
Haven
Tisbury Oak Bluffs
Edgartown
Joseph Harbor
Sylvia Beach Edgartown
North Tisbury Chappaquiddick
Island
Menemsha Katama
Aquinnah Chilmark Martha's South
(Gay Head) Vineyard Beach

Muskeget
Channel

Wauwinet
Nantucket
Madaket
Siasconset
Nantucket
Island

ATLANTIC OCEAN

N

0   5   10 miles

where to go

Martha's Vineyard Chamber of Commerce. 24 Beach Rd., Vineyard Haven; (508) 693-0085; mvy.com. There is a small information booth located at the Vineyard Haven ferry docks. Be sure to pick up a copy of *This Week on Martha's Vineyard* to find out the latest island happenings.

The Farm Institute. 14 Aero Ave., Edgartown; farminstitute.org. Farm-to-table is all the buzz. The Farm Institute is a teaching farm that is open to the public for farm tours. Families with young children who are on the island for several days may want to sign their kids up for "farmer for the day" workshops, where kids can spend time in the fields planting, weeding, and harvesting. There is a farm stand on the premises, too. Farm stand hours late June through late Sept, Mon through Sat 9 a.m. to 4 p.m. Program costs vary.

Flying Horses Carousel. 15 Lake Ave., Oak Bluffs. This 1876 amusement ride is the oldest operating platform carousel in the country. To the sounds of calliope music, take a ride on these elaborately carved antique steeds. Catch the brass ring and you get a free ride. Open Memorial Day weekend through Labor Day daily 10 a.m. to 10 p.m.; spring and fall, Sat and Sun 11 a.m. to 4:30 p.m. Tickets $3.

Island Alpaca. 1 Head of Pond Rd., Vineyard Haven; (508) 693-5554; islandalpaca.com. A must-visit for families, gentle alpacas have a charm all their own. Founded in 2006, this 19-acre working farm located just 2 miles out of town raises a large herd of nearly 80 alpacas. The staff is incredibly attentive toward the animals and is eager to share their passion with visitors. Be sure to check out the gift shop, which sells alpaca sweaters, scarves, socks, stuffed toys, and gorgeous throws. Open daily; summer hours 10 a.m. to 5 p.m.; rest of the year 10 a.m. to 4 p.m. Admission $5 per person.

Joseph Sylvia State Beach. Beach Road, Edgartown. Midway between Oak Bluffs and Edgartown, this is a lovely 2-mile beach with protected, clear, shallow waters and small waves.

Katama Beach. Katama Rd., Edgartown. Sweeping barrier dunes form this picture-perfect 3-mile stretch of remote sand, just a 15-minute VTA bus ride from Edgartown. Also known as South Beach, it is an Atlantic-facing shoreline with sometimes pounding waves. The beach is lifeguarded and has restrooms and changing facilities. Admire the natural beauty and if you don't have to catch a ferry, stick around for the sunset.

Wesleyan Grove National Historic District. Oak Bluffs. A former Methodist revival campground, the small colorful cottages (most are private homes) with ornate gingerbread trim and flower-filled window boxes are sure to enchant. Take a peek at a cottage interior at the Cottage Museum and Shop (at Highland Avenue and Trinity Park). Museum open seasonally Mon through Sat 10 a.m. to 4 p.m., Sun 1 to 4 p.m. Admission $2 adults, $0.50 ages 3 to 12.

where to shop

Granary Gallery. 636 Old County Rd., West Tisbury; (508) 693-0455; granarygallery.com. Established more than 50 years ago, the Granary "at the red barn" is the island's oldest and largest art gallery. The Granary represents many of the island's highly regarded artists who work in sculpture, photography, and painting. You'll also find a good mix of fine art and antiques here. Open year-round Mon through Sat 10 a.m. to 5 p.m., Sun 11 a.m. to 4 p.m.

Morning Glory Farm. 120 Meshacket Rd., Edgartown; (508) 627-9674; morninggloryfarm .com. Since 1975, this 55-acre farm has really grown. More than just a farm stand, this is a one-stop shop for organic produce (much from the fields out back) and gourmet foods. Find imported olive oil, fresh bread and pasta, cheeses, prepared dinners, freshly baked desserts, and stunning bouquets of field-grown flowers. Open summer Mon through Sat 9 a.m. to 6 p.m., Sun 9 a.m. to 5 p.m.; check website for spring and fall hours. Closed Jan through Apr.

Orange Peel Bakery. 22 State Rd., Aquinnah; (508) 645-2025. On the way to the Aquinnah Cliffs, look for the sign of the Orange Peel Bakery. Juli Vanderhoop's licensed home-based bakery is island-famous for its rustic breads, croissants, and cookies, made on the premises and baked in the giant outdoor beehive oven in the driveway. Orange Peel is self-serve and operates on an honor system—look for the bakery case and money jar on the table at the side of the road. In the summer, Wednesday BYO (bring your own toppings) Pizza Nights attract islanders and summerers for fresh-from-the-oven pizza, live music, and community.

where to eat

The Bite. 29 Basin Rd., Menemsha; (508) 645-9239; thebitemenemsha.com. This true roadside clam shack is as honest a place as you will ever find. And you'll gladly endure waiting in line for the Bite's tender sweet clams and clam chowder. There are only 2 picnic tables, so resign yourself to taking your carton of plump, sweet fried clams to Menemsha Beach down the street. Ahh, the Vineyard. Open daily in season 11 a.m. to 8 p.m. $.

Barn Bowl & Bistro. 13 Uncas Ave., Oak Bluffs; (508) 696-9800; thebarnmv.com. Burgers, pizza, drinks and bowling. What's not to love? This bowling alley cum restaurant is one of

dancing alabaster sculptures

Just down the road from the Granary, the permanent outdoor sculpture garden on the grounds of the Field Gallery (1050 State Rd., West Tisbury; 508-693-5595) features cavorting nudes by Tom Maley that are whimsical, luscious, and fun—and a great photo op.

the island's best family-friendly, cheap-eats, funky-casual spots. There is also more creative fare on the menu, like hazelnut cod in a wine sauce with Swiss chard and rice and a grilled vegetable lasagna in a red pepper puree. At lunch, $9.99 specials take over with dishes like a Greek salad wrap and a toasted Italian sub. The bowling experience is classic 10-pin (big ball, with finger holes) offering lots of fun on a rainy island day with room to spare. Open Sun through Thurs 11 a.m. to 11 p.m., Fri and Sat 11 a.m. to midnight. $

The Black Dog Tavern. 20 Beach St., Vineyard Haven; (508) 693-9223; theblackdog.com. Perhaps the Vineyard's most well-known restaurant, the Black Dog Tavern turns out to be a belly-busting bargain for the Vineyard with a terrific waterfront location (and lots of window seats), a large outdoor patio, reasonable prices (dinner entrees average less than $30), and huge portions. The next-door store has the full line of the restaurant's iconic Black Dog gear. Open daily year-round 7 a.m. to 10 p.m. $$.

Copper Wok. 9 Main St.; Vineyard Haven; (508) 693-3416; copperwokmv.com. Cape Cod seafood is even better with an Asian accent. This new Vineyard hot spot pairs a lively atmosphere (read: scorpion bowls for two) with an anything goes Chinese and Asian-influenced menu of spiced potato samosas, pulled pork buns that have just the right touch of hoisin sauce and coconut curry shrimp. The dining room also has a sushi bar with traditional rolls and inventive specialties. Open daily 11:30 a.m. to 10 p.m. $$.

Giordano's. 18 Lake Ave., Oak Bluffs; (508) 693-0184; giosmv.com. Located across from the Flying Horses Carousel, Gio's, as it's known to islanders, is an old-school Italian restaurant that serves Neapolitan-style pizza topped with swirls of house-made sauce, cheese, and classic toppings like sausage, peppers, and anchovies. The memorabilia-laden dining room is family friendly—or there's always the take-out window as a fallback. The menu also features fried seafood and traditional pasta dishes like fettuccine alfredo. Open sometime in Apr through Columbus Day weekend, daily 11:30 a.m. to 10:30 p.m. $$.

Lucky Hank's. 218 Upper Main St., Edgartown; (508) 939-4082; luckyhanksmv.com. Located in a cozy 1910 home, this Edgartown spot is small on seating but huge on rustic farm-to-table seasonal cuisine. The kitchen turns out especially fine breakfasts—like the cod cakes with lobster tartar sauce. At dinner, local produce is the star of many of the dishes. The vegetable-centric "farm share" is the chef's whim—recently quinoa with heirloom tomatoes, peppers, roasted zucchini, and ricotta salata. The welcoming service even draws the locals here—nearly every night of the week. Open year-round, daily 8 a.m. to 2:30 p.m. and 5 to 9 p.m. $$.

Offshore Ale Company. 30 Kennebec Ave., Oak Bluffs; (508) 693-2626; offshoreale .com. Go straight to the source of Martha's Vineyard's favorite beers, Offshore Amber and Offshore IPA. This is the (sometimes raucous) place to be for expertly crafted beers that appeal to every palate. The menu specializes in gastropub fare such as roast chicken, meat loaf, and artisan pizzas along with the usual bar food offerings of burgers, wings, and sandwiches. In summer, daily brew tours are available with beer sampling sessions; check website for times. Open year-round Thurs through Tues 11:30 a.m. to 4 p.m. and 5:30 to 10 p.m.; Wed 5:30 to 10 p.m. $$.

Rockfish. 11 North Water St., Edgartown; (508) 627-9967; rockfishedgartown.com. The Coogan family, owners of the Wharf Pub, identified a Vineyard need and filled it: a hip, bar-centered environment offering consistently excellent wood-fired flat breads, local seafood and farmhouse chic dishes—all at off-island prices. Start off your meal with the fried oysters and remoulade sauce. Enjoy plates of shrimp, bacon, and grits or the harissa grilled chicken thighs with couscous. Open year-round, check website as hours vary by season. $$.

Slice of Life Cafe. 50 Circuit Ave., Oak Bluffs; (508) 693-3838; sliceoflifemv.com. This is the place on the island for reliable all-day dining in welcoming digs. Breakfasts feature egg scrambles and bagel sandwiches, and light lunches and dinners include choices like an Asian salmon salad and a grilled sirloin sandwich. Open Tues through Sat 8 a.m. to 10 p.m., Sun 8 a.m. to 2 p.m. $$.

where to stay

Hob Knob. 128 Main St., Edgartown; (508) 627-9510; hobknob.com. This gorgeous 19th-century Gothic Revival inn has 17 plush rooms that include lots of boutique hotel perks. Indulge yourself at the on-site spa or retreat to the sauna. An organic full farm breakfast and afternoon tea and cookies come standard with a stay. $$$–$$$$.

Nobnocket Inn. 60 Mount Aldworth Rd.; Vineyard Haven; (508) 696-0859; nobnocket .com. This modern B&B is tucked into a 2-acre garden landscape. The handsome arts and crafts style inn has 7 contemporary rooms that feature Frette linens and marble and glass baths. Breakfast is made to order from local farm ingredients and is served in the sunroom (or choose to have breakfast in bed). Inn owners Simon and Annabelle Hunton live on the premises and are committed to making your stay outstanding with extras like homemade brownies and the next day's weather report on your bedside table at turndown. $$

Peqout Hotel. 19 Pequot Ave., Oak Bluffs; (508) 693-5087; pequothotel.com. This pretty 32-room Victorian-style hotel is just steps from the Oak Bluffs ferry landing and the beach. The rooms come in different shapes and sizes and are decorated in a cheerful mix of styles. The hotel's gingerbread-trimmed front porch is a perfect spot for sitting and rocking. Rates include an expanded continental breakfast and afternoon tea and cookies. $$–$$$.

Winnetu. 31 Dunes Rd., Edgartown; (508) 310-1733; winnetu.com. This is the Vineyard's premier accommodation choice for families. It's a sprawling resort located directly on South Beach, and it boasts loads of activities to keep the kiddies busy, including 2 pools, a playground, and complimentary supervised children's programs. Room configurations run the gamut from 1- to 4-bedroom hotel rooms (all with kitchenettes or kitchens) to 3- to 5-bedroom private homes, all done up in variations of classic New England coastal style. For families not on a budget, this is perhaps as good as it gets. $$$$.

day trip 12

cape cod

romance of the sea:
nantucket, ma

nantucket, ma

Known as the "Grey Lady" because of the almost daily early morning fog, Nantucket is an island retreat loaded with laid-back charm. The word "Nantucket" comes from the Native American language meaning "far-away island." Located 30 miles off the Massachusetts coast, Nantucket—once an important whaling port—is day-trip doable. Arriving by ferry puts you in the center of Nantucket town with its 18th-century sea captain's homes, the Nantucket Whaling Museum, cobblestoned streets lined with quaint shops, and an impressive number of very good restaurants. The island's pristine beaches and natural beauty make for a perfect island getaway.

getting there

The **Steamship Authority** (508-495-3278; steamshipauthority.com) and **Hy-Line Cruises** (800-492-8082; hy-linecruises.com) both offer year-round direct high-speed (1 hour) and traditional (2 hour) ferries from Hyannis. **Freedom Cruise Line** (508-432-8999; nantucket islandferry.com) runs seasonal (spring through fall) high-speed ferry service from Chatham.

where to go

Nantucket Visitors Center and Information Bureau. 25 Federal St.; (508) 228-0925. The weather-worn shingled cottage that serves as the island's information center is near the

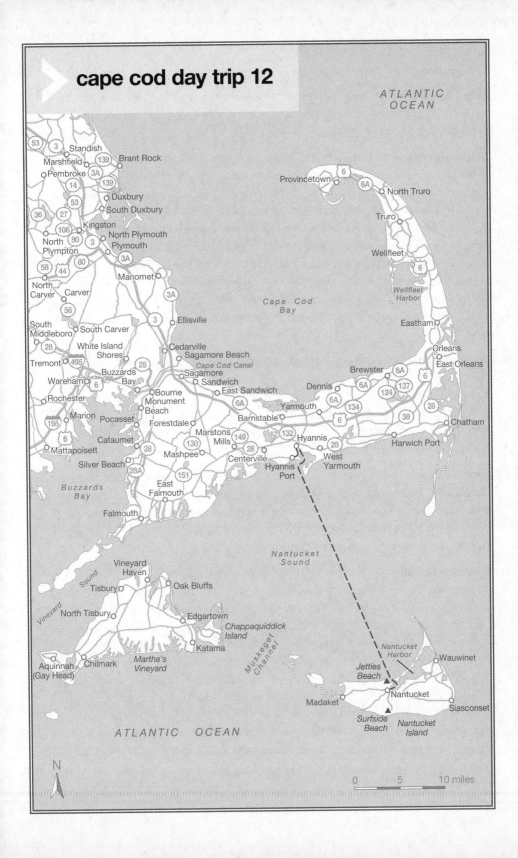

cape cod day trip 12

ATLANTIC OCEAN

Standish
53 3
Marshfield
Pembroke 3A 139 Brant Rock
14
139
53 Duxbury
27 South Duxbury
36 106 Kingston
80 North Plymouth
North 3 Plymouth
Plympton 80 3A
58 44
North Manomet
Carver Carver 3A
58
South Ellisville
Middleboro
South Carver
28 White Island
Tremont 495 Shores Cedarville
Sagamore Beach
Buzzards Cape Cod Canal
Wareham Bay Sagamore
6 Sandwich
Rochester Bourne East Sandwich
Monument
Marion Beach 6A
195 Pocasset Forestdale
6 Barnstable
Cataumet Marstons 149
Mattapoisett 130 Mills
28 Mashpee 28
Silver Beach Centerville
28A 151 Hyannis
East Port
Falmouth

Falmouth

Provincetown 6
6A North Truro
Truro

Wellfleet
6

Cape Cod Wellfleet
Bay Harbor

Eastham

Orleans
Brewster 6A East Orleans
Dennis 6A 137 6
124
Yarmouth 6A
134
6 39 28
132 Chatham
Hyannis
28 Harwich Port
West
Yarmouth

Nantucket
Sound

Vineyard
Haven
Sound
Tisbury Oak Bluffs
Vineyard North Tisbury
Edgartown
Chappaquiddick
Island
Katama
Aquinnah Chilmark Martha's
(Gay Head) Vineyard

Muskeget Channel

Nantucket
Harbor Wauwinet
Jetties
Beach
Nantucket
Madaket
Surfside Siasconset
Beach Nantucket
Island

ATLANTIC OCEAN

N

0   5   10 miles

ferry terminals and is always busy. There are maps and brochures, and yes, they can make same-day hotel reservations if you decide to stay the night. Open Mon through Sat 9 a.m. to 6 p.m., Sun 10 a.m. to 4 p.m.

Cisco Brewers. 5 Bartlett Farm Rd.; (508) 325-5929; ciscobrewers.com. There's a lot of brewing going on here. In a small cluster of buildings set among pine and fields, Cisco Brewery, Triple Eight Distillery, and Nantucket Vineyards produce handcrafted beer, vodka, and wine. Their best-known brand is probably their Whale's Tale Pale Ale. There is live music daily, and although there isn't a kitchen on-site, patrons are encouraged to bring their own food. There are also regularly scheduled food trucks that come by. Cisco now runs a free, scheduled shuttle bus to the brewery that leaves from the Nantucket visitor center. The behind-the-scene tours are informative and relaxed; they last about 1.5 hours and conclude with a flight tasting of either beer, wine, or vodka (your choice). Tour admission $20 per adult, there is no charge for kids. Tours by appointment. Brewpub open year-round Mon through Sat 10 a.m. to 7 p.m., Sun noon to 6 p.m.

Jetties Beach. 4 Bathing Beach Rd. Jetties Beach is the island's most popular public beach for day-trippers. It's just a short walk, bike ride, or shuttle bus trip from town and features soft beige sand and mild surf. It's a lifeguarded beach with changing rooms and restrooms. Beachfront, The Jetties (thejetties.com) has all the other amenities you need to spend the day: a beach shop with chair rentals, a full restaurant serving casual lunch and dinner, and live music on the deck in the evening. Open Memorial Day weekend to Labor Day.

Surfside Beach. Surfside Road. For bigger waves head out to Surfside. Another golden-hued beach, this one is also hugely popular for families and beginning windsurfers (good windsurfing always means there is great kite flying). Surfside is 2 miles from town; it's an easy bike ride with a dedicated paved bike path or take the shuttle. Surfside has lifeguards, changing facilities, and a concession stand.

Whaling Museum. 13 Broad St.; (508) 228-1894, nha.org. This small but fascinating museum tells the tale of Nantucket's whaling days in the early to mid-1800s when the island prospered from the lucrative business of hunting whales for their oil. The museum's center-piece attraction is the 46-foot sperm whale skeleton that hangs from the ceiling (this whale was not hunted, but it washed up on Nantucket's shore on New Year's Day 1998). You can watch a film on whale hunting, see a full-size whale dory, check out the restored candle-making factory equipment, and peruse the museum's collection of antique scrimshaw and vintage Nantucket baskets. Be sure to climb up to the museum's roof-top observation deck before you leave to get a widow's-walk-like view of Nantucket Harbor. Open daily 10 a.m. to 5 p.m. from mid-May through mid-Oct; check website for days/hours during other times of the year. Admission $20 adults, $18 seniors and students, $5 ages 6 to 17, free for children ages 5 and under.

go green in nantucket

You really don't need a car in Nantucket. Nantucket is tiny; you can walk, use public transportation, or bike everywhere on the island. The ferry puts you in the middle of town near most of the island's shops and restaurants. The Nantucket Regional Transit Authority's (NRTA) town-operated shuttle bus runs frequently to all parts of the island (including the beaches) and charges a fare of $1 to $2 per person. Another option to explore Nantucket is by bicycle. The exercise is an added bonus!

where to shop

There are lots of unique shops to while away the time before you catch the ferry back to the mainland. Here are some of the best.

Bartlett's Farms. 33 Bartlett Farm Rd.; (508) 228-9408; bartlettsfarm.com. Since the 19th century, the sprawling barn at Bartlett's Farm has supplied its homegrown vegetables to Nantucket residents and visitors. Today, food-loving islanders come also for Bartlett's selection of fruits, flowers, and ready-made gourmet entrees. Bartlett's is convenient to both Cisco Beach and Cisco Brewery and is a popular stop for sandwiches and salads and other picnic provisions. The on-site nursery produces Nantucket-hardy plant varieties and other gardening necessities. Open daily 10 a.m. to 6 p.m.

Coskata-Coatue Wildlife Refuge. Wauwinet Road; (508) 228-5646; thetrustees.org. On Nantucket's north shore, tucked between the Atlantic Ocean and Nantucket Sound, Coskata-Coatue is a walk on the wild side. You can rent a jeep from town and explore the ruggedly beautiful remote beaches, wooded walking trails, and Great Point Lighthouse on your own, or better yet, sign up for one of the Trustees of Reservations' excellent 2.5-hour guided 4x4 adventures. Open year-round, tours offered seasonally; check website for days/times.

Milly & Grace. 2 Washington St.; (508) 901-5051; millyandgrace.com. This too-pretty-for-words boutique sells well-styled dresses, skirts, tops, and lovingly hand-picked accessories (including an exceptional selection of cashmere wraps). Open daily 10 a.m. to 6 p.m.

Murray's Toggery Shop. 62 Main St.; (508) 228-0437; nantucketreds.com. Murray's Toggery Shop is the home of Nantucket Reds. Originally made as men's chino pants, the distinctive rusty red fades to salmon-ish pink with time. Today, the line has expanded to also include women's and children's clothing and home accents like pillows and throws. Open Mon through Sat 10 a.m. to 5 p.m., closed Sun.

Nantucket Bookworks. 25 Broad St.; (508) 228-4000; nantucketbookworks.com. Poke around this charming bookstore, which stocks a wonderful selections of beach reads, children's books, and books by Nantucket authors. Open Mon through Thurs 10 a.m. to 7 p.m., Fri and Sat 10 a.m. to 9 p.m., Sun 10 a.m. to 7 p.m.

Nantucket Looms. 51 Main St.; (508) 228-1908; nantucketlooms.com. Established in 1968, Nantucket Looms has built its reputation on creating textiles of both timeless beauty and utility. Hand-loomed in the upstairs studios, their sumptuous mohair, cotton, or cashmere throws and blankets are heirloom quality and are to be handed down through generations. The store also carries other home accessories and showcases work from several Nantucket artists. Open Mon through Sat 10 a.m. to 5 p.m., Sun 10 a.m. to 4 p.m.

where to eat

American Seasons. 80 Centre St.; (508) 228-7111; americanseasons.com. Sometimes you just have to book a table way in advance for that big dining experience. This is one of those times. A long-standing Nantucket restaurant (now in its 25th year), American Seasons still retains its ability to seduce diners with morsels like pig ear fries with cilantro, chili, and lime and tobacco-roasted duck breast with farro, and then it lures them into can't-refuse desserts like the dark-chocolate cinnamon cheesecake with coffee sorbet. Open summer daily 5:30 p.m. to close. Rest of the year open Thurs through Mon 5:30 to close. $$$–$$$$.

Black-Eyed Susan's. 10 India St.; (508) 325-0308; black-eyedsusans.com. You'll experience casually upscale dining that features a truly eclectic menu. It's seasonal food at easy prices, like seared Maine diver scallops with limoncello fettuccine or massaman curry with roasted pork and mango. Almost everybody who lives or visits Nantucket agrees, Black-Eyed Susan's is the place to meet up for weekend brunch. Their sourdough french toast with Jack Daniel's butter is nothing short of fantastic. A few rules: It's BYOB, cash only, and reservations are taken (in person) only for the 6 p.m. seating, after which you can put your name on the list. Open Mon through Sat, 7 a.m. to 1 p.m. and 6 to 10 p.m., Sun 7 a.m. to 1 p.m. $$.

Fog Island Cafe. 7 S. Water St.; (508) 228-1818; fogisland.com. A full-service sit-down breakfast and lunch spot that serves hearty breakfasts like cranberry pancakes and cheddar-cheese egg scrambles with home fries. Lunch skews to more eclectic offerings like soba noodle salad, gazpacho soup, and a fish-cake sandwich with ginger slaw, and here's the kicker: Everything is reasonably priced. Open Mon through Sat 8 a.m. to 2 p.m., Sun 8 a.m. to 1 p.m. $–$$.

Nantucket Culinary Center. 22 Federal St., (508) 228-2665; nantucketculinary.com Opened in 2015 by husband and wife team Greg and Joy Margolis (he's the chef, she's the managing director), this is Nantucket's best place to eat like a local. NCC is a unique culinary destination experience that incorporates both the casual Corner Table Café and a cooking school. In the morning there are granola parfaits and breakfast burritos. Lunch brings soups, salads, and sandwiches (the Puritan sandwich of house-roasted turkey and cranberry jalapeno compote is a favorite). Dinner offers dishes like green chicken chili to eat in or take out. Everything on the menu has a focus on a slow-food derived appreciation for Nantucket ingredients. The state-of-the art kitchen hosts an impressive line-up of cooking classes. NCC proves that everything really does taste better when it is served with a sense of community. Café open daily 7 a.m. to 9 p.m.

Oran Mor. 2 S. Beach St.; (508) 228-8655; oranmorbistro.com. Some of Nantucket's most exciting food—roasted halibut with smoked mussels and lobster broth, grilled lamb T-bone, and lamb sausage with quinoa tabbouleh—is served in this welcoming and intimate Nantucket home setting. The conceptual yet satisfying desserts—like a dark chocolate brownie, peanut brittle, and toasted marshmallow cream—are not to be missed. Open Apr through Dec daily 6 to 10 p.m. $$$.

Something Natural. 50 Cliff Rd.; (508) 228-0504; somethingnatural.com. The sandwiches and baked goods are anything but ordinary at this sandwich shop/bakery located within biking distance of Jetties Beach. Sheila's Favorite is nearly everyone's favorite: tomatoes, carrots, pickles, mayo, and swiss piled high on the bakery's homemade oatmeal bread. And a giant peanut butter–chocolate chip cookie for dessert? Why yes! Open late Apr through Oct, Mon through Thurs 8 a.m. to 4 p.m., Fri through Sun 8 a.m. to 5:30 p.m. Cash only. $.

where to stay

Greydon House. 17 Broad St.; (508) 228-2468; greydonhouse.com. Nantucket's newest boutique hotel has a prime spot close to the Whaling Museum and is a short walk from the ferries. There are 20 rooms and suites with modern bathrooms and bespoke furnishings spread throughout the original 1850s Greek Revival residence and a 3-story 2016 addition. The décor reflects the global eclecticism that is Nantucket's seafaring heritage with Portuguese tiles, occasional chairs from the Ivory Coast, whaling artifacts and Native American art pieces. Glamorous details abound in the common rooms with a paneled library that features a custom–designed Chinese port mural and a front porch furnished with rattan chairs and ferns. All room rates include continental breakfast. The on-site Restaurant & Bar at Greydon House is small, but is open year-round and features beautifully plated dishes like grilled Maine prawns in coconut broth and roasted chicken with hen of the woods mushrooms and butternut squash. The bar has quickly become an island destination for pre-dinner drinks with an excellent cocktail program of classics and seasonally influenced originals. The Little Grey Lady—gin, St. Germaine, lemon and fortified wine—is one unique favorite. $$$.

Nantucket Inn. 1 Millers Ln.; (508) 228-6900; nantucketinn.net. The 100 rooms of this modest establishment are large and comfortably traditional. A family-friendly choice, the property boasts both an indoor and outdoor pool and tennis courts, and offers complimentary shuttle service to both Surfside Beach and the ferry docks. Rates include a full breakfast. $$$.

The Wauwinet. 120 Wauwinet Rd.; (508) 228-0145; wauwinet.com. This waterfront resort with sweeping vistas over Nantucket Harbor has 2 exquisite private sand beaches (bayside and Atlantic). Rooms are casually elegant with time-worn antiques, Pratesi sheets, tawny walls, and cream trim. There are extensive spa facilities, a full roster of low-key hotel activities (bikes and kayaks, fishing poles and waders to borrow, cooking demonstrations and boat tours), and on-site 4-star dining at Topper's. Rates include continental breakfast and afternoon port. No children under age 12. Open mid-May through Oct. $$$–$$$$.

Veranda House. 3 Step Ln.; (508) 228-0695; theverandahouse.com. With its sleekly designed rooms (fresh modern color palette, Simon Pearce lamps, flat-panel TV/DVD), and little spa bathrooms, this hip 20-room boutique inn is anything but a fusty B&B. Perched above the harbor, this 3-story, circa 1684 building sits minutes from the heart of Nantucket. The hotel boasts 3 wraparound porches, and many of the rooms have harbor views. Breakfast is a lovely spread of seasonal fruits, artisan cheeses, and fresh-baked pastries. $$$.

providence

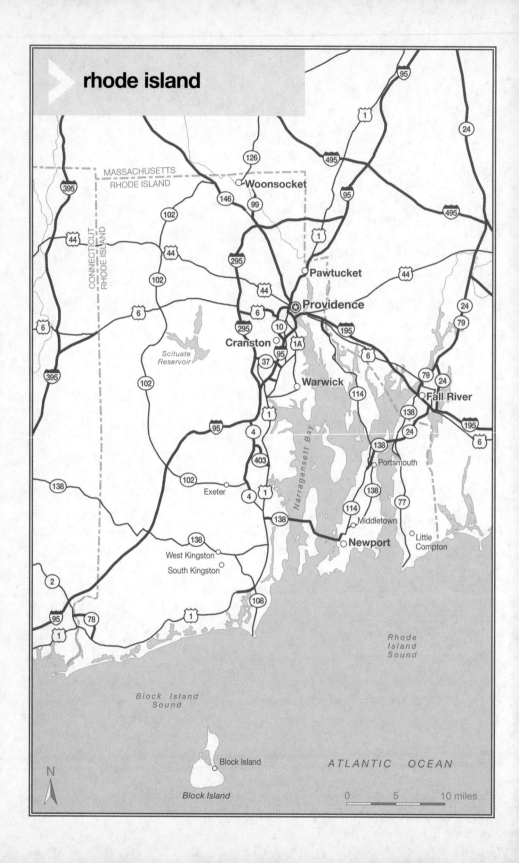

day trip 13

providence

>>> **the creative capital:**
providence, ri

providence, ri

New England's third largest city, Providence, is known as the "Creative Capital," a quirky fusion of a vibrant arts community, a thriving dining scene, and a large student population— all mixed with a good dose of colonial history.

Admire the Rhode Island state capital's colonial past along brick-paved Benefit Street and on the leafy campus of Brown University. Federal Hill, the city's Italian neighborhood, bustles with restaurants, bakeries, and cafes. Modern-day Providence is home to scores of trendy restaurants, progressive galleries, and a variety of one-of-a-kind museums like the RISD Museum of Art and the Johnson & Wales Museum of Culinary Arts.

Rhode Island is the smallest state, which is also one of its strengths. It's easy to take day trips from Providence, especially because you are never more than an hour away from anywhere else in the state.

getting there

From either Boston or New York, drive to Providence via I-95 and take exit 22A to downtown. From points east, take I-195 West, follow to merge with I-95 North and follow into Providence. From the west, take US 6 East and follow until it merges with RI 10 North, and follow signs to downtown Providence.

where to go

Providence Warwick Convention & Visitors Bureau Visitor Information Center.
1 Sabin St.; (401) 751-1177 or (800) 233-1636; goprovidence.com. Located inside the Providence Convention Center, the Providence visitor center is staffed by helpful specialists and is a good place to pick up brochures and maps. Open Mon through Sat 9 a.m. to 5 p.m.

The Rhode Island State House. 82 Smith St.; (401) 330-3111. Begin your visit of Providence at the state capitol. Climb the steps of the south entrance for an impressive view of downtown and Narragansett Bay. The inscription above the door, "To hold forth a lively experiment that a most civil state may stand and be best maintained with full liberty in religious concernment," comes from the state's Royal Charter of 1663 and refers to Roger Williams's then-radical idea of the separation of church and state. It's a graceful building, designed by renowned New York architectural firm McKim, Mead, and White. The exterior is made of white Georgia marble, and it has the fourth-largest self-supporting marble dome in the world. Crowning the dome is an 11-foot-tall, 500-pound gilded bronze statue known as *Independent Man,* holding a spear with a ship anchor—the state symbol—at his feet. Open Mon through Fri 8:30 a.m. to 4:30 p.m.

Alex and Ani City Center. 2 Kennedy Plaza; (401) 331-5544, alexandanicitycenter.com. Lace up some skates and join in! The Alex and Ani City Center outdoor oval is Providence's version of Rockefeller Center, with figures twirling and gliding against an enchanting cityscape backdrop. Thanks to its refrigerated surface, skating is available all winter, generally late Nov through mid-Mar daily 10 a.m. to 10 p.m. Skate rentals available for $6, admission $7 adults, $4 for kids ages 12 and under.

Benefit Street. Providence Preservation Society, 24 Meeting St.; (401) 831-7440; ppsri .org. In colonial times, bustling Main Street was Providence's major thoroughfare. As the city prospered, the path parallel to Main Street was made into a second street, "for the common benefit of all." Still a mostly residential neighborhood, a stroll along Providence's "Mile of History" is an opportunity to admire one of the country's largest concentrations of restored 18th- and 19th-century colonial homes. Stop by the Providence Preservation Society for a self-guided Benefit Street tour booklet.

Brown University. 45 Prospect St.; (401) 863-1000; brown.edu. Founded in 1764, this is one of America's most prestigious universities, named in honor of its principal benefactors, the Brown family of colonial Providence. The stately campus is open to visitors and is worth a spin. The college green features a mix of academic and residential buildings. Among these, University Hall is the oldest structure. Built in 1771, it was used as barracks for French troops during the Revolutionary War. Across the way, the great iron Van Wickle Gates are traditionally opened just twice a year: to welcome new students in the fall and in the spring as the new graduates depart. But the most popular visitor stop on the quad is "Bruno," the 7-foot bronze brown bear statue that stands on a slate rock said to be where Roger Williams first staked the land that would later become Providence.

Federal Hill. Along Atwells Avenue. Providence's Italian neighborhood dates back to the late 19th century when Italian immigrants came to work in the local mills. Today the neighborhood is an almost island-like district, cut off from the city by I-95. But cross Atwells Avenue from downtown, and La Pigna ("pine cone") gateway arch welcomes. Federal Hill's attractions are mostly food related; the neighborhood is packed tight with dozens of restaurants that draw pasta-hungry locals and visitors. Finish your meal by heading over to one of the neighborhood's many *caffes* to have an espresso and cannoli.

First Baptist Church. 75 Main St.; (401) 454-3418; fbcia.org. This is the country's oldest Baptist church, built in 1775 for the congregation established by Roger Williams, and one of Rhode Island's most distinguished buildings. The church is an impressive example of Georgian architecture with a pretty white spire and a graceful interior that features a Waterford chandelier that dates from 1792. Still an active Baptist congregation, guided and/or self-guided tours are available at select times Memorial Day weekend through Columbus Day Mon through Fri 10 a.m. to 3 p.m. Admission is $2 per person.

John Brown House Museum. 52 Power St.; (401) 273-7507; rihs.org. At the top of College Hill and next to the university that bears his family's name, this handsome 3-story Georgian home was built in 1786 for John Brown, a prominent entrepreneur and statesman who made his fortune in iron, banking, shipping, and the slave trade in the years immediately following the American Revolution. This was the city's first mansion, and it is chock-full of wonderful examples of Rhode Island furniture craftsmanship of the period. Tour times Apr 1 to Nov 30 Tues through Fri 1:30 p.m. and 3 p.m., Sat 10:30 a.m., noon, 1:30 p.m., and 3 p.m.; Dec 1 to Mar 31, Sat 10:30 a.m., noon, 1:30 p.m., and 3 p.m. Admission $10 adults, $8 seniors and students, $6 children ages 7 to 17.

Museum of Art, Rhode Island School of Design. 224 Benefit St.; (401) 454-6500; risdmuseum.org. The Rhode Island School of Design, which is almost always abbreviated as RISD and universally referred to as "RIZ-dee," is one of the country's leading fine arts and design colleges. The school and its students are known for being avant-garde, but its art museum houses a wide-ranging collection of art. It's all here, from ancient Greek and Roman sculpture, to a 9-foot Buddha sculpture, to many important French Impressionist paintings. As you would expect, the museum is particularly strong in contemporary works with pieces from Andy Warhol, Robert Mangold, and sculptor Howard Ben Tré (a Providence resident and RISD alum). Admission includes access to the adjacent Pendleton House, with re-created period rooms that display a collection of Gorham silver, fine examples of block-and-shell furniture from famed Newport cabinetmakers Goddard and Townsend, and paintings from Rhode Island native son Gilbert Stuart. Open Tues through Sun 10 a.m. to 5 p.m.; closed Mon. Admission $12 adults, $10 seniors, $3 children ages 5 to 18.

Providence Athenaeum Library. 251 Benefit St.; (401) 421-6970; providenceathenaeum .org. Housed in a striking 1838 Greek Revival building, the august Providence Athenaeum was established in 1753, making it one of the country's oldest independent lending libraries. Only members can borrow, but the library is open to the public for browsing or reading. Hours Mon through Thurs 9 a.m. to 7 p.m., Fri and Sat 9 a.m. to 5 p.m., Sun 1 to 5 p.m. Public tours are held Weds at 10:30 a.m. and Sat at 2:30 p.m.

The Providence Children's Museum. 100 South St.; (401) 273-5437; childrenmuseum .org. Learning is a strictly hands-on affair at the Providence Children's Museum, where kids and adults can play and learn together. At the Water Ways exhibit, kids can float boats, build fountains, and generally just get wet. Littlewoods is an indoor play space where preschoolers will find dress-up materials, puppets, and storybooks. Outdoors, kids will delight in the Children's Garden, which features a fanciful 22-foot play structure made of brightly painted green, curved platform leaves to climb, reminiscent of Jack and the Beanstalk. Open Sept through Mar Tues through Sun 9 a.m. to 6 p.m.; Apr through Labor Day daily 9 a.m. to 6 p.m. Also, open some Friday nights until 8 p.m. Admission $9 per person, free under 12 months.

Roger Williams Park. 1000 Elmwood Ave.; (401) 785-3510; rogerwilliamsparkzoo.com. Known as the "jewel of Providence," this 400-acre park features the Roger Williams Zoo, a premier attraction for both local and out-of-town families. The animals at Roger Williams span the globe; the zoo features a diverse collection of more than 130 different species in a naturalistic, parklike setting. Don't miss the Fabric of Africa exhibit; the zebras, elephants, and giraffes here are real crowd-pleasers. Also part of the grounds are a carousel, paddleboat rentals, a greenhouse, and the city's Museum of Natural History and Planetarium. This place is huge, so wear your most comfortable walking shoes, and if you have little kids, bring that stroller! Zoo open daily Apr through Sept 9 a.m. to 5 p.m., Oct through Mar 9 a.m. to 4 p.m. Admission $14.95 adults, $12.95 seniors, $9.95 children ages 2 to 12.

Waterplace Park and Riverwalk. Financial Way, Memorial Boulevard, Francis Street, and Exchange Street. Located at the foot of Smith Hill, Waterplace Park has become Providence's 21st-century gathering spot. Created in 1994 as part of a massive urban renewal project to revitalize downtown, this 4-acre park at the convergence of the Providence, Woonasquatucket, and Moshassuck Rivers features the cobblestoned and brick-paved Riverwalk, an amphitheater that hosts free festivals, and a tidal basin that is best known as the site of the city's popular WaterFire Festival.

> ## waterfire

On some summer evenings, the Providence River glows with 100 burning wood bonfires rising from the water, stoked by black-clad fire tenders in boats that quietly glide among the braziers, while an eclectic mix of ambient music plays in the background. It's a magnificent spectacle.

Begun in 1994 by artist Barnaby Evans, this public art installation has become Providence's signature event and is emblematic of the city's creative spirit. Each WaterFire event typically draws tens of thousands of visitors to the banks of the Providence River, so plan accordingly. The WaterFire season typically runs on Saturday evenings, twice a month from May through October, beginning at sunset and ending at 1 a.m. Weather dependent, of course. Waterplace Park; (401) 273-1155; waterfire.org.

where to shop

As you would expect from a city that attracts creative and artistic types, Providence has a bunch of homegrown shops that offer one-of-a-kind clothing, gifts, and furniture. Here are a few worth seeking out.

Homestyle. 229 Westminster St.; (401) 227-1159; homestyleri.com. Bringing a SoHo sensibility to the Downcity neighborhood, expect well-priced pieces by contemporary artists, unique finds like a vintage porcelain garden stool, plus funky sculptural notepads and elegant soy candles. Open Mon through Sat 10 a.m. to 6 p.m., Sun noon to 5 p.m.

Providence Place. 1 Providence Place; (401) 270-1000; providenceplace.com. With more than 170 stores, restaurants, and a cinema, this is not your average downtown shopping mall. Open Mon through Sat 10 a.m. to 9 p.m., Sun 11 a.m. to 6 p.m.

Rhode Island School of Design Bookstore. 30 N. Main St.; (401) 454-6464; risdstore .com. Channel your inner artist at RISD's campus bookstore. Open to the public, the bookstore stocks a mind-boggling array of art, drawing, drafting supplies, and art books, all at prices that are affordable even to a struggling art student. Open Mon through Fri 8 a.m. to 7 p.m.; Sat and Sun 10 a.m. to 5 p.m.

RISD Works. 20 North Main St.; (401) 277-4949; risdworks.com. This is the gift shop for the RISD Museum of Art, and all the items are created or designed by current RISD students, faculty, or alum. You'll find affordable fine art pieces, functional design items for the home, and stylish clothing and accessories. Open Tues through Sun 10 a.m. to 5 p.m., closed Mon.

only in rhode island: iconic local foods

For a small state, Rhode Island has a huge homegrown food subculture. Local menus feature many dishes that have become (proudly) state tradition. Here's a translation.

- *Quahog. Pronounced "ko-hog," this hard-shell clam is found abundantly in the waters of Narragansett Bay.*

- *Stuffies. Quahog shells filled with a mixture of chopped clam meat, breadcrumbs, and spices and then baked.*

- *Johnny cakes. White cornmeal pancakes, locally almost universally made with Kenyon brand cornmeal. The name is said to derive from "jonakin," the native word for corn.*

- *Cabinent. What Rhode Islanders call milkshakes (or frappes in the rest of New England), made with milk, flavored syrup, and ice cream.*

- *Coffee milk. This is Rhode Island's official state drink. It's milk flavored with coffee syrup—Autocrat and Eclipse are the brands of choice.*

Venda Ravioli. 275 Atwells Ave.; (401) 421-9105; vendaraviolistore.com. This Old World–style Italian market has been a staple of the Federal Hill neighborhood for more than 70 years. Venda Ravioli specializes in—you guessed it—ravioli. They make dozens of kinds, including a lobster ravioli, and it's not unusual to see locals stock up on a dozen boxes for the freezer. They also carry olive oils and vinegars, cured meats, international cheeses, and imported delights of all kinds. They will even make sandwiches and have prepared meals to go. Picnic anyone? There is a 30-seat cafe in the back of the store, and in the warm months you can dine alfresco at the piazza in the front. Open Mon through Sat 8:30 a.m. to 7 p.m., Sun 8:30 a.m. to 5 p.m.

where to eat

Al Forno. 577 S. Water St.; (401) 273-9760; alforno.com. This is the place that everybody knows about, universally acclaimed as the restaurant that put Providence on the culinary map when it opened in 1980. Al Forno (which means "from the oven") does a rustic Italian menu that simply wows. If it's your first visit, you must order their signature dish: the wood-grilled pizza Margherita topped with scallions. Other top choices include the spicy clams with sausage and the pasta baked with tomato, cream, and five cheeses. The desserts are knockouts, too, especially the hand-churned ice cream and seasonal fruit tarts. ***Note:*** Al

Forno doesn't take reservations, and long waits are common. Open Tues through Fri 5 to 10 p.m., Sat 4 to 10 p.m. $$$.

Camille's. 71 Bradford St.; (401) 751-4812; camillesonthehill.com. On Federal Hill since 1914 and spiffed up in recent years, Camille's serves old-school Italian-American cuisine. You'll find pasta with meatballs and gravy (that's what Rhode Islanders call tomato sauce), rich carbonaras, and grilled seafood and meats. Many of the dishes come from old family recipes, and you certainly can taste the love. Open Mon through Thurs 11:30 a.m. to 3 p.m., 5 to 10 p.m.; Fri 11:30 a.m. to 3 p.m., 5 to 11 p.m.; and Sat 5 to 11 p.m. Closed Sun. $$$.

Chez Pascal. 960 Hope St.; (401) 421-4422; chez-pascal.com. The menu here is a cut above—an almost perfect combination of rustic and modern seasonal bistro fare. Find inventive charcuterie boards for sharing along with dishes like steak with blue cheese bread pudding, mushrooms, and bacon jam. For dessert, a tasting of three French custards is a decadent finish. Chez Pascal excels at street food, too, especially house-made sausages that along with from-scratch condiments have become the starting point for some interesting offerings like rabbit and Dijon sausages and kielbasa with horseradish cream. Find these "haute" dogs and more at either the newly opened walk-up Wurst window or at the Wurst Kitchen, both located inside Chez Pascal. Tues through Thurs 11:30 a.m. to 2:30 p.m. and 5:30 to 9:30 p.m. and Fri through Sat 11:30 a.m. to 2:30 p.m. and 5:30 to 10 p.m. $–$$$.

Julian's Providence. 318 Broadway; (401) 861-1770; juliansprovidence.com. Choose this charmingly offbeat spot for a good meal any time of the day. On weekends there is always a queue down the street for their fantastic (reasonably priced) weekend brunch. From the well-seasoned griddle, try the popular french toast or the indulgent Nova Scotia salmon Benedict. Dinner is a lot more sane featuring well-prepared New American fare like house-cured corned beef with fingerling potatoes and maple glazed carrots. Julian's is somewhat of an oasis for local vegetarians and vegans with more than a few token choices including espresso walnut and dried cherry vegan pancakes and a vegetarian black bean burger with pepper jack cheese. The excellent array of 20 draft beers is poured by a knowledgeable bar crew. Open Mon through Fri 9 a.m. to 11 p.m., Sat and Sun 8 a.m. to 11 p.m. $–$$.

Nicks on Broadway. 500 Broadway; (401) 421-0286; nicksonbroadway.com. Young chef-owner Derek Wagner is passionate about his commitment to local ingredients, creating inspired contemporary dishes that are served by an enthusiastic and knowledgeable staff. The space has a hip, open-kitchen concept, and the best seats in the house are at the dining bar, where you can watch the kitchen crew at work. Breakfast features dishes like vanilla brioche french toast and omelets with home fries. For a casual lunch, order the yellowfin tuna sandwich with feta or a seasonal soup. For dinner you can order a la carte; try the house-made charcuterie plate, the herbed grilled duck, or the skillet-roasted sea bass. But for a real culinary blow-out, go for the 4-course tasting menu. Open Wed through Sat 8 a.m. to 3 p.m. and 5:30 to 10 p.m.; Sun 8 a.m. to 3 p.m. $$$.

North. 3 Luongo Memorial Square; (401) 421-1100; foodbynorth.com. Although it is close to Federal Hill, North is barely marked, so it is the sort of hole-in-the wall that you have to be told about to find. It is always hopping for good reason. First, because the small plates menu focuses on brilliant takes on global fare: tiny ham biscuits with mustard; dan dan noodles with mutton, squid and chile; crispy potato bravas with charred scallion and soft egg. Another reason: the prices are reasonable for such well-made food, created with high-caliber, mostly local ingredients. Finally, the space is tiny: just 6 tables and 6 bar stools, and they don't take reservations. Open daily 5:30 p.m. to midnight. $$.

Parkside. 76 S. Main St.; (401) 331-0003; parksideprovidence.com. You'll find urban sophistication at this bistro. The signature rotisserie dishes, executed with precision, set Parkside apart. The lemon-garlic half chicken is especially good. Finish with the banana tart a la mode served warm from the oven. Open Mon through Thurs 11:30 a.m. to 10 p.m., Fri 11:30 a.m. to 11 p.m., Sat 5 to 11 p.m., and Sun 4 to 9 p.m. $$$.

Seven Stars. 820 Hope St.; (401) 521-2200; sevenstarsbakery.com. Seven Stars is pretty much the ideal neighborhood bakery offering buttery chocolate almond croissants, fragrant olive bread, hefty sandwiches, and saucer-size cookies. Don't you wish you lived next door? (There is another location at 342 Broadway.) Open Mon through Fri 6:30 a.m. to 7 p.m., Sat and Sun 7 a.m. to 7 p.m. $.

where to stay

Christopher Dodge House. 1858 W. Park St.; (401) 351-6111; providence-hotel.com. This 3-story brick Italianate mansion is in a quiet neighborhood within a short walk to downtown and Federal Hill. The good-size rooms in this homey guesthouse are outfitted in unfussy early American style with private bath; several rooms have fireplaces. There is free Wi-Fi throughout the house, and rates include both breakfast and free parking. $$.

Dean Hotel. 122 Fountain St.; (401) 455-3326; thedeanhotel.com. For the hip and budget-conscious traveler more concerned with Providence's creative culture scene than luxury, the Dean Hotel makes for a perfect overnight or weekend stay. The hotel has a moody, contemporary, masculine vibe—think lots of wood and metals. The 52 minimalist-chic rooms come in several configurations to include standard queen- and king-bedded rooms as well as quad bunk bed rooms with a fun sleepover theme—perfect for a group of friends or family. All the rooms have private baths, but there are no closets or dressers, so pack light. The hotel boasts four gathering spaces just off the lobby. Bolt offers a coffeehouse experience by a master barista. The hotel's main restaurant Faust is an über-trendy, decidedly Teutonic spot with schnitzels, wursts and chicken paprika. Magdalenae is the sultry cocktail bar, and Boombox is the hotel's raucous Karoke lounge. After so much in-house entertainment, be thankful that you can flop down in that bed just up the stairs. $$.

Hotel Providence. 139 Mathewson St.; (401) 861-8000 or (800) 861-8990; thehotelprovidence.com. Drop your bags at this boutique property set in a historic 1897 building, and you will enjoy rooms with a blend of modernized Second Empire decor and New England character. Beds are piled high with down comforters, bathrooms are decadent with rain showerheads, and rooms, decorated with works from local talents, include all the high-tech essentials. The hotel's stylish restaurant, Rosmarin, is helmed by father and son Swiss chefs Massimiliano and Stefano Mariotta. The seasonally inspired menu is somewhere between classic and conservative contemporary: veal tenderloin with champagne cream sauce and roast potatoes, beef tenderloin with carrots, house-made noodle and pepper jus. $$$. This hotel represents an excellent value for the location in the heart of the cultural district. $$–$$$.

The Providence Biltmore Hotel. 11 Dorrance St.; (401) 421-0700; providencebiltmore.com. A chandeliered gilt-and-burgundy lobby and a sweeping center staircase grace this grand dame hotel, built in 1922 at the height of the Jazz Age. The rooms are spacious, decorated in taupes and soft greens with cherrywood furnishings, and beds are topped with luxe linens. There's free Wi-Fi throughout the property, and you can't beat the location, in the heart of downtown and just steps from Waterplace Park. Now part of the Hilton brand, savvy vacationers will find good weekend bargains. The onsite spa makes this a popular hotel choice for bachelorette parties. $$–$$$.

Renaissance Providence. 5 Avenue of the Arts; (401) 919-5000 or (800) 468-3571; marriott.com/hotels/travel/pvdbr-renaissance-providence-hotel. Contemporary and luxurious style are the hallmarks of the city's premier boutique property. The 1929 neoclassical building was originally built as a Masonic temple, and the structure's restoration carefully and deliberately juxtaposes the old and new. Style-wise, the generously sized rooms are nicely turned out with cushy beds, marble bathrooms, and flat-screen TVs. Some rooms have a view of the State House. $$–$$$.

worth more time

The Pawtucket Red Sox. McCoy Stadium; 1 Columbus Ave., Pawtucket; (401) 724-7300; pawsox.com. Catch a Red Sox game—kind of. Just 5 miles north of Providence, the Pawtucket Red Sox, the minor league AAA affiliate of the Boston Red Sox, make their home at McCoy Stadium. The Paw Sox are just one step from the big leagues, so you may even see one of the players from the Red Sox on rehab assignment. World Series MVP David Ortiz did a PawSox stint in 2013. The tickets are cheap, concession prices are reasonable, and parking is free. This is pure baseball. After the game, kids are encouraged to come to the infield and run around the bases. General admission $9 adults, $6 seniors and children ages 12 and under, box seats $14.

day trip 14

providence

>>>

legendary seaside mansions:
newport, ri

newport, ri

Set off for Newport, known as "America's First Resort," about an hour drive—as the gull flies—from downtown Providence. The opportunity to tour the opulent homes that were once the summer playground of America's wealthy industrialists draws most visitors to the city. But be sure to explore the other facets of this charming colonial seaport town, too: its many fine restorations of 18th-century buildings, its vibrant harbor and waterfront scene, and fine shops and restaurants.

getting there

Follow I-195 East from Providence for 17 miles to MA 24 South (crossing into Massachusetts) to RI 114 South (also called W. Main Road) through the towns of Portsmouth and Middletown. In Newport, RI 114 South becomes Broadway; follow signs to the Newport Visitor Center.

where to go

Newport Visitor Information Center. 23 America's Cup Ave., (401) 845-9131; discovernewport.com. Getting around on foot is the way to go in Newport. Many of the city's attractions are close together, and for those that are farther out—the mansions, beaches, and Cliff Walk—your best bet is to take the Rhode Island Public Transportation Authority

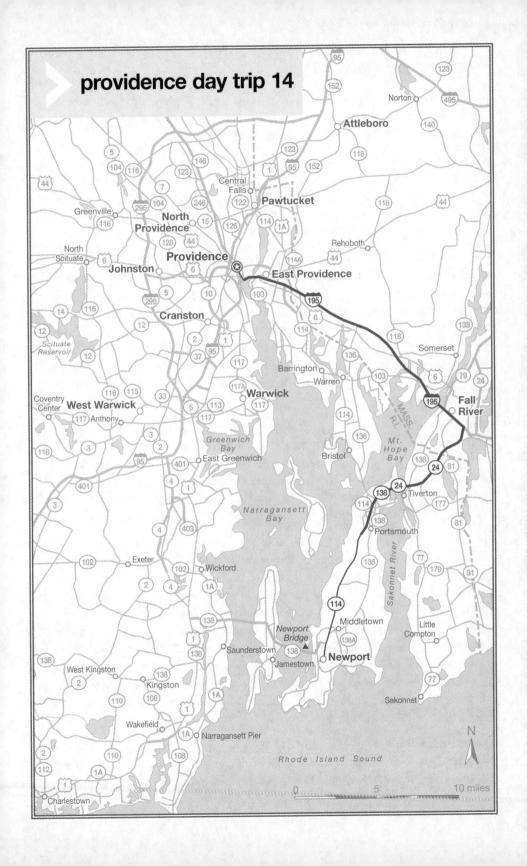

providence day trip 14

(RIPTA) trolley. Take advantage of the Gateway Parking lot and garage, which offers plentiful and convenient metered parking. You can also save time and avoid lines by buying your tickets to the mansions here. Open daily 9 a.m. to 5 p.m.

Newport Mansions & the Preservation Society of Newport County. 424 Bellevue Ave.; (401) 847-1000; newportmansions.org. The Preservation Society manages several of Newport's mansions, including the Breakers, and is an excellent resource for planning your mansion itinerary. Their mansion tickets can be purchased singularly or as a multi-mansion pass combination online or at the door. Open daily 10 a.m. to 4 p.m.

The Breakers. 44 Ochre Point Ave.; (401) 847-1000; newportmansions.org. This is the largest and grandest of the Newport mansions—and Rhode Island's most visited attraction. The Beaux Arts mansion by architect Richard Morris Hunt is dramatically set on a promontory with a commanding view of the Atlantic Ocean. The 70-room, 5-story mansion was built in 1895 for Cornelius Vanderbilt II, president of the New York Central Railroad. Its Great Hall with its grand center staircase measures 50 feet in all directions and makes quite a first impression. Self-guided audio tours are provided for visitors. Open year-round; Jan through Mar daily 9 a.m. to 4 p.m.; Apr through Dec 9 a.m. to 5 p.m. Admission $24 adults, $8 children ages 6 to 17.

Chateau-sur-Mer. 474 Bellevue Ave.; (401) 847-1000; newportmansions.org. The oldest of Bellevue Avenue's stately homes, Chateau-sur-Mer was built in 1852 for William Wetmore, a merchant who made his fortune in the Far East. The French-style villa was constructed of granite block and has a more staid Victorian feel than its neighbors. On the grounds, a massive circular stone Chinese Moon Gate is a popular spot for photos. Open seasonally, check website for times. Admission $17.50 adults, $8 children ages 6 to 17.

The Elms. 367 Bellevue Ave.; (401) 847-1000; newportmansions.org. Built at the turn of the 20th century for Pennsylvania coal baron Edward Julius Berwind, the Elms was modeled after an 18th-century French chateau, with what was then cutting-edge technology: electricity. The self-guided audio tour of the main home is offered year-round. Special guide-led "Servant Life" tours are offered, too—it's all very *Downton Abbey*. The grounds at the Elms are exceptionally lovely, featuring a sunken garden, fountains, sculptures, and a wonderful old stand of weeping beech trees. From late May through Columbus Day, the Carriage House Cafe is open daily for lunch, offering sandwiches and other light fare. Eat in the Carriage House or on the terrace and "pretend that you are manor born." Open year-round, check website for times. Admission $17.50 adults, $8 children ages 6 to 17. Servant-Life tours, $18 adults, $7.50 children ages 6 to 17.

Marble House. 596 Bellevue Ave.; (401) 847-1000; newportmansions.org. This is another Vanderbilt estate, and another Richard Morris Hunt design, built in 1892 for William Vanderbilt, Cornelius's brother. The Marble House is notable for its gold-mirrored ballroom and for the lavish China Tea House behind the property. Open year-round, check website for times. Admission $17.50 adults, $8 children ages 6 to 17.

Audrain Auto Museum. 222 Bellevue Ave.; (401) 856-4420; audrainautomuseum.org. If you need a lure for a mansion-hating spouse, this is the place. The 1903 Gilded Age Audrain office building makes a stunning showroom to display historic—not to mention drop-dead gorgeous—cars including an 1899 steam powered Crouch runabout and a 1929 Rolls Royce Phantom. The museum mounts three exhibits a year drawing from its collection of nearly 200 cars with 15-20 on display at any one time. Open daily 10 a.m. to 4 p.m. Admission $14 adults, $10 seniors and students, $8 children ages 6 to 17.

Classic Cruises of Newport. Bannister's Wharf; (401) 847-0298; cruisenewport.com. You can't really say that you've experienced Newport unless you have been out on the water. The classic schooner sailing yacht the *Madeleine* casts off several times a day during the summer season for a scenic 90-minute cruise around Newport Harbor. Or board the classic motor yacht, the *Rum Runner II,* for a 70-minute narrated tour. The season runs May through Oct daily. Check website for departure times. Tickets for the *Madeleine* are $32 for the daytime cruise, $41 for the sunset cruise; tickets for the *Rum Runner II* are $25 for the daytime cruise and $35 for the sunset cruise.

Cliff Walk. Memorial Drive; cliffwalk.com. When you've had your fill of sightseeing and shopping, stroll along all or part of the 3.5-mile walkway that hugs along the high, rocky coastline and skirts across the backyards of several of the Newport mansions. It's quite a ramble, with breathtaking views of Atlantic Ocean waves crashing over granite outcroppings. The normal start is at Memorial Boulevard, ending at Bailey's Beach, taking most 2.5 hours to finish, with a planned return via RIPTA trolley to downtown Newport. Some of the walk is rugged; be sure to wear real shoes, not flip-flops or sandals. Also, know that there is a lack of shade along the route so wear sunscreen and bring water. Open daily, sunrise to sunset.

The Colony House. Washington Square; (401) 846-0813; newporthistorytours.org. Dating from 1739, this sturdy brick Georgian-style building served as Rhode Island's state capitol building until 1900. It was here that Rhode Islanders first heard the Declaration of Independence read publicly. The Colony House is a remarkably intact example of colonial American architecture; the interior was used in filming the courtroom scenes of the 1997 film *Amistad.* Guided site tours are offered throughout the year; check website for days and times. The Newport Historical Society also does guided walking tours of the neighborhood. Walking tour tickets $12 adults, $5 children ages 12 and under.

Easton's Beach. 175 Memorial Blvd.; (401) 848-5810; cityofnewport.com. Somewhat surprisingly, Newport has only one true ocean beach. Located adjacent to the Cliff Walk, Easton's Beach (also called First Beach) is a 0.75-mile warm-water beach with just-right surf; it has all the facilities for a full-day outing with lifeguards, changing rooms, concession stand, and playground. At the end of the day, a ride on the 1950s carousel ($2) is fun for the young—and for the young at heart. Beach open Memorial Day through Labor Day daily, 9 a.m. to 6 p.m. Parking $10 per car weekdays, $20 per car weekends.

International Tennis Hall of Fame. 194 Bellevue Ave.; (401) 849-3990; tennisfame.com. Discover the history and experience the legacy of tennis. Located In a sprawling 1880s Victorian shingle-style mansion that was once the Newport Casino, a members-only social and recreational club, this museum houses a diverse collection of tennis artifacts that chronicle the history of the game from the 12th century to the present day. The facilities grounds contain 13 manicured grass courts that are available for public play. If you can hold your own, consider booking court time. Open July through Labor Day daily 10 a.m. to 6 p.m., after Labor Day through June. Admission $15 adults, kids free.

Redwood Library & Athenaeum. 50 Bellevue Ave.; (401) 847-0292; redwoodlibrary.org. Bibliophiles must not miss visiting the Redwood Library, the oldest continuously operating library in America. Founded in 1747, the original collection of 751 volumes was purchased in London with a donation from wealthy Newport merchant Abraham Redwood. The library building, also designed by Peter Harrison and modeled after a Roman Doric temple, was completed in 1750. It is said to be the first classical public building in America. The oldest part of the library, the Harrison Room, houses the library's original collection and several paintings by Gilbert Stuart. Pretty heady stuff! Open to the public Mon, Tues, Thurs, Fri, and Sat 9:30 a.m. to 5:30 p.m., Weds 9:30 a.m. to 8 p.m., Sun 1 to 5 p.m.

Touro Synagogue and Loeb Visitor's Center. 85 Touro St.; (401) 847-4794; tourosynagogue.org. This is America's oldest synagogue, designed by preeminent colonial architect Peter Harrison and dedicated in 1763. Newport's Jewish community is one of America's oldest congregations and can trace its roots back to 1658 when a group of Spanish and Portuguese Sephardic Jews arrived from the West Indies. In 1790, George Washington wrote a letter to the congregation, pledging to give "to bigotry, no sanction, to persecution, no assistance." In this spirit, the Loeb Visitor's Center adjacent to the synagogue features interactive exhibits on the story of religious freedom in the US and the history of Jews in colonial America. Open year-round; check website for days and times. Note that the synagogue is an active congregation, so there are no tours on Saturday or on Jewish holidays. Admission $12 adults, $8 students, $10 seniors, children ages 13 and under free.

where to shop

Thames Street with its many galleries and home-design and antiques shops is worthy of investigation. Along the waterfront, Bowen's and Bannister's Wharves attract both casual lookers and serious shoppers. Spring Street and Bellevue Avenue have a large concentration of upmarket shops, too.

Also, the Preservation Society of Newport County operates gift shops at several of their properties, including the Breakers, Marble House, Rosecliff, and the Elms, as well as a shop at 1 Bannister's Wharf. These stores offer high-quality and unique gift and home-decor items inspired by the Newport mansions and gardens.

Alex and Ani. One Bowen's Wharf; (401) 849-3002; alexandani.com. This is the flagship store of the well-known Rhode Island–based jewelry manufacturer and retailer. Founded by Carolyn Rafaelian and named after her two oldest daughters, Alex and Ani, the brand is mostly known for its affordable line of trend-setting customizable bracelets with inspirational charms. The pieces are handmade in Rhode Island, which has a strong jewelry-making tradition. If you are on a stacking bracelet binge, this is the place for you. Open Mon through Fri 10 a.m. to 6 p.m., Fri and Sat 10 a.m. to 7 p.m., and Sun 11 a.m. to 5 p.m.

Farmaesthetics. 144 Bellevue Ave.; (401) 619-4199; farmaesthetics.com. This exquisite apothecary boutique carries its own line of natural beauty products made only from organic oils, herbs, flowers, and grains. The company's glass bottle and tin packaging is not only beautifully restrained but sustainable. Summer hours daily 10 a.m. to 6 p.m.; winter hours Weds through Sat 11 a.m. to 5 p.m.

Resails. 33 America's Cup Ave.; (401) 849-0084; resails.com. Designed and manufactured in Newport since 1996, Resails makes custom totes, duffle bags, and jackets from repurposed sails. It's nautical redux—and very cool. Recently the product line has expanded to include products made from new sailcloth. Summer hours daily 10 a.m. to 9 p.m.; winter hours Mon through Thurs 10 a.m. to 5 p.m., Fri and Sat 10 a.m. to 6 p.m., Sun 11 a.m. to 5 p.m.

Thames Glassblowing Studio & Gallery. 688 Thames St.; (401) 846-0576; thamesglass. com. Inside this working studio visitors can watch molten strands of crystal being blown into colorful vases, platters, bowls and candlesticks. Owner Matthew Buechner and his small team of master craftsman handcraft each piece. Or you can experience glassblowing first hand and make your own. You will be shown how to gather glass from the 2,000 degree furnace and shape it into a colorful ornament or paperweight to take home as a souvenir. Open Thurs noon to 5 p.m., Fri through Mon 11 a.m. to 5 p.m., closed Tues and Wed.

where to eat

Flo's Clam Shack. 4 Wave Ave., Middletown; (401) 847-8141; flosclamshacks.com. After a day at First Beach, swimmers swarm this divey fish shack (is there any other kind?) to savor simple seafood at picnic tables and watch the sunset. For a juicy taste of the sea, order the fried whole-belly clams. Besides fried clams, you can tuck into brothy Rhode Island clam chowder, no-nonsense "lobsta" rolls, and shellfish from the upstairs raw bar. Open Memorial Day weekend through Labor Day Sun through Thurs 11 a.m. to 9 p.m. and Fri and Sat 11 a.m. to 10 p.m.; check website for days and hours in spring and fall. Closed Dec through Mar. Cash only. $.

Fluke Wine Bar and Kitchen. 41 Bowen's Wharf; (401) 849-7778; flukewinebar.com. Conventional wisdom holds that waterfront restaurants are subpar. Ditto for spots in historical districts. Fluke defies both rules with an urbane menu that features dishes like fire-roasted octopus with linguica and chickpeas and grilled spice pork tenderloin with dates and figs. Open daily May through Oct 5 p.m. to 1 a.m.; Nov through Apr Wed through Sat 5 p.m. to 1 a.m. $$–$$$.

Jo's American Bistro. 24 Memorial Blvd. West; (401) 847-5506; josamericanbistro.com. This booming bistro turns out straightforwardly delicious American and French fare (classics like a bacon burger with onion jam, duck breast with fig and orange, plus grilled salmon served with spaetzle, oyster mushrooms and leeks). The accessible, affordable wine list makes it easy to indulge in a glass or two of your favorites. And the live weekend jazz and laid back atmosphere make this a comfortable but stylish place to dine. Open Sun through Thurs 5 to 10 p.m., Fri 5 to 10 p.m., Sat noon to 3:30 and 5 to 10 p.m. $$.

The Mooring Seafood Kitchen and Bar. 1 Sayers Wharf; (401) 846-2260; mooringres taurant.com. Located at Newport's historic waterfront with spectacular views of the harbor from its outdoor patio, the Mooring is the kind of casual place where regional fish dishes are king. For lunch you'll find a nice range of soups, salads, and sandwiches. Dinner favorites include the seafood pie, Guinness-battered fish-and-chips, and cedar-roasted salmon. And no matter what time of the day, nearly every table orders the Bag of Doughnuts appetizer: lobster, crab, and shrimp fritters with chipotle-maple aioli. Sun through Thurs 11:30 a.m. to 9 p.m.; Fri through Sat 11:30 a.m. to 10 p.m. $$–$$$.

Perro Salado. 19 Charles St.; (401) 619-4777; perrosalado.com. Located in the heart of Newport, the "Salty Dog" specializes in high-end Mexican with beautifully presented seafood-centric entrees (fish tacos and chili-dusted scallops) along with addictive quesadillas and tacos with lots of embellishments. For tipplers there is sangria, several types of margaritas and a great tequila selection. Open Mon through Sat 5 to 10 p.m., Sun noon to 3 p.m. and 5 to 10 p.m. $$.

Rosemary & Thyme. 382 Spring St.; (401) 619-3338; rosemaryandthymecafe.com. Culinary-inspired and effortlessly seasonal, this artisan bakery does a roaring business with tourists and locals alike. Their signature European sandwich—smoked turkey, ham, and aged gouda—is a real meal. Their creations also include breads—a tasty sourdough and an airy ciabatta and pastries that range from flaky croissants to just-right sweet ginger and lemon scones. Open Tues through Sat 7:30 a.m. to 4 p.m., Sun 7:30 a.m. to 11:30 a.m. Closed in Jan and Feb. $.

where to stay

Castle Hill and Resort. 590 Ocean Dr.; (401) 849-3800 or (888) 466-1355; castlehillinn .com. Perched on a wooded hill overlooking Narragansett Bay, this luxuriously updated 1874 property was once the summer home of Harvard scientist Alexander Agassiz. This is an exclusive resort with just 25 rooms and suites; stay here and you will feel like a member of a very posh private club. Guests can choose from accommodations in the mansion or a private beach cottage. Each room is distinctive and designed with understated elegance and extraordinary attention to detail. The inn's much-acclaimed restaurant gets raves for its contemporary American cuisine and spectacular views. $$$$.

Gilded. 23 Brinley St.; (401) 619-7758; gildedhotel.com. An instant hot spot since opening its doors in 2015, Gilded offers a taste of forgotten glamour and a modern twist on Newport excess. Every inch of this hotel was run through a design filter from an unexpected teal, fuchsia and purple color scheme, to the richly draped velvet upholstery to the gold gilt mirrors. This place doesn't skimp on the goodies either; rates include free parking, snacks all day and a breakfast featuring stylish small plates like overnight oatmeal with berries, Mexican hot chocolate scones and Caprese baked eggs. Rooms are fully up-to-date with luxury expectations, so you'll find plenty of outlets, USB charging stations, LED smart TVs and free Wi-Fi. And to help you live the life you always imagined, there is a billiard room as well as a croquet practice green in the garden. $$–$$$.

Hotel Viking. 1 Bellevue Ave.; (401) 847-3300 or (800) 556-7126; hotelviking.com. Grace characterizes this 1926 hotel located just a short walk from Newport Harbor. The rooms are romantic but restrained, done up with custom repro antique furniture, fine linens, and Oriental rugs. Modern comforts are not forgotten either; all the rooms have complimentary high-speed Internet and flat-screen TVs. Amenities include an on-site indoor pool, spa, and fitness center. $$–$$$.

The Newport Beach Hotel and Suites. 1 Wave Ave.; (401) 846-0310; newportbeach hotelandsuites.com. It can be pricey to stay in Newport, especially during the summer season, so this oceanfront hotel is a real find. Just across the street from Easton's Beach and 1 mile from downtown Newport, this hotel strikes the perfect balance between nautical get-away and city stay. The rooms in the historic hotel have been recently renovated to include luxurious bedding and marble bathrooms. Rooms in the all-suite annex addition to the property include whirlpool tubs, a separate living room, and kitchen. An indoor pool, fire pit, and rooftop hot tub are nice pluses. $$–$$$.

worth more time

Green Animals Topiary Gardens. 380 Cory's Ln., Portsmouth; (401) 847-1000; newport mansions.org. Mansioned out? Located on a 7-acre country estate overlooking Narragansett Bay, Green Animals is the oldest topiary garden in the US; some of the earliest sculptures here date from 1910. Stroll among the 80 whimsical, larger-than-life topiaries, which include teddy bears, a giraffe, and an elephant that have been sculpted from privet and yew shrubs. Children will find that the winding paths among the topiaries lend themselves to spirited games of hide-and-seek. You can explore the vegetable, herb, and flower gardens, too. To get there from Newport, follow RI 114 North for 9 miles to Portsmouth, and follow signs to the garden. Open daily mid-May through Oct; check website for times. Admission $17.50 adults, $8 children ages 6 to 17.

Newport International Polo Series. 715 East Main Rd., Portsmouth; (401) 846-0200; nptpolo.com. Polo, anyone? Polo in Newport dates from 1876. Matches are open to the public and held from June through September, drawing players and spectators from around the world. The bucolic green fields ringed by linden trees provide a gorgeous backdrop for a tailgate picnic and a day spent watching the ponies. Matches are held Sat at 5 p.m. (4 p.m. in Sept). General admission lawn seats are from $12.

day trip 15

providence

block island, ri

With 17 miles of white sand beaches, dramatic bluffs, and grassy moors, Block Island is a captivating destination for nature lovers and just an hour ferry ride from Rhode Island's coast.

Take time to adjust to a slower pace and explore—on foot or by bicycle—the island's unspoiled beaches, lighthouses, and acres of conservation land. New Shoreham was incorporated in 1672 and is the island's only town. It has a year-round population of 1,000 residents, which swells to nearly 20,000 in the summer. Be sure to enjoy some seafood and watch the sunset before taking the last ferry back to the mainland. Better yet, stay the night.

getting there

Most vacationers arrive by ferry. The **Block Island Ferry** (401-783-4613; blockislandferry .com) operates year-round and during the season offers both traditional car passenger service and high-speed passenger-only service between Narragansett's Port of Galilee and Old Harbor. Block Island Ferry also runs a traditional passenger service between both Newport and Fall River, Massachusetts, and Old Harbor during the summer. There is seasonal passenger-only ferry service from **Block Island Express** out of New London, Connecticut, and by the **Viking Fleet** out of Montauk, New York. You can reach the island by air arriving at the Block Island State Airport.

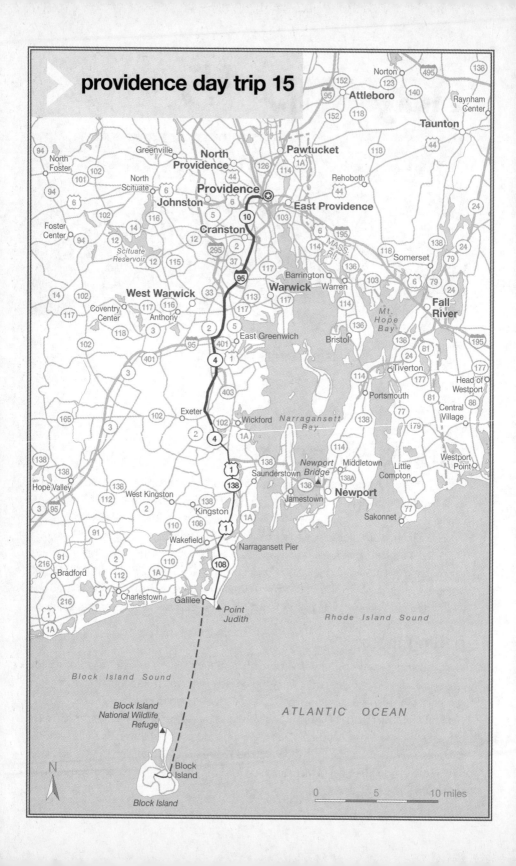

From Providence take I-95 South, then take exit 9 (Narragansett) to RI 4 South. Stay on RI 4 South to US 1 South. On US 1 South take the exit toward Narragansett, RI 108 exit; continue for 3 miles until you see the signs for the Block Island Ferry.

where to go

Block Island Chamber of Commerce. Old Harbor Ferry Dock; (800) 383-2474; block islandchamber.com. Stop by the visitor center for maps and information on the island. And if you decide at the last minute to stay the night, they can help with that, too. Summer hours daily 9 a.m. to 5 p.m.

Crescent Beach. Off Corn Neck Road. Just a short stroll or bike ride from the ferry terminal, 3-mile Crescent Beach stretches northward along the eastern side of the island and consists of three named beaches, each with a distinct personality. The Frederick J. Benson Town Beach, or Kid Beach, is closest to town with warm water and calm waves perfect for the little ones. Scotch Beach attracts an active, young crowd that likes to play volleyball and lie in the sun. Mansion Beach is more remote, but it's a great all-around beach with white sand, clear water, and just-right waves. There's a concession stand here where you can rent chairs, umbrellas, and boogie boards for the day.

Mohegan Bluffs. Off Sunset Road. Against a backdrop of 250-foot cliffs, sweeping views of the Atlantic Ocean beckon. Walk down the wood steps to a small rocky beach—it's steep, so be sure you can climb back up. Nearby, you can tour the Southeast Lighthouse Museum. Perched high on the cliff, this redbrick Victorian beacon is a gem. Lighthouse museum open Memorial Day through Labor Day, daily 10 a.m. to 4 p.m.

North Lighthouse. Off Sandy Point Road. Since 1867, this granite lighthouse on the northernmost tip of the island has been guiding the way. At the adjacent Block Island Wildlife Refuge, deer and rabbits inhabit the area, along with thousands of birds, making this area especially popular with birders during the spring and fall migrating seasons.

Rodman's Hollow. Access off Cooneymus Road. Take a hike and enjoy Block Island's still-wild beauty. In the southwest corner of the island, Rodman's Hollow was created by a glacial depression and features several walking trails that wind through thicket and meadows and eventually lead to the ocean.

where to eat

Ballard's. Old Harbor Dock; (401) 466-2231; ballardsinn.com. A full-service restaurant and bar that serves your drinks while you lounge on the beach is a rarity in New England. In the evening, when there's live music and dancing, this place heaves. Open May through Sept daily 11 a.m. to 1 a.m. $$.

Eli's. 456 Chapel St.; (401) 466-5230, elisblockisland.com. This casual and popular spot serves some of the island's most inventive cuisine, including some Asian-inspired dishes. Their tuna nachos are a signature dish; so, too, is the oregano-and-almond-encrusted rack of lamb. Reservations are not accepted, so be prepared to wait, or come early. Open mid-March through mid-Nov Mon through Thurs 6 to 9 p.m., Fri through Sat 6 to 10 p.m., Sun 6 to 9 p.m. $$–$$$.

Ice Cream Place. 232 Water St. (401) 466-2145. A Block Island institution for 30 years that is totally worth the time standing in line. Walk under the archway, and the smell of home-baked waffles cones draws you inside. The list of flavors like campfire s'mores and maple walnut is irresistible. Open seasonally May through mid-Oct. $.

Mohegan Cafe & Brewery. 213 Water St.; (401) 466-5911; moheganbi.com. For better food and much better beer, a brewpub is often a good choice. This welcoming pub is close to the ferry dock (with good views) and popular with both locals and tourists. This is elevated pub grub: a salad with grilled tuna, a cod and corn chowder, and a steak with a chimichurri sauce. Their draft list consists only of beer that is made on the premises—a good excuse to order another round. Open daily spring through fall. $$.

The Oar. 221 Job's Hill Rd.; (401) 466-8820. Located in New Harbor, with terrific views of Great Salt Pond, the Oar is a solid choice for casual dining with options like Southern fried chicken, lobster club sandwiches, and hamburgers. Open daily May through Oct. $$–$$$.

Persephone's Kitchen. 235 Dodge St.; (401) 466-5070; persephonekitchenbi.com. This tiny breakfast and lunch spot is an oasis for coffee, smoothies and sandwiches with both indoor and outdoor seating or for takeout. The splendid egg sandwich with avocado, tomato, and bacon on whole wheat bread is perfect for toting over to the beach. Open May through Oct daily 7 a.m. to 5 p.m. $.

where to stay

The Atlantic Inn. 359 High St.; (401) 466-5883 or (800) 224-7422; atlanticinn.com. This 21-room Victorian inn set high on a grassy hill has a long front porch that overlooks the Atlantic Ocean. Rooms are romantic, furnished with antiques, quilts, and floral wallpaper. Hotel guests and island day-trippers come to have drinks and appetizers and watch the sunset from Adirondack chairs on the lawn. The inn's dining room serves a 4-course prix-fixe menu (2 appetizers, entree, and dessert). It's a table everyone on the island wants; do make reservations. Room rates include continental breakfast. Inn and restaurant open late Apr through mid-Oct. $$–$$$.

Darius Hotel. 62 Dodge St.; (401) 466-2722; dariusblockisland.com. In the 1800s this was the home of the island's druggist, Captain Darius Dodge. Opened in 2013 as the 11-room Darius Inn, owners and sisters Becca and Christy Zendt have decorated the rooms in a shabby-chic style featuring bright colors, lots of patterns and original art. Some of the rooms have kitchenettes and a sofa bed to accommodate families. There are pet-friendly rooms and rooms with private porches, too. The inn is just steps from the beach and the bars and restaurants on Water Street. Rates include breakfast—frittata, fruit and homemade bread, coffee and juice and an afternoon happy hour on the front porch with wine and beer. $.

Hotel Manisses. 251 Spring St.; (401) 466-9898; hotelmanisses.com. A great value, and located just a pebble's throw to the ferry landing, the Hotel Manisses owners recently revamped the public spaces and 17 coastal–themed rooms to reflect a traditional but polished look. Rooms are outfitted with crisp linens and soft aqua walls, flat-screen TVs and air-conditioning. From some rooms you can watch the boats come and go from your private terrace. The hotel's restaurant and bar is a good option when you don't want to fight the island's crowds with a mix of regional fare and Italian specialties. $$–$$$.

National Hotel. Water Street; (401) 466-2901 or (800) 225-2449; blockislandhotels.com. Just a minute's walk from the ferry in the middle of all the action, this quaint beachside hotel has cozy, no-frills rooms with ocean views. Open Apr through Oct. $$–$$$.

Sea Breeze Inn. 71 Spring St.; (401) 466-2275; seabreezeblockisland.com. A budget choice in expensive Block Island, this inn has just 10 rooms; 5 rooms in the shingled main house (with shared baths) and 5 neighboring small cottages. The simple and spacious rooms are furnished with antiques and have an artistic flair. Know that the inn does not have TV or Wi-Fi, but it is well placed to walk to Pebbly Beach and town. Rates include continental breakfast. Open Apr through Oct. $$.

new haven

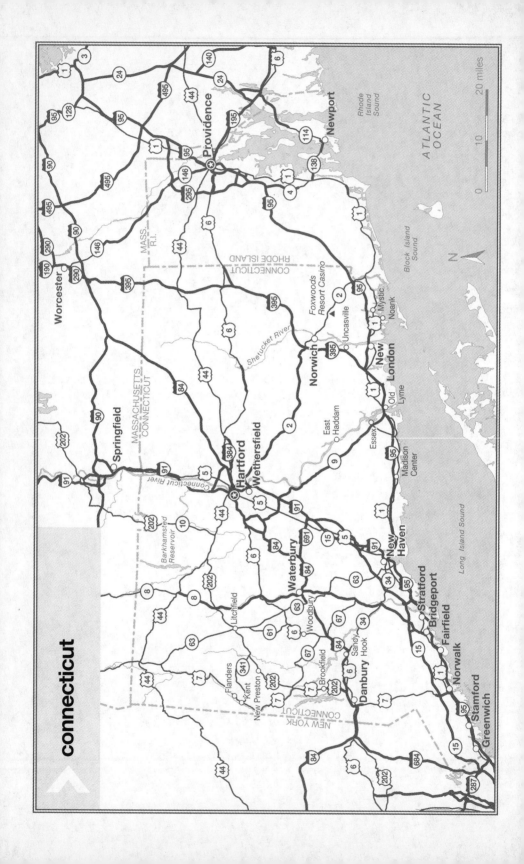

connecticut

day trip 16

new haven

the elm city:
new haven, ct

new haven, ct

Standing on neatly manicured New Haven Green, you get a sense of the city's 17th-century legacy. Founded by the Puritans, New Haven depended first on sea trade to become a leading East Coast mercantile port. By the 19th century, the city was a leading manufacturing center of guns, carriages, and clocks. New Haven is also famously home to Yale University, making the city an academic enclave that is also college-town cool with bars, shopping, and fabulous restaurants. The Yale University Art Gallery and the Yale Center for British Art both greatly enhance the New Haven cultural landscape.

getting there

New Haven is located at the junction of I-95 and I-91 and is easy to access by car from any direction. From the north, take I-91 South to exit 1 and downtown New Haven. From the east, take I-95 South toward New Haven. Just after the bridge, take exit 47 to the CT 34 connector and take exit 1 into New Haven. From the west, take I-95 North to exit 1 and downtown New Haven.

where to go

Downtown New Haven Visitor Information Center. 1000 Chapel St.; (203) 773-9494; infonewhaven.com. Pick up maps, brochures, and guides for dining, lodging, and special events in New Haven. Open Mon through Sat 10 a.m. to 9 p.m., Sun noon to 5 p.m.

New Haven Green. Bordered by College, Chapel, Church, and Elm Streets. New Haven is one of the country's first planned cities with a grid-like street layout. The 16-acre parcel at its center dates from 1638 and is as old as the city itself. The Green is the site of three hand-some and architecturally distinct churches that were all built in the early 1800s and reflect New Haven's theocratic roots. The redbrick Georgian-style Center Congregational Church was established in 1639 and is oldest of the three congregations. The church building is notable for its pretty spire and because it is built over the New Haven Crypt, which contains the remains of the city's first Puritan settlers. The United Church with its distinctive cupola is an excellent example of Federal-style architecture. The congregation dates from 1796 and is particularly known for its early involvement in the abolition movement. Trinity Church is built in a Gothic Revival style and is the most elaborate of the three, designed by architect Ithiel Town for a congregation that was founded in 1752. To the west of the Green is the Yale University campus and to the east, New Haven City Hall. Across from the Green and directly in front of City Hall is New Haven's *Amistad* Memorial, a three-sided bronze sculpture that marks the former site of the jail where the illegally kidnapped Africans were imprisoned for the two years of their trial. The elms that bordered these streets at one time gave the city the nickname "Elm City." Lost to Dutch elm disease in the first half of the 20th century, the elms have since been replaced. Today, the Green remains a fine public space that is the center of New Haven city life.

Yale Peabody Museum of Natural History. 170 Whitney Ave.; (203) 432-5050; peabody .yale.edu. After a visit here your kids will agree—old-fashioned artifacts are cool. Head to the third floor to see the museum's first-rate North American and southern New England wildlife dioramas. The second floor Discovery Room is the place for hands-on fun; kids can touch a 100-million-year-old fossil, watch brightly colored poison dart frogs from South America; and walk in the tracks of a dinosaur. End your visit in the Hall of Dinosaurs. Kids will be drawn to the apatosaurus that dominates the room, and they'll probably recognize the nearby stegosaurus skeleton, too. Grown-ups will find the 110-foot Age of Reptiles mural to be particularly interesting—painted in the 1940s, it offers fascinating insight about changes in scientific understanding over the years. Open Mon through Sat 10 a.m. to 5 p.m., Sun noon to 5 p.m. Admission $13 adults, $9 seniors, $6 ages 3 to 18.

Sea Mist Thimble Islands Cruise. Stony Creek Dock; Stony Creek; (203) 488-8905; thimbleislandcruise.com. Just off the Connecticut coast, this cluster of islands (as many as 365 depending on whether you are counting at high or low tide!) is said to be the hiding place of Captain Kidd's treasure. Hear sailor's tales, pirate's lore, and stories of the hurricane of 1938 on a scenic 45-minute cruise around the 25 larger, inhabited islands. Cruise season runs June through Oct; check website for days and departure times. Cash only. $13 adults, $12 seniors, $6 ages 12 and under.

Yale Center for British Art. 1080 Chapel St.; (203) 432-2800; britishart.yale.edu. Housed in a light-filled building designed by modernist architect Louis I. Kahn, this is the largest collection of British art outside the United Kingdom. A gift from Yale alum Paul Mellon, the museum traces English life from the Elizabethan period onward with works by Thomas Gainsborough, J. M. W. Turner, and John Constable. Sporting art is among the museum's strengths, and George Stubbs's *Horse Attacked by Lion* is sought out by many. Anglophiles will find a lot to like about the museum's bookstore: art books and museum prints, artisan gifts, and British kitsch. Open Tues through Sat 10 a.m. to 5 p.m., Sun noon to 5 p.m. Closed Mon. Admission free.

Yale Repertory Theater. 1120 Chapel St.; (203) 432-1234; yalerep.org. With its 3 venues—Yale Repertory Theatre, University Theatre, and the Iseman Theater—Yale Rep not only dominates New Haven's performing arts scene, but its reach goes to New York City. Since its founding as part of the Yale School of Drama in 1966, 12 productions have gone on to Broadway.

Yale University. Yale University Visitor Center, 149 Elm St.; (203) 432-2300; yale.edu/visitor. In 1701, the colony of Connecticut voted funds to establish the Collegiate School to train clergy and political leaders. The school was named in 1718 for Elihu Yale, a successful merchant of the British East India Company in honor of his donation to the fledgling college. Yale's Visitor Center is located in New Haven's oldest residential building, the 1767 Pierpont House, where student-led guided tours that cover Yale's history, art, and architecture are offered daily. Another option? Download Yale's free MP3 tour before your visit and pick up a campus map at the visitor center for a self-guided walking tour. Visitor center open Mon through Fri 9 a.m. to 4:30 p.m., Sat and Sun 11 a.m. to 4 p.m. Tours offered Mon through Fri 10:30 a.m. and 2 p.m., Sat and Sun at 1:30 p.m.

handsome dan: bow, wow, wow!

Yale has a long tradition of English bulldogs serving as the school's mascot. The taxidermied bulldog in the glass case at the Visitor Center is Handsome Dan II who served from 1933–1937. Yale's current mascot, the 18th Handsome Dan, is just a puppy—he was born in September 2016 and is very handsome indeed.

day trip to new york city:

Shopping, sightseeing, even dinner and a Broadway show: one of the most popular side trips from New Haven is to head to New York City for the day. Of course, you can drive into the city—it normally takes 90 minutes to 2 hours (or more during rush hour) and parking is expensive. Traveling to the city by train is the better—both quicker and less stressful—option. MetroNorth (877-690-5116, http://new.mta.info/mnr) commuter rail trains leave frequently from New Haven's Union Station, arriving approximately 100 minutes later at New York's Grand Central Station. Amtrak (800-872-7245; amtrak.com) is a faster (the trip to Manhattan from New Haven takes 90 minutes) but more expensive option. It's impossible to see everything that New York has to offer, even if you stayed forever. To make the most of a limited stay, visit the New York City information center in Times Square (Broadway Plaza between 43rd and 44th Streets) for maps, brochures and discount attraction passes. Both the New York CityPASS and the New York City Explorer Pass are efficient, allowing visitors to save money on the city's most popular attractions and skip New York City's epic admission lines. In midtown, every hotel chain that you can imagine is located within a one-block radius of Grand Central Station. How to choose? You can't go wrong with the iconic Algonquin with its jazz-age glamour or Hotel 48 Lex, a trendy, boutique property that appeals to eco-minded travelers.

Situated just blocks from Times Square, but without the chaos, the Sofitel New York (45 West 44th St., sofitelnewyork.com) is a 30-story glass and limestone tower that effortlessly blends French chic and New York contemporary style for a sophisticated Big Apple experience. Best of all—it's not as expensive as it seems. The large, light-filled lobby is splendid, with burnished wood walls, museum-quality art and fresh flowers. Its 400 rooms are modernly elegant, averaging 350 square feet, which is big by New York standards. Bathrooms feature lots of marble and separate bath and toilet areas. The room to book though is one of the terrace suites with views of the Chrysler building. Gaby, the hotel's Gallic-inspired bar and restaurant, is both sleek and whimsical, offering classic cocktails and bistro fare.

Yale University Art Gallery. 1111 Chapel St.; (203) 432-0600; yale.edu/artgallery. A striking 2012 renovation and expansion has brought together three of Yale's landmark buildings into a seamless facility, creating a more cohesive museum experience. Founded in 1832, this is the oldest university art museum in the Western Hemisphere as well as one of the largest, boasting an encyclopedic collection of some 185,000 pieces from Greek antiquities to Peter Paul Rubens to an extensive collection of Picasso prints and drawings. Open Tues through Fri 10 a.m. to 5 p.m., Sat and Sun 11 a.m. to 5 p.m. Admission free.

where to shop

Delmonico Hatter. 47 Elm St.; (203) 787-4086. Millinery is on trend thanks to the royal wedding of Kate Middleton and Prince William. And although Delmonico's has been in business since 1908, there's nothing old hat here; you can find everything from a custom-made Stetson to outback hats, to elaborate Kentucky Derby dress straws, and more. And yes, Delmonico carries fascinators, too. Open Tues through Fri 11 a.m. to 5:30 p.m., Sat 10 a.m. to 5 p.m., closed Sun and Mon.

J. Press. 206 College St.; (203) 772-1310; jpressonline.com. Venerable New Haven–based men's clothier J. Press knows that timeless American style is never out of fashion. Always well known for its conservative suits and sportswear, the brand has recently introduced the J. Press Blue label which offers a modern, more youthful take on preppy style. Open Mon through Fri 9 a.m. to 6 p.m., Sat 9 a.m. to 5:30 p.m.

The Shops at Yale. shopsatyale.com. Around Yale, there are nearly 50 shops and boutiques that line Chapel Street and Broadway. Of course, you'll find college campus shopping faves like Apple (65 Broadway; 203-498-8950; apple.com) and J. Crew (29 Broadway; 203-624-7101; jcrew.com). There are also a good number of independent stores like Hello Boutique (1090 Chapel St.; 203-562-0204; helloboutique.com), a go-to source for high-end women's clothing, and New Haven's own Gant (268 York St.; 203-776-1949; gant.com) for the well-dressed guy. Yale students take their ice cream seriously, with some factions professing allegiance to Arethusa Farm Dairy (1020 Chapel St.; 203-390-5114; arethusafarm. com), and others loyal to Ashley's (280 York St.; 203-776-7744; ashleysicecream.net). Try them both and decide. General store hours are Mon through Wed, Fri, and Sat 10 a.m. to 6 p.m.; Thurs 10 a.m. to 8 p.m.; Sun noon to 5 p.m.

where to eat

Atticus Bookstore Cafe. 1082 Chapel St.; (203) 776-4040; atticusbookstorecafe.com. A New Haven institution for more than three decades, this cafe and bookstore is perfect for coffee, a quick bite, or a full meal. For breakfast choose the egg and sausage strata or the cranberry-pecan french toast. The black bean soup is a customer favorite; get a cup along with half a sandwich for a light lunch. At dinner, comfort food classics like chicken potpie, boneless beef short ribs, or barbecue pork turnovers and coleslaw are good bets. Open Sun 8 a.m. to 8 p.m., Mon through Sat 7 a.m. to 9 p.m. $.

Caseus. 93 Whitney Ave.; (203) 624-3373; caseusnewhaven.com. It's a lovely thing, really, to eat in a cheese shop. Part specialty food store, part bistro, Caseus serves a small menu of neatly prepared French fare in cozy surrounds. Steak frites with a tarragon Dijon sauce, mussels with chorizo and chilies, and a sumptuous mac and cheese are among the pleasures. To start your meal, there's a well-rounded wine list and carefully composed cheese and charcuterie boards. If they are on offer, don't miss the *zeppole* (fried fritters) served with caramel and chocolate dipping sauce for dessert. Also look for the Caseus Cheese Truck (thecheesetruck.com) around town serving gourmet grilled cheese sandwiches, tomato soup (the always perfect go-with), and grilled sausages. Restaurant open Mon and Tues 11:30 a.m. to 2:30 p.m.; Wed and Thurs 11:30 a.m. to 2:30 and 5:30 to 9 p.m.; Fri and Sat 11:30 a.m. to 2:30 and 5:30 to 9:45 p.m. Closed Sun. $$–$$$.

Crepes Choupette. 24 Whitney Ave.; (475) 441-7966; crepeschoupette.com. A bit of Paris comes to New Haven in the form of this authentic French creperie. The whole-wheat crepes are stuffed with sweet fillings of sugar, butter and lemon or Nutella and banana, but it is the traditional savory buckwheat crepes like the egg, smoked salmon and crème fraiche that truly set this cafe apart. Open Mon through Wed 7:30 a.m. to 6 p.m., Thurs and Fri 7:30 a.m. to 8 p.m., Sat 7:30 a.m. to 5 p.m., Sun 8 a.m. to 5 p.m. $.

Frank Pepe Napoletana. 157 Wooster St.; (203) 865-5762; pepespizzeria.com. New Haven has a reputation as home to some of America's best pizza. And Pepe's, dating from 1925, is the most legendary New Haven pizzeria of all. First timer? Don't hesitate. Order the white clam pie: chopped littleneck clams, fresh garlic, oregano, and pecorino cheese on a thin, chewy crust with a nice bottom char—judge for yourself. Open daily 10:30 a.m. to 10 p.m. $–$$.

Louis' Lunch. 263 Crown St.; (203) 562-5507; louislunch.com. Another New Haven landmark, Louis' Lunch is said to be the birthplace of the hamburger; they have served their juicy hand-packed patties on toast since 1900. The burgers are cooked in an antique cast-iron broiler and served only with grilled onion, tomato, and cheese. There's no ketchup. Or mustard either. They don't have it (and don't ask, the staff can be gruff). But these hamburgers are so good, you won't mind a bit. And the dark, atmospheric digs only add to the charm. Open Tues and Wed 11 a.m. to 3:45 p.m., Thurs through Sat noon to 2 a.m., closed Sun and Mon and the month of Aug. Cash only. $.

Miya's Sushi. 68 Howe St.; (203) 777-9760; miyassushi.com. Chef-owner (and 2013 James Beard Foundation–nominated chef) Bun Lai's quest for the perfect balance of East-meets-West sushi has resulted in brilliant culinary creations like pumpkin miso soup, a kimchee-seared wild Arctic char roll, and a water piglet roll made of fried tuna, goat cheese, and cranberries. Miya's is the first sustainable sushi restaurant on the East Coast, too—so it's both delicious and guilt free! Open Tues and Wed 5 to 11 p.m., Thurs through Sat 5 to midnight, closed Sun and Mon. $$.

Skappo Italian Wine Bar. 59 Crown St.; (203) 773-1394; skappo.com. The Sincavage clan, husband-and-wife team Thomas and Anna along with their three grown children, run this cozy Italian wine bar that showcases the food of Umbria, with dishes like braised rabbit, meatballs with raisins and pignoli, and butternut squash gnocchi with walnut sauce. The fare is simple, the atmosphere is friendly, and the wine list interesting and reasonable. Open Wed and Thurs 4:30 to 10:30 p.m., Fri and Sat 4:30 to 11 p.m., Sun 5:30 to 9:30 p.m. Closed Mon and Tues. $$.

Zinc. 964 Chapel St.; (203) 624-0507; zincfood.com. Seasonal ingredients anchor the menu at this New Haven stalwart (which opened in 1998) that continues to draw students, professors, and visiting intelligentsia. Regulars can't help but to order the duck nachos whenever they're on the menu. Other favorites include the Vietnamese chicken with black Thai rice and the sea scallops with root vegetables and truffle vinaigrette. Open Mon 5 to 9 p.m.; Tues through Fri noon to 2:30 p.m. and 5 to 9 p.m.; Sat 5 to 10 p.m.; closed Sun. $$–$$$.

where to stay

New Haven Hotel. 229 George St.; (203) 498-3100; newhavenhotel.com. The New Haven Hotel sparkles after a total interior renovation that has brought custom-made furnishings, marble baths, flat-screen TVs, and a contemporary color scheme to each of its 118 rooms. The revamped lobby features a soaring fireplace, original artwork, and sophisticated seating groupings that create a comfortable, modern vibe. $$.

Omni New Haven Hotel at Yale. 155 Temple St.; (203) 772-6664; omnihotels.com. Just steps from Yale, all 306 rooms in this classic hotel have an understated elegance. The good-size rooms distinguish this hotel from its neighbors. Rooms on the upper floors offer views of Yale or Long Island Sound. $$.

Study at Yale. 1157 Chapel St.; (203) 503-3900; studyatyale.com. Superbly located just blocks from the Yale campus, this is easily New Haven's most hip hotel. The 133 rooms are smartly decorated with contemporary furnishings in tones of blue and neutrals that are softened by homey touches like a soft wool throw at the end of the bed and a leather reading chair. Rooms come with free Wi-Fi and a flat-screen TV, too. $$.

day trip 17

new haven

authors' homes, art & roses:
hartford, ct

hartford, ct

Insurance company buildings pierce the sky over Connecticut's capital, but Hartford, founded in 1636, is one of the country's oldest cities. As a state capital, Hartford is unique; although Hartford has been the capital of Connecticut since 1662, it jointly shared state-capital duties with New Haven from 1701 to 1874. Fans of literature and history will want to visit the house museums of Mark Twain and Harriet Beecher Stowe. Art lovers will rave about the Wadsworth Athenaeum. In summer, the Elizabeth Park Rose Garden is breathtaking. And the Connecticut Science Center draws families to the revitalized Connecticut riverfront.

getting there

From New Haven, take I-91 North for 37 miles. At exit 29A merge left toward Capitol Area/downtown Hartford.

where to go

Greater Hartford Welcome Center. 100 Pearl St.; (860) 244-0253. The volunteers here are terrifically helpful. Pick up maps, directions, brochures, and event listings for Hartford and surrounding towns. Check out, too, the adjacent gallery space that exhibits work from local artists. Open Mon through Fri 9 a.m. to 5 p.m.

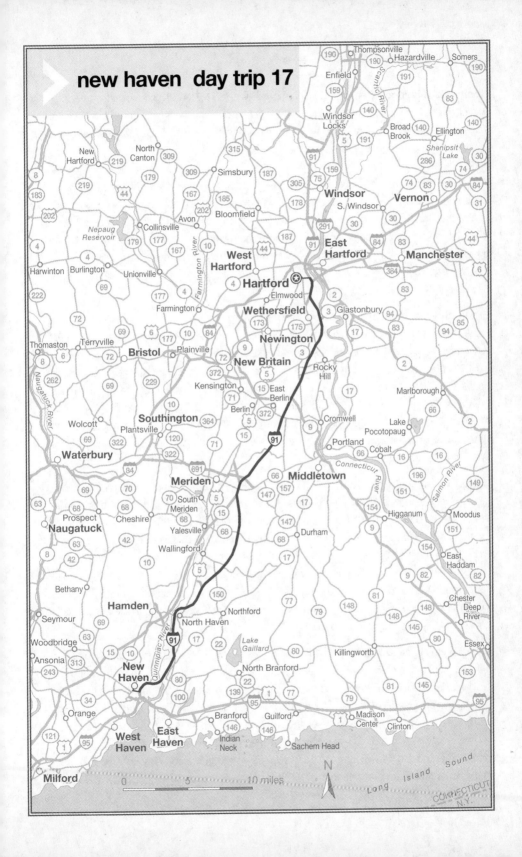

new haven day trip 17

Connecticut Science Center. 250 Columbus Blvd.; (860) 724-3623; ctsciencecenter.org. A modern-day landmark, this daring 2009 building overlooking the Connecticut River at Adriaen's Landing has transformed the Hartford skyline. It's also a LEED Gold-certified green building, generating most of its energy needs from an on-site fuel cell. With more than 165 hands-on exhibits and experiments, this is Hartford's most popular attraction for families. Whether exploring a supernova by virtual navigation, feeling sound and hearing light in the Sight and Sound Gallery, or experiencing larger-than-life 3D films that journey to the rain forest, the Connecticut Science Center knows how to make learning fun. Good to know, too, that the museum's cafe serves way-better-than-average kiddie museum fare: cheese quesadillas, salads from locally grown produce, and sandwiches made from artisan bread. Open Tues through Sun 10 a.m. to 5 p.m., closed Mon. General admission $23.95 adults, $21.95 seniors, $16.97 children ages 3 to 17, children under 3 free.

Elizabeth Park. Asylum Avenue; elizabethparkct.org. In a residential area straddling the Hartford/West Hartford line, Elizabeth Park is an urban masterpiece, a perfect spot for quiet contemplation or a stroll. Admire too, the park's formal beds of herbs, annuals, and perennials. Its centerpiece attraction though is its rose garden, the first municipal rose garden in the country. In June, the rose garden is nothing short of fantastic, drawing huge crowds when the roses (800 varieties and a total of 15,000 plants at last count) bloom in profusion. The excellent Pondhouse Cafe (pondhousecafe.com; 860-231-8823) is on the premises, serving light New American meals as it caters to all senses in a garden/greenhouse setting. Gardens open daily dawn to dusk. Free admission.

Harriet Beecher Stowe Center. 77 Forest St.; (860) 522-9258; harrietbeecherstowecenter.org. Harriet Beecher Stowe lived in this Gothic Victorian "cottage" (it has 14 rooms) from 1873 until her death in 1896; it's located next door to Mark Twain's house. Primarily known as the best-selling author of the antislavery novel *Uncle Tom's Cabin,* Stowe was a prolific writer (she published 30 books)—and the mother of seven! Guided house tours offer insight into Stowe's influence on American literature and social activism in the 19th century. Open Jan through Mar, Mon and Wed through Sat 9:30 a.m. to 5 p.m., Sun noon to 5 p.m.; Apr through Dec, Mon through Sat 9:30 a.m. to 5 p.m., Sun noon to 5 p.m. Admission $14 adults, $12 seniors, $8 children ages 5 to 16.

Mark Twain House & Museum. 351 Farmington Ave.; (860) 247-0998; marktwainhouse.org. Samuel Clemens, better known as Mark Twain, had this elaborate Victorian mansion built in 1871 and lived here with his wife and three daughters for 17 years. Start your tour at the visitor center, and be sure to see the excellent 30-minute Ken Burns *Mark Twain* biopic. Tours of the home are by guided tour only. You'll see the stunning entrance hall that was designed by Louis C. Tiffany as well as more modest rooms like the second-floor classroom where his daughters were homeschooled. You'll learn, too, that "man caves" are not a new concept. The third floor of the house was Twain's private domain. This is where he retired to pen *Huckleberry Finn* and

Tom Sawyer as well as entertain his friends with drinking, smoking cigars, and playing billiards. Museum open Mon through Sat 9:30 a.m. to 5:30 p.m., Sun noon to 5:30 p.m., closed Tues Jan through Mar. Admission $20 adults, $18 seniors, $11 ages 6 to 16.

Old State House. 800 Main St.; (860) 522-6766; ctosh.org. This Charles Bulfinch–designed Federal-style building was completed in 1796, making it the newly independent nation's first capitol building. Tour the restored chambers to see the Gilbert Stuart portrait of George Washington, visit the courtroom that witnessed the opening of the 1839 trial of the *Amistad* prisoners. On the second floor, don't miss the re-creation of the 1797 Mr. Steward's Museum of Natural and Other Curiosities. You won't soon forget the two-headed calf! A farmers' market is held outside from late June through late October. Market days are Tues and Fri from 10 a.m. to 2 p.m. Old State House hours are Mon through Fri 10 a.m. to 5 p.m. Admission $6 adults, $3 seniors, students and children ages 6 to 17.

State Capitol. 210 Capitol Ave.; (860) 240-0222; cga.ct.gov/capitoltours. Adjacent to Bushnell Park, the Victorian Gothic white marble edifice with its gold leaf dome, turreted spires, and carved facade is almost too fanciful for a state capitol building. Built in 1878, it is Connecticut's third state house since the Revolution and is the current home of the Connecticut state government. Open to the public, visitors can pick up a brochure at the Information and Tours Desk for a self-guided tour or join one of the scheduled docent-led guided tours that take place Mon through Fri; check website for exact times. Free admission.

wethersfield for even more colonial history & architecture

Founded in 1633–1634, "Ye most auncient towne" in Connecticut is very old indeed. A farming community, Wethersfield became known as "Oniontown" for its famous red onion variety. In a compact area of this suburban village there are more than 300 historic houses with an amazing variety of architectural styles: colonial, Federal, Victorian, late Georgian, Gothic, and Greek Revival. Among them, the **Webb-Deane-Stevens Museum** *(211 Main St.; 860-529-0612; webb-deane-stevens .org) comprises three well-preserved 18th-century homes next door to each other. It was at the Webb House in May 1781 that George Washington and Jean Baptiste Rochambeau planned the battle of Yorktown, the last major battle of the Revolutionary War that led to the defeat of the British. From Hartford, Wethersfield is a short 6-mile jaunt down I-91 S to exit 26. For a suggested walking itinerary and map, visit the Wethersfield Historic Society, Keeney Memorial Cultural Center, 150 Main St.; (860) 529-7656; wethhist.org.*

Wadsworth Atheneum of Art. 600 Main St.; (860) 278-2670; thewadsworth.org. Wander the galleries of "the Wad," America's oldest public art museum. The castle-like Wadsworth Atheneum was founded in 1842, with holdings of more than 50,000 objects spanning five centuries, and it's notable for its collection of 19th-century Hudson River landscape paintings, as well as its European and American Impressionists works. The Samuel Colt firearms collection is uniquely Connecticut and the museum's Amistad Center is strong in African-American art and artifacts. The museum's cafe is a good choice for a quick and inexpensive lunch break. Open Wed through Fri 11 a.m. to 5 p.m., Sat and Sun 10 a.m. to 5 p.m. Admission $15 , $12 seniors, $5 students, free for children ages 18 and under.

where to eat

Black Eyed Sally's. 350 Asylum St.; (860) 278-7427; blackeyedsallys.com. Find an appealing combination of live blues and soulful cooking at this Hartford icon. The reasonably priced dishes include crowd-pleasing options like barbecued beef brisket, fried chicken, and shrimp and grits. Among the desserts, bourbon pecan pie is always a fine ending to any Southern meal. Open Mon through Thurs 11:30 a.m. to 10 p.m., Fri and Sat 11:30 a.m. to 11 p.m.,Sun 11:30 a.m. to 8 p.m. $$.

Salute. 100 Trumbull St.; (860) 899-1350; salutect.com. Salute is a sophisticated but unpretentious place for nouveau Italian that has quite a following. From the jumbo lump crab cake with roasted red-pepper remoulade to chicken gnocchi with pesto cream sauce and grilled Atlantic salmon with potato lasagna, you can't go wrong. Be sure to save room for the tiramisu. Open Mon through Sat 11:30 a.m. to midnight, Sun 3 to 10 p.m. $$.

Trumbull Kitchen. 150 Trumbull St.; (860) 493-7412; maxrestaurantgroup.com. Conventioneer expense accounters and local hipsters mingle at this bustling, smart restaurant that incorporates a bi-level open dining space and an expansive bar. You'll find tremendous flavors from a mostly mid-priced menu of small plates accompanied by wines by the glass and fancy-schmancy cocktails. The menu is eclectic and as stylish as the surrounds: Quebec vintage cheddar fondue, shrimp and sweet potato fritters with *nuoc cham* dipping sauce, grilled filet mignon with truffled *pommes frites,* and Creole tuna sashimi. Suggestion? Order far more appetizers than you think you can eat and then just finish them all. Open Mon through Fri 11:30 a.m. to 11 p.m., Sat noon to midnight, Sun 4 to 10 p.m. $$–$$$.

Woody's. 915 Main St.; (860) 278-5499; woodyshotdog.com. A hot dog may sound like no big deal, but Woody's Deputy Dog, an all-beef foot-long hot dog that is smothered with both pulled pork and cheddar, is special. Hands drenched with barbecue sauce, cheddar dripping onto the table—best to roll up your sleeves before you get down to business. Open Mon through Wed 11:30 a.m. to 3 p.m., Thurs and Fri 11:30 a.m. to 10 p.m., Sat noon to 10 p.m. Closed Sun (except during football season, when Woody's opens at noon—this is a Miami Dolphins bar). $.

where to stay

Hartford Marriott. 200 Columbus Blvd.; (860) 249-8000 or (866) 373-9806; marriott.com. This 22-story business hotel attached to the Hartford Convention Center has large rooms featuring oversize work desks. The indoor roof-top pool is a draw for vacationing families who come for weekend getaways to visit the nearby Connecticut Science Center. Rooms come with top-of-the-line linens, flat-screen TVs, and many have river views. On weeknights, the hotel's glam L Bar is full of happy hour regulars, and the hotel's restaurant Vivo Seasonal Trattoria entices with rustic Italian done very well. $$–$$$.

Residence Inn Hartford-Downtown. 942 Main St.; (860) 524-5550 or (800) 960-5045; marriott.com. The massive brownstone building with contrasting limestone trim is distinctive of H. H. Richardson, the renowned architect of Trinity Church, Boston. The building looms over its corner along Main Street and is located close to many of Hartford's attractions. The hotel's 120 suites are extra-spacious and quite comfortable. Each guest room has a living room (with sofa bed), a separate bedroom, a fully equipped kitchen, flat-screen TVs, and free Wi-Fi. You'll find good pub grub at microbrewery City Steam (860-525-1600; citysteam-brewerycafe.com) . Adding to the hotel's value is the daily complimentary hot breakfast and Mon through Wed complimentary happy hour. A business-oriented hotel, it typically slashes weekend prices to lure leisure travelers. $$.

day trip 18

new haven

along the river & shore:
madison, ct; essex, ct; old lyme, ct; mystic, ct

East of New Haven, the southeastern Connecticut coast extends from the well-to-do suburb of Madison to just south of the Rhode Island border. Travel the stretch of towns along the Connecticut coast and you will encounter the state's longest public beach, Connecticut River artist colonies, and a city dedicated to all things maritime. The region is especially bustling during the summer, with an appealing, almost rural serenity, during the rest of the year.

madison, ct

Located midway between New Haven Harbor and the mouth of the Connecticut River, Madison enjoys both urban convenience and beach town amenities. First settled in 1641, the town retains a New England village feel with a large green surrounded by boutiques and restaurants. The town is most known, though, as the home of Hammonasset State Park, one of Connecticut's few public beaches.

getting there

From New Haven take I-95 North toward New London/US 1 and follow for 16 miles. Take exit 61 to pick up US 1 (also called the Boston Post Road) to Madison.

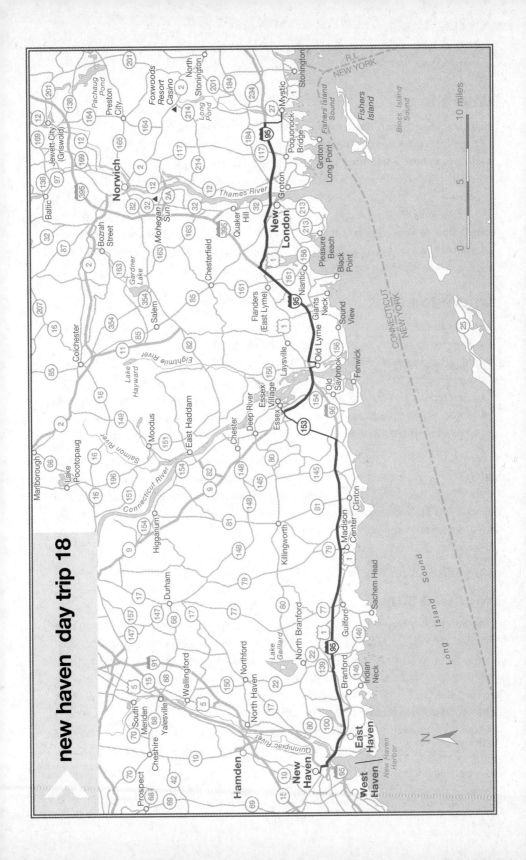

new haven day trip 18

where to go

Hammonasset Beach State Park. 1288 Boston Post Rd.; (203) 245-2785. This is Connecticut's longest beach with 2 miles of sandy shoreline along Long Island Sound. It's a warm-water beach with almost no waves, so the beach is hugely popular with both local and day-tripping families. You really could spend a day here. Walk along the almost 0.75-mile boardwalk to the rocky outcrop at Meigs Point or follow the walking trails through the 900 acres of woods. Within the park, the Meigs Point Nature Center (meigspointnaturecenter .org) houses exhibits relating to the natural history of the Connecticut shore. There's also a 550-site (tent and RV) campground, a bathhouse, and concession stand. Open daily 8 a.m. to sunset. Admission fee per vehicle $22 weekend, $15 weekdays.

where to eat

Bar Bouchee. 8 Scotland Ave.; (203) 318-8004; barbouchee.com. At this comfy neighborhood bistro, dishes show both elegance and technique. There's hand-chopped steak tartare, escargots with herbed butter, and braised rabbit with polenta and lardoons. For those seeking comfort food, there's the winning *foie gras* burger with tomato confit and pan-roasted chicken with kohlrabi puree. The desserts, especially the *fromage blanc* mousse with seasonal fruit compote, are hard to resist. In season, the pretty patio is a pleasant place for an alfresco dinner. Open Mon through Sat 4 to 10 p.m., Sun 4 to 9:30 p.m. $$–$$$.

Lenny & Joe's Fish Tale. 1301 Boston Post Rd.; (203) 245-7289; ljfishtale.com. A great stop after Hammonasset Beach, this is where locals go to get their seafood; it's especially known for its fried whole clams, scallops, and cod platters. Lenny & Joe's attracts lots of families with its ice-cream stand and the wooden flying carousel out in the back (rides cost $1.50 with all proceeds going to local charities). Order at the counter and sit inside or outside at the many picnic tables. BYOB. Open Sun through Thurs 11 a.m. to 9 p.m., Fri and Sat 11 a.m. to 9:30 p.m. $–$$.

where to stay

Madison Beach Hotel. 94 W. Wharf Rd.; (203) 245-1404; madisonbeachhotel.com. The historic, Victorian-era Madison Beach Hotel was once a boardinghouse for shipbuilders. Renovated in 2012, today it is part of the Hilton Curio Collection. Each of its 33 rooms has a private balcony where you can gaze out at the sweep of sand and, just beyond, water views of Long Island Sound. Rooms are comfortably elegant with sleigh beds, high thread-count sheets and wooden shutters on the windows. All rooms come with flat-screen TVs and small refrigerators. Several rooms have a gas fireplace and/or soaking tubs. By day, enjoy the hotel's private beach, and at night, there's only the sound of the waves. $$.

essex, ct

Travel the backroads through the lower Connecticut River Valley to reach postcard-pretty Essex, an important 19th-century shipbuilding center. The town actually consists of three distinct villages: in the early 1900s tiny Ivoryton became prosperous from the import of ivory tusks used in the manufacture of buttons, combs, and piano keys; Centerbrook's village center has several restaurants and shops; and in Essex the impeccably maintained Georgian- and Federal-style homes that were built for the shipyard owners still line the length of Main Street all the way to Steamboat Landing and the Connecticut River Museum. Among these, perhaps there is no more authentic colonial homestead in all of New England than the Revolutionary-era Griswold Inn.

getting there

Take the scenic route along the shore. Follow US 1 North for 8 miles. Turn left onto CT 153 North (also known as Essex Road) for 5 miles into Essex.

where to go

Connecticut River Museum. 67 Main St.; (860) 767-8269; ctrivermuseum.org. Located at the end of Main Street in an 1878 steamboat warehouse overlooking scenic Essex Harbor, this museum tells the story of Essex and the Connecticut River with nautical artwork, ship models, and collections of shipbuilding and fishing tools. Among the museum's exhibits is a full-scale replica of the *American Turtle*, a 1776 invention by Connecticut native (and Yale graduate) David Bushnell and the world's first functioning submarine. Open June through Oct daily 10 a.m. to 5 p.m.; rest of year Tues through Sun 10 a.m. to 5 p.m. Museum admission $10 adults, $8 seniors, $6 ages 6 to 12, free ages 5 and under.

Essex Steam Train and Riverboat. 1 Railroad Ave.; (860) 767-0103; essexsteamtrain .com. Climb aboard the lovingly restored vintage steam train at Essex station for the 1-hour narrated trip through the Connecticut countryside. At Deep River Landing you will transfer to the steamboat *Becky Thatcher* for an hour cruise along the Connecticut River, passing local landmarks like Gillette Castle and the wedding-cake-like Victorian-era Goodspeed Opera House (it was in *Man of La Mancha* in 1964 and *Annie* in 1976) before returning by train back to Essex. Special train events are scheduled throughout the season; be sure to reserve early for foliage-season trains. Season May through Dec; check website for departure times. Steam train and riverboat tickets $29 adults, $19 children ages 2 to 11.

Ivoryton Playhouse. 103 Main St., Ivoryton; (806) 767-7318 ivorytonplayhouse.org. Established in 1930, this is one of the country's oldest straw-hat circuit theaters. Still thriving, Ivoryton produces a full schedule of dramas, comedies, and musicals during its March through December season. Recent lineups have included staples such as *Biloxi Blues* and *West Side*

Story, as well as new works such as *I Hate Musicals! The Musical* by Emmy award–winning comedy writer (and Bristol native) Mike Reiss.

where to eat

Blue Hound Cookery & Taproom. 107 Main St.; Ivoryton; (860) 767-0260; bluehound cookery.com. Located across the street from the Ivorytown Playhouse. The menu is best described as global southern. Enjoy a little bit of everything from an expertly prepared tuna crudo, Carolina pork spring rolls, jerk chicken with grilled pineapple and Creole seafood fra diavola in the downstairs restaurant. If you are attending a show and didn't make a reservation, the upstairs bar serves flatbread pizzas, grilled sandwiches, black bean soup and salads to tide you over. Restaurant open Mon, Wed, Sat 11:30 a.m. to 2 p.m, 5 to 9 p.m.; Sun 4 to 8 p.m. Taproom open Mon, Wed, Thurs 4 to 11 p.m., Fri and Sat 4 to midnight, Sun. Both closed Tues. $$.

where to stay

The Griswold Inn. 35 Main St.; (860) 767-1776; griswoldinn.com. A landmark in Essex since 1801, this is one of the oldest inns in the US. The "Gris" exudes atmosphere with 33 rooms, each with a private bath, period antique furniture, and floors that are slightly, charmingly settled. Room rates include a simple continental breakfast. Dine on American comfort food like chicken potpie and sticky toffee pudding in the historic dining room or artisanal cheese and small plate cuisine in the Wine Bar. Be sure to check out the Griswold's Tap Room, which displays an impressive collection of marine art, antique guns, Currier and Ives steamboat prints, and temperance posters. The Tap Room has been rated by *Esquire* magazine as "one of the top bars in America" and hosts a lively weekly Monday night sing-along. $$.

worth more time

Gillette Castle State Park. 67 River Rd., East Haddam; (860) 526-2336. This one-of-a-kind fieldstone castle was the 24-room mansion of William Gillette, a turn-of-the-20th-century stage actor best known for his portrayal of Sherlock Holmes. Apparently a bit of an eccentric, Gillette designed the castle's hidden compartments, secret stairway, and a somewhat creepy system of mirrors that let him see his guests before they saw him. Tours of the castle are self-guided, but volunteers are available to answer questions. There are walking trails throughout the 184-acre property. Bring a picnic to enjoy sweeping views from high above the banks of the Connecticut River. Park open daily 8 a.m. to sunset; castle open Memorial Day through Labor Day Thurs through Sun 11 a.m. to 5 p.m. Admission $6 adults, $2 ages 6 to 12.

If you are driving from Essex, taking the **Chester-Hadlyme Ferry** is a fun way to reach Gillette Castle. The Chester-Hadlyme route has been an established ferry crossing since 1769. Today, the *Selden III* makes the trip, landing just a short walk from Gillette Castle.

Season is Apr 1 through Nov 30 (weather permitting), $5 per vehicle weekdays, $6 weekends or $2 per pedestrian. If the ferry is not running, take CT 82 across the East Haddam Bridge.

old lyme, ct

Located at the mouth of the Connecticut River as it flows into Long Island Sound, Old Lyme is renowned as a center of 19th-century Impressionism in the US—a kind of American Giverny. For more than 30 summers, the artists of the Lyme Art Colony stayed at the Florence Griswold boardinghouse and captured on canvas the beauty of the rocky shores and bucolic countryside of southern Connecticut.

getting there

From Essex take CT 9 South for 3 miles. Merge onto US 1 North crossing the Connecticut River into Old Lyme.

where to go

Florence Griswold Museum. 96 Lyme St.; (860) 434-5542; flogris.org. In the late 19th century, this famed boardinghouse is where several of the artists of the Lyme Art Colony lived and painted, and Florence Griswold, "Miss Florence," was the colony's guiding force. The daughter of one of Old Lyme's most established families, she opened her home to artists, among them, Henry Ward Ranger, Clark Voorhees, Willard Metcalf, and Childe Hassam, who were drawn to the area by the natural beauty of the coast and the village charm of Old Lyme. The 1817 mansion is a delight and has been restored to reflect its 1910 appearance. The dining room is of special interest, with 38 mural panels that were painted by several of the famed artist-boarders. The museum's riverfront Krieble Gallery is a modern space that houses changing art exhibitions from the permanent collection. For a quick bite, visit Cafe Flo, which is open May through Oct Tues through Sat 11:30 a.m. to 3 p.m. and Sun 1 to 4 p.m., and serves light fare: soups, salads, and sandwiches. Museum open Tues through Sat 10 a.m. to 5 p.m., Sun 1 to 5 p.m. Admission $15 adults, $14 seniors, $13 students, free ages 12 and under.

where to eat

Morning Glory Café. 11 Halls Rd.; (860) 434-0480. Set on the banks of the reed-lined Lieutenant River, this casual breakfast and lunch eatery offers a casual, mostly American menu with a welcome touch of Asian flair. Omelets, benedicts, and muffins highlight the breakfast menu. Sandwiches, burgers, and dishes like Pho, spring rolls and a veggie satay from the owner's native Laos lead at lunch. Eat inside, or better yet, outside on the deck. Open daily 8 a.m. to 3:30 p.m. $.

where to stay

Bee & Thistle Inn. 100 Lyme St.; (860) 434-1667; beeandthistleinn.com. This historic 1756 property is located on 5 beautifully landscaped acres along the Lieutenant River. The 10 stylish rooms at this B&B are beyond gracious, featuring four-poster beds, antique reproduction furniture, Persian rugs, luxurious bedding, and local artwork. Rates include a gourmet breakfast, which you can request to have in bed. The inn's fine dining restaurant, the Chestnut Grille, serves creative cuisine like pan-roasted duck with roasted fennel and garden rhubarb-and-fresh-cherry compote in equally charming surroundings. $$–$$$.

mystic, ct

This classic seafaring town in the southeastern part of the state has loads to see and do, with both the Mystic Aquarium and Mystic Seaport considered the area's big-deal attractions. The town especially puts out the welcome mat for families looking to stay for a get-away weekend, with hotel packages that bundle admissions and include extras like free breakfast and welcome gifts. For a totally different New England vacation experience, try your luck at Connecticut's two Native American–run casinos. Located just 11 miles from each other, both Foxwoods and Mohegan Sun offer self-contained resort-style gaming with luxury hotels, celebrity restaurants, and nightclub entertainment.

getting there

This section of the shore is slow going. From Old Lyme, the speedy route to Mystic is to pick up I-95 North for 20 miles.

where to go

Mystic and Shoreline Information Center. 27 Coogan Blvd.; (860) 536-1641; mysticinfo center.com. Located at Olde Mistick Village, make this your first stop before you head into town. You can pick up brochures and maps, and the staff will help you make last-minute overnight hotel reservations. You can also purchase attraction admission tickets here and save time waiting in line. Open summer Mon through Sat 9 a.m. to 6 p.m., Sun 9 a.m. to 4:30 p.m., winter daily 9 a.m. to 3:30 p.m.

Mystic Aquarium & Institute for Exploration. 55 Coogan Blvd.; (860) 572-5955; mystic aquarium.org. Mystic Aquarium has more than 70 exhibits, both indoors and out, so set aside plenty of time to see it all. Mystic Aquarium's Arctic Coast exhibit is a crowd favorite; the 1-acre outdoor whale habitat allows viewing from above ground and below through 20-foot-long windows and is home to 3 beluga whales. The sea lion shows entertain (and inform) several times during the day. The must-do exhibit is the "hands-in" touch pool, where kids can actually feel a cownose ray. Very cool! Open Apr through Aug daily 9 a.m. to 6 p.m.,

Sept through Nov 9 a.m. to 5 p.m., Dec through Mar 10 a.m. to 5 p.m. Admission (good for 2 consecutive days) is $34.99 adults, $29.99 seniors, $28.99 ages 13 to 17, $24.99 ages 3 to 12, free for ages 2 and under.

Mystic Seaport. 75 Greenmanville Ave.; (860) 572-0711; mysticseaport.com. From 1784 to 1919, Mystic was at the center of the maritime trade, building more than 600 ships. Get a sense of the era by visiting a re-created 19th-century seafaring village with its homes and dozens of tradesmen buildings, among them a cooperage, ship carver, and ship smith shops. Climb aboard historic vessels including the *Charles W. Morgan,* the world's last surviving wooden whaling boat, and the 1882 tall ship, the *Joseph Conrad.* View the working shipyard where craftspeople use 19th-century tools to preserve as well as build re-created historic vessels. The *Mayflower II,* the 60-year-old replica of the 1620 ship that brought the Pilgrims to America is undergoing renovation at the preservation shipyard through 2019. The museum is spread over 19 acres, and the exhibits and attractions are both indoors and outside. You'll be walking a lot, so wear comfortable walking shoes and dress for the weather. Open late Apr to Oct daily 9 a.m. to 5 p.m.; Nov through Mar Thurs through Sun 10 a.m. to 4 p.m. Admission (good for 2 consecutive days) is $29.95 adults, $26.95 seniors and students, $18.95 ages 4 to 14, $24.99 kids ages 3 and under free.

Schooner *Argia*. Steamboat Wharf; (860) 536-0416; argiamystic.com. Set sail for a harbor cruise on the 81-foot wooden schooner *Argia* and see Mystic the way that so many sea captains did. These 2.5-hour cruises sail down the Mystic River (the Bascule Bridge drawbridge opens twice for each *Argia* cruise) and out to Fishers Island Sound, past lighthouses, and around Ram Island. All cruises include snacks and refreshments. Cruise season May through Oct, departure times 9:30 a.m., noon, and 3:30 and 6 p.m. daily. Tickets $50 adults, $47 seniors, $40 children ages 18 and under.

where to shop

Olde Mistick Village. 27 Coogan Blvd.; (860) 536-4941; oldemistickvillage.com. A parklike colonial village is the setting for 40 unique shops and restaurants, among them **Franklin's General Store** (860-536-1038, mysticfudge.com), **Garden Specialties** (860-572-0077, garden-specialties.com), and the **Toy Soldier** (860-536-1554, toysoldiermystic.com). Open Memorial Day weekend through Labor Day weekend and the month of Dec Mon through Sat 10 a.m. to 8 p.m., Sun 11 a.m. to 8 p.m. The rest of the year Mon through Sat 10 a.m. to 6 p.m., Sun 11 a.m. to 5 p.m.

where to eat

Abbot's Lobster in the Rough. 117 Pearl St., Noank; (860) 536-7719; abbottslobster .com. No decor, but atmosphere aplenty, this seafood shanty offers gorgeous views of Noank Harbor as mountains of seafood in the rough—lobster, clams, and mussels—are set before the crowds who share picnic tables on the pier. This is the place to try a Connecticut lobster roll: whole lobster on a round toasted roll with melted butter. Indulge! BYOB is encouraged. Open Memorial Day through Labor Day daily 11:30 a.m. to 9 p.m., May and Sept through Columbus Day Fri through Sun 11:30 a.m. to 7 p.m. $$.

Captain Daniel Packer Inne Restaurant and Pub. 32 Water St.; (860) 536-3555; daniel packer.com. Since 1756, when it was a traveler's inn on the road between New York and Boston, there's always been a good story to be had from dining at the "DPI." Between the elegant main dining room and its boisterous first-floor pub, there's something for everyone. Both serve updated New England fare with casual salads, sandwiches, and appetizers (try the honey chipotle wings) in the pub and more refined dishes like veal scaloppine with lobster and lemon-peppered chicken upstairs. Open daily 11 a.m. to 4 p.m. and 5 to 10 p.m. $$–$$$.

Kitchen Little. 36 Quarry Rd.; (860) 536-2122; kitchenlittle.org. My, how Kitchen Little has grown. Recently moved to the Mystic Marina and as cute as ever, this breakfast-centric spot serves an array of New American noshes; from a California Benedict with lump crabmeat, asparagus, and hollandaise to a pancake sandwich made with 2 eggs, ham, and cheese. Lunches and now bistro dinners are excellent, too, with dishes like fresh fried scallop plates and a clear-broth clam chowder. Try to score a seat on the covered patio for a view of the Mystic River to enjoy with your beer. Open Mon through Fri 7:30 a.m. to 2 p.m., Sat and Sun 6:30 a.m. to 1 p.m. $–$$.

Mystic Pizza. 56 W. Main St.; (860) 536-3700; mysticpizza.com. The real Mystic Pizza, from the movie with the same name, does indeed exist. Although not actually filmed in the restaurant, the movie is set here. This is thick-style pizza and heavy on the toppings, but the shop with its film posters and memorabilia is a must-visit for movie fans. Open 10 a.m. to 11 p.m. $.

where to stay

Hilton Mystic. 20 Coogan Blvd.; (860) 572-0731; hiltonmystic.com. For family vacations predictability can be a very good thing. The Hilton Mystic welcomes parents and kids with modern, well-appointed, and spacious accommodations, on-site dining, and an indoor pool. And while there are scores of family-friendly chain hotels in Mystic, you can't beat the Hilton's location across the street from Mystic Aquarium. You can practically roll out of bed and visit the aquarium before the crowds arrive, and you have just a quick dash back to the hotel for afternoon naps and/or pool time. $$.

Steamboat Inn. 73 Steamboat Wharf; (860) 536-8300; steamboatinnmystic.com. Located directly on the Mystic River, 9 of the inn's 11 rooms have sensational water views. Rooms are individually decorated in an updated traditional style. A full breakfast is included in the rate, and in the afternoon sherry and cookies are offered. The inn is well placed for Mystic's restaurants and the Mystic Seaport Museum. Located next to the Bascule Bridge drawbridge, the first horn of the day sounds at 7:40 a.m., but watching the boats pass by your bedroom window is part of the charm of a stay here. $$–$$$.

Whaler's Inn. 20 E. Main St.; (860) 536-1506; whalersinnmystic.com. A hybrid between a motel and inn, the 49-room Whaler's Inn has a convenient location just a short stroll from downtown Mystic and the Mystic Seaport Museum. Rooms in the Hoxie House are handsomely appointed—almost chic—with Federal-style reproduction antiques, whirlpool tubs, and gas fireplaces. Rooms located in the main building and 1865 House are cheerful and pretty with flower wallpaper, wing chairs, and canopy beds. The Noank and Stonington buildings are more casual and ideal for families. All rates include continental breakfast, afternoon snacks, parking and free Wi-Fi. The inn's on-site restaurant, Bravo, is one of Mystic's top fine-dining rooms, a local favorite for its fabulous pastas and seafood with Italian zest— make reservations. $$.

worth more time

Feeling flush? You'll find world-class gaming at not one but two mega-casinos just 20 minutes from downtown Mystic.

Foxwoods Resort Casino. 350 Trolley Line Blvd., Mashantucket; (800) 369-9663; foxwoods.com. Located in the back woods of southeastern Connecticut, Foxwoods is one of the largest gambling casinos in the country. Surprised? Opened in 1992 and managed by the Mashantucket Pequot Tribe, this mammoth (6 million square feet!) Native American– themed gambling center boasts 6 casinos with 4,800 slot machines, 250 tables, one of the world's largest bingo halls, and a poker room. Foxwoods offers a lot more than slots with the spectacular 36-hole Lake of Isles golf course, a retail concourse, 2 spas, and nonstop live entertainment, including appearances by popular artists like John Legend and Amy Schumer. Choose to overnight, and you can stay in the middle of all the action at the Great Cedar Hotel, experience luxurious accommodations at the Grand Pequot Tower, enjoy glitzy suites at the Foxwood Villas, or retreat to the rustic Two Trees Inn. There are countless eating options that run the gamut from the Hard Rock Cafe and California Pizza Kitchen to a classic all-you-can-eat casino buffet to high-end Italian at Alta Strada and no less than 3 high-roller steak houses.

Mashantucket Pequot Museum. 110 Pequot Trail, Mashantucket; (800) 411-9671; pequotmuseum.org. A mile down the road from Foxwoods, this museum gathers together an impressive collection of native Pequot artifacts including woodcarvings, masks, and pottery. It's a "living" museum as well, with traditional storytelling and workshop demonstrations of weaving and basket making throughout the day. The on-site cafe presents Native Indian cuisine featuring indigenous ingredients in dishes like turtle soup and butternut squash fry bread. **Note:** Museum admission is not required to visit the cafe. Open Apr through Nov Wed through Sat 9 a.m. to 5 p.m. Admission $20 adults, $15 seniors, $12 children ages 6 to 18.

Mohegan Sun. 1 Mohegan Sun Blvd., Uncasville; (888) 226-7711; mohegansun.com. Located on the banks of the Thames River in Uncasville, Mohegan Sun (owned by the Mohegan Indian Tribe) is a more understated gaming experience with 3 casinos featuring a total of 5,000 slot machines, 350 table games, and a poker room. Mohegan Sun offers some terrific entertainment choices, including the 10,000-seat Mohegan Sun Arena, which hosts boxing and national touring acts, and the 300-seat Wolf Den, which offers free live music nightly. The family-friendly Kids Quest/Cyber Quest indoor supervised playground allows you to drop off the tots so that you can play while the kids play. Non-gaming diversions include shopping, a golf course, and two spas. The 1,600 rooms at the Mohegan Sun Hotel are spacious and smartly decorated in a contemporary style with marble bathrooms. The hotel also boasts a Vegas-worthy indoor/outdoor pool and solarium. Mohegan Sun has more than 45 eateries, from an outpost of Frank Pepe's Pizzeria Napoletana (see Day Trip 16) to lots of big-name restaurants including Bobby Flay's Bar Americain, Todd English's Tuscany, and Michael Jordan's Steakhouse.

day trip 19

new haven

so very town & country:
woodbury, ct; litchfield, ct; kent, ct

Along the quiet back roads of the Housatonic River Valley, this trio of towns offers many low-key diversions. Spend a lazy afternoon at the antiques galleries in Woodbury. Litchfield boasts more than a few upmarket restaurants, a vineyard, and the gorgeous White Flower Farm. Along the Appalachian Trail, Kent appeals to outdoor enthusiasts for fly fishing and hiking.

woodbury, ct

Charming Woodbury is the heart of Connecticut's antiques country. And 30 antiques dealers in one posh, well-kept village pretty much guarantees that you'll find something worth carting home.

getting there

Woodbury is one of several gateway towns to the Litchfield Hills region and a pleasant 45-minute drive from New Haven. Take CT 63 North for 3 miles, branch off onto CT 67 West for 16 miles. Exit at US 6 East for 3 miles into Woodbury.

where to go

Glebe House Museum and Gertrude Jekyll Garden. 49 Hollow Rd.; (203) 263-2855; theglebehousemuseum.org. This glebe, or parsonage house, is a fine example of

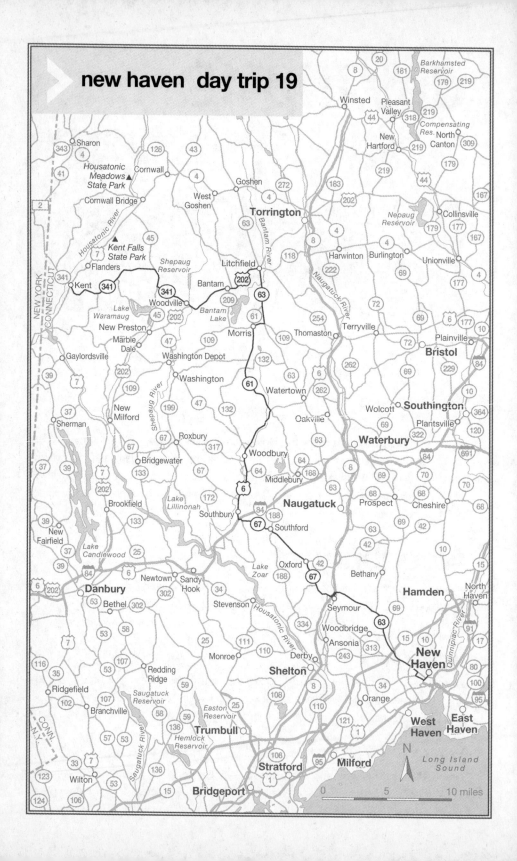

new haven day trip 19

pre-Revolutionary architecture. The large gambrel-roof colonial was built around 1750 for the Reverend John Marshall, Woodbury's first Episcopalian minister, his wife Sarah, and their nine children. The home was restored in 1923 and is furnished in its period, becoming one of the first house museums in the country. The real treasure on this site, though, is the 1920s Gertrude Jekyll garden—one of only three that the famed English gardener designed in the US. It's a cottage garden: a mix of border and foundation plantings, roses, and a stone terrace. And although it is small, the Jekyll garden is the pride of Woodbury. Open May through Oct Wed through Sun, 1 to 4 p.m. Admission $7 adults, $2 children ages 6 to 12, $2 garden only.

where to shop

Many of the shops are located in historic homes and barns on and around Main Street (US 6) and make for an idyllic morning or afternoon of browsing in the countryside. And although there is nothing quite like the satisfaction of a serendipitous find, be sure to pick up the **Woodbury Antiques Dealers Association** (antiqueswoodbury.com) directory (available at any of the shops) as soon as you arrive. Along with spending some time on their website, it's a good idea to rough out a shopping route, while still leaving room for inspiration to strike.

Abrash Galleries. 40 Main St. North; (203) 263-7847; abrashgalleries.com. The store is an exotic visual feast with an impressive selection of antique and semi-antique rugs from Iran, Turkey, India, and China. Open Tues through Sat 10 a.m. to 5 p.m., Sun by appointment.

Main Street Antiques Center. 113 Main St. South; (203) 263-0046. Four separate dealers occupy 2 floors that are chock-a-block with everything from 18th- and 19th-century American and European furniture and paintings to books, maps, and collectibles. Open Wed through Mon 11 a.m. to 5 p.m., closed Tues.

Pantry & Hearth. 994 Main St. South; (203) 263-8555; pantryandhearth.com. Located in a 1775 barn, this is the place to find New England treasures of yore. Specializing in 17th- and 18th-century American furniture and accessories; you'll find everything from museum-quality Queen Anne case goods, to rustic painted candle-stand tables to small folk-art pieces like needlework samplers. Open daily 11 a.m. to 5 p.m.

Woodbury Pewter. 860 Main St. South; (800) 648-2014; woodburypewter.com. A family-owned Woodbury business since 1952, this factory outlet store sells reproduction American pieces: tankards, soup tureens, and baby gifts. Not yet antiques, but perhaps heirlooms in the making. Open Mon through Sat 9 a.m. to 5 p.m., Sun 11 a.m. to 5 p.m.

where to eat

Dottie's Diner. 787 Main St.; (203) 263-2516. Cinnamon-sugar cake doughnuts and chocolate-dipped cinnamon doughnuts—legendary homemade doughnuts these. This bright, cheery neo-diner is a destination for all sorts of culinary delights including killer huevos rancheros, a rich-as-can-be chicken potpie, and bread pudding made with crème anglaise, fresh fruit, and—wait for it—leftover cinnamon doughnuts. Open Mon 6 a.m. to 3 p.m., Tues through Sat 6 am to 8:30 pm. Sun 7 a.m. to 3 p.m. Cash only. $.

Good News Cafe. 694 Main St.; (203) 266-266-4663; good-news-cafe.com. Renowned chef and co-owner Carole Peck's French cuisine gets a New England twist at this dining destination that is still abuzz with well-heeled locals and big-city weekenders even after nearly two decades in the Litchfield Hills. Savor dishes like the braised beef short ribs and yucca cake and an anything-but-ordinary Tahitian vanilla cake with pink guava pomegranate and grapefruit. Open Mon and Wed through Sat 11:30 a.m. to 10 p.m., Sun noon to 10 p.m., closed Tues. $$–$$$.

John's Cafe. 693 Main St.; (203) 263-0188; johnscafe.com. Pleasing local foodies and visitors just passing through, John's Cafe turns out sophisticated fare in a cozy-casual atmosphere. The New American–leaning menu offers something for every type of diner with wood-fired pizza, burgers, pasta, and steaks. A standout? The grilled center-cut pork chop with cheddar-scalloped potatoes and house-made apple butter. Open Mon through Sat 11:30 a.m. to 2:30 p.m., 5:30 to 9 p.m., Sun 4:30 to 8:30 p.m. $$.

litchfield, ct

Settled in 1721, the town of Litchfield is nestled among the rolling hills with a village green that is dominated by the iconic steepled and white-columned First Congregational Church and streets that are bordered by historic colonial and Greek Revival homes. One of these, the Tapping Reeve House, was the home of the first formal law school in the US. A popular weekend-home community for New Yorkers, Litchfield is the epicenter of high-end dining and shopping in the region.

getting there

From Woodbury, take US 6 East for 4 miles, pick up CT 61 North for 8 miles and then CT 63 for another 4 miles into Litchfield. These are two-lane country roads so the driving time is close to 30 minutes for 16 miles of enjoyable scenic driving.

where to go

Litchfield Hills Visitor's Booth. US 202, on the Village Green; (800) 663-1273; litchfield hills.com. Pick up maps and brochures at this booth. Open May through mid-Oct Mon through Wed 9:30 a.m. to 4:30 p.m.; Thurs through Sat 9:30 a.m. to 1 p.m.; closed Sun.

Haight-Brown Vineyard. 29 Chestnut Hill Rd.; (860) 567-4045; haightvineyards.com. Located just outside of Litchfield center, this is Connecticut's oldest winery—since 1975.

Small and laid-back with a European ambience, Haight-Brown provides visitors a first-class wine experience with a personal touch. They produce 10 or so wines—Chardonnay, Riesling, and Merlot—as well as seasonal varieties. The tasting room is open daily for walk-in sampling. A basic wine tasting is $9. Tasting room open May through Nov, Mon through Thurs noon to 5 p.m., Fri and Sat noon to 6 p.m.; check website for days and hours during the rest of the year.

Tapping Reeve House and **Litchfield Law School.** 82 South St.; (860) 567-4501; litchfieldhistoricalsociety.org. In 1773, Judge Tapping Reeve began to tutor the young men who came to clerk for him in his law practice. He eventually built a one-room schoolhouse on his property and established a formal curriculum of legal studies to prepare students to take the bar exam. More than 1,000 students attended the school before it closed in 1833. Among them were Aaron Burr (Reeve's brother-in-law and first student), Vice President John C. Calhoun, Horace Mann, three Supreme Court justices, 28 US senators, as well as US congressmen by the score. Open mid-Apr through Nov Tues through Sat 11 a.m. to 5 p.m., Sun 1 to 5 p.m. Admission free.

White Flower Farm. 167 Litchfield Rd., Morris; (860) 567-8789; whiteflowerfarm.com. The headquarters of the well-known mail-order nursery is in the town of Morris, just 3 miles from Litchfield Green, and is open to the public. Pick up a walking map of the gardens at the visitor center near the parking lot. Word to the wise: If you are even mildly interested in gardening, you will be seduced by the 5 acres of lavish display gardens. Inspired? You can buy plants for your own garden at the retail store. Open Apr through Oct 9 a.m. to 5 p.m.

where to eat

@ the Corner. 3 West St.; (860) 567-8882; athecorner.com. This bistro-style spot has a warm neighborhood vibe. For lunch you'll find creative light fare like vegetarian pea and bean chili, aged cheddar and lobster panini, and a spinach salad with goat-cheese crisps. For dinner, the menu features crowd-pleasers like pork tenderloin with apple-ginger chutney and filet mignon with frizzled onions—all for a reasonable tab. The pleasant, cozy room is fine for a spur-of-the moment lunch, but it fills quickly at night, so make reservations. The next-door bakery storefront has a few tables and serves coffee, muffins, and cookies. Restaurant open Sun through Fri 11:30 a.m. to 9 p.m., Sat 11:30 a.m. 10 p.m. $–$$.

West Street Grill. 43 West St.; (860) 567-3885; weststreetgrill.com. Still the place to see and be seen, this upscale New American spot delivers thoughtfully prepared, updated bistro classics made interesting with seasonal delights. Grilled New York strip steak with sweet potato strudel and mushroom bordelaise, salmon with leeks and a pea-tendril salad, and a dreamy chocolate bread pudding that will make you forget about ever having any other dessert are among the dishes you might find on the menu. Open Mon through Thurs 11:30 a.m. to 2:30 p.m. and 5:30 to 9 p.m.; Fri 11:30 a.m. to 2:30 p.m. and 5:30 to 10 p.m.; Sat

11:30 a.m. to 3:30 p.m. and 5:30 to 10 p.m.; Sun 11:30 a.m. to 3:30 p.m. and 5:30 to 9 p.m. $$–$$$.

where to stay

Litchfield Inn. 432 Bantam Rd.; (860) 567-4503; litchfieldinnct.com. Set off the main road, the circular driveway of the white clapboard Litchfield Inn calls to mind classic country get-away. Inside, the grand foyer with its spiral staircase is the centerpiece of the inn's 2013 multimillion-dollar renovation. Each of the inn's 32 guest rooms is attractively furnished with a pillow-top mattress, high-thread-count linens, and a 37-inch flat-screen TV. Cookies upon arrival are a welcome touch. The inn's Tavern off the Green is pleasantly busy and worth a visit for drinks or dinner. $$.

kent, ct

Tucked into the far western reaches of Litchfield County near the New York border, Kent is another pre-Revolutionary Connecticut village that attracts a fair number of visitors for its scenic beauty. Hike the Appalachian Trail's popular Housatonic River Walk or drive along the US 7 byway to visit the West Cornwall Bridge and Bull's Bridge; both are centuries old and are Connecticut's only covered bridges still open to traffic.

getting there

From Litchfield follow US 202 West for 7 miles. Merge onto CT 341 West for 13 miles into Kent.

where to go

Housatonic River Walk. Among the most popular stretches of the entire 2,000-mile Appalachian Trail, this easy, flat 5-mile, well-marked trail hugs the Housatonic as it passes through dense forest from Kent to Cornwall. The trailhead entrance is off CT 341 West at Skiff Mountain Road.

Kent Falls State Park. 462 Kent Cornwall Rd.; (860) 927-3238. The park is nearly 300 acres, but the main attraction for most visitors is Kent Falls, which is just a short walk from the parking lot. As you enter the park, cross the small covered footbridge to pick up the 0.25-mile trail that, although steep, has steps and wooden lookouts along the way. The impressive series of waterfalls cascade through the valley before joining the nearby Housa-tonic River. Open daily 8 a.m. to sunset. Admission $15 vehicle fee weekends from Memorial Day weekend through Oct.

Eric Sloane Museum. 31 Kent Cornwall Rd.; (860) 927-3849. This quirky but intriguing little museum began with a donation by artist and collector Eric Sloane (1905–1985) of his early-American tool collection and is housed in a barn donated by Connecticut-based Stanley tools. A resident of nearby Warren for many years, Sloane was an accomplished historian and the author and illustrator of some 30 books, many of which chronicled colonial-era life, barns, covered bridges, tools, and folklore. The gift shop sells Sloane's books, including his most popular title, *A Reverence for Wood*. Open May through Oct Thurs through Sun 10 a.m. to 4 p.m. Admission $8 adults, $6 seniors and students, $5 ages 6 to 17.

where to eat

Gifford's. 9 Maple St.; (860) 592-0262; giffordsrestaurant.com. J. P. Gifford Market's Mike Moriarty and James Neunziz are at it again with Kent's newest restaurant, an approachable spot that caters to the New York crowd and local young families, couples, and groups of friends. The stellar menu tempts with elegant, hearty entrees like a vegetarian Indian spiced chickpea, roasted eggplant and tomato spinach ragout, and grilled New York strip steak with goat cheese and grilled onions. Open Fri 5 to 9 p.m., Sat noon to 9 p.m. and Sun 11 to 7 p.m. $$.

J. P. Gifford Market & Catering. 12 N. Main St.; (860) 592-0200; jpgifford.com. Fresh scones and muffins for breakfast, roasted poblano white-bean enchiladas and roasted butternut squash and apple bisque at lunch, and grilled salmon for dinner. J. P. Gifford has brought culinary joy for visitors to Kent looking for gourmet to go. Open Mon through Sat 7 a.m. to 7 p.m., Sun 7 a.m. to 3 p.m. $-$$.

where to stay

Inn at Kent Falls. 107 Kent Cornwall Rd.; (860) 927-3197; theinnatkentfalls.com. This polished rural retreat features a historic 1741 building, 11 country-luxe decorated rooms, and outdoor pool in a garden setting. Rates include a gourmet breakfast that includes dishes like frittata, along with fresh orange juice with homemade granola. Guests entertain themselves in the evenings by reading in the library and taking turns at the grand piano in the living room. $$$.

burlington

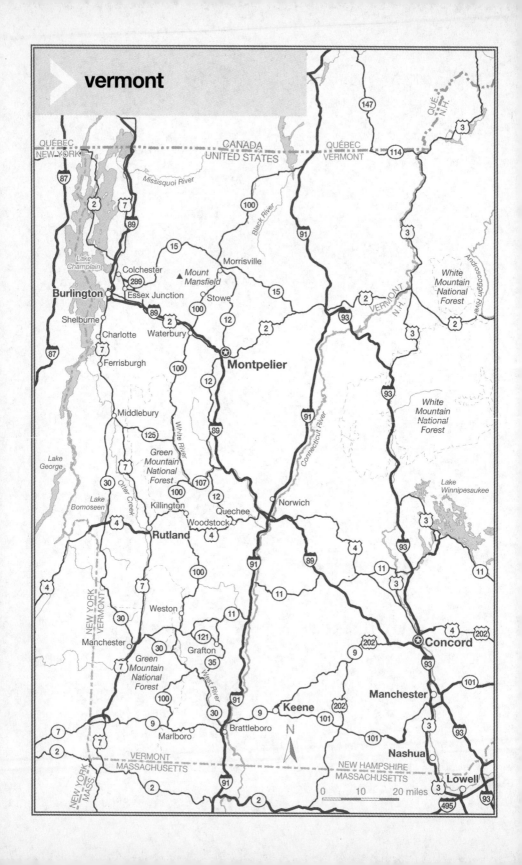

day trip 20

burlington

>>> **made-in-vermont:**
burlington, vt

burlington, vt

Head north—way north—to Burlington, Vermont's largest city. Located on the shores of Lake Champlain, Burlington is an ideal base to explore the outdoor paradise that is the Green Mountains.

With a population of 39,000, Burlington still retains a New England small-town feel and has a reputation as being one of the country's most livable cities. Burlington is also home to the University of Vermont, which gives the city a creative and youthful vibe. With its idyllic setting and thriving downtown Church Street Marketplace, the city has much to offer visitors.

For Burlington residents, as in the rest of Vermont, social responsibility and environmental awareness really are a way of life. Vermonters are particularly passionate about locally sourced food. Many restaurants proudly participate in the Vermont Fresh Network, a partnership between chefs and farmers to bring locally grown produce to the table. Another highlight of visiting the Burlington area are the many farm and factory tours of "made-in-Vermont" products.

getting there

Burlington is located at the junction of I-89, US 7, and US 2, and is an easy drive from all the New England states. The most common approach to the city is via I-89 E.

where to go

Lake Champlain Regional Chamber of Commerce. 60 Main St.; (802) 863-3489; vermont.org. Around the corner from Church Street Marketplace, pick up materials on sights, lodgings, and events. Open Mon through Fri 8:30 a.m. to 5 p.m.

Echo Lake Aquarium and Science Center. 1 College St.; (802) 864-1848; echovermont .org. Opened in 2003, this science museum is geared to young children and their families and has a Lake Champlain focus. Kids can practice being a weather reporter in front of a green screen; find out about the science behind "Champ," Vermont's mythical lake serpent; and see assorted freshwater fish and lake creatures like a 40-pound sturgeon in natural-habitat-like conditions. Open daily 10 a.m. to 5 p.m. Admission $16.50 adults, $14.50 seniors and students, $13.50 children ages 3 to 17.

Magic Hat Brewing Company. 5 Bartlett Bay Rd., South Burlington; (802) 658-2739; magichat.net. Brewery tours are always a good time. Best known for its #9 brew, Magic Hat Brewery's Artifactory is just outside Burlington in an unassuming industrial park. The self-guided tour is a 10-minute walk-through; the guided tours are a highly entertaining 30-minute spiel. Both tours cover all aspects of Magic Hat's beer production, before the welcome free samples at tour's end. Check on-line for guided tour hours and factory open times. Admission free.

***Spirit of Ethan Allen III* Lake Champlain Cruises.** 1 College St., Burlington Boathouse; (802) 862-8300; soea.com. Named for the 17th-century French explorer Samuel de Champlain, this nearly 490-square-mile freshwater body—Lake Champlain—is Burlington's crown jewel. Spend some time on the water aboard the 400-passenger *Spirit of Ethan Allen,* which offers daily narrated lunch, sunset, and scenic cruises. Season runs from May through Oct; check website for schedule. Narrated tours from $21 adults, $8.43 children ages 3 to 11.

where to shop

Church Street Marketplace. Along Church Street, from Main Street to Pearl Street; (802) 863-1648; churchstmarketplace.com. Explore the more than 100 shops, restaurants, and pushcart vendors located at this pedestrian-only open-air market in the heart of downtown Burlington. Among the notable local merchants is the artist cooperative **Frog Hollow Vermont State Craft Center** (85 Church St.; 802-863-6458; froghollow.org). **Sweet Lady Jane** (40 Church St.; 802-862-5051; sweetladyjane.biz) is a women's clothing and accessory boutique with tremendous design sense geared to the young and fashionable. **Homeport** (52 Church St.; 802-863-4644; homeportonline.com) has 3 stories of furniture, useful housewares, and gifty niceties.

where to eat

American Flatbread. 115 St. Paul St.; (802) 861-2999; americanflatbread.com. Is it pizza? It doesn't really matter. These organic, free-form wood-fired pizzas are absolutely divine. Try the Punctuated Equilibrium with kalamata olives, roasted red peppers, rosemary, and goat cheese. A dynamic selection of 10 house brews on tap keeps the local college student population coming back (and hence that maddening line). Open Mon through Fri 11:30 a.m. to 3 p.m. and 5 to 11:30 p.m.; Sat and Sun 11:30 a.m. to 11:30 p.m. $–$$.

Farmhouse Tap & Grill. 160 Bank St.; (802) 859-0888; farmhousetg.com. It's a casual-meets-refined atmosphere perfect for enjoying locally sourced gourmet burgers, Vermont cheeses, and house-made charcuteriere. One to order—the pork burger with pickled fennel and root-beer barbecue sauce, topped with a sunny-side up egg. There's a deep selection of beer—including 20 casks—as well as local and international bottles. The beer garden in the back is a Burlington warm-weather sanctuary. In the winter, regulars head to the downstairs parlor for their beer and burgers fireside. Open Mon through Thurs 11:30 a.m. to 11 p.m., Fri 11:30 a.m. to midnight, Sat 10 a.m. to midnight, Sun 10 a.m. to 11 p.m. $$.

Leunig's Bistro & Cafe. 115 Church St.; (802) 863-3759; leunigsbistro.com. Burlington's version of *le vrai français,* this classic bistro re-creates a workaday Parisian experience with luscious dishes like escargots, beef bourguignon, and roasted quail with spaetzle. Leunig's has every day early-bird and night-owl two-course prix fixe dinners that are easy on the vacation wallet. Open Mon through Thurs 11 a.m. to 10 p.m., Fri 11 a.m. to 11 p.m., Sat 9 a.m. to 11 p.m., Sun 9 a.m. to 10 p.m. $$–$$$.

Penny Cluse Cafe. 169 Cherry St.; (802) 651-8834; pennycluse.com. Bright and cheery, locals and visitors crowd into this much-loved cafe that serves breakfast all day. The gingerbread pancakes smothered with blueberries are like a warm hug, and a glass of freshly squeezed tangerine juice is a treat. Lunch choices are just as sensational, with a vegetable Reuben sandwich fit for connoisseurs and always-interesting lunch plates like homemade pork sausage with potato salad or grilled chicken with warm orzo salad. Open Mon through Fri 6:45 a.m. to 3 p.m., Sat and Sun 8 a.m. to 3 p.m. $.

Revolution Kitchen. 9 Center St.; (802) 448-3657; revolutionkitchen.com. Charmingly weird, this is where vegetarians dine in Burlington for a big night out. The menu is always changing, but always consists of dishes that are better that the usual tofu and beans: goat cheese and fig wontons with maple citrus vinaigrette, laksa noodle bowl with broccoli bok choy and carrots in a spicy coconut broth, grilled sweet potato and oyster mushrooms with sautéed kale guacamole. The large portions, beautiful presentation and fun dining room vibe have won over a following even among carnivores. Open Tues through Sat 5 to 10 p.m., closed Sun and Mon. $$.

Trattoria Delia. 152 St. Paul St.; (802) 864-5253; trattoriadelia.com. Remember that cute little trattoria you discovered on your trip to Italy? Trattoria Delia is that place with a rustic beamed grotto-like setting and earthy dishes that take particular inspiration from Calabria, where owner Thomas Delia's family is from. Standouts include the osso bucco (braised veal shanks) and the gnocchi with truffles. Open daily 5 to 10 p.m. $$–$$$.

where to stay

Courtyard by Marriott Burlington Harbor. 25 Cherry St.; (802) 864-4700; marriott.com/ hotels/travel/btvdt-courtyard-burlington-harbor. Sometimes, you just want the reliability of a full-service chain hotel. The Courtyard Burlington has a a prime location within walking distance of the Church Street Marketplace. The rooms are spacious, with large desks and free Wi-Fi, and many have views of Lake Champlain. At the end of the day, unwind at the hotel's fire pit or indoor pool and soaking tub, or hit the on-site fitness facility. The hotel's restaurant has received plenty of buzz. Bleu Northeast Seafood (802-864-8600; bleuvt.com) is a simple but quietly upscale space that focuses (unsurprisingly) regional fish and seafood. $$.

Hotel Vermont. 41 Cherry St.; (802) 651-7337; hotelvt.com. Showcasing all that is distinctive and authentic about Burlington, the Hotel Vermont has both a cosmopolitan vibe and youthful sensibility. Each of the 125 guest rooms is decorated in pale woods and clean lines; even the small details are steadfastly local, from Johnson Woolen Mills throws on the beds to the Vermont Soap Company toiletries in the bathrooms. The hotel has not one, but two first-rate farm-to-table restaurants including the second location of celebrated **Hen of the Wood** (802-540-0534; henofthewood.com). $$.

Lang House. 360 Main St.; (877) 919-9799; langhouse.com. A classic 1881 Victorian home converted to a B&B with 11 rooms (all with private bath) that are individually decorated with period antiques and nice linens. There's a gourmet breakfast worth waking up for and homemade treats in the afternoon. It's all a short walk from downtown and the University of Vermont campus. This is a rare child-friendly B&B—some rooms will accommodate cots. $$.

Made Inn Vermont. 204 S. Willard St.; (802) 399-2788; madeinnvermont. With its cupola tower and stained glass windows, this Queen Anne-style Victorian is one of the grandest houses in the Hill District neighborhood, but there is nothing frumpy about this bed and breakfast. Opened in 2012, each of the 4 consciously quirky, modern bedrooms have a wood accent wall and industrial chic pieces like platform beds, restored chandeliers and a masculine slate/cream color scheme. The common spaces include front and rear porches and two garden areas along with an all season 6-person hot tub. $$. *Note:* Each classically modern room comes with a private, keyed bathroom that is across the hall from your sleeping quarters. Rates include a gourmet Vermont breakfast, a welcome, seasonal drink and complimentary snacks throughout the day.

Willard Street Inn. 349 S. Willard St.; (802) 651-8710; willardstreetinn.com. This Victorian mansion effortlessly blends gracious 19th-century hospitality with 21st-century comforts. Period detailing gives the inn charm, and each of the inn's 14 rooms (all with private bath) is unique; one has climbing rose-trellis wallpaper, another a high lace canopy bed. Breakfast showcases Vermont ingredients and is served in the marble-floored solarium overlooking the inn's English gardens. $$.

day trip 21

burlington

down on the farm:
shelburne, vt; middlebury, vt

Nestled in the heart of the fertile Champlain Valley, visit dairy and educational center Shelburne Farms, the Vermont Wildflower Farm, and the University of Vermont Morgan Horse Farm.

shelburne, vt

Just a few miles south of Burlington along the shore of Lake Champlain, Shelburne was once a farming town but is now a Burlington bedroom community that brims with activity as the home of some of Vermont's most popular attractions including Shelburne Farms, the Shelburne Museum, and family favorite, the Vermont Teddy Bear Company.

getting there

The drive from Burlington is just 5 miles along busy US 7. This is one of Vermont's few commercial corridors with several shopping plazas and chain stores so the drive is a little slow going and will take 10 to 15 minutes.

where to go

Shelburne Farms. 1611 Harbor Rd.; (802) 985-8686; shelburnefarms.org. Created in 1886 by William Webb and Lila Vanderbilt Webb as a "gentlemen's country estate" along the shores of Lake Champlain, this 1,400-acre working farm serves as an educational

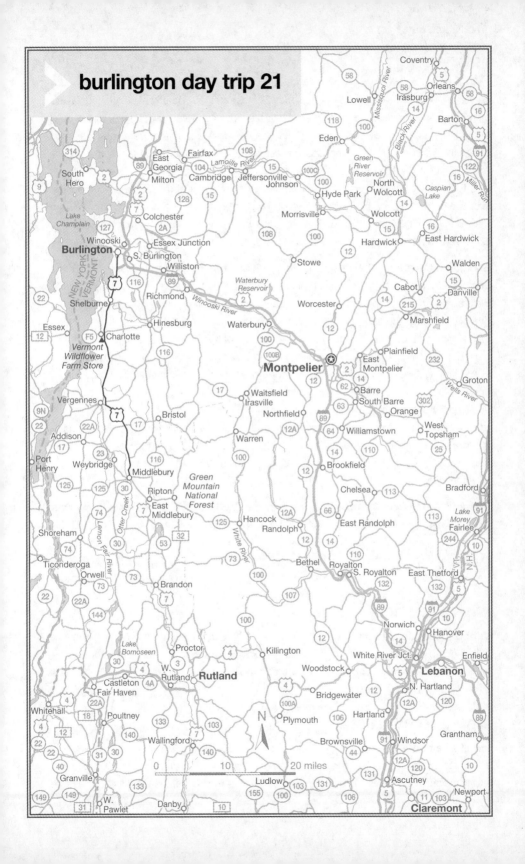

burlington day trip 21

center to promote sustainable agriculture. The farm has a children's barnyard where friendly volunteers introduce kids to farm activities; kids can help collect eggs, milk a cow, or bottle-feed a new baby animal. From the glass window in the Farm Barn you can watch Shelburne Farms' award-winning cheddar being made by hand. This is farmstead cheese made exclusively from the milk of Shelburne Farms' own herd of Brown Swiss cows. Be sure to sample and (and purchase) Shelburne Farms' cheddar at the Welcome Center. The property is crisscrossed by 8 miles of walking trails that make for a pleasant ramble. Open May through Oct 9 a.m. to 5 p.m.; Nov through Apr 10 a.m. to 4 p.m. Admission $8 adults, $6 seniors, $5 children ages 3 to 17.

Shelburne Museum. 6000 Shelburne Rd.; (802) 985-3346; shelburnemuseum.org. This is one of the country's most outstanding private collections of Americana. New York socialite Elektra Havemeyer Webb (she married William and Lila's son, James Watson Webb) was one of the first to recognize the value of American folk art and artifacts. Decoys, horse-drawn carriages, furniture, quilts, and textiles are at the core of this highly diversified collection. The museum also holds a number of paintings by American artists including works by Winslow Homer, Mary Cassatt, Grandma Moses, and Andrew Wyeth. The collection is housed in an array of 39 historical buildings, arranged as in a New England village, several of which Webb acquired from throughout the area and moved to Shelburne. Among them, a 200-year-old tavern, a one-room schoolhouse, a log cabin, and the steamship *Ticonderoga*. Not all buildings are open during the winter. Open 10 am to 5 pm daily May through Dec, Wed through Sun for Jan through Apr. Admission $24 adults, seniors $22, $14 children ages 13 to 17, $12 ages 5 to 12.

Vermont Teddy Bear Company. 6655 Shelburne Rd.; (802) 985-3001; vermontteddybear .com. This is another terrific made-in-Vermont factory tour. See how the Vermont Teddy Bear's line-up of themed (sports, holiday, and occupation) handcrafted bears are "born." Open June through mid-Sept 15, daily from 9 a.m. to 6 p.m.; mid-Sept through May, daily from 10 a.m. to 4 p.m. Admission $4 adults, $3 seniors, free for children ages 12 and under.

where to shop

Vermont Soap. 616 Exchange St.; (802) 388-4302; vermontsoap.com. Find all manner of handmade bars, shower gels, foaming hand soap, and gift sets (responsibly packaged, of course). If you like what you buy here, you can replenish your supplies online. Open Tues through Sat 10 a.m. to 4 p.m.

where to eat & stay

Inn at Shelburne Farms. 1611 Harbor Rd.; (802) 985-8498; shelburnefarms.org. Built in 1899, this country estate was the home of William Webb and Lila Vanderbilt Webb. The inn's 24 rooms and 4 cottages have an elegant, genteel charm and feature some furnishings that are original family heirlooms. All rooms feature views of either Lake Champlain or the estate's perennial gardens, and rates include continental breakfast. Tranquility reigns here; there are no TVs, central heat, or air-conditioning. But the inn does have Wi-Fi. Some rooms share a bath. But far and away, the inn's best amenity is the bucolic Shelburne Farms just outside the inn's door. The inn's restaurant serves breakfast and dinner with a menu that honors the season and features mostly produce from its own market garden. Inn and restaurant open May through Oct. Restaurant hours Mon through Sat 7:30 a.m. to 11:30 a.m. and 5:30 to 9:30 p.m.; Sun 8 a.m. to 1 p.m. and 5 to 9:30 p.m. Reservations essential. Hotel: $$$–$$$$. Restaurant: $$$.

middlebury, vt

Part of the lower Champlain Valley, nestled between the Adirondack and Green Mountains, Middlebury is a classic New England college town and home to esteemed Middlebury College. The town has a New England storybook quality to it, with the requisite town green bordered by a white steepled church and several inns along a main street lined with shops and restaurants.

getting there

It's a pleasant 45-minute drive from Shelburne along US 7 South for 27 miles to Middlebury.

where to go

Robert Frost Interpretive Trail. Trailhead on VT 125, Ripton. Poet Robert Frost summered in a simple, rustic cabin in the nearby town of Ripton for 23 years and was quite familiar with these woods. This easy 1-mile looping walking trail is an ideal introduction to the Green Mountain National Forest. His poems, "The Road Not Taken," "Pasture," and others are mounted on markers along the way, making for a most inspirational walk.

UVM Morgan Horse Farm. 74 Battell Dr., Weybridge; (802) 388-2011; uvm.edu/morgan. The sturdy Morgan horse is Vermont's state animal. The historic University of Vermont (UVM) Morgan Horse Farm, located just outside of Middlebury, has been training and breeding champion Morgan horses for more than 150 years. Guided tours include a video presentation about the history of the Morgan and an opportunity to admire the breed as you walk through the farm's impressive barns. Open daily May through Oct 9 a.m. to 4 p.m. Admission $5 per person.

where to shop

Danforth Pewter Workshop & Store. 52 Seymour St.; (802) 388-0098; danforthpewter .com. Danforth specializes in handcrafted, contemporary-styled pewter tableware and gifts.

Watch the artisans at work from the viewing window over the workshop floor. Open Mon through Sat 9:30 a.m. to 5:30 p.m., Sun 11 a.m. to 4 p.m.

Edgewater Gallery. 1 Mill St; (802) 458-0098; edgewatergallery-vt.com. For generations, the tradition of craftsmanship has drawn a large number of artists to Vermont. The showroom displays the work of regional craftspeople and includes paintings, pottery, jewelry, weaving, sculpture, and furniture at several price levels. Open Mon through Sat 11 a.m. to 5 p.m., Sun 11 a.m. to 4 p.m.

where to eat

Storm Cafe. 3 Mill St.; (802) 388-1063; thestormcafe.com. With a view of Otter Creek Falls, this cafe offers quick service for lunch that features soups, salads, and sandwiches. If it's on offer, be sure to order the roasted garlic and potato soup. Dinner is a more leisurely experience, with entrees like pan-seared chicken breast with braised leeks and butternut squash. This is a Middlebury College student favorite when Mom and Dad are paying. Tues through Sun 9 a.m. to 2:30 p.m. and 5 to 9 p.m. closed Mon. $$.

where to stay

Inn on the Green. 71 S. Pleasant St.; (802) 388-7512; innonthegreen.com. At the very heart of things in Middlebury, the 11 rooms of the 1803 Federal-style home and next-door carriage house have wide-plank hardwood floors with braided rugs, quilt-covered beds, and comfortable reading chairs. A continental breakfast with fruit and yogurt is included in all rates and delivered to your room each morning. $$–$$$.

worth more time

Midway between Burlington and Middlebury, the **Vermont Wildflower Farm**'s beautifully landscaped 6-acre trial gardens showcase the products of the mail-order seed catalog merchant. There's a large nursery and a garden store that stocks plants, bulbs, seeds, and garden-related gifts. 3488 Ethan Allen Hwy., Charlotte; (802) 425-3641; vermontwildflower-farm.com. Open daily 10 a.m. to 5 p.m.

day trip 22

burlington

> **powered by ice cream—**
> **from foothills to mountain peaks:**
> waterbury, vt; montpelier, vt; stowe, vt

A visit to Vermont is incomplete without a tour of the Ben & Jerry's ice cream factory in Waterbury. Poke around friendly Montpelier and experience year-round mountain fun around Mount Mansfield in the upscale ski community of Stowe.

waterbury, vt

Most visitors are passing through Waterbury to visit the Ben & Jerry's mothership, but several other food-related retailers have set up shop along VT 100 and are well worth a stop for shopping and sampling.

getting there

From Burlington, merge onto I-89 South toward Montpelier and follow for 24 miles. Take exit 10 to merge onto VT 100, which is also known as Waterbury-Stowe Road.

where to go

Ben & Jerry's Ice Cream. 1281 Waterbury-Stowe Rd.; (802) 882-2047; benjerry.com. Direct from the cow to you. This is easily the state's most visited tourist attraction. The 30-minute tours of Ben & Jerry's factory headquarters start with a video of the company's humble beginnings by founders Ben Cohen and Jerry Greenfield, followed with a walk-by along a glass-enclosed catwalk of the production facilities, and end with a generous sample

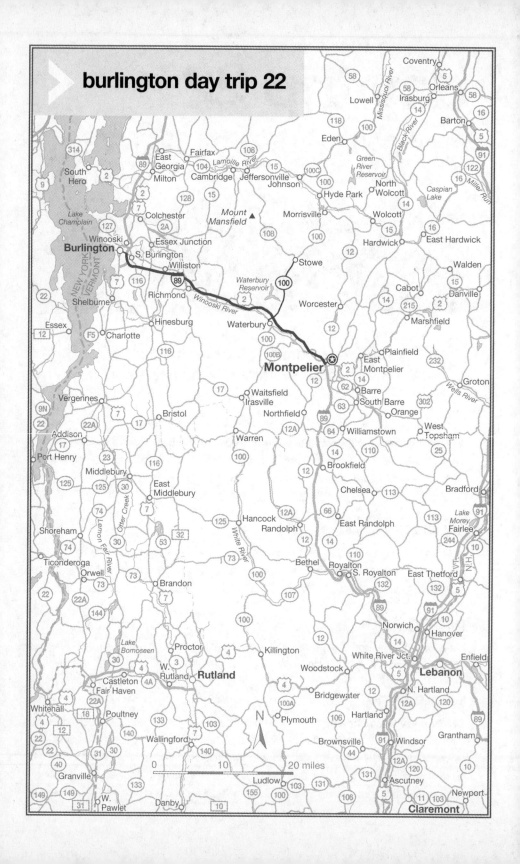

of the flavor of the day. Open daily year-round, check website for details. Admission $4 adults, $3 seniors, free for children ages 12 and under.

The Blue Stone. 15 Stowe St.; (802) 882-8185; bluestonepizza.com. This farmhouse industrial-chic space is trendy but unpretentious and always busy with groups of families and friends munching on thin-crust artisan pizza and dressed-up comfort food. There's also a huge selection of local beers on tap. Open daily 11:30 a.m. to close. $.

where to shop

Cabot Cheese Annex. 2657 Waterbury-Stowe Rd.; (802) 244-6334; cabotcheese.coop. You can't come to Vermont without taking home some cheese. Cabot Creamery is one of the state's largest dairy cooperatives. This Cabot company store is not only stocked with every type of the company's award-winning cheddar but also has cured meats, handmade jams, and interesting crackers. Open daily 9 a.m. to 6 p.m.

Cold Hollow Cider Mill. 3600 Waterbury-Stowe Rd.; (800) 327-7537; coldhollow.com. During the course of the year Cold Hollow uses 6 million pounds of apples to make its award-winning cider. You can watch the fresh-pressed cider being made year-round from the viewing room. Cider Hollow also makes amazing cider doughnuts—as many as 16,000 doughnuts per day during the weekends of the fall foliage season. The mega barn-size farm stand is stocked full of other Vermont-made products, including maple syrup, cheese, and other gourmet goodies. Excellent soups and salads augment an inventive menu of sandwiches made with local artisanal ingredients on warm home-made bread. The lemon tarragon chicken salad pairs perfectly with the mill's hard cider, Barn Dance. Open daily June through Aug 8 a.m. to 7 p.m., Sept through May 8 a.m. to 6 p.m.

Green Mountain Coffee Cafe & Visitor Center. 1 Rotarian Place; (877) 879-2325; waterburystation.com. Headquartered in Waterbury, Green Mountain Coffee is one of Vermont's largest employers. The manufacturer of the popular Keurig brand of coffee machines and specialty coffee roaster maintains a visitor center in the restored historic Waterbury train station. The visitor center is worth a stop to sample coffee and learn about Green Mountain's roasting process. The cafe features a full line of Green Mountain coffee products as well as a selection of pastries and sandwiches. Open Mon through Fri 7 a.m. to 5 p.m., Sat and Sun 8 a.m. to 5 p.m.

where to eat

Hen of the Wood. 92 Stowe St.; (802) 244-7300; henofthewood.com. In a historic gristmill next to a stream, Hen of the Wood is a romantic destination restaurant worth the trek. The dining room is rustic chic with exposed beams, centuries-old stone walls, and flickering candles. The season is very much part of the dining experience, and chef Eric Warnstedt rewrites the menu daily depending on what he has nabbed from area farms and markets, but his signature Hen of the Woods Mushroom Tartine is always on the menu and is a must-order. The restaurant stands apart, too, for its attentive and professional service, not common in ski country. Open Tues through Sat 5 to 9 p.m. Reservations essential. $$$–$$$$.

montpelier, vt

Located in a picturesque valley beside the Winooski River, Montpelier—with a population of around just 8,000—is by far the country's smallest state capital. Montpelier is a friendly town with a quiet "busyness" as state workers go about their day and is home to the well-regarded New England Culinary Institute. Stop here to visit the Vermont capitol building, the Vermont Museum, and experience some excellent dining.

getting there

Take I-89 South for 10 miles toward Montpelier. Take exit 8 for US 2 and downtown Montpelier.

where to go

Vermont Museum. 109 State St.; (802) 828-2291; vermonthistory.org. Located next to the State House, the Vermont Historical Society presents its award-winning multimedia exhibit Freedom & Unity, which chronicles 250-plus years of Vermont state history. Highlights include a full-scale model of a native Abenaki wigwam, exhibits about Ethan Allen and the Green Mountain Boys, and a re-created World War II–era living room. Open Tues through Sat 10 a.m. to 4 p.m. Admission $5 adults, $3 seniors, students, and children ages 6 to 17.

Vermont State House. 115 State St.; (802) 828-2228; vtstatehouse.org. The foothills of the Green Mountains provide an idyllic backdrop for the bright gold dome of the Vermont State House. Built in 1859, this is Vermont's third state house building on this site, yet it is still one of the country's oldest and best-preserved capitol buildings. Guided tours July through Oct, Mon through Fri 10 a.m. to 3:30 p.m., Sat 11 a.m. to 2:30 p.m.; Nov through June Mon through Fri 9 a.m. to 3 p.m. Admission free.

where to eat

La Brioche. 89 Main St.; (802) 229-0443; neci.edu/labrioche. A teaching laboratory for students of the New England Culinary Institute, this airy, casual all-day spot serves not only artisan-style breads, croissants, and scones but a full lunch menu of soups, salads, and sandwiches. Open Mon through Fri 7 a.m. to 6 p.m., Sat 7 a.m. to 3 p.m., closed Sun. $.

New England Culinary Institute on Main. 118 Main St.; (802) 223-3188; neci.edu/neci-on-main. This is a student kitchen for the New England Culinary Institute. Under the watchful eyes of their chef-instructors, students practice what they have learned in the classroom. You'll feast on some very sophisticated dishes, like cassoulet with duck confit and passion

vermont's rabble rouser

Leader of the settlers' militia eventually known as the Green Mountain Boys, Revolutionary War hero who captured Fort Ticonderoga from the British, and one of the state's founders—Vermonters sure are proud of Ethan Allen. The folk hero invokes the spirit of independence in keeping with the reputation of state residents as unconventional freethinkers. Vermonters also revel in their history as a separate state: the Republic of Vermont existed for 14 years before joining the Union as the 14th state in 1791.

fruit soufflé, while paying far less than elsewhere. Open Tues through Sat 11:30 a.m. to 9 p.m., Sunday brunch buffet 10 a.m. to 2 p.m., closed Sun and Mon. $$.

Skinny Pancake. 89 Main St.; (802) 262-2253; skinnypancake.com. The Skinny Pancake is a local creperie chain that specializes in fun, messy concoctions like the Lumberjack with ham, cheddar, and sliced apples. It's a tasty and inexpensive dining option—and still totally locally sourced. Open Sun through Thurs 8 a.m. to 8 p.m., Fri and Sat 8 a.m. to 9 p.m. $.

Three Penny Taproom. 108 Main St.; (802) 223-8277; threepennytaproom.com. Three Penny Taproom is often packed thanks to its laid back atmosphere and a menu that includes small plates, shareable, tasty sides, and home-style mains. Offerings include cod croquettes with squid ink aioli, roasted harissa peanuts, chili cheese fries, a ploughman's board and grilled cheese with white bean soup. They offer more than 20 beers on tap and virtually all are from Vermont. So it's no surprise that this is a local favorite for a casual dinner or an early drink. Kitchen open Mon through Thurs 11 a.m. to 9 p.m., Fri 11 a.m. to 10 p.m., Sat noon to 10 p.m., Sun 11 a.m. to 4 p.m. Bar open later. $.

where to stay

Inn at Montpelier. 147 Main St.; (802) 223-2727; innatmontpelier.com. Within walking distance of everything that Montpelier has to offer, the 19 rooms at this inn are comfortable affairs decorated in cozy New England style. The wide wraparound front porch has wicker furniture and is just right for enjoying a book and watching passersby. All rates include an expanded continental breakfast featuring breakfast breads from La Brioche (see above). $$.

stowe, vt

Bring your sense of adventure to Stowe. Home to Mount Mansfield, Vermont's highest peak, Stowe is an all-season outdoor playground with the world class Stowe Mountain Resort serving as a base for skiing and snowboarding in winter, and hiking, biking, and family-fun activities during the non-ski season. The village of Stowe is one of the East Coast's more lively ski towns. It's busy year-round and packed with shops, restaurants, and a mix of quaint inns and high-end lodging.

getting there

Head back toward Burlington along I-89 North for 11 miles. Take exit 10 to VT 100 North and follow for 10 miles to Stowe. In the village, Mountain Road is the main drag, and during the winter ski season, the summer months, and the fall foliage season, expect traffic congestion and slow going.

where to go

Stowe Area Association. 51 Main St.; (802) 253-7321; gostowe.com. Located in the center of Stowe village, this is where you want to come if you arrive in town without a reservation. Open Mon through Sat 9 a.m. to 5 p.m., Sun 11 a.m. to 5 p.m. during ski season, Mon through Sat 9 a.m. to 9 p.m., Sun 11 a.m. to 9 p.m. during the summer.

Stowe Mountain Resort. 5781 Mountain Rd.; (802) 253-3000; stowe.com. Stowe is known as the "ski capital of the East" in part because of this resort's unmatched ability to provide a ski experience that caters to every level of skier. Stowe features 116 trails with nearly 60 percent of the runs rated as intermediate; its nearly 4-mile-long and gentle Toll Road is extremely popular. Beginners have a dedicated mountain, Spruce Peak, just for them. And Stowe is a terrific mountain for riders. The resort has a strong relationship with Burton, the Vermont-based snowboard manufacturer, and has 5 terrain parks. There's snowmaking coverage on 80 percent of the mountain, which allows the resort a long snow season, typically beginning in mid-November and often lasting until late April.

The resort hosts a myriad of activities after the winter. You can ride a gondola to Mount Mansfield's summit or ride the alpine slide to the bottom, take in majestic views from the golf course, or drive the 4.5-mile Mount Mansfield Auto Toll Road. Resort types will love Stowe's base facilities with several restaurants and bars. There are 2 slope-side hotel options, the luxury Stowe Mountain Lodge and the more modest Inn at Stowe Mountain. Looking for some action? The resort's newly opened Spruce Peak Performing Arts Center offers nightlife diversions year-round.

Stowe Recreation Path. This 5.5-mile greenway through Stowe village is the perfect setting for biking, jogging, or a walk. In the winter, the trail is used for cross-country skiing. The trail parallels Mountain Road, meandering through woods and fields and crossing 11 small bridges along the West Branch River.

Vermont Ski and Snowboard Museum. 1 S. Main St.; (802) 253-9911; vtssm.org. Located in Stowe's 1818 Old Town Hall, the exhibits in this small museum detail the history of downhill skiing, snowboarding, and Nordic (cross-country) skiing in Vermont with artifacts and memorabilia. Open Wed through Sun noon to 5 p.m., closed Mon and Tues.

where to shop

Umiak Outdoor Outfitters. 849 S. Main St.; (802) 253-2317; umiak.com. From alpine and cross-country skis to canoe and kayak rentals, Umiak can set you up. Umiak also runs a full range of guided trips including moonlit family snowshoe tours, dog-sledding adventures, and paddling. Open daily 9 a.m. to 6 p.m.

where to eat

McCarthy's Restaurant. 454 Mountain Rd.; (802) 253-8626; mccarthysrestaurant.com. If you believe that breakfast is the most important meal of the day, then this is the spot for you. The bargain-priced breakfast menu highlights dishes like eggs any style with bacon, home fries and hash, or honey oat French toast with Vermont maple syrup. Burgers and a range of tasty sandwiches lead at lunch. Cash only. Open daily 6 a.m. to 2 p.m. $.

Plate. 91 Main St.; (802) 253-2691; platestowe.com. The menu here is influenced by California—husband and wife owners Mark Rosman and Jamie Persky are natives of Los Angeles—and sourced from Vermont. The menu changes frequently but standouts include cheddar soufflé with maple-bourbon cream, a bourbon-brined pork chop and the must-order banana pudding served in a Mason jar. Open Sun, Wed and Thurs 5 to 9 p.m., closed Mon and Tues. $$.

Trattoria La Festa. 4080 Mountain Rd.; (802) 253-8480; trattoriastowe.com. This is an unpretentious place for good Italian food and wine, and, unlike most of the restaurants in Stowe, it has a pedigree as the Devito family has been part of the Stowe dining scene since 1986. The restaurant is popular with hungry skiers after a day on the slopes for its generous portions of well-executed Italian staples—pillowy gnocchi with a hearty meat sauce, fall-apart tender osso buco, and an impossibly rich baked manicotti. Open Mon through Sat 5 to 9 p.m. $$.

where to stay

Golden Eagle Resort. 511 Mountain Rd.; (802) 253-4811; goldeneagleresort.com. Not fancy but more than adequate for an affordable mountain resort vacation, Golden Eagle's accommodations range from standard guest rooms to 1- and 2-bedroom suites with a kitchen and fireplace. The rooms are motel-like, but generally spacious and have been recently refreshed with a color palette of taupe, brown and cream, new carpeting and furniture.The hotel has both an indoor and outdoor pool as well as a sauna and hot tub. Families will be happy to know that there is a game room and playground on the premises. The hotel enjoys proximity to the Stowe Recreation Path. Nice touch: complimentary tea and cookies in the afternoon. $$.

Green Mountain Inn. 18 Main St.; (800) 253-7302; greenmountaininn.com. Located in the heart of Stowe village and close to shops and galleries, the accommodations in this inviting 100-room inn feature canopy beds with country quilts and wingback reading chairs; some rooms have fireplaces and whirlpool tubs. The inn's fitness and sauna areas and outdoor pool have all been recently updated. And the on-site Whip Bar & Grill is one of Stowe's most popular gathering spots. And all for very un-Stowe-like rates. $$–$$$.

Trapp Family Lodge. 700 Trapp Hill Rd.; (802) 253-8511; trappfamily.com. The story of the Von Trapp family was immortalized in the 1965 movie *The Sound of Music*. The Von Trapps settled in Vermont in the 1940s and opened their Stowe lodge in 1950. Now a 2,400-acre complex that includes a 96-room hotel and 100 stand-alone chalets, the resort is managed by Maria and the Captain's youngest son, Johannes, and is a Vermont tourist attraction in its own right. Guest rooms vary in size but are all decorated in a cheery Alpine style and many have grand mountain views. It would take several days to exhaust all the resort activities; in the winter there is an excellent cross-country facility and horse-drawn sleigh rides. In summer, enjoy the 2 outdoor swimming pools, tennis courts, and the Trapp concert series in the meadow. Year-round there is an indoor pool, a fitness center, and a popular history tour of the property. There are four dining options at the resort including the brand-new post and beam Bierhall, which features ales and lagers from the Von Trapp on-site brewery and traditional Austrian fare like pretzels and bratwurst and schnitzel. It's an airy, modern, industrial like space with long communal tables along with an outdoor patio overlooking a pond and a view of Mount Mansfield. It's all very gemutlich $$$.

day trip 23

burlington

mountain hamlets:
norwich, vt; quechee, vt; woodstock, vt; killington, vt

Find natural beauty in the covered bridges, tidy town greens, and waterfalls that are scattered across the landscape. Hiking, biking, and ski opportunities abound at Killington. Special to this area are the Simon Pearce artisan glass and pottery factory in Quechee and the King Arthur Flour Baker's Store in Norwich. Central Vermont is a fair distance from Burlington, about a 1.5-hour drive. But all four towns are close to each other and can really be visited in any order.

norwich, vt

Yet another charming Vermont village, Norwich is the sister "city" to the better-known town of Hanover, New Hampshire—home to Dartmouth College—just a mile away across the Connecticut River. Don't be limited by state borders; there are places to visit in both towns.

getting there

From Burlington merge onto I-89 South for about 88 miles to White River Junction. Take I-91 North for 5 miles to Norwich.

where to go

Hood Museum. Wheeler Street, Dartmouth College, Hanover, NH; (603) 646-2808; hood museum.dartmouth.edu. Housed in an award-winning, post-modern redbrick building near

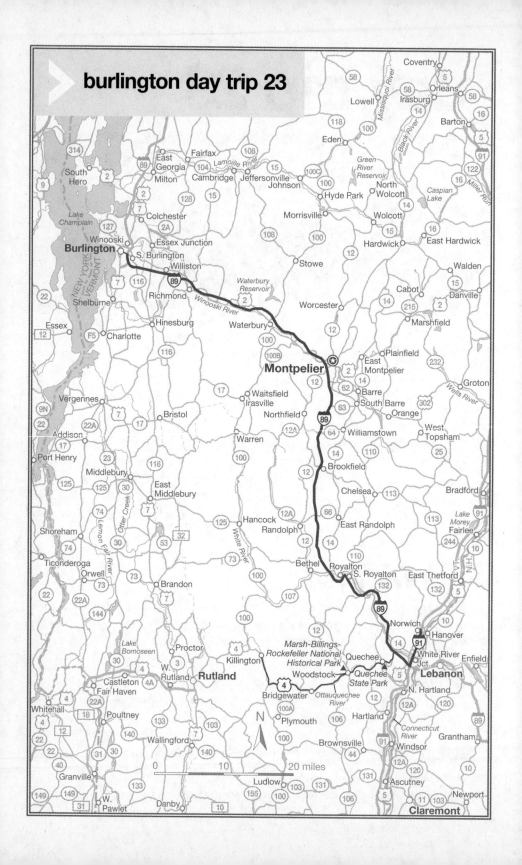

burlington day trip 23

Dartmouth's green, this is one of the country's oldest and largest college museums. It is a wide-ranging collection that boasts outstanding exhibits of American paintings and decorative arts, European old masters paintings, and ancient African and Native American art. The museum is currently closed for a major restoration and expansion and is scheduled to reopen in the fall of 2019—just in time for Dartmouth's 250th anniversary. While construction is underway, Dartmouth has leased gallery space, at 53 Main Street and dubbed it *Hood Downtown.* The gallery is free and open to the public and will feature an ongoing series of exhibits with a focus on contemporary art: paintings, photographs and video. Open Wed through Sat 11 a.m. to 7 p.m., Sun 1 to 5 p.m. Free admission.

Montshire Museum of Science. 1 Montshire Rd.; (802) 649-2200; montshire.org. With two floors of hands-on, interactive science and nature exhibits, there's plenty here to keep the kids occupied for several hours. Be sure to venture outside—the museum's walking trails and parklike setting are a big part of the visitor experience. In the summer, the museum's outdoor water park lets kids splash about and get wet while learning about water pressure and flow. (Hit the water park last, though; otherwise you'll have a hard time getting your kids to go inside the museum!) Open daily 10 a.m. to 5 p.m. Admission $17 adults, $14 children ages 2 to 17.

where to shop

King Arthur Flour Baker's Store. 135 US 5 South; (802) 649-3361; kingarthurflour.com. In the home baking world, King Arthur Flour is the serious baker's favorite flour brand and a trusted resource. Founded in 1790, this is the company's flagship store and a mecca for baking enthusiasts who come to shop for the ingredients and top-quality baking equipment featured in the company's popular Baker's Catalogue. The store also houses a demonstration kitchen and an education center that offers classes to the general public. There's a cafe on-site, too, serving sandwiches on artisan-made bread and as you would expect, really good cakes and pastries. Open daily 7:30 a.m. to 6 p.m.

where to eat & stay

Norwich Inn. 325 Main St.; (802) 649-1143; norwichinn.com. Less than 2 miles from Dartmouth's campus, the Norwich Inn has recently expanded and now has a total of 39 rooms divided among the historic 1890 main inn and two new buildings behind the property. Accommodations in the main inn are cozy Victorian in style, those in the new Walker House and Ivy Lodge have an updated but traditional feel, and all feature expanded bathrooms and gas fireplaces. The hotel has an all-day dining room and a microbrewery, Jasper Murdock's Alehouse, that is a convenient spot for light lunch fare and dinner. Hotel: $$–$$$. Restaurant: $$.

quechee, vt

Quechee, pronounced "QUEE-chee," is best known for its scenic gorge and for the Simon Pearce glassblowing, retail, and restaurant facility in a converted mill building over the falls.

getting there

From Norwich drive on I-91 South for 5 miles. Take the exit onto I-89 North for 3 miles and then take exit 1 for US 4, also known as Woodstock Road. Follow US 4 West for 2 miles to Quechee.

where to go

Quechee Gorge State Park. Along US 4 (Woodstock Road). Be awed by the sheer power of this 165-foot chasm—Vermont's deepest and longest river gorge. There's a breathtaking view of the Ottauquechee River as it rushes and roars toward White River Junction 4 miles downstream, where it joins the Connecticut River. You can park at the gift shop on US 4; the trailhead sign is just beyond. Nearby the worn path parallels the gorge and has several overlooks perfect for picture taking.

where to shop

Simon Pearce. 1760 Quechee Main St.; (802) 295-2711; simonpearce.com. Simon Pearce is well known for its gorgeous handblown glass and handmade pottery. At this factory store you can watch the artisans at work, visit the large retail showroom, and stop for lunch or dinner at the fine dining restaurant. The entire complex is powered by hydroelectric power, so be sure to check out the power plant in the building's basement. Open daily 10 a.m. to 9 p.m.

where to eat

The Mill at Simon Pearce. 1760 Quechee Main St.; (802) 295-1470; simonpearce.com. Overlooking the Quechee falls, dining at Simon Pearce rates as one of Vermont's most memorable vacation experiences. Ask for (and wait if you must) for a table on the porch. The cuisine is creative contemporary American. For lunch the soups are particularly worth mentioning; both the cheddar and carrot-ginger soup are standouts. At dinner, the horseradish-crusted cod with crispy leeks is the dish to order. If you didn't reserve a table in the dining room, you can grab a meal and drink at the new bar, which features inventive small plates like steamed barbecue pork buns and crispy duck confit with lentils and pancetta—not a bad plan B. Open Mon through Sat 11:30 a.m. to 2:45 p.m. and 5:30 to 9 p.m.; Sun 10:30 to 2:45 p.m. and 5:30 to 9 p.m., bar open daily 11 a.m. to 10 p.m. $$–$$$.

woodstock, vt

The stately Woodstock Inn & Resort is centered on the village green, and nearby a covered bridge spans the Ottauquechee River that flows through town. Woodstock is Vermont as you imagine it—nostalgically quaint—but with an old-money air.

getting there

The road to and from Quechee and Woodstock is well traveled. From Quechee take US 4 West (Woodstock Road) for 6 miles to Woodstock center. In normal traffic it's a 15-minute drive.

where to go

Woodstock Welcome Center. Mechanic Street; (802) 432-1100; woodstockvt.com. This welcome center is staffed Mon through Fri 9 a.m. to 5 p.m.

Billings Farm & Museum. VT 12 and River Road; (802) 457-2355; billingsfarm.org. Founded in 1871 by Vermont lawyer and railroad magnate Frederick Billings and now an educational working farm, you can learn about Vermont dairying and see farm work first-hand. Explore the horse barn, milk room, calf nursery, and dairy barn with Jersey cows (watch your step!). Visit the property's original 1890 farmhouse, which served as a home to the farm manager and his family; the farm office; and creamery. In a series of connected barns, the Vermont Farm Life exhibits showcase the region's rural heritage with displays and artifacts related to ice cutting, maple sugaring, milking, haying, and more. Open Apr through Oct daily 10 a.m. to 5 p.m., Nov through Feb Sat and Sun 10 a.m. to 4 p.m. Admission $14 adults, $13 seniors, $9 students, $8 ages 5 to 15, $4 ages 3 to 4.

Marsh-Billings-Rockefeller National Historical Park. 54 Elm St.; (802) 457-3368; nps .gov/mabi. In the shadow of Mount Tom, one of the country's first managed forests, this park is named for the three influential families that once owned this land. The property, along with its Queen Anne–style mansion house, was donated to the National Park Service by Laurence and Mary Rockefeller (a granddaughter of Frederick Billings), and it is Vermont's only national park. The 550 acres of majestic forest feature miles of carriage roads that make for an easy (2-hour) walk to reach the Pogue, a man-made pond near the mountain's summit. The mansion is open for ranger-led tours Memorial Day weekend through Oct daily 10 a.m. to 5 p.m.; park grounds open daily year-round, dawn to dusk.

where to shop

F. H. Gillingham & Sons. 16 Elm St.; (802) 457-2100; gillinghams.com. Located in the center of Woodstock and a local institution for more than 125 years, this emporium of practical and hard-to-find goods really does have something for everyone: oil lanterns, ukuleles,

Vermont specialty foods, books, groceries, and a dizzying array of gadgets. Open Mon through Sat 8:30 a.m. to 6:30 p.m., Sun 10 a.m. to 5 p.m.

Woodstock Farmers' Market. 979 W. Woodstock Rd.; (800) 344-6668; woodstockfarmers market.com. Woodstock's cherished farm stand is a spacious and inviting place to shop for a well-curated selection of meats, cheeses, chocolates, and more, all produced in the region. Its prepared-food department features excellent picnic victuals, including 26 different kinds of specialty sandwiches and a first-rate beer and wine department. Open Tues through Sat 7:30 a.m. to 7 p.m., Sun 8 a.m. to 6 p.m., closed Mon.

where to eat

Mountain Creamery. 33 Central St.; (802) 457-1715; mountaincreameryvt.com. This is the spot in Woodstock for down-home goodness. From the breakfast menu, the omelet with cheddar cheese, sausage, and apples is exceptional. Lunch dishes include items like pulled pork sandwiches, tuna melts, or a chef's salad. You just may want to come back later for the Creamery's homemade ice cream. Ice cream by the scoop is available at the take-out shop downstairs throughout the day and into the evening. Cafe is open daily 7 a.m. to 3 p.m.; ice-cream shop open seasonally Mon through Fri 8:30 a.m. to 5 p.m., Sat and Sun 8:30 a.m. to 10 p.m. Cash only. $.

Worthy Kitchen. 442 Woodstock Rd.; (802) 457-7281; worthyvermont.com. People come here for the burgers and the welcoming, community vibe, but just about everything on the menu pleases, including the farm-fresh salads and a beer list that features small operation Vermont brewers. Open Mon through Thurs 4 to 9 p.m., Fri 4 to 10 p.m., Sat 11:30 a.m. to 10 p.m., Sun 11:30 a.m. to 9 p.m. $$.

Prince & the Pauper. 24 Elm St.; (802) 457-1818; princeandpauper.com. Settle in to enjoy a dining experience where the prix-fixe menu reflects all the goodness that a cozy bistro should offer: goat cheese soufflé, rack of lamb with a bordelaise sauce, and almond pear tart, as well as a nontraditional surprise or two. There's also a casual bar menu with wood-fired pizza, crab cakes, and the like available in the lounge. Open daily 5:30 to 9 p.m. Lounge opens at 5 p.m. $$.

where to stay

Kedron Valley Inn. 4778 South Rd., South Woodstock; (802) 457-1473; kedronvalley inn.com. Located on 15 idyllic acres of field and woods just outside of Woodstock, this 25-room inn charms with fireplaces in nearly every guest room. Reasonably priced room rates include breakfast. The inn's intimate candle-lit tavern/dining room serves New England fare with only the freshest of ingredients. $$.

Woodstock Inn & Resort. 14 The Green; (802) 332-6853; woodstockinn.com. Located on Woodstock's village green, surely one of the loveliest spots in all of Vermont, the Woodstock Inn is an ideal getaway with 142 rooms that spoil guests with upscale New England country-house decor that has been reinvigorated with updated furnishings and a historic blue/green palette that incorporates pops of fresh color. The inn's common areas are impressive; the lobby features a massive 6-foot fieldstone fireplace and original Vermont artwork. On-site there is an outdoor pool, a luxurious spa, and several excellent restaurants, including the acclaimed Red Rooster. Down the road, enjoy the resort's golf, tennis, and a fitness club with an indoor pool. $$$–$$$$.

killington, vt

Without a defined village center, Killington Resort and the town are really one and the same. Killington is an especially popular mountain for serious skiers and riders. And like many New England ski resorts, winter segues to late spring and summer golf activities while in the autumn the resort's K-1 gondola ride takes leaf-peepers to the summit for a sweeping view of the Green Mountain National Forest.

getting there

From Woodstock, take US 4 West for 17 miles to Killington. You can save some driving time on the return trip to Burlington by taking VT 100 North and then VT 107 East to pick up I-89 North.

where to go

Killington Resort. 4763 Killington Rd.; (802) 422-6200; killington.com. Killington is Vermont's largest ski resort built across 6 mountain summits with a network of 150 downhill skiing trails that are serviced by more than 20 chairlifts, and 2 high-speed gondolas—so there is hardly ever a wait to get to the top. With the resort's golf course, biking, and hiking trails, Killington attracts active vacationers year-round. There's much to enjoy at the Killington Grand resort—slopeside ski access, a heated outdoor pool and hot tub, and 200 guest rooms (all still shining after a recent refresh).

manchester

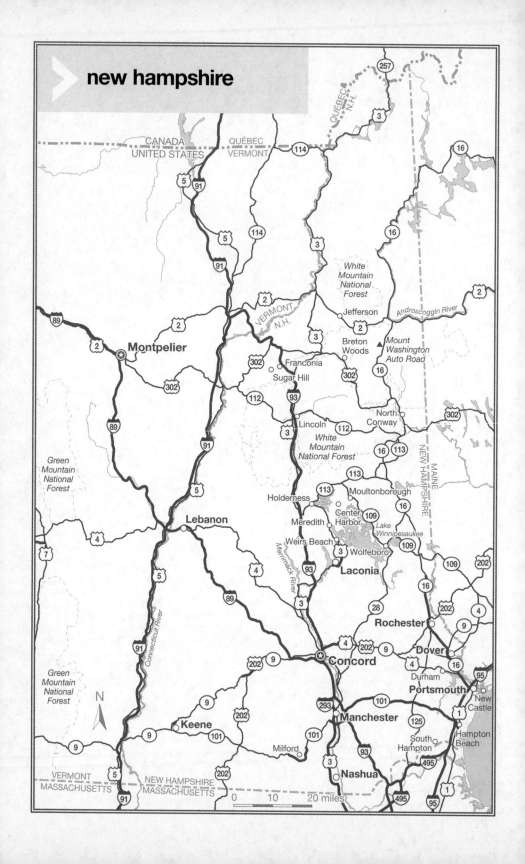

day trip 24

manchester

>>> **the queen city:**
manchester, nh

manchester, nh

Located along the Merrimack River, Manchester—with 109,000 residents—is northern New England's largest city. Its sturdy mill buildings are reminders of Manchester's past as one of the world's largest producers of textiles. Over the years, Manchester has retooled itself as the state's business and commerce center, and the old mill buildings have been converted to offices, shops, restaurants, and museums—most notably the Currier Museum of Art. Just an hour from both New Hampshire's seacoast and the Lakes Region, Manchester is a convenient base to explore the area.

getting there

Manchester is located at the junction of several highways. From the south, follow I-93 North; from the north, I-93 South will bring you into the city. From the east or west, follow NH 101 to Manchester. Once near the city, I-293 parallels the Merrimack River and will bring you to downtown.

where to go

Greater Manchester Chamber of Commerce. 54 Hanover St.; (603) 666-6660; manchester-chamber.org. Staffed by trained volunteers this walk-in center has maps, brochures, and an excellent city magazine. Open Mon through Thurs 8:30 a.m. to 5 p.m., Fri 8:30 a.m. to 4 p.m.

Currier Museum of Art. 150 Ash St.; (603) 669-6144; currier.org. The Currier Museum of Art is a regional gem. A recent expansion has added new gallery space to the original 1929 building and spectacularly showcases the museum's world-class collection of European and American paintings, decorative arts, and sculpture. Highlights include paintings by 18th- and 19th-century American artists as well as works by Monet, Matisse, and Picasso. Unique to the Currier is its extensive paperweight collection. The Currier also owns the Zimmerman House, the only Frank Lloyd Wright residence open for public tours in New England. The house is open by guided tour only (you'll be driven to the house by van), and reservations are required in advance. Open Sun, Mon, and Wed through Fri 11 a.m. to 5 p.m.; Sat 10 a.m. to 5 p.m., closed Tues. Admission $15 adults, $13 seniors, $10 students, $5 children ages 13 to 17, free ages 12 and under. Admission with Zimmerman House Tour, $20 adults, $19 seniors, $16 students, $8 ages 7 to 17.

Millyard Museum. 200 Bedford St., Mill No. 3; (603) 622-7531; manchesterhistoric.org. Located in one of the former buildings of the Amoskeag Mills, the Millyard Museum's principal exhibit, Woven-in Time: 11,000 years at Amoskeag Falls, tells the story of the Manchester area from the days when Native Americans fished along the river to the area's early American farming communities to the role of the Amoskeag Mills in making Manchester an industrial powerhouse. Open Tues through Sat 10 a.m. to 4 p.m. Admission $8 adults, $6 seniors and students, $4 ages 12 to 18, free for children ages 11 and under.

where to eat

Hooked. 110 Hanover St.; (603) 606-1189; hookednh.com. A sophisticated seafooder where the decor has a subtle nautical theme and the menu delivers fresh and clever New American seafood dishes like calamari with a cayenne aioli, tarragon sea scallops, and haddock piccata. Open Mon through Wed 4 to 9 p.m., Thurs 11 a.m. to 9 p.m., Fri 11 a.m. to 10 p.m., Sat 4 to 10 p.m., closed Sun. $$.

Lala's Hungarian Pastry. 836 Elm St.; (603) 647-7100. A family-run restaurant that treats you like one of its own while tempting you with painstakingly prepared Hungarian home cooking like stuffed cabbage, beef goulash, and sour cherry soup. Whatever you order, save room for dessert and order the eight-layer Dobos torte. Open Mon and Tues 7 a.m. to 5 p.m., Wed through Sat 7 a.m. to 8 p.m., closed Sun. $–$$.

Red Arrow Diner. 61 Lowell St.; (603) 626-1118; redarrowdiner.com. Dating from 1922, this old-time diner is a popular stop for presidential hopefuls during the primary season and is a favorite haunt of Manchester-native Adam Sandler. It's a small place but with an enormous menu that features breakfast all day, sandwiches and burgers at lunch, and dinner blue-plate specials that are pure comfort food: chicken potpie, mac and cheese with ham steak, and lasagna to name a few. The homemade pies—including the brownie cream pie—are a point of pride. Open 24 hours. $.

Republic Cafe. 1069 Elm St.; (603) 666-3723; republiccafe.com. For all occasions, Republic Cafe is a great destination where locals and visitors gather for an approachable menu of European-style fare. On weekend mornings, linger over espresso and homemade granola with yogurt. When the sun sets, there's a dimly lit ambience, and daring yet carefully crafted plates reign—falafel fried fish, Moroccan red lentil stew, and five-hour braised ribs with heirloom new potatoes. Open Mon through Fri 11 a.m. to 9 p.m., Sat and Sun 9 a.m. to 10 p.m. $–$$.

where to stay

Ash Street Inn. 118 Ash St.; (603) 668-9908; ashstreetinn.com. Tucked away on a residential street close to the Currier Museum, the 5 rooms in this turreted 1885 Victorian B&B feature antique furnishings and polished hardwood floors overlaid with Oriental rugs. All the rooms have a private bath, some rooms have fireplaces and/or original stained-glass windows. Make it down to the parlor early for a full made-to-order breakfast. $$.

Radisson Hotel Manchester. 700 Elm St.; (603) 625-1000 or (800) 395-7046; radisson .com. The only real choice for full-service downtown Manchester accommodations, this 250-room hotel offers convenience along with the buzz of a busy lobby. Rooms are better than functional with super-cushy beds, crisp triple-sheeting, and spacious bathrooms. Upper floor rooms have views of Manchester. The hotel's indoor pool, whirlpool and sauna, and fitness room add to the hotel's appeal. $$.

day trip 25

manchester

historically charming & hip:
portsmouth, nh

portsmouth, nh

Located at the mouth of the Piscataqua River as it approaches the Atlantic Ocean, Portsmouth anchors New Hampshire's seacoast region. First settled by the English in 1630, Portsmouth is one of America's oldest cities. Its deep, natural harbor proved ideal for trade and shipbuilding, and the city prospered during the 18th century. Discover the many facets of Portsmouth—it's a great walking city. The Strawbery Banke historic district features beautifully maintained sea captain's homes along brick cobbled streets, while the newly revitalized downtown district buzzes with an abundance of off-beat shops, cafes, and restaurants. Hampton Beach, the state's major seaside destination, is just 20 minutes from downtown. And from Portsmouth, it's only a 5-minute drive to the Maine coastal town of Kittery, just across the harbor.

getting there

Portsmouth is an hour east of Manchester. From I-93 South take exit 7 to merge onto NH 101 East and follow for 31 miles. Take I-95 North for 10 miles toward Portsmouth and take exit 6 for Portsmouth.

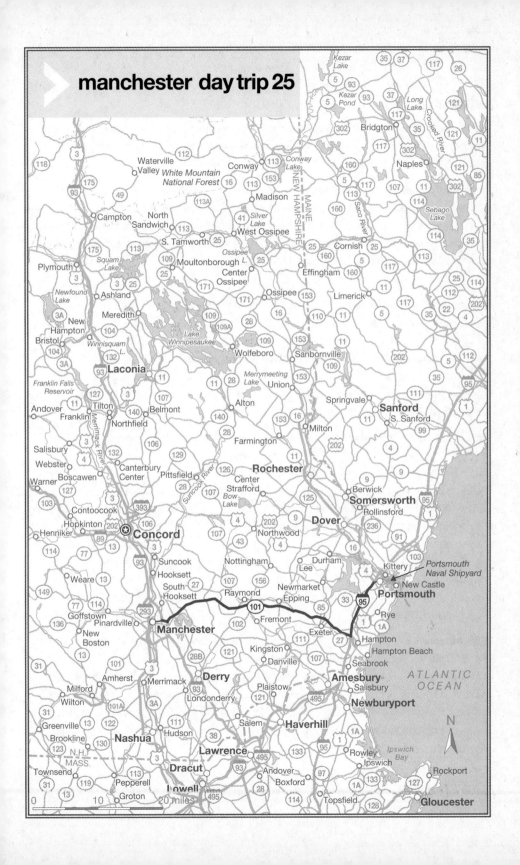

where to go

Portsmouth Chamber of Commerce. Stock up on brochures at the kiosk at Market Square. Staff is on hand to answer questions and give directions. Open mid-May through Oct, daily 10 a.m. to 5 p.m.

John Paul Jones House. 43 Middle St.; (603) 436-8420; portsmouthhistory.org. John Paul Jones, the celebrated naval hero of the Revolutionary War, was a tenant at this yellow clapboard Georgian house during his 1781 stay in Portsmouth to supervise the building of the *America.* The house now serves as the headquarters for the Portsmouth Historical Society. Open May through Columbus Day, daily 11 a.m. to 5 p.m. Admission $6 adults, $5 seniors, free for children ages 12 and under.

Portsmouth Harbor Cruises. 64 Ceres St.; (603) 436-8084; portsmouthharbor.com. Go on a seafaring adventure aboard the 49-passenger *Heritage,* a 1963 cruiser, and experience an entertaining and informative 1.5-hour narrated tour that explores Portsmouth's maritime history and cruises near the Portsmouth Naval Yard, the Portsmouth Lighthouse, and the Wentworth Marina. Sunset, inland river, and fall foliage tours are also offered. Season runs from May through Oct, check website for departure times. Harbor cruises $19 adults, $17 seniors, $13 children.

Strawbery Banke Museum. 14 Hancock St.; (603) 433-1100; strawberybanke.org. The first English settlers called this area Strawbery Banke after the native strawberries that grew wild here. Today, at the site of Portsmouth's first settlement, this outdoor living-history museum brings together a collection of some 40 restored buildings to create a vivid sense of daily neighborhood life spanning the years from 1695 to 1950. The museum is spread over 10 beautifully landscaped waterfront acres, and as you tour at your own pace, costumed guides are on hand to lend perspective. Among the structures are several colonial merchant houses, a Victorian mansion, a World War II corner grocery store and 2 (!) taverns. Open May through Oct daily 10 a.m. to 5 p.m. Admission $19.50 adults, $9 ages 5 to 17, ages 4 and under free. Museum admission is good for 2 consecutive days. Open additional days in Dec; check website for hours.

USS *Albacore.* 600 Market St.; (603) 436-3680; ussalbacore.org. In permanent dry-dock, the 1953 Navy research submarine the USS *Albacore* offers self-guided tours. Climb aboard and walk inside—you'll get an idea of how 50 submariners lived and worked in very tight quarters. Definitely not for the claustrophobic. Open daily Memorial Day weekend through Columbus Day weekend 9:30 a.m. to 5 p.m., Jan and Feb open Sat and Sun 9:30 a.m. to 4 p.m., Mar through May daily 9:30 a.m. to 4 p.m. Admission $7 adults, $3 children ages 7 to 17, $14 family rate.

where to shop

Market Square is a handsome space and has been Portsmouth's economic and commercial center since the 1700s. With period lighting, the tree-lined streets and brick sidewalks are home to historic buildings and mostly locally owned businesses. It's a delightful place to do some shopping.

Nahcotta. 110 Congress St.; (603) 433-1705; nahcotta.com. No ho-hum pieces here. This is an exceptionally well-edited selection of gifts, jewelry, and home and kitchen accessories. Open Mon through Sat 10 a.m. to 6 p.m., Sun 11 a.m. to 5 p.m.

Pickwick's Mercantile. 64 State St.; (603) 427-8671; pickwicksmercantile.com. While in Portsmouth, pop into Pickwick's for what is surely one of New England's most unique shopping experiences. This is a magical store where the cedar shelves are stuffed with all sorts of amusements from souvenirs to toys and antiques. Among the store's specialties are small-batch perfume and old-school grooming aids such as shaving soap, badger brushes and, of course, mustache wax. To add to the fun, Pickwick's shopkeepers are dressed the part in edgy, reimagined Victorian-era costumes. Open Sun through Thurs 10 a.m. to 6 p.m., Fri and Sat 10 a.m. to 9 p.m.

Riverrun Bookstore. 142 Fleet St.; (603) 431-2100; riverrunbookstore.com. This is a classic independent, neighborhood bookstore with a nice selection of new books, local and regional titles, and a full schedule of author readings. You'll also find well-chosen book picks by a knowledgeable and enthusiastic staff. Open Mon through Sat 9 a.m. to 7 p.m., Sun 10 a.m. to 7 p.m.

where to eat

Black Trumpet Bistro. 29 Ceres St.; (603) 431-0887; blacktrumpetbistro.com. Chef-owner Evan Mallett transforms New England cuisine with the flavors of the Mediterranean and Latin America in this rustic two-level bistro and wine bar with a killer view of Portsmouth Harbor. Sup on roasted half spring chicken with pistachio pilaf and rhubarb jam and swoon over the fig and cherry clafouti. The softly lit dining space with exposed brick walls, wood beams, and gleaming copper-topped tables really add to the bistro's perfect date-night ambience. Open Sun through Thurs 5 to 9 p.m., Fri and Sat 5 to 10 p.m. $$–$$$.

Cava. 10 Commercial Alley; (603) 319-1575; cavatapasandwinebar.com. Amid Portsmouth's historical district, this alley hideaway recalls a Madrid *taberna*. There's both a subterranean wine cave and a first-floor dining room. You'll find classic tapas like grilled octopus with hearts of palm—and more unusual ones like a lobster tortilla española. The fare also includes some Spanish entrees like a paella with chicken chorizo, clams, and just enough *sofrito* to lend a perfect bite. There's a superb Iberian wine list, and in warm weather, the enchanting vine-covered patio is the place to be. Open Mon through Thurs 5 to 9 p.m., Fri 5 to 10 p.m., Sat 2 to 5 p.m., Sun 5 to 10 p.m. $$.

The Friendly Toast. 113 Congress St.; (603) 430-2154; thefriendlytoast.net. Breakfast is king, but lunch and dinner also shine at this kitsch-filled hipster and family-friendly hangout. The menu features updated favorites like Drunkard's French Toast in a Grand Marnier and raspberry sauce, and green (herbed) eggs and ham for breakfast. The D.G.G.C. (Damn Good Grilled Cheese) is exactly that; with American and cheddar cheese on cayenne cheese bread, with an olive spread, and a strawberry-habañero dipping sauce. Burgers, burritos, and salads round out the menu. Open Sun through Wed 7 a.m. to 8 p.m., Thurs 7 a.m. to 9 p.m., Fri and Sat 7 a.m. to 2 a.m. $-$$.

Lexie's Joint. 212 Islington St.; (603) 319-4055; lexiesjoint.com. Whether you order the Jack (with pepper jack and fried jalapeños), the Bleu Angel (with bacon and blue cheese), or customize your own burger, there are loads of options at this quick-serve spot. Other choices include house-cut fries, fried onion rings, and unbelievable shakes, and just about everything is local. Open daily 11:30 a.m. to 8 p.m. $.

Popovers on the Square. 8 Congress St.; (603) 431-1119; popoversonthesquare.com. Located on Market Square, this ultracasual, friendly, eclectic Portsmouth bakery/cafe is a local gathering spot for casual meals. For breakfast, steel-cut oatmeal with berries and the fried egg sandwiches are favorites. For lunch try the New England clam chowder or the turkey panini on honey wheat bread. Be sure to order the signature popover slathered with maple butter. Yum! Open Mon through Thurs 7 a.m. to 8 p.m., Fri 7 a.m. to 10 p.m., Sat 8 a.m. to 10 p.m., Sun 8 a.m. to 7 p.m. $.

where to stay

Ale House Inn. 121 Bow St; (603) 431-7760; alehouseinn.com. Housed in a former brewery warehouse building, this 10-room urban boutique hotel has a definite hipster sensibility—with a lot of appeal for those who would rather spend money on a good meal than a hotel bill. The rooms are on the small side, but there are plenty of modern comforts: pillow-top mattresses, free Wi-Fi, free parking, and a complimentary in-room iPad for guests' use. $$-$$$.

Hotel Portsmouth 40 Court St.; (603) 433-1200; hotelportsmouth.com. siseinn.com. You'll find modern B&B charm at Portsmouth's newest boutique hotel, located in an 1881 Queen Anne–style home close to Market Square. The inn's foyer and breakfast room retains the rich oak-wood detailing and the grace of the Victorian era. Rooms are a perfect hybrid of upscale luxury and New England charm complete with flat-screen TVs, in-room iPads, down duvets and contemporary maple furniture. Rates include free Wi-Fi, a small plates breakfast and parking. $$.

Wentworth by the Sea. 588 Wentworth Rd., New Castle; (603) 422-7322; wentworth .com. Just a 10-minute drive from Portsmouth, cross the Sagamore River Bridge to experience a New England island getaway. This iconic grand dame hotel is now part of the Marriott chain and the New Hampshire seacoast's only oceanfront resort. The hotel is also a National Historic Landmark. It was the site of the Russo-Japanese peace conference that concluded with the signing of 1905 Treaty of Portsmouth. Built in 1874, the hotel has been elegantly updated for a new era; the 161 guest rooms now have marble bathroom floors with radiant heat, and most have ocean or marina views. SALT Kitchen & Bar crafts meals that change seasonally and are determined by the local harvest. Artisanal cocktails and a superb wine list complement an outstanding menu from the signature appetizer of torched tuna with blood orange served on a slab of salt to toasted peppercorn crusted steak and Meyer lemon panna cotta. Decadent meals are all served under the hotel's restored rotunda mural of cherubs and flower garlands in a pearly blue sky. The resort also has a brand-new 8,500-foot spa, and both indoor and outdoor pools. $$$.

worth more time

Hampton Beach. Ocean Boulevard; (603) 926-8717; hamptonbeach.org. New Hampshire has just 18 miles of coastline, but it sure does make the most of it. Just 16 miles south of Portsmouth, Hampton Beach is quite the scene, attracting a youngish mix of locals and day-trippers who come to soak up the sun during the day. As the sun goes down in the evening, the action at the beach really heats up with a free summer concert most evenings and a weekly Wednesday night fireworks show.

day trip 26

manchester

lakeside pleasures:
wolfeboro, nh; meredith, nh;
weirs beach, nh

Lake Winnipesaukee, the Native American word for "smile of the Great Spirit," is located very nearly in the exact center of New Hampshire. It really is an enormous lake, and the sixth largest body of water in the US. Known as the "Lakes Region," this is a boater's paradise with motor boating, water skiing, and Jet Skiing as especially popular ways to get out on the water. Or you may enjoy the serenity of sailing, kayaking, and canoeing among the area's nearly 300 ponds, lakes, and streams. You'll also find swimming, fishing, walks in the nearby woods, and a surprising number of shopping opportunities. And it's all available within a 63-mile drive along the shores of Lake Winnipesaukee.

wolfeboro, nh

Family adventure or romantic getaway, upscale Wolfeboro makes a perfect home base to explore Lake Winnipesaukee. Located on the eastern shore of the lake, Wolfeboro is a charming town with several eclectic museums and a nice mix of restaurants and shops along its main street.

getting there

The shortest and most direct route from Manchester is to take NH 28 North for 50 miles to Wolfeboro center. The ride should take just about 1 hour.

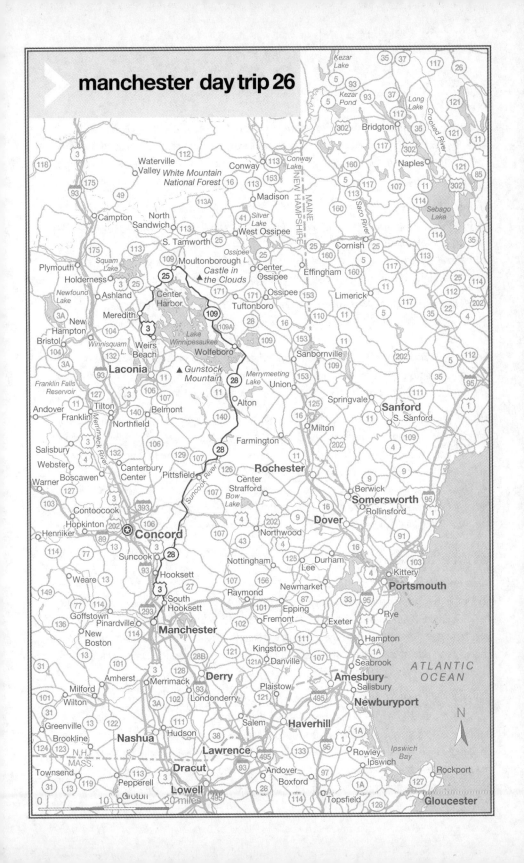

where to go

Wolfeboro Chamber of Commerce Information Center. 32 Central Ave.; (603) 569-2200; wolfeboro.com/chamber. Located in the town's gingerbread-trimmed Victorian-era railroad station, friendly volunteers can help with Lakes Region dining, hotel, and even boat-rental information. Open Mon through Fri 10 a.m. to 3 p.m., Sat 10 a.m. to noon.

Abenaki Tower. Parking lot on NH 109, Tuftonboro. Drive 7 miles out of Wolfeboro toward the town of Tuftonboro. This 80-foot timber public-lookout tower was originally built in 1929 and vaguely references the Abenaki native people who once inhabited the area. A climb up the narrow staircase rewards with an excellent view of the eastern shore of Lake Winnipesaukee and the Ossipee Mountains in the distance. Try to come at sunset. Admission is free.

New Hampshire Boat Museum. 399 Centre St.; (603) 569-4554; nhbm.org. Dedicated to the boating heritage of New Hampshire's lakes, this museum displays an impressive collection of wooden vintage boats of all types; runabouts (including Chris Craft, Lyman, and Garwood), sailboats, and canoes. It's a must-visit for antique-boat folks. Open Memorial Day weekend to Columbus Day Mon through Sat 10 a.m. to 4 p.m., Sun noon to 4 p.m. Admission $7 adults, $5 seniors, $3 ages 7 to 17, free ages 6 and under.

Wright Museum. 77 Center St.; (603) 569-1212; wrightmuseum.org. This small museum chronicles the American World War II experience from 1939 to 1945. The museum serves as a repository for battle memorabilia with dozens of operational military vehicles including tanks, jeeps, motorcycles, and more. The Home Front exhibits include displays of a corner soda fountain, a dentist office, gas station, and a World War II–era kitchen. Open May through Oct Mon through Sat 10 a.m. to 4 p.m., Sun noon to 4 p.m.; closed Nov through Apr. Admission $10 adults, $8 seniors, $6 ages 5 to 17, free ages 4 and under.

where to eat

Mise en Place. 96 Lehner St.; (603) 569-5788; miseenplacenh.com. There's a lot to like about this neighborhood bistro where you can savor eclectic cuisine with a definite French flair. For lunch there is baby spinach salad with pancetta and a poached egg or a caramelized onion tart. For dinner enjoy the mussels with fennel in saffron broth, veal medallions with capers, and bananas Foster for dessert. Open summer Tues through Sat 5 p.m. to close; check website for hours during the rest of the year. $$.

Seven Suns Coffee & Tea. 21 Railroad Ave.; (603) 515-1010; sevensunscoffee.com. Across the street from the picturesque Wolfeboro train station, this homey shop serves fair trade, organic coffee, espresso, cappuccinos and lattes as well as perfectly brewed tea (hot and iced) and ultra-healthy veggie/juice smoothies. The crepe menu includes traditional and gluten-free options filled with the savory offerings like the very popular lobster, or combinations like peanut butter, honey, banana and chocolate for the sweet. There is free Wi-Fi, and the outdoor sidewalk seating is a bonus. Open Mon through Fri 7 a.m. to 6 p.m., Sat and Sun 7 a.m. to 4 p.m. $.

Wolfetrap Grill and Raw Bar. 19 Bay St.; (603) 569-1047; wolfetrapgrillandrawbar.com. Sit out on the deck and enjoy a spectacular sunset over Lake Winnipesaukee while choosing from a menu that includes fried options of every kind of seafood along with other crowd-pleasers like a Caesar salad with fresh lobster meat and fish tacos. Or just order a beer and fried onion rings, and savor the end of the day. Open May through Oct, Sun through Wed 11 a.m. to 10 p.m., Thurs 11 a.m. to 11 p.m., Fri and Sat 11 a.m. to midnight. $$.

where to stay

Wolfeboro Inn. 90 N. Main St.; (603) 569-3016; wolfeboroinn.com. Located directly on Lake Winnipesaukee (and with its own private beach), the Wolfeboro Inn has the perfect blend of casual sophistication and rustic New England inn ambience. The property dates from 1812, and all 44 guest rooms have been remodeled with pillow-top mattresses, high-count sheets, and flat-screen TVs. The inn's popular Wolf's Tavern serves favorites like grilled sirloin tips and newer dishes like a roasted eggplant–vegetable torte with fried risotto cakes and fresh tomato cream. Hotel: $$–$$$. Restaurant: $$.

meredith, nh

Meredith, on the western shore of Lake Winnipesaukee, has long lured anglers for its bass and trout fishing. Much more quiet than nearby Weirs Beach, Meredith retains a somewhat more exclusive air and is also the region's premier shopping destination.

getting there

It's a pretty drive along NH 109 North around the lake to Meredith. The drive is around 28 miles and should take 45 minutes without stopping, but a detour along the way to Castle in the Clouds (see p. 229) in Moultonborough is highly recommended.

where to go

Meredith Marina. 2 Bayshore Dr.; (603) 279-7921; meredithmarina.com. Getting out on the water is a big part of the Lake Winnipesaukee vacation experience. Meredith Marina rents all types of pleasure craft including powerboats and Jet Skis. Open mid-May through Columbus Day daily 8 a.m. to 5 p.m.

Wild Meadow Canoes & Kayaks. Route 25, Center Harbor; (603) 253-7536; wildmeadow canoes.com. If you prefer a quiet paddle along Lake Winnipesaukee's secluded coves, Wild Meadow can set you up with a canoe, kayak or paddle board rental. They also offer scenic guided tours during the foliage season. Open May through Oct daily 9 a.m. to 5 p.m.

where to shop

Annalee's Outlet Store. 339 Daniel Webster Hwy.; (800) 433-6557. New Hampshire–based Annalee poseable felt dolls are as cute as a button. At the outlet store you can find the company's complete line of handmade seasonal mice, elves, bunnies, and more. Or pick up discontinued or last season's dolls at a very good price. Open daily 10 a.m. to 5 p.m.

Keepsake Quilting. 12 Main St., Center Harbor; (603) 253-4026; keepsakequilting.com. A place of pilgrimage for quilters, Keepsake Quilting is said to be the largest quilt store in the US. The store stocks over 10,000 bolts of fabric and offers a comprehensive selection of quilt kits, patterns, tools, and notions. Finished quilts are also available for purchase. And like all quilt stores, the staff is super friendly and helpful. Open June through Oct Mon through Sat 9 a.m. to 6 p.m., Sun 9 a.m. to 5 p.m., Nov through May, Mon through Sat 10 a.m. to 5 p.m., Sun 11 a.m. to 5 p.m.

Mill Falls Marketplace. 312 Daniel Webster Hwy.; (800) 622-6455; millfalls.com/market place. Part of the Inns at Mills Fall complex, find more than a dozen local boutiques and specialty shops including Cozy Cabin Rustics (cozycabinrustics.com) for custom hand-crafted furniture; Great Northern Trading Company (greatnortherntradingcompany.com) for New Hampshire–themed gifts, home decor, and casual wear; and the Innisfree Bookshop, along with several eateries. General marketplace hours Sun through Thurs 10 a.m. to 5:30 p.m., Fri and Sat 10 a.m. to 9 p.m.

where to eat

George's Diner. 10 Plymouth St.; (603) 270-8723; georgesdiner.com. There's no better place to eat like a local than George's Diner. Fill up on the house special for breakfast: 2 eggs, bacon, sausage, home fries, toast, and beans. The lunch/dinner menu features burgers and sandwiches (including a very good Reuben) and daily specials like a Yankee pot roast that falls apart with the pull of the fork—just as it should. Open daily 6 a.m. to 8 p.m. $.

Hart's Turkey Farm Restaurant. 233 Daniel Webster Hwy.; (603) 270-6212; hartsturkey farm.com. This New Hampshire landmark has roosted here since 1954. The old-timey restaurant features knotty pine walls decorated with a huge turkey plate collection. Know that this is one of the region's largest restaurants—it seats 500—making it a popular stop for the tour-bus crowd. The must order is the home-style turkey dinner. On a busy day, Hart's will serve up more than a ton of roast turkey; 1,000 pounds of potatoes; 40 gallons of gravy; and 4,000 rolls—but it really is what Hart's does best.Open Sun through Thurs 11:15 to 8 p.m., Fri and Sat 11:15 to 8:30 p.m. $–$$.

Town Docks. 289 Daniel Webster Hwy.; (603) 279-3445; thecman.com/restaurants/town-docks. Located over at Mills Falls (see below) and a Lakes Region hangout for its laid-back vibe, the restaurant's big draw is its unbeatable lakefront location, complete with a guest dock for diners to park their boats. The food is appealing casual fare: grilled burgers and hot dogs, wraps and salads, fried fisherman's platters, and steamed lobster. Open Memorial Day weekend through Oct daily 7 a.m. to 9 p.m. $$.

where to stay

Mills Falls at the Lake. 312 Daniel Webster Hwy.; (603) 279-7006 or (800) 622-6455; mill falls.com. Along the shores of Lake Winnipesaukee, this charming village-style community of 4 New England inns (the Inn at Mill Falls, Bay Point, Chase House, and Church Landing), 7 restaurants, a spa, and marketplace (with 15 shops) are under the same ownership. It's a resort complex geared to guests who enjoy boating, hiking, snowmobiling, and other woodsy activities, but don't necessarily want the dirt that comes with them. Property-wide, among the 4 inns there are more than 156 rooms, and the vast majority have both lake views and fireplaces. Other amenities include 2 indoor pools, 3 hot tubs, a spa, and a fitness center. Guests can use the facilities at any Mill Falls property, and the resort offers package deals galore for every type of vacationer. $$$.

worth more time

Squam Lakes Natural Science Center. 23 Science Center Rd., Holderness; (603) 968-7194; nhnature.org. Just 8 miles northwest of Meredith, this is a wonderfully laid-out science center that offers live animal exhibits (including black bears and mountain lions), and well-marked walking trails that range from just 0.33 mile to 1 mile through forest and meadow. Enjoy the serenity of Big Squam Lake on a 90-minute naturalist-led canopied pontoon cruise, where you will learn about Squam Lake folklore, see some of the locations where *On Golden Pond* was filmed, and you may spot loons or a bald eagle. Science Center and trails open May 1 through November 1 daily 9:30 a.m. to 4:30 p.m., cruises operate late May through mid-Oct daily, check website for times. Science Center and trail admission $19 adults, $16 seniors, $14 children ages 3 to 15. Cruise only $25 adults, $23 seniors, $21 children. Trail and cruise combo pass $38 adults, $33 seniors, $29 children.

weirs beach, nh

Weirs Beach is the Lakes Region's playground, attracting fun seekers of all ages. Its long and generous beach is never crowded. A flurry of summer activities from Jet Skiing and wind surfing on Lake Winnipesaukee to every type of boardwalk arcade game, fair ground ride, and water slide ensure that no one ever gets bored. Weirs Beach is also the homeport for the excursion vessel the M/S *Lake Winnipesaukee*.

ice out

Winter in New Hampshire is extremely frigid—with single-digit temperatures on the wrong side of zero for long stretches of time. Even Lake Winnipesaukee freezes over to a depth of 3 to 4 feet, typically in late December or early January. And while die-hard sports enthusiasts take to winter lake sports like ice-skating, ice fishing, and snowmobiling, most Granite-staters look forward to the first sign of spring when the ice on Lake Winnipesaukee breaks up enough for the M/S Mount Washington to travel its route around the lake. Typically ice-out occurs in mid- to late April, and soon after the docks go in the water and the boating season begins.

getting there

Take US 3 South for 5 miles to Weirs Beach in just 10 minutes. For a return to Manchester, save time and pick up I-93 South.

where to go

Fun Spot. 579 Endicott St.; (603) 366-4377; funspotnh.com. With 500 video games, bowling, minigolf, bumper boats, a driving range, bingo hall, and more, Fun Spot is the perfect outing for families who like to explore their separate interests together. In other words, it's a great place for families with teens. Open mid-June through Labor Day Sun through Fri 9 a.m. to 11 p.m., Sat 9 a.m. to midnight; Sept through mid-June Sun through Thurs 10 a.m. to 10 p.m., Fri 10 a.m. to 11 p.m., Sat 10 a.m. to midnight.

Gunstock. 719 Cherry Valley Rd., Guilford; (603) 293-4341; gunstock.com. Overlooking Lake Winnipesaukee, Gunstock is well known regionally as a family ski mountain with more than 50 downhill trails, night skiing, a terrain park, and a tubing hill. In summer, adrenaline-fueled activities continue with an adventure park that offers zip-line tours and guided Segway mountain tours. At the sport activity center enjoy a climbing wall, minigolf, and mountain biking.

M/S *Mount Washington* Cruises. 211 Lakeside Ave.; (603) 366-5531; cruisenh.com. Replacing an 1872 vessel of the same name, the M/S *Mount Washington* has been plying the waters of Lake Winnipesaukee since the 1940s. The 500-passenger, 3-level ship takes passengers on a 2.5-hour leisurely cruise with awesome views of the shoreline and the nearby White Mountain foothills. There are also sunset dinner cruises and a Sunday brunch cruise. Cruise season is May through Oct; check website for departure times. Day cruise tickets from $32 adults, $16 ages 5 to 12.

Winnipesaukee Scenic Railroad. 211 Lakeside Ave.; (603) 745-2135; hoborr.com. All aboard for a scenic train ride that hugs the western Lake Winnipesaukee shore. You'll ride in vintage coaches and you can board at either Weirs Beach or in Meredith for the 1- or 2-hour excursion rides. Be sure to reserve ahead of time during foliage season. Season runs from late May through Oct; check website for train departure times. Tickets for round-trip 2-hour train ride $17 adults, $13 ages 3 to 11, and free children 2 and under.

where to eat

Kitchen Cravings. 15 Airport Rd., Gilford; (603) 528-0001; kitchencravingsnh.com. Even if you're not flying anywhere, this diner, located just outside the Laconia airport, is worth the trip for its breakfasts (try the fluffy 3-egg French-style omelets), award-winning chili, burgers, and specialty sandwiches. Kids adore the moose-shaped pancakes. Open daily 6 a.m. to 2 p.m. $.

where to stay

Cozy Inn and Cottages. 12 Maple St.; (603) 366-4310; cozyinn-nh.com. This is an affordable accommodation choice for families that is conveniently close to the Weirs Beach action—but not too close. The decor of the 15 cottages is basic, but all of the units have at least some cooking facilities and are well maintained. The property also has individual rooms available in its 2 inns. And you can take a break from lake swimming at either of the property's 2 outdoor swimming pools. $$.

worth more time

Castle in the Clouds. 455 Old Mountain Rd., Moultonborough; (603) 476-5900; castlein theclouds.org. "Lucknow," a spectacular mountaintop estate on 5,500 acres overlooking Lake Winnipesaukee was built at the turn of the 20th century by Boston shoe-factory tycoon Thomas Plant. From the visitor parking lot, you'll experience a sense of anticipation as the trolley (included in admission) winds its way up the mountain road to reveal exhilarating views of Lake Winnipesaukee. Tours of the grand Arts and Crafts–style interior are self-guided. Afterward explore some of the miles of hiking and walking trails that traverse the property. The half-mile Brook Path along the boardwalk to view the property's natural 50-foot waterfall is a must-see. Enjoy lunch alfresco on the patio at the Carriage House, which was named by *Yankee Magazine* as one of the region's best cafes. Open May through mid-June Sat and Sun only 10 a.m. to 4 p.m.; mid-June through Oct daily 10 a.m. to 4:30 p.m. Admission $17 adults, $14 seniors, $10 ages 5 to 17, free ages 4 and under. Grounds-only pass $8.

portland

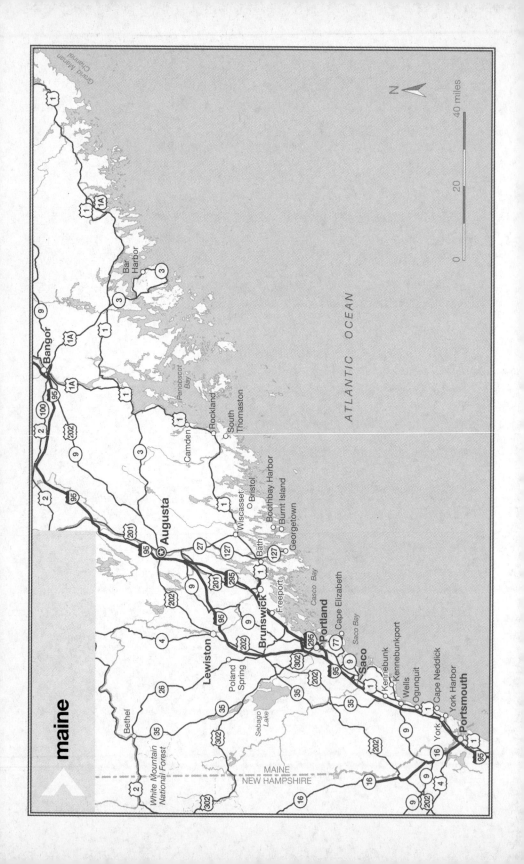

day trip 27

portland

>>>

maine's cultural capital:
portland, me

portland, me

Overlooking picturesque Casco Bay, Maine's largest city has a deep, natural harbor and a maritime tradition as both a busy fishing port and shipbuilding center. Today, Old Port still supports a vibrant working waterfront that includes a commercial fishing fleet, international cargo ship handling, and the cruise ship industry.

Portland may have been discovered in 1633, but it was in the 1800s that the modern city started to take shape. When Portland was rebuilt after the Great Fire of July 4, 1866 (said to have started from a firecracker), city leaders focused on more fire-resistant architecture, and much of the city's handsome brick and granite buildings in the Old Port and West End districts date from that time.

Portland's motto is *Resurgam* or "I shall rise again." And over the decades, the city has done just that, establishing itself as Maine's major economic center with a serious locavore food scene, an eclectic mix of shops, and a first-rate art museum.

Maine is the biggest state in New England. In fact, it is bigger than all the other five New England states combined. There really is no better place than Portland from which to explore Maine. It's an easy drive along US 1 to reach the sandy beaches and charming villages of Maine's southern coast, or you can head along US 1 in the opposite direction past lighthouses and lobster shacks to discover the small fishing villages that dot the mid-coast.

And just a 30-minute drive inland finds quiet and scenic beauty in the dense woods and clear lakes of the state's western mountains.

getting there

Most visitors driving to Portland come from other Northeast cities. Portland is adjacent to I-95. Take exit 44 and follow I-295 North for 5 miles into town.

where to go

Portland Convention and Visitors Bureau. 14 Ocean Gateway Pier; (207) 772-5800; visitportland.com. This information center is well staffed and is open year-round. Open Nov through Apr Mon through Sat 10 to 3 p.m.; May Mon through Fri 9 a.m. to 4 p.m., Sat 10 a.m. to 3 p.m. June through Oct Mon through Fri 9 a.m. to 5 p.m., Sat 9 a.m. to 4 p.m.

Casco Bay Lines. 56 Commercial St.; (207) 774-7871; cascobaylines.com. All-aboard for a 20-minute ferry ride to poke around the shops and restaurants on Peaks Island, the clos-est of the large Casco Bay islands. Just 3 miles from the mainland, the island is actually a neighborhood of Portland with a year-round population of just under 1,000 residents. It's also a terrific day-trip destination for nature lovers, with miles of trails to explore by walking or biking. Another option? Enjoy a few hours of paddling along the shoreline with full-service outfitter **Maine Island Kayak** (207-766-2373; maineislandkayak.com).

Children's Museum & Theatre of Maine. 142 Free St.; (207) 828-1234; childrensmuseum ofme.org. This children's museum is geared to toddlers through age 10 and features lots of hands-on, interactive activities, among them unique Maine-themed exhibits including a lobster boat, ranger station, and a lumberyard. The museum's outdoor shipyard and pirate ship encourage lots of active play as kids clamber up, down, and about. Open Memorial Day through Labor Day daily 10 a.m. to 5 p.m.; day after Labor Day through day before Memo-rial Day Tues through Sun 10 a.m. to 5 p.m.; closed Mon fall and winter (except Monday holidays). Admission $10 per person, under 18 months, free.

Portland Head Light. 1000 Shore Rd., Cape Elizabeth; (207) 799-2661; portlandhead light.com. With its stunning location 80 feet above the rocky shore of Portland Harbor, Portland Head Light is among the most photographed lighthouses in New England. Com-missioned by President George Washington and dating from 1791, this was also Maine's first lighthouse. It was automated in 1989 and remains an active aid to navigation today. The lighthouse itself is only rarely open to the public, but the grounds are open for you to take your own screen-saver-worthy photographs. You can also visit the attached former keeper's quarters, which house the Museum at Portland Head Light and a small gift shop. The lighthouse is part of Fort Williams Park, which has plenty of parking, walking trails, and picnic benches. Grounds open year-round, dawn to dusk. Museum is open June through Oct daily 10 a.m. to 4 p.m.; weekends Apr through May and Nov through Dec. Grounds are free; museum admission $2 adults, $1 children ages 6 to 16.

Portland Museum of Art. 7 Congress St.; (207) 775-6148; portlandmuseum.org. This first-rate art museum is especially known for its American collection of paintings. Works that showcase the artistic heritage of Maine such as those by Winslow Homer, Rockwell Kent, and N. C. Wyeth are especially prominent. The museum's European collection is also strong; works include a bronze by August Rodin and paintings by Claude Monet, Pierre Auguste Renoir and Pablo Picasso. Open Tues through Thurs, Sat, and Sun 10 a.m. to 6 p.m.; Fri 10 a.m. to 8 p.m. Admission $15 adults, $13 seniors and students, $10 ages students, free for children ages 14 and under.

Victoria Mansion. 109 Danforth St.; (207) 772-4841; victoriamansion.org. This handsome Italianate brownstone mansion was constructed between 1858 and 1860 as a summer home for Maine hotelier Ruggles Sylvester Morse and his wife, Olive. It is a superb example of American residential architecture and design during the Victorian era, with nearly 90 percent of its original furnishings and fixtures intact. Highlights of the home include a magnificent mahogany flying staircase, an elaborate Turkish-style smoking room, and palace-worthy frescoes, plasterwork, and stained-glass windows. Open May through Oct Mon through Sat 10 a.m. to 4 p.m., Sun 1 to 5 p.m.; late Nov through early Jan daily 11 a.m. to 4:30 p.m. Admission and guided tour $15 adults, $13.50 seniors, $5 ages 6 to 17.

where to shop

Angela Adams. 131 Middle St.; (800) 255-9454; angelaadams.com. This is the only brick-and-mortar store of Angela Adams, the internationally recognized Maine-based designer known for her abstract patterns and modern color palette. Stop in and you'll find a terrific selection of Adams's signature hand-tufted rugs, bedding, tote bags, and stationery. Open Mon through Sat 10 a.m. to 6 p.m., closed Sun.

Portland Architectural Salvage. 131 Preble St.; (207) 780-0634; portlandsalvage.com. There's real treasure to be found at this architectural warehouse. Find high-end hardware (doorknobs and hinges), mantles, solid wood doors, and stained glass windows all just begging for a new home. Open Mon through Fri 10 a.m. to 5 p.m., Sat 10 a.m. to 4 p.m.

Shipwreck and Cargo. 207 Commercial St.; (207) 828-8065; shipwreckandcargo.com. A shop especially for those who love the sea, you'll find ship models, functional weather instruments, and nautical antiques of all types including ships lanterns and compasses. Open daily Mon through Fri 9 a.m. to 7 p.m., Sat and Sun 9 a.m. to 5 p.m.

where to eat

Duckfat. 43 Middle St.; (207) 774-8080; duckfat.com. There is always a lot of fuss about Duckfat and for good reason. Their signature dish is amazing: Belgian-style fries made from Maine potatoes that are deep-fried twice in duck fat and served in a paper cone along with a choice of several dipping sauces (get the truffle ketchup). Or you can go all out and order *poutine*—their amped-up version of the Quebecoise dish is made with duck-fat fries smothered with duck-fat gravy and melty cheese curds. The rest of bistro's menu features mostly light fare like tomato and fennel soup and various panini. But they are known, too, for their Duckfat milk shake, which is not made with duck fat! Open daily 11 a.m. to 10 p.m. $$.

Eventide Oyster Company. 86 Middle St.; (207) 774-8538; eventideoysterco.com. This isn't seafood for a day at the beach; it's seafood for a celebration. Eventide brings the urban excitement of a seafood tapas bar to Portland in a modern, coastal-inspired space. Eventide is a sophisticated spot for primo seafood and offers innovative twists on New England classics. The raw bar features a dozen (or more) varieties of oysters on the half shell—most from local waters—to go along with an artisan cocktail list, as well as a perfectly balanced gin & tonic. You could make a meal from Eventide's small plates offerings with dishes like the cured salmon with hazelnut citrus, beets and potato chips and a delicate fluke ceviche. But if all you're really after is a Maine clambake or fried seafood, that is here too. Reservations are not accepted for parties smaller than 6, so be prepared to wait. Open daily 11 a.m. to midnight. $$.

Gilbert's Chowder House. 92 Commercial St.; (207) 871-5636; gilbertschowderhouse .com. Grab a seat on the back porch overlooking the waterfront and have a beer while you chow down on no-nonsense fried and broiled seafood, clam chowder, and lobster rolls. Try Gilbert's tasty clam cakes, too. Open daily 11 a.m. to 9 p.m. $.

Miyake. 468 Fore St.; (207) 871-9170. Chef Max Miyake turns out artful arrangements of raw fish; what is offered daily depends on what is freshest at this Japanese fusion sushi restaurant. Bento boxes anchor the daytime menu. In the evening the 5-course (or even better, 7-course) *omakase* or chef's-tasting menu is the way to go, featuring both raw and cooked dishes such as lobster sashimi, duck two ways, and seared sweet scallops. Open Mon through Sat 11:30 a.m. to 2:30 p.m. and 5:30 to 10 p.m., closed Sun. $$–$$$.

Otto Pizza. 576 Congress St.; (207) 773-7099 (storefront); and 225 Congress St.; (207) 358-7870 (waitress service); ottoportland.com. Portland has its share of gourmet pizza places. Convenient to the Portland Museum of Art, Otto's bakes razor-thin pies with artful, interesting toppings like pulled pork and mango and mushroom and cauliflower. The mashed potato, bacon, and scallion pizza is weirdly, addictively good. Open Sun through Thurs 11 a.m. to 10 p.m., Fri and Sat 11 a.m. to 11 p.m. $–$$.

Two Fat Cats Bakery. 47 India St.; (207) 347-5144. You can't visit Maine without trying a whoopee pie—it's Maine's official state treat. A whoopee pie isn't a pie at all, though; it's more like a cake sandwich made with a cream filling. Traditionally it's made with chocolate cake and a vanilla or sometimes marshmallow filling and is about the size of the palm of your hand. Two Fat Cats makes to-die-for whoopee pies and a killer blueberry pie (Maine's official state dessert). Open Sun 10 a.m. to 2 p.m., Mon through Fri 8 a.m. to 6 p.m., Sat 8 a.m. to 5 p.m. Sun 8 a.m. to 4 p.m. $.

where to stay

Danforth Inn. 163 Danforth St.; (207) 879-8755 or (800) 991-6557; danforthinn.com. Each of the 10 rooms in this 1823 Federal mansion is designed with stylish furnishings and fresh colors, all have a private bath, and most have fireplaces. Rates include breakfast, which is served the old-fashioned way—in the dining room. The hotel's onsite restaurant Tempo Dulu specializes in high-end Malay, Singapore and Indonesian cuisine. This is fusion fare that is sharp and fun, like the Penang poached lobster tail with coconut turmeric rice and roasted lychees. $$$. The Danforth boasts exceptional common spaces, too: a glam salon, a billiard room, conservatory, and lush backyard garden. It's all just a short walk from the Old Port district. $$–$$$.

Pomegranate Inn. 49 Neal St.; (207) 772-1006 or (800) 356-0408; pomegranateinn.com. Set within Portland's Western Promenade neighborhood, the 8 whimsically artistic rooms in this Italianate Victorian inn are a far cry from your typical New England B&B. Both the common spaces and guest rooms are gallery-like and filled with art (some of which is from local artists and is available for purchase). Walls are a focal point in each room's decor; one guest room features hand-painted oversized hydrangeas, another room is done with a more subtle Asian medallion theme. All the rooms feature flat-screen TVs, sitting areas with fine antiques that recall an older era, sumptuous beds, and crisp white bathrooms. Breakfast is included in all rates and given the full upscale treatment: grapefruit brûlée, blackberry cream scones, and asparagus Parmesan crepes. $$–$$$.

Portland Harbor Hotel. 468 Fore St.; (207) 775-9090 or (888) 798-9090; portlandharbor hotel.com. Blending historic charm with modern conveniences for a boutique-like feel, the Portland Harbor is a great compromise to the area's big-box chain hotels. The recently refreshed rooms feature luxe linens and free Wi-Fi; some rooms have pretty garden views. The hotel offers complimentary bike rental so you can explore the Old Port and waterfront just outside the door. The hotel's popular restaurant, Eve's at the Garden, is open for breakfast, lunch, and dinner. $$$.

Portland Regency Hotel. 20 Milk St.; (207) 774-4200 or (800) 727-3436; theregency.com. This 1895 building was formerly the armory of Portland's National Guard, but nowadays the 84 rooms and 11 suites are poshly done with dark woods, high thread-count sheets, fluffy towels, and high-end toiletries. The hotel has both a fitness room and an on-site spa for pampering. Twenty Milk Street is open for all-day dining, and the Armory Lounge is a local evening destination for its menu of infused martinis. $$$.

day trip 28

portland

coastal maine quaint:
the kennebunks, me; wells, me;
ogunquit, me; the yorks, me

Just north of both the Massachusetts and New Hampshire borders, Maine's south-ernmost coastal resort towns are among the state's most popular vacation destinations. Miles of coastline and dazzling ocean views are just part of the beauty of this area of Maine. There are harbor towns with darling B&Bs, the state's only real sandy beaches for a bracing swim, and waterfront seafood shacks that always feature a catch-of-the-day.

the kennebunks, me

Located along Maine's southern coast, the delightful towns of **Kennebunk** and **Kennebunkport** may be separated by a bridge over the Kennebunk River, but together they are known simply as "the Kennebunks." During your visit allow time for a swim or a stroll along the town's broad beaches, board a sightseeing trolley or check out the antique trolleys at the Seashore Trolley Museum, and shop and dine in pretty Dock Square.

getting there

From Portland, pick up I-95 South (known locally as the Maine Turnpike) for 7 miles. Take exit 36 to I-195 East for 2 miles and merge onto US 1 South for 9 miles and follow signs to the towns of Kennebunk and Kennebunkport. The ride should take just about 45 minutes.

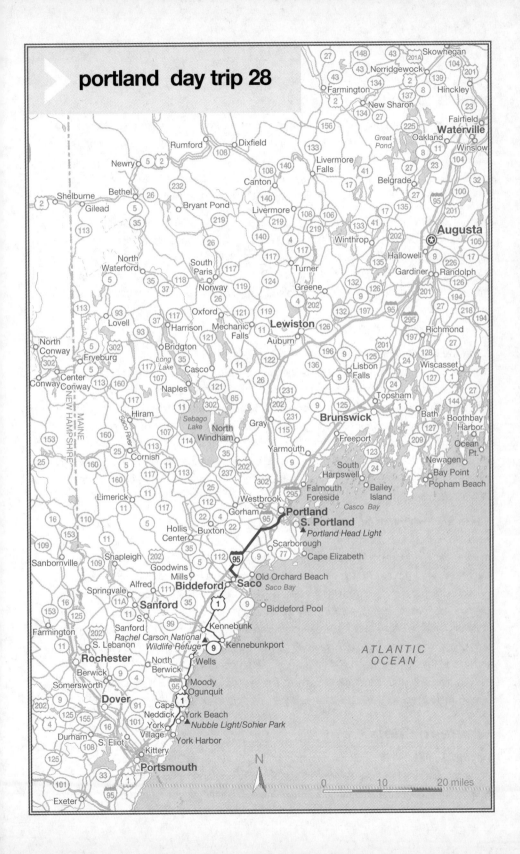

portland day trip 28

where to go

Kennebunk & Kennebunkport Chamber of Commerce. 1 Chase Hill Rd., Kennebunk; (207) 967-0857; visitthekennebunks.com. Located just over the bridge in Kennebunk and within walking distance of Kennebunkport's Dock Square, this information center provides a guidebook and brochures for both towns and sells parking permits for the town's beaches. Open Mon through Fri 10 a.m. to 5 p.m., Sat and Sun 10 a.m. to 4 p.m.

Intown Trolley. 21 Ocean Ave., Kennebunkport; (207) 967-3686; intowntrolley.com. This 45-minute narrated hop-on/hop-off trolley serves a dual purpose as transportation to the town beaches and as a pleasant way to get an overview of both towns. You'll learn about the area's history as a shipbuilding center, its development as a summer resort destination in the late 1800s, and have an opportunity to snap pictures (at a distance!) of the Bush family's summer home at Walker's Point. Trolley season runs from Memorial Day weekend through Columbus Day weekend, daily 10 a.m. to 5 p.m. Tickets $16 adults, $6 ages 3 to 17.

Kennebunk's Beaches. Along Beach Avenue. The broad swath of white sandy beaches that are shared by Kennebunk and Kennebunkport are among the best in New England; three beaches are conveniently adjacent to each other. **Mother's Beach** is a small sheltered area with shallow water and is ideal for young children. **Middle Beach** is quiet but a little rocky, while **Gooch's Beach**, the largest and most popular of the three beaches, attracts both swimmers and sun worshipers. Parking stickers are required at town beaches; purchase a day sticker ($25 per day) at the chamber of commerce. If you are staying overnight, most lodging places will have a pass available for guests. Or you can bike or take the trolley to the beaches.

Seashore Trolley Museum. 195 Log Cabin Rd., Kennebunkport; (207) 967-2800; trolley museum.org. "Clang, clang, clang went the trolley." This museum is a must-visit for rail fans of all ages. The museum has the largest collection of its kind, with more than 250 mass-transit vehicles from around the world, among them vintage trolleys from Boston, New York, Baltimore, and other major American cities; a 1939 double-decker streetcar from Liverpool; and a 1926 tram from Sydney. You can walk through some of the vehicles; others are in a state of disrepair. Restoration of the vehicles is an on-going process, and you can watch the volunteers work safely from a viewing platform. The highlight of your visit is sure to be the 2-mile ride through the woods on a turn-of-the-20th-century, open-air trolley. Open Memorial Day through Labor Day, daily 10 a.m. to 5 p.m. Admission $10 adults, $8 seniors, $7.50 ages 6 to 16, free ages 5 and under.

where to shop

Daytrip Society. 4 Dock Sq., Kennebunkport; (207) 967-4440; daytripsociety.com. This gift and accessory boutique reflects both a love of the outdoors and an appreciation for the finer things in life. Find hand-loomed Swan's Island blankets, doormats made from recycled marine rope, and stylish solar-powered paper lanterns. Also check out Daytrip Jr. around the corner at 9 Ocean Ave. for super-cute kids clothing, toys, and games. (Great name for a store, too!) Open daily 10 a.m. to 6 p.m.

where to eat

Alisson's. 11 Dock Sq., Kennebunkport; (207) 967-4841; alissons.com. With its dark-wood decor and lots of booth seating, Alisson's is a handsome yet comfy neighborhood place that offers everything from specialty sandwiches and massive salads to pub food and classic Maine seafood dishes on its sprawling menu. The petite lobster roll and clam chowder combo is available at both lunch and dinner and is highly recommended. The pub is a popular local watering hole with large-screen TVs for watching the game (Red Sox, of course!), and it offers weeknight happy hour specials and live music on weekends. Open daily 11:30 a.m. to 9:30 p.m. $$.

Bandaloop. Dock Square, Kennebunkport; (207) 967-4994; bandaloop.biz. This chef-owned bistro is a standout in the area for its green-leaning, well-prepared eclectic fare. Revel in adventurous and artfully presented dishes like pickled-ginger crab cakes, corn and three-onion risotto, pepper-crusted salmon with saffron basmati rice, and a Belgian chocolate torte with raspberry Chambord granita. Open Sun and Tues through Thurs 5 to 10 p.m., Fri and Sat 5 to 11 p.m., closed Tues and Sun in the winter. $$–$$$.

Clam Shack. On the Bridge, Kennebunkport; (207) 967-3321; theclamshack.net. This spot may be called the Clam Shack, but the legendary lobster rolls are the thing to get. These lobster rolls are made from round rolls (which is not the norm for Maine) and are chock-full of the whole tail and claw meat from an entire lobster. It's a walk-up window only, but there are some benches and wood crates near the shack's parking spaces. Open May through Oct only Sun through Thurs 11 a.m. to 6 p.m., Fri and Sat 11 a.m. to 8 p.m. $$.

David's KPT. 21 Ocean Ave., Kennebunkport; (201) 967-8225; boathouseme.com. This is Kennebunkport's must-visit restaurant. Armed with some of the East Coast's freshest seafood, chef David Turin creates all matter of reinvented classics. Take the lobster ravioli. You've seen it before, but never like this, open face with hunks of Maine lobster, day boat scallops, gulf shrimp and herbed ricotta and a sherry cream. If you prefer turf over surf, there's Turin's signature Portland sirloin with port reduction and garlic mashed potatoes or barbecue chicken pizza with queso fresco and caramelized onion and bacon. At happy hour, soak up the energy at Kennebunkport's only raw bar where you will have a front row seat to both the shucking and cocktail making action. Open Sun through Thurs 11 a.m. to 9 p.m., Fri and Sat 11 a.m. to 10 p.m. $$.

H.B. Provisions. 15 Western Ave., Kennebunk; (207) 967-5762; hbprovisions.com. Eating a home-style breakfast in a quaint general store is a wonderfully unique New England experience. Order the red flannel hash and eggs (it's hash made with the addition of beets) or the blueberry pancakes. At lunch or dinner, the Maine crab melt is mighty tasty. Afterward stock up on groceries, Maine souvenirs, and necessary vacation odds and ends like Wiffle ball bats and jigsaw puzzles. Open June through Sept 6 a.m. to 10 p.m., Oct through May 6 a.m. to 9 p.m. $.

where to stay

Captain Fairfield Inn. 8 Pleasant St., Kennebunkport; (207) 967-4454; captainfairfield.com. Located in an 1813 Federal-style mansion, the 9 guest rooms of this inn perfectly blend the warmth and hospitality of a B&B with the feel of a luxurious boutique hotel. The rooms have been masterfully designed with historic authenticity and feature a mix of antiques and contemporary pieces, wide-plank pine floors with Persian carpets, white-on-white linens, private marble bathrooms, flat-screen TVs, and free Wi-Fi. Feast on the inn's gourmet breakfast each morning and indulge in still-warm chocolate chip cookies in the afternoon. The inn is also an easy 5-minute walk to everything Kennebunkport has to offer. $$–$$$.

Colony Hotel. 140 Ocean Ave., Kennebunkport; (207) 967-3331 or (800) 552-2363; the colonyhotel.com/maine. Large verandahs with wicker chairs, and manicured lawn and gardens that spill to the ocean, the 19th-century Colony Hotel is the quintessential old-school Maine coastal resort. Rooms are traditional in style with floral wallpaper, hardwood floors, and hooked rugs. Most rooms don't have a TV, but the hotel does have a heated saltwater pool and the best amenity of all—a private stretch of beach. All rates include a buffet breakfast. Open May through Oct. $$–$$$.

Franciscan Guest House. 26 Beach Ave., Kennebunk; (207) 967-4865; franciscanguest house.com. Both the beaches and the village of Kennebunkport are just a short walk away from this budget-friendly lodging choice. Associated with the next-door Franciscan Monastery (with its estate-like grounds), the 65 rooms are modest—but not spartan. All have a private bathroom and also include cable TV and free Wi-Fi, air-conditioning, and daily linen and towel service. For the price, there are a surprising number of amenities, too—breakfast (featuring Lithuanian pastries) is included in the rate, there is a small on-site outdoor pool, and you have use of a parking pass for the Kennebunk beaches. Open Apr through Dec. $–$$.

Kennebunkport Inn. 1 Dock Sq., Kennebunkport; (207) 967-2621; kennebunkportinn .com. With an enviable location overlooking Dock Square, lots of extras, and rates considerably lower than most Kennebunkport hotels, the Kennebunkport Inn is an awesome value. The inn's 49 rooms are tastefully appointed and vary in style. The main inn's rooms are done with a traditional New England theme; the Wharfside rooms are more casual and have a Maine cottage look, and some of these are multi-bedroom suites that are ideal for families. The inn's pub aims to please with small plates like grilled flatbreads and "Maine plates" of foolproof classics like lobster ravioli along with weekend live music. All room rates include a generous continental breakfast. Open year-round. $$–$$$.

wells, me

Wells boasts some of Maine's best and most accessible beaches. The headquarters of the Rachel Carson National Wildlife Refuge is here, too. Its leisurely 1-mile walking trail is a just-right afternoon activity between beach and ice cream.

getting there

From Kennebunkport to Wells is a short 10 minute drive along ME 9 West for 4 miles to US 1.

where to go

Wells Chamber of Commerce. 696 Sanford Rd. (ME 109); (207) 646-2451; wellschamber .org. The Wells Transportation Center is located just off the Maine Turnpike (I-95) at the town's Amtrak train station and serves as the town's visitor information center. Pick up brochures and maps on Wells and the seacoast region. This is also a stop for the Wells Shoreline Trolley (shorelineexplorer.com). Avoid the hassle and expense of parking at the town's beaches. There is ample free parking for your car here, and you can take the town trolley to the beach; fares are $1 one-way for adults, children under 18 are free.

Rachel Carson National Wildlife Refuge. 321 Port Rd.; (207) 646-9226; fws.gov/ northeast/rachelcarson. The refuge is named for Rachel Carson, the biologist and environ-mentalist best known for her book *Silent Spring,* who summered for many years on nearby Southport Island. The refuge itself is quite large, spanning 50 miles of southern Maine coast-line from Kittery to Cape Elizabeth. Begin the 1-mile Carson Trail at the headquarters' visitor center and follow it as it winds along the salt marsh of the Little River. There are floating boardwalks and observation decks along the trail that allow close views of waterfowl and migrating birds. Trails open daily dawn to dusk. Visitor center open summer daily 8 a.m. to 4:30 p.m., rest of year Mon through Fri 8 a.m. to 5 p.m. Admission is free.

Wells Beach. End of Mile Road at Atlantic Avenue. Wells has 7 miles of beaches, and this section is the largest of the town's 3 public beaches. It's backed by salt marsh, has dramatic rock outcrops in places, and its length makes it ideal for jogging or for long walks. Know that Wells is a famously cold swimming beach—unless it's August, the water temperature rarely breaks 60 degrees. Open daily. Admission fee June through Sept, $20 per vehicle.

where to eat

Congdon's Doughnuts. 1090 Post Rd.; (207) 646-4219; congdons.com. Since 1955, generations of Mainers have grown up on Congdon's handmade doughnuts. They make nearly 30 flavors, and while the honey-dip doughnut is very good, the chocolate-dipped chocolate is great. Congdon's also serves breakfast and lunch; blueberry pancakes are one of their specialties. Open Thurs through Sun 6 a.m. to 3 p.m., closed Wed. $.

Fisherman's Catch. 134 Harbor Rd.; (207) 646-8780; fishermanscatchwells.com. On the way to Wells Harbor, the Catch is a local, casual seafood restaurant where the food rivals the view. The decor of the knotty-pine dining room is campy coastal: brightly painted picnic tables, buoys, and fishing nets. Count on fresh-as-can-be seafood including a lobster stew, steamed lobster dinner, and fried seafood platter. In warm weather, eat outside on the back patio overlooking the marsh. Perfection! Open daily May through mid-Oct 11:30 a.m. to 9 p.m. $$.

ogunquit, me

For more than a century, Ogunquit's sandy beaches and breathtaking scenery have attracted artists who come to paint *en plein air*. The village brims with art, whether it's the paintings of John Marin at the Ogunquit Museum of American Art or works by local artists at one of the many galleries in Perkins Cove. End your visit to this "beautiful place by the sea" with a stroll along the Marginal Way for unparalleled ocean views.

getting there

It's only a 5-mile drive south from Wells to Ogunquit, but this particular section of US 1 is crowded with lots of motels, hotels, and restaurants and can be slow going in the summer.

where to go

Ogunquit Chamber of Commerce Visitor Center. 36 Main St. (US 1); (207) 646-2939; ogunquit.org. This is a staffed visitor center with plenty of free parking. Pick up the Ogunquit Trolley (ogunquittrolley.com) for both Perkins Cove and Ogunquit Beach. One-way fares are $2 adults, $1.50 children ages 10 and under. Open Mon through Fri 9 a.m. to 5 p.m., Sat and Sun 10 a.m. to 3 p.m.

The Marginal Way. Enjoy the smell of salt air and the scent of *Rosa rugosa* along this 1-mile paved trail while taking in the spectacular views of the Atlantic Ocean and the crashing waves against the cliffs below. Pick up the trail (there's a sign) near the shops at Perkins Cove; as you stroll there are lots of benches along the way, and you can choose to retrace your steps when your reach Ogunquit Beach or return by walking along shop- and restaurant-lined Shore Road.

Ogunquit Beach. Beach Street. Ogunquit Beach is lovely—a 3.5-mile white sand natural barrier between the Ogunquit River and the Atlantic. The inner sandbar is quite shallow, making this beach particularly popular with families with small kids. Admission fee June through Sept, $30 per vehicle.

Ogunquit Museum of American Art. 543 Shore Rd.; (207) 646-4909; ogunquitmuseum .org. Perched on a cliff overlooking Narrow Cove, this small, nationally recognized museum specializes in exhibiting American art of the 19th century to the present. Highlights of the collection include works by Marsden Hartley, Rockwell Kent, and Reginald Marsh. The museum's beautifully landscaped grounds are also a visual delight. Open May 1 through October daily 10 a.m. to 5 p.m. Admission $10 adults, $9 seniors and students, free children ages 12 and under.

Ogunquit Playhouse. 10 Main St.; (207) 646-5511; ogunquitplayhouse.org. One of the longest-running repertory theaters in the country and part of what was once known as the "straw-hat circuit," the Ogunquit Playhouse still attracts audiences for its May through October musical season. Recent productions have included *Mama Mia!, Grease,* and *Billy Elliot.*

where to shop

Abacus Gallery. 213 Main St.; (207) 646-0399; abacusgallery.com. This shop's wares feature a frequently changing roster of stylish art objects and gift items. Find classic and offbeat home goods and accessories from cocktail glasses to a delicate sea-foam opal necklace to affordable *giclée* prints. Many of the pieces are the work of local artists. Open Sun through Thurs 10 a.m. to 6 p.m., Fri and Sat 10 a.m. to 9 p.m.

where to eat

Barnacle Billy's. 50–70 Perkins Cove; (207) 646-5575; barnbilly.com. You know exactly what to expect from a restaurant with the name Barnacle Billy's in coastal Maine—lobster rolls, clam chowder, and steamed lobsters. But the corny name doesn't do justice to the restaurant's gorgeous water views of picturesque Perkins Cove. ***Note:*** There are two "Billy's." Barnacle Billy's is the original, order-at-the-counter and find-a-seat place. Billy's Etc. is the full-service restaurant next door with more expanded offerings including dishes like baked stuffed shrimp and barbecue chicken. Open Apr through Oct daily 11:30 a.m. to 9 p.m. $$–$$$.

Cafe Prego. 44 Shore Rd.; (207) 646-7734; caffeprego.com. A casual, authentic take on a neighborhood Italian *caffe*—complete with a large outdoor (heated) terrace and gardens. Offering enticing pastas, sandwiches, salads, and especially brick-oven pizza, this is one of Ogunquit's most popular restaurants. Tourists often order the lobster pizza; purists gravitate toward traditional Margherita. Follow your meal with espresso and house-made gelato. Open May through Oct, Mon through Fri 11:30 a.m. to 11 p.m., Sat and Sun 11:30 a.m. to 9:30 p.m. $$.

Roost Cafe & Bistro. 262 Shore Rd.; (207) 646-9898; roostcafeandbistro.com. The happy, simple farmhouse vibe at Roost makes it a pleasure to visit. For breakfast, tuck into classic eggs Benedict or blueberry pancakes. At lunch or dinner find well-executed, reasonably priced bistro fare like coq au vin and lamb shanks with root vegetables. Open year-round Wed through Thurs 5 to 9 p.m., Fri and Sat 8 a.m. to 2 p.m. and 5 to 9 p.m., Sun 8 a.m. to 2 p.m. $–$$.

where to stay

Beachmere Inn. 62 Beachmere Place; (800) 336-3983; beachmereinn.com. This family-owned and family-friendly oceanfront hotel has lots of appeal with a location just steps from the Marginal Way. The 53 basic motel rooms are updated and are spread among a Victorian inn and 2 annexes. Rooms come in a wide variety of sizes and configurations, but all come with kitchenettes and some have a balcony and/or fireplace. Bonus: The inn has a small, private beach for guests' use. Rates include continental breakfast. $$–$$$.

Gazebo Inn. 572 Main St.; (207) 646-3733; gazeboinnogt.com. Although it has just 14 rooms, the Gazebo Inn has many amenities offered by a larger inn: outdoor pool, gym, sauna, and library. The rooms have an upscale, rustic feel with exposed beams, while some barn-room suites have fireplaces, sitting areas, and whirlpool tubs. The inn's location is prime, too—just a short walk from Footbridge Beach. Rates include a large buffet breakfast. $$.

the yorks, me

First settled in 1624, **York** is one of the oldest towns in Maine. It includes the towns of **York Village, York Beach, York Harbor,** and **Cape Neddick.** Located on Maine's southeastern shore, just over the border from New Hampshire, York is a summer resort town that is particularly popular with families. With its wide sandy shores, beachside arcades, and the York Wild Kingdom Animal Park, a York beach vacation harkens back to simpler times.

getting there

Drive along US 1 South for 7 miles to York. US 1 is slightly less crowded here; the ride should take 10 minutes.

where to go

Greater York Region Chamber of Commerce Visitors Center. 1 Stonewall Ln., York; (207) 363-4422; gatewaytomaine.org. Located off US 1 and next to Stonewall Kitchen, this is a large visitor center, fully staffed with racks of brochures with information about York and the next-door town of **Kittery** (outlet central). On Saturday mornings from June through early October, the visitor center parking lot is the site of the Gateway farmers' market, where you can buy everything from organic produce to artisanal baked goods to handmade soaps and candles. This is also a stop for the York Trolley Company (yorktrolley.com), a convenient way to get to the beaches and around York. Fares are $4 per person. Check website for current hours.

Museums of Old York. 3 Lindsay Rd., York; (207) 363-1756; oldyork.org. Within walking distance of present-day York Village, this cluster of 9 historic buildings chronicles 300 years of York history. You'll recognize the Old York Gaol immediately from the pillory out in the front. The building dates from 1719, and inside you can check out the cells, the dungeon, and the quarters for the jailer and his family. Among the other buildings on the property are a one-room schoolhouse dating from 1845, and a 1740 York River warehouse that once belonged to American patriot John Hancock. The 3 residential house buildings showcase the museum's collection of early American furniture, textiles, and decorative arts. Open June through Columbus Day Tues through Sat 10 a.m. to 5 p.m., Sun 1 to 5 p.m., closed Mon. Admission $12 adults, $8 children ages 5 to 16, free children 4 and under.

Stonewall Kitchen. 2 Stonewall Ln., York; (207) 351-2712; stonewallkitchen.com. This is both the flagship store and factory headquarters for Stonewall Kitchen, the New England all-natural gourmet food company. In the retail store, the shelves are stocked with the company's jams, mustards, and salsas. Best of all, there are lots of samples to try! One to consider? The roasted-garlic and onion jam. In the factory, there is a viewing area where you can watch products being made. Epicures will enjoy attending a class at the cooking school (register ahead). The Stonewall Cafe offers light breakfast fare—croissants and breakfast breads and coffee—and lunches like lobster bisque, a cobb salad, and several types of interesting panini that offer a pleasant break from shopping; it's all the more serene when eaten outside in the garden. Retail store open Mon through Sat 8 a.m. to 8 p.m., Sun 9 a.m. to 6 p.m. Cafe open Mon through Sat 8 a.m. to 5 p.m., Sun 9 a.m. to 4 p.m.

York's Beaches. York's two main beaches attract a family-oriented crowd. Short Sands Beach (along Ocean Avenue) is a small stretch that is popular for its sheltered swimming and the old-timey atmosphere of the beachfront T-shirt shops, ice-cream stands, and Funorama Arcade. Cape Neddick Light, called Nubble Light by locals, is just across the waters of Cape Neddick Point. Nubble doesn't have public access, but there are benches and a viewing telescope at Sohier Park. Long Sands Beach (Long Beach Avenue) is a 1.5-mile wide beach with a nice length of sand, perfect for a relaxing afternoon. It faces the open Atlantic Ocean and has calm waves; its dedicated surfing area attracts surfing novices.

York's Wild Kingdom. 1 Animal Park Rd., York; (207) 363-4911; yorkswildkingdom.com. If you're in York for more than a day, and if your kids beg and plead long enough, you are bound to give in to taking them to this hybrid zoo and amusement park. There are more than a dozen classic rides geared to little thrill seekers, including bumper boats, a Ferris wheel, a carousel, and a haunted house. Zebras, a Bengal tiger, an American black bear, and kangaroos are just some of the animals you'll encounter here. Open Memorial Day weekend through late Sept; check website for times. Adults $14.75 zoo only, $21.25 zoo and rides; ages 4 to 12 $9 zoo only, $16.25 zoo and rides.

where to eat

Bob's Clam Hut. 315 Route 1, Kittery; (207) 439-4233; bobsclamhut.com. When you can't face another discounted designer handbag, retreat to this popular Route 1 spot. Bob's is actually a few steps up from a hut, with year-round indoor seating for nearly 70 diners and the requisite New England seaside ambience. A devoted following of tourists and locals come for the full menu of regional seafood specialties including first-rate lobster rolls and plump, tender, fried whole belly clams. Open Sun through Thurs 11 a.m. to 7 p.m., Fri and Sat 11 a.m. to 8 p.m. $.

Dunne's Ice Cream. 232 Nubble Rd., Cape Neddick; (207) 363-1277. Just a stone's throw from Nubble Light, enjoy your cone with a view of the sea. In business for more than 40 years, this stand is a local institution. You'll find it hard to choose from among the more than 40 flavors, including not-so-usual throwback favorites like rum raisin and frozen pudding. Open May through Columbus Day daily noon to 9 p.m. Cash only. $.

Flo's Steamed Hot Dogs. 1359 US 1, Cape Neddick; floshotdogs.com. Not for nothing does the line spill out the door of this shack along a busy stretch of US 1 between Ogunquit and York. Flo's has long enjoyed a cult following for its steamed hot dogs. For the total Flo's experience, get yours "loaded" (that's with relish, mayo, and celery salt). Open Thurs through Tues 11 a.m. to 3 p.m., closed Wed. Cash only. $.

Frankie and Johnny's. 1594 US 1, Cape Neddick; (207) 363-1909; frankie-johnnys.com. The humble environs of this charming side-of-the-road eatery belie its gourmet greatness. Toasted peppercorn seared tuna and grilled rack of lamb with minted lentils are just a sampling of the exceptional menu of farm-to-table fare. The menu has several vegan-friendly options, too. It's also BYOB. Open July and Aug Wed through Sun 5 to 9 p.m.; Thurs through Sun 5 to 9 p.m. rest of the year; closed late Dec through mid-Feb. Cash only. $$-$$$.

Goldenrod. 2 Railroad Ave., York; (207) 363-2621; thegoldenrod.com. Overlooking this corner of Main Street and Railroad Avenue since 1896, Goldenrod is famous for saltwater taffy. Today, like in the past, people line up in front of the store's windows to watch the taffy-pulling machines make their magic. Be sure to buy a box and check out the genuine penny-candy counter inside. The nostalgia continues in the Goldenrod dining room, where the hearty breakfasts, lunches, and dinners are loaded with down-home goodness. Or sit on a stool at the old-fashioned marble soda fountain and have a hot fudge sundae. Open Memorial Day weekend through Columbus Day 11 a.m. to 9 p.m. Closed day after Columbus Day through May. $.

Robert's Main Grill. 326 Route 1, Kittery; (207) 439-0300; robertsmainegrill.com. This two-story roadside restaurant isn't far from the Kittery outlets and remains open throughout the year. You have your choice of authentic seafood restaurants all along coastal Maine, but few are as food-forward and upscale as Robert's. There's a trendy large bar in the center of the main dining room which is outfitted with pendant lights, simple wooden tables and large picture windows that look out onto the Spruce Creek estuary. New England classics like fried seafood and lobster rolls share menu space with fun stuff like lobster pizza and Moxie bourbon steak tips. Desserts are simple with lots of pies including raspberry and good ol' Maine blueberry. Open Mon through Thurs 11:30 a.m. to 8:30 p.m., Fri and Sat 11:30 a.m. to 9 p.m., Sun 11:30 a.m. to 7:30 p.m. $$.

where to stay

Stage Neck Inn. 8 Stage Neck Rd., York Harbor; (207) 363-3850; stageneck.com. This small resort complex, located directly on York Harbor Beach and with both an indoor and an outdoor pool, is a good bet for a happy family vacation without breaking the bank. The rooms are comfortably done up with British colonial furniture and white matelasse bedspreads; the bathrooms have been recently renovated and are supplied with ecofriendly toiletries. $$.

day trip 29

portland

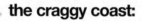

the craggy coast:
freeport, me; bath, me;
rockland, me; camden, me

Lobster hauls, rocky beaches, and salty seaside villages—this journey is among the most picturesque in all of New England. An L. L. Bean gear-up at the flagship store in Freeport is a Maine vacation must-do. Learn about Bath's famed shipbuilding heritage at the Maine Maritime Museum and sail along the rockbound coast on a windjammer. This region has long inspired artists, and you, too, will find breathtaking views of sea and shore. And with fish shacks by the water at the end of nearly every finger of land, there are lots of opportunities to eat lobster straight from the source.

freeport, me

Located just north of Portland on the shore of Casco Bay, Freeport is a serious shopper's dream destination as the home of L. L. Bean and more than a hundred outlet stores.

getting there

Take I-295 North to exit 22. Follow US 1 North into the Freeport.

where to go

L. L. Bean Outdoor Discovery Schools. 95 Main St.; (888) 552-3621. Try something new while on vacation. L. L. Bean Discovery Schools offer a slew of walk-on programs, from kayaking to sporting clays to archery. Whatever activity you choose, all the very best

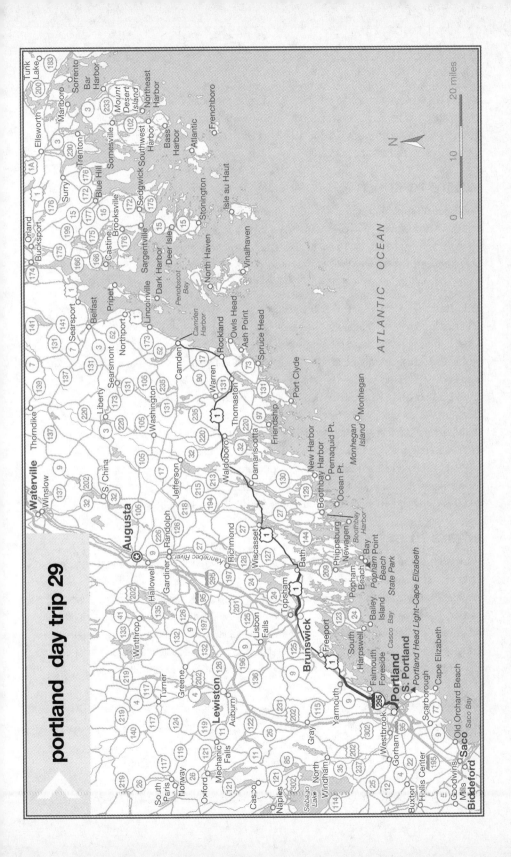

portland day trip 29

equipment and instruction are provided. Sign up at the kiosk in the lobby of the main store or call ahead to register in advance. The Discovery School also offers longer day tours and guided weekend adventures. Participants must be 8 years of age or older, and walk-on class prices begin at $25 per person.

where to shop

Freeport Shopping Outlets. Along Main Street; (207) 865-1212; freeportusa.com. You'll find great deals from an impressive selection of stores along Freeport's Main Street. Maine-based home goods stores **Thos. Moser Cabinetmakers** (149 Main St., thosmoser.com) and **Georgetown Pottery** (148 Main St., georgetownpottery.com) are worth visiting among the outlet mall standards like Nike, J. Crew, and Polo Ralph Lauren.

L. L. Bean. 95 Main St.; (877) 755-2326; llbean.com. This is the flagship store and head-quarters for the world-famous outfitter that Leon Leonwood Bean began in 1912 as a mail-order company selling hunting boots. Nowadays L. L. Bean is a total outdoor-lifestyle brand that sells a whole lot more than the "Bean boot." The Freeport store is actually a complex of several L. L. Bean stores: the flagship store, L. L. Bean Hunting and Fishing, L. L. Bean Bike, Boating, and Ski; and L. L. Bean Outlet. Besides offering a dizzying array of merchandise, L. L. Bean cultivates a festival atmosphere with in-store demonstrations, an in-store trout pond, and a cafe—it's among Maine's most visited attractions. On Saturday evenings from late June through early September, the store sponsors the very popular Summer in the Park concert series in front of the Freeport stores. Concerts range from rock to folk to Shakespeare. L. L. Bean stores are open 24 hours, 365 days a year. (And it has been a middle-of-the-night road trip for generations of New England college students!)

where to eat

Harraseeket Lunch & Lobster Co. 36 Main St., South Freeport; (207) 865-4888; harraseeketlunchandlobster.com. Ten minutes south of L. L. Bean land, this is a real-deal Maine lobster pound with counter service, indoor seating, and picnic tables overlooking a working harbor. There are actually two lines: The biggest at the front is for lobster rolls, clam chowder, and fried seafood. The back counter is the lobster pound where you go to order the "lobster delight," a 1-pound steamed lobster, a dozen steamed clams, and an ear of corn. Open May through Oct, daily check website for hours. Cash only. $$.

where to stay

Harraseeket Inn. 162 Main St.; (207) 865-9377 or (800) 342-6423; harraseeketinn.com. Just blocks from L. L. Bean, the Harraseeket Inn is the perfect home base for a sportsman, shopping, or family vacation. The inn features 93 rooms, and all room rates include a hearty, locally sourced Maine breakfast and an expanded afternoon tea with cookies, cheese, and fruit in the mahogany drawing room. Rooms are pleasantly decorated with comfortable

New England furniture; some rooms have Jacuzzis, others have fireplaces. The inn's Maine Harvest Dining Room offers formal dining in the evening, or head to the inn's other eatery, the Broad Arrow Tavern, for more casual fare like a great-value daily lunch buffet and dinner choices like panko-crusted haddock and flat-iron steak with roasted vegetables. $$.

bath, me

Historic Bath still retains the charm of its 19th-century seafaring days with the elegant homes of shipyard owners and sea captains lining the streets. The rhythm of life continues to rely on the shipyard. Bath Iron Works is Maine's biggest civilian employer, building the destroyers that are the warhorse ships of the US Navy.

getting there

Once out of Freeport's bumper-to-bumper shopping-outlet traffic, the ride to Bath is quick, just 17 miles and 20 minutes along US 1 North.

where to go

Maine Maritime Museum. 243 Washington St.; (207) 443-1316; mainemaritimemuseum .org. Located on the Kennebec River, learn about Maine's shipbuilding history past and present at the Maine Maritime Museum. See the 19th-century shipyard buildings, where some of the world's largest wooden schooners were built, and watch wood boat construction in the working shop. The history of the Maine lobstering industry is another exhibit highlight. There are seasonal lighthouse and nature cruises (additional fee) as well as a guided "Behind the Scenes" trolley tour of the Bath Iron Works (also an additional fee, and make reservations in advance). Special to this museum is a staff that is exceedingly well-informed and passionate; many are former Bath Iron Works employees. Open daily 9:30 a.m. to 5 p.m. Admission $15 adults, $16 seniors, and students, $14.50 children ages 6 to 12, children 5 and under are free.

Popham Beach State Park. ME 209, Phillipsburg; (207) 389-1335. This 3-mile stretch of tawny sand at the mouth of the Kennebec River is one of Maine's prettiest and least-crowded beaches. It is a lifeguarded beach, but there is a strong undertow. You can walk out across the sandbar to Fox Island and look for shells, but you can be stranded if you are not aware of the tides. Admission fee June through Sept $8 per person.

where to eat

Beale Street Barbecue. 215 Water St.; (207) 442-9514; mainebbq.com. Even though you are way north of the Mason-Dixon Line, Beale Street does very good barbecue. Order the barbecue sampler platter; with your choice of slow-cooked barbecue meats, a half slab of ribs, a quarter chicken, sausage, and 2 sides, you won't leave hungry. You'll probably need extra napkins, too. Open daily 11 a.m. to 9 p.m. $$.

where to stay

Sebasco Harbor Resort. 29 Kenyon Rd., Sebasco Estates; (207) 389-1161; sebasco .com. While Adirondack chairs invite on the great lawn, this updated 1930s-era oceanfront resort is tailor made for modern-day family vacation fun. The 133 rooms carry out variations of a tasteful nautical theme across all its many room types: Main Lodge, multi-bedroom cottages, and the resort's unique lighthouse building. Golf is a huge draw with dramatic fairways that hug the ocean. In the late afternoon, the ecofriendly outdoor saltwater pool overlooking the harbor is the place to be. Kids will love the rec center, campfire s'mores, and day camp activities. The hotel has 2 excellent on-site restaurants, and you may want to take advantage of room packages that include meal and activity options. Season is May through Oct. $$$.

rockland, me

The gateway to Penobscot Bay, Rockland is the self-proclaimed "lobster capital of the world," hosting Maine's annual summer lobster festival the first weekend of August. This area of Maine is also Wyeth country; three generations of Wyeth artists—N. C., Andrew, and Jamie—have spent their summers here. You can see paintings from this American art dynasty at Rockland's Farnsworth Museum as well as works from other area artists.

getting there

From Bath to Rockland is a true mid-coast Maine scenic drive; 45 miles along US 1 North through Wiscasset and Damariscotta—both claim to be Maine's "prettiest" town; decide for yourself.

where to go

Farnsworth Art Museum. 16 Museum St.; (207) 596-6457; farnsworthmuseum.org. The Farnsworth Art Museum is a small treasure, a nationally recognized collection of Maine-related American art, with paintings by Fitz Henry Lane, Childe Hassam, and Edward Hopper, and sculpture by Louise Nevelson. The museum, though, is most well known for its holdings of art by the Wyeth family. The family patriarch, illustrator N. C. Wyeth, first came to mid-coast Maine in the 1930s. His son Andrew became one of America's best-loved painters. The Olson House, portrayed in his iconic work *Christina's World* (owned by the Museum of Modern Art in New York), is also a Farnsworth property; guided visits occur in season on the hour. The museum owns more than 60 works by the Wyeth family. Its Wyeth Center is devoted to the work of Andrew's son Jamie, who is a well-known artist, and works by N. C. Wyeth. Open June through Oct daily 10 a.m. to 5 p.m. Check website for days and times the rest of the year. Admission $15, adults, $13 seniors, $10 students, children ages 16 and under free.

Maine Lighthouse Museum. 1 Park Dr.; (207) 594-3301; mainelighthousemuseum.org. Learn everything there is to know about lighthouses, Fresnel lenses, and the rigorous life of a lighthouse keeper. ***Note:*** The museum shares building space with the Rockland Chamber of Commerce Visitor Center. Open Mon through Fri 9 a.m. to 5 p.m., Sat and Sun 10 a.m. to 4 p.m. Admission $8 adults, $6 seniors, free for children ages 12 and under.

where to eat

Cafe Miranda. 15 Oak St.; (207) 594-2034; cafemiranda.com. Just steps from the Farnsworth, this funky (Elvis and flamingos figure in the design mix) local eatery is a favorite place to enjoy laid-back meals with bold flavors. The cafe's wood-fire oven really does make everything taste better, like local scallops with smokehouse bacon, tomato, and fennel over homemade pasta and fire-baked mac 'n' cheese. This is an ecofriendly restaurant, too, with some provender coming from the cafe's own farm. Mon through Sat 11:30 a.m. to 2 p.m. and 5 to 9 p.m.; Sun 10:30 a.m. to 2 p.m. and 5 to 8:30 p.m. $$.

Home Kitchen Cafe. 650 Main St.; (207) 596-2449; homekitchencafe.com. In a Maine vacation lobster-roll rut? It can happen. For a taste of Mexico meets Maine, try Home Kitchen Cafe's lobster tacos: fresh lobster claw meat with purple cabbage, cilantro, avocado, and *crema fresca* on a homemade corn tortilla. Come for either breakfast or lunch; the wide-ranging menu features the likes of eggs Benedict, gourmet sandwiches, salads, and burgers. Open Mon and Wed through Sat 7 a.m. to 3 p.m. and 5 to 9 p.m.; Sun 8 a.m. to 2 p.m. Closed Tues. $.

Primo. 2 S. Main St.; (207) 596-0770; primorestaurant.com. If you are a devotee of Italian food, it would be a mistake to miss out on a visit to Primo. Chef-owner Melissa Kelley's cuisine is inspired by Italy and a love of local, seasonal ingredients. The restaurant even maintains acres of gardens on-site. Dishes may include halibut with corn and lobster risotto or pork saltimbocca on garlic mash with garden spinach, prosciutto, and sage. Whatever you do, don't skip dessert. Order the house-made cannoli and gelato and leave happy. Kelley is the 2013 James Beard Best Chef in the Northeast winner, so reservations are hard to get and essential for the dining room, but spur-of-the-moment dining is possible at the upstairs bar. Open daily June through Oct 5:30 to 9 p.m.; check website for days and hours in the off-season. $$$.

where to stay

The Berry Manor Inn. 81 Talbot Ave.; (207) 596-7696; berrymanorinn.com. This 1898 Victorian mansion features 12 cozily appointed rooms, superb breakfasts, and some of the friendliest innkeepers in Maine. The rooms are decorated in warm, rich tones with antique reproduction furniture—and a flat-screen TV. Each of the rooms has a luxurious bathroom, and 11 of the rooms have fireplaces. Here though, every guest's favorite amenity is the pie. Husband-and-wife owners Cheryl and Mike, stock the inn's guest pantry daily with fresh-baked homemade pies (along with Gifford's vanilla ice cream). $$–$$$.

Samoset Resort. 220 Warrenton St., Rockport; (207) 594-2511 or (800) 341-1650; samoset resort.com. There's plenty to do at this sprawling modern resort overlooking Penobscot Bay. Samoset has a home-style getaway vibe that makes it a great pick for family vacations. Partake in a round of golf, take a dip in the oceanfront (and heated!) infinity-edge pool, play a game of tennis, join in lawn games, linger by the nightly bonfire, or splurge on services at the spa. The 178 recently renovated rooms each have a balcony and impressive views of either the ocean or grounds, and there are 3 on-site restaurants, making it easy for the family to regroup for dinner after a day of play. Since 2012, the Samoset has returned to year-round operation; look for great package deals for winter stays. $$$.

camden, me

Camden is the quintessential coastal Maine village with views of a sparkling harbor dotted with windjammer sloops in full sail. Camden's other visitor charms are of the low-key variety, with a Main Street lined with excellent restaurants, B&Bs, and galleries.

getting there

It isn't far from Rockland to Camden, just 8 miles along US 1 North.

where to go

Camden Chamber of Commerce. 2 Public Landing; (207) 236-4404; camdenrockland. com. Located next to the harbor, pick up brochures and walking maps for both Camden and Rockport here. Open Memorial Day through Labor Day Mon through Fri 9 a.m. to 5 p.m.

Camden Hills State Park. 280 Belfast Rd.; (207) 236-3109. Just a few minutes north of town, the 1-mile Mount Battie Trail hike rewards with an exceptionally worthwhile view of Camden, Penobscot Bay, and, on a clear day, as far away as Mount Cadillac at Acadia National Park. *Note:* It's a short hike, but steep and rocky, so wear proper footgear—no flip-flops.

The Windjammer Cruises. A trip to mid-coast Maine isn't complete without a day sail on a turn-of-the-20th-century wooden windjammer around Penobscot Bay. You may be offered the opportunity to help hoist the sails or take a turn at the helm. Camden Habor–based windjammers that offer day sails include the Schooner *Surprise* (207-236-4687; camden mainesailing.com); Schooner *Olad* (207-236-2323; maineschooners.com); and Schooner *Appledore,* a 1978-built replica ship (207-236-8353; appledore2.com).

where to eat

Long Grain. 31 Elm St.; (207) 236-9001. Reimagined with local Maine ingredients, this is authentic Asian cuisine (chile-laced curries, restorative soups, and delicate dumplings) of the kind you would usually buy from street vendors. If available, the haddock curry fishcake and stir-fried pork belly with homemade kimchee are musts. Open Tues through Sat 11:30 a.m. to 3 p.m. and 4:30 to 9 p.m., closed Sun and Mon. $–$$.

where to stay

Camden Harbour Inn. 83 Bayview St.; (866) 626-1504; camdenharbourinn.com. From the front, this inn has all the characteristics of a period 1874 mansion—white clapboards, a wide front porch, and mansard roof. Head inside, and the inn has a distinctly different feel, taking its design inspiration from contemporary European urban boutique hotels. Each of the 18 rooms is different, but with every conceivable comfort, king-size feather beds, and water views of Camden Harbor. All rates include a breakfast of fresh-baked pastries and a buffet of cheeses, homemade granola, fruit, and yogurt. One of the inn's best amenities is its gourmet restaurant, Natalie's, which serves an internationally influenced menu with dishes like carpaccio of beets with goat cheese panna cotta and halibut with a mustard crust and white asparagus and English pea puree. $$$–$$$$.

Hartstone Inn. 41 Elm St.; (207) 236-4259; hartstoneinn.com. This regal 1835 mansarded Victorian is run by husband-and-wife team Michael and Mary Jo Salmon and boasts 21 handsomely designed rooms, each with a private bath and extra flourishes like original art-work and fresh flowers. Michael Salmon is also a renowned chef and offers cooking classes at the inn's fine dining restaurant. All room rates include a full gourmet breakfast and after-noon cocktail hour. $$$.

day trip 30

portland

>>> **moose in the woods:**
poland spring, me; bethel, me;
sebago lake, me

Maine's stunning mountain wilderness offers four-season adventures for vacation explorers. Enjoy leaf peeping, skiing, fishing, hiking, biking, paddling, swimming, and golf. Mountain lodging choices run the gamut from camping to cottages to inns to full-scale resorts.

poland spring, me

In the 19th century Poland Spring became a world-renowned vacation destination to escape the summer heat of the city and take the "curative" mineral water discovered in the area's springs. Today, Poland Spring Resort attracts value-seeking vacationers who consider the hotel an ideal base to visit the historic Poland Spring bottling plant, tour the Sabbathday Shaker Village, and see a real (!) moose at the Maine Wildlife Park.

getting there

From Portland, take I-95 North to exit 63. Follow ME 26 North for 10 miles to Poland Spring Resort.

where to go

Maine Wildlife Park. 56 Game Farm Rd., Gray; (207) 657-4977; maine.gov/ifw/education/ wildlifepark. In partnership with the Maine Department of Inland Fisheries and Wildlife, this

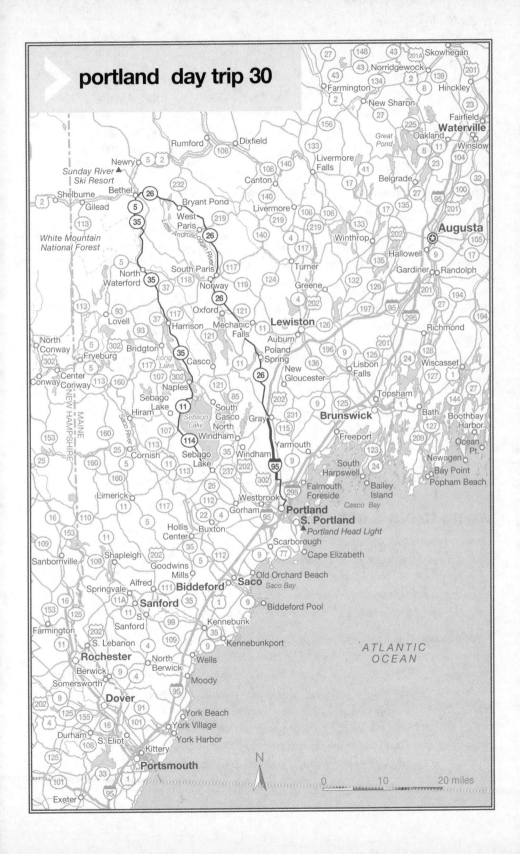

portland day trip 30

small "zoo" features 30 native Maine animals, among them a bald eagle, a black bear, and a moose in a naturalistic parklike setting. Most of the animals that live at the sanctuary are here because they have been injured or orphaned and can't return to the wild. Open mid-Apr through mid-Nov daily 9:30 a.m. to 4:30 p.m. Admission $7 adults, $5 seniors and children ages 4 to 12.

Poland Spring Preservation Park. 37 Preservation Way; (207) 498-4142. The 1907 bottling plant has been restored to house a museum that tells the story of Poland Spring water and the subsequent development of the town. The museum also maintains 5 miles of grounds for hiking and cross-country skiing. Grounds open year-round, dawn to dusk. Museum and springhouse open May through Oct Tues through Sat 9 a.m. to 4 p.m. Admission free.

Sabbathday Lake Shaker Village & Musuem. 707 Shaker Rd., New Gloucester; (207) 926-4597; maineshakers.com. In an idyllic country setting of rolling farmland and orchards, the cluster of neat white clapboard buildings and barns mark what is left (just 2 members) of America's oldest active Shaker community. A sect of the Quaker religion, founded in England in the late 1700s by Mother Ann Lee, this community was established in 1783 and at one time numbered some 200 people who lived communally and followed the Shaker's beliefs of hard-work, self-sufficiency, and celibacy. Guided tours of the village reveal the history of the community and offer insight into the Shaker way of life. Exhibits include Shaker furniture, oval boxes, basketry, and tools. There is also a gift shop selling Shaker-made goods. Open Memorial Day weekend through Labor Day Mon through Sat 10:30 a.m. to 4:30 p.m. (guided tours on the half hour). Admission $10 adults, $2 children ages 2 to 12.

where to eat & stay

Cyndi's Dockside. 640 Main St.; (207) 998-5008; dockside.me. Located next door to Poland Spring Resort, this year-rounder is simply decorated and specializes in lobster dinners and American fun food like fried ravioli, burgers, buffalo chicken wings and brownie sundaes. Open May through Oct Sun through Thurs 11:30 a.m. to 8 p.m., Fri and Sat 11:30 a.m. to 9 p.m. Check website for hours in the off-season. $$.

Poland Spring Resort. 543 Main St.; (207) 998-4351; polandspringinns.com. Woodlands and lawn surround this rustic retreat just 30 minutes, but seemingly worlds away, from downtown Portland. Not quite a resort—the rooms are short on amenities with minimal decor—but all rates include basic, yet hearty and plentiful, breakfast and dinner buffets (with communal seating) each day. There's an endless array of activities: a championship golf course, tennis courts, a huge outdoor pool, and boat rentals on a nearby lake. Shuffleboard, badminton, and bocce are on offer, too. In the evening, the best activity of all may be watching the sunset over the White Mountains. Open May through October. Hotel and restaurant: $$.

bethel, me

Located in the Maine's western mountains, Bethel is considered the gateway town to Sunday River, Maine's largest ski resort. It's a classic New England ski village with white steepled churches, quaint clapboard houses, and scenic views all around. In the summer, the town is a destination for the active with hiking, biking, canoeing, kayaking, fishing, and perhaps some relaxing by the Androscoggin River.

getting there

From Poland Spring to Bethel it is a 40-mile drive along scenic ME 26 North.

where to go

Bethel Outdoor Adventure. 121 Mayville Rd.; (207) 824-4224; betheloutdooradventure .com. This full-service, four-season outfitter rents canoes, kayaks, and mountain bikes to adventurers of all abilities. They also specialize in fun beginner-friendly guided paddle tours of the Androscoggin River, and in the winter they rent snowmobiles.

Grafton Notch State Park. 1941 Bear River Rd., Newry. Along ME 26 and just north of Bethel, this 3,000-acre park is a popular scenic drive-through. All along the road are turn-outs where you can stop; the tumbling Auger Screw Falls, impressive Mother Walker Falls and granite-flanked Moose Cave are all just a short walk from the parking areas. For more intrepid trekkers, the 2.5-mile Table Rock Loop is a moderately hilly climb that offers views of Old Speck Mountain—and the bonus of bragging rights that you've hiked a portion of the Appalachian Trail. Open year-round, staffed March 15 through October 15. Admission fee $4 adults, $1 seniors and children ages 5 to 12.

Sunday River. 97 Ridge Rd., Newry; (207) 824-3000; sundayriver.com. With 132 trails over 8 peaks, there's something for everyone at Sunday River. Sunday River is a favorite all-around ski New England mountain with extensive ski school programming for novices as well as snow parks, glades, and bumps to please serious powder hounds. The resort also has terrific snowmaking and grooming, making it one of New England's first ski resorts to open for the season and one of the last to close. In summer, enjoy the valley to mountain vista as you ride the high-speed chondola lift (a hybrid chair-lift/gondola) to the top of North Peak. After you snap a few photos and enjoy the views, you can either take the gondola back or hike back down to the base on marked trails.

where to eat

Cho Sun. 141 Main St.; (207) 824-7370; chosunrestaurant.com. Seoul food fan? Korean food is the real star of this menu. Order the beef *bibimbap*: a warm stone crock filled with rice and topped with mushrooms, spinach, carrots, chili pepper paste, and a fried egg. It may change how you think of ski grub. Open Tues through Sun 5 to 9:30 p.m. $$.

where to stay

Bethel Inn Resort. 22 Broad St.; (207) 824-2175; bethelinn.com. This classic four-season resort hotel just minutes from Sunday River offers tons of activities for the sports crazed. In winter there is excellent on-site cross-country skiing. In summer there's golf on the property. And in any season, guests enjoy the outdoor heated pool, hot tub, and health club with sauna. For even more diversion the inn can arrange snowmobiling, dog sledding, fly fishing, ATV adventures, and (photographic) moose safaris. An older New England–style ski resort, accommodation choices include either modest hotel rooms or fairway townhouses. Breakfast is included in all rates. $$–$$$.

sebago lake, me

Just 20 minutes from downtown Portland, the Sebago Lake region is a beautiful place to relax in the outdoors. Sebago Lake is the deepest and second-biggest lake in the state and is particularly known for its nearly clear water. Whether you stretch out along the sandy beaches of Sebago Lake Park, fish for trout, or go day-boating, there's no end to the adventures you'll encounter here.

getting there

From Bethel, a visit to Sebago Lake on the way back to Portland is an easy 40-mile detour along ME 35 and ME 5 South.

where to go

Sebago Lakes Region Chamber of Commerce. 747 Roosevelt Trail, Windham; (207) 892-8265; sebagolakeschamber.com. This information center is fully staffed and stocked with maps, brochures, and visitors' guides for the 10 communities of the Sebago Lake region. They also maintain an updated accommodation availability list for the area. Open Memorial Day through Labor Day Mon through Sat 9 a.m. to 4 p.m.

Sebago Lake State Park. 11 Park Access Rd., Casco; parksandlands.com. Sebago Lake is the region's centerpiece attraction and bustles with activity. Hiking, swimming, boating, picnicking, and fishing are popular in the summer and fall months. In the winter, 5 miles of trails are groomed for cross-country skiing. There is also a 250-site campground within the park. Open year-round. Admission $6.50 adults, $2 seniors, $1 children ages 5 to 12.

Songo River Queen II. 841 Roosevelt Trail; (207) 693-6861; songoriverqueen.net. Cruise Lake Sebago aboard the *Songo River Queen II,* a 2-level, 300-passenger replica Mississippi

River paddle wheeler. Scenic cruises are offered each day, but for a unique experience take the 2.5-Songo River/Lock trip, which passes through Long Lake and Brandy Pond and on to the still hand-operated Songo Lock at Sebago Lake. Cruise season is Memorial Day through Columbus Day; check website for departure times and prices.

where to eat & stay

Migis Lodge. 30 Migis Lodge Rd., South Casco; (207) 655-4524; migis.com. With a dramatic natural setting on the shores of Lake Sebago, Migis Lodge provides a luxury family camp-style vacation of endless summer fun. Choose accommodations from lodge rooms or cottages; all are done in upmarket New England country style. Food is front and center as part of your vacation experience, and meals are gourmet affairs. Whether you take a boxed picnic lunch over to the resort's private island, secure a table indoors for a fine-dining experience at dinner, or enjoy blueberry pancakes and coffee at the lake's edge, you will find the meals and settings here too perfect for words. The restaurant also accepts outside guests, and reservations are requested. The private beach offers swimming and boating of all kinds, including canoes and kayaks, pedal boats, and Sunfish. Open mid-June through mid-Oct. Rates include meals and activities. The Lodge also doesn't accept credit cards; most bring a check. Hotel: $$$–$$$$. Restaurant: $$$.

historic trips

day trip 31

historic trips

colonial history:
boston, ma; cambridge, ma;
lexington, ma; concord, ma; deerfield, ma

Any colonial history tour of New England must begin in Boston. Discover Boston's role in the American Revolution and why the neighboring towns of Lexington and Concord confronted the British in April 1775. Then drive along the Mohawk Drive to peaceful Deerfield and spend the day exploring a rural 18th-century village.

boston, ma

Considered the birthplace of the nation, the young colony's early struggle for American independence from Britain can be seen in sites throughout downtown.

getting there

From the west, the Massachusetts Turnpike (I-90) runs directly to the city. From the south, take I-95 North to I-93 North to downtown. From Vermont and points northwest, take I-93 South to downtown. From Maine and points northeast, take I-95 South to I-93 South to downtown.

where to go

Freedom Trail. Boston Common Visitor Center, 139 Tremont St., Downtown, Boston. Walk with history along the Freedom Trail, Boston's centerpiece "attraction." The 2.5-mile red-brick path links 16 historical sites that played an important role in the events of the American Revolution. Among them: the site of the Boston Massacre, where in the shadow of the Old State House and the lion and the unicorn (the lion is the symbol for England, the unicorn for Scotland), the first shots of the Revolution rang out; the Old South Meeting House, where a mob of angry protesters marched to the waterfront and dumped three shiploads of tea into the harbor; and the Granary Burying Ground, where legendary patriots Paul Revere, John Hancock, and Sam Adams are buried.

One could wax poetic about each of the sites, but you should find out for yourself. Whether you choose to follow the Freedom Trail on your own or take a guided walking tour (see the Freedom Trail primer in Day Trip 01 for details), try to see them all—it's a fascinating introduction to American history.

Massachusetts Historical Society. 1154 Boylston St., Back Bay; (617) 536-1608; masshist.org. This is one of Boston's hidden gems. The roots of the Massachusetts Historic Society go back to 1791, making this the country's first historic society. Every state has a historic society, but because of Massachusetts' unique role in the founding of the country, the scope of the society includes the history of America from its very beginnings. The society is an independent research library that collects, preserves and makes available documents and artifacts that relate to the history of Massachusetts. Among the highlights of the collection for researchers are the Adams (John Adams and John Quincy Adams) family papers and the personal papers of Thomas Jefferson. A free, guided art and architecture tour of the library is offered most Saturdays at 10 a.m., but visitors can drop in at any time to visit the exhibits. The collection includes portraits of key early American figures like the Marquise de Lafayette and Dr. Joseph Warren. In the display cases there are interesting artifacts like bullets from the Boston Massacre, Washington's epaulets and the pen Lincoln used to sign the Emancipation Proclamation. If you are a real American history fan, consider attending one of the evening public lectures—many include a pre-talk reception where you can meet with the speaker and other attendees. Open Mon through Fri 9 a.m. to 4:45 p.m., Sat 9 a.m. to 4 p.m., closed Sun. Admission free.

Museum of Fine Arts. 465 Huntington Ave., Back Bay; (617) 267-9300; mfa.org. Step off the Freedom Trail and check out the MFA's Art of the Americas wing. The MFA has a superlative collection of Revolutionary-era art, including Thomas Sully's *The Passage of the Delaware,* Paul Revere's 1770 engraving of the Boston Massacre, and Gilbert Stuart's unfinished 1796 portrait of George Washington that you'll surely recognize—it was used as the basis for the US $1 bill. Open Mon, Tues, Sat, and Sun 10 a.m. to 4:45 p.m., Wed through Fri 10 a.m. to 9:45 p.m. Admission $25 adults, $23 seniors and students, free for ages 7 to

17 after 3 p.m. and on weekends; otherwise $10, free children ages 6 and under. Admission by donation Wed after 4 p.m.

where to eat

Warren Tavern. 2 Pleasant St., Charlestown; (617) 241-8142; warrentavern.com. Raise a glass to the Founding Fathers at one of Boston's oldest taverns. Built in 1780, it was named in honor of Dr. Joseph Warren, the Sons of Liberty leader who died at the Battle of Bunker Hill. The Federal-style building, with its timber beams and low ceiling, has tremendous colonial ambience. You drink in good company, too; the tavern was a regular watering hole for Paul Revere, and George Washington visited here as well. It's a convenient stop for lunch after visiting the USS *Constitution* and Bunker Hill Monument. Their Angus burgers are especially good. Open Sun through Fri 11 a.m. to 1 a.m., Sat and Sun 10 a.m. to 1 a.m. $.

cambridge, ma

In Revolutionary times, Cambridge was a hotbed of Loyalist sentiment. The mansions along Brattle Street were known as "Tory Row" because the residents were supporters of King George III. In the months leading up to the Revolution, many of the homes were abandoned, their owners often settling in Canada.

getting there

Travel west on Storrow Drive, which becomes Soldiers Field Road. Take the Harvard Square/Cambridge ramp, crossing the Charles River at the Anderson Bridge, and continue along JFK Street into the heart of Harvard Square. The distance from Boston to Cambridge is only about 4 miles, but it will take about 12 minutes to drive. Another alternative to Cambridge from Boston is to take the T (Red Line) to the Harvard Square station.

where to go

Harvard University. The Harvard Information Center, 30 Dunster St.; (617) 495-1573; harvard.edu/visitors. One of the world's most prestigious universities, Harvard was the first college established in America. Named for its first benefactor, John Harvard, the college was founded in 1636 to educate the religious and civil leaders of the Massachusetts Bay Colony. The oldest surviving building on campus is Massachusetts Hall (next to Johnston Gate on Mass Ave) a 4-story brick building dating from 1720. It was once a dormitory and over the years has housed some illustrious students, among them John Adams, John Hancock, and Sam Adams. Today, the building houses the offices of university president Drew Faust. Student-led guided historical tours of Harvard geared to the general public are offered Mon through Sat at 10 a.m. to 4 p.m. (on the hour). Free.

Longfellow House–Washington Headquarters National Historic Site. 105 Brattle St.; (617) 876-4491; nps.gov/long. George Washington slept here. For quite a long time, actually. This gracious home was Washington's headquarters during the planning stages of the Siege of Boston from July 1775 to April 1776, and it hosted many guests during that time, including Washington's wife, Martha, as well as fellow patriots and dignitaries. In later years it was the home of Henry Wadsworth Longfellow, who lived here with his wife and brood of six. Longfellow was proud of his home's history and its association with Washington. After all, in his poems he helped create American legends. This became Longfellow's home for most of his life, and many of his most famous works, "Paul Revere's Ride," "The Legend of Hiawatha," and "The Courtship of Miles Standish," were penned here. The grounds are open daily dawn to dusk. The home is open seasonally June through Oct Wed through Sun, by guided tour only. Check website for exact times. Admission free.

lexington, ma

Colonial history isn't confined to the city limits of Boston. Just a few miles northwest of Boston, in the towns of Lexington and Concord, farmers took up their muskets against their own government in 1775.

getting there

From Cambridge, turn right onto Mass Ave and follow for 2 miles. Turn right onto MA 2 West for 3 miles. Take exit 56 for MA 225 West and follow signs to Lexington center.

where to go

Battle Green. Massachusetts Avenue and Bedford Street. This is where it all began. On April 19, 1775, the first exchange of fire between the colonists and the British took place on Lexington Common. Every year, on Patriots' Day (the third Mon in Apr), a band of patriots and an army of redcoats reenact the "shot heard round the world."

Minute Man National Historical Park. Minute Man Visitor Center, 250 N. Great Rd., Lincoln; (978) 369-6993; nps.gov/mima. Extending through the towns of Lexington, Lincoln, and Concord, the park interprets the events that led up to the Revolutionary War. Be sure to see the free orientation film, *The Road to Revolution,* and check the schedule for the generally excellent park ranger–led talks and walks. Minute Man Visitor Center open Apr through Oct, daily 9 a.m. to 5 p.m.; month of Nov, 9 a.m. to 4 p.m.; Dec through Mar 11 a.m. to 3 p.m. Grounds open dawn to dusk. Free.

Lexington Historical Society. Lexington Depot, 13 Depot Sq.; (781) 862-1703; lexington history.org. Visit the Lexington Historical Society to purchase tickets for the town's three historic home sites. Admission for all three properties $15 adult, $8 children ages 6 to 16, free for children under age 6. Admission for any one property $8 adult, $5 children ages 6 to 16, free for children under age 6.

Buckman Tavern. 1 Bedford St.; (781) 862-5598. Anticipating a fight, in the early morning of April 19, 1775, the Lexington militia gathered at Buckman Tavern. Check out the musket hole in the old front door. Open Apr through Oct daily 10 a.m. to 4 p.m., tours on the half hour.

Hancock-Clarke House. 36 Hancock St.; (781) 861-0928. This was a parsonage, the one-time home of John Hancock's grandfather, the Reverend John Hancock. Hancock knew the house well, and on the eve of the battle, Hancock and Sam Adams were the guests of the then-minister Jonas Clarke. Late in the evening of April 18, 1775, Paul Revere and William Dawes arrived to warn them that the British troops were on the move. Open Apr and May Sat and Sun 10 a.m. to 4 p.m.; June through Oct daily 10 a.m. to 4 p.m.

Munroe Tavern. 1332 Massachusetts Ave.; (781) 862-6295. Colonial Lexington's other tavern, British troops used it as a field hospital and headquarters in the hours after the battle at the North Bridge. Just 14 years later, President George Washington dined at the tavern as the Munroe family's very special guest. Drop-in 30-minute guided tours (on the hour) tell the story of the British troops' return march to Boston. Open Apr through Nov, daily noon to 4 p.m.

Liberty Ride. Departs from the Lexington Visitor Center, 1875 Massachusetts Ave.; (339) 223-5623; libertyride.us. For an overview of everything historical in both Lexington and Concord, consider the Liberty Ride with narrated commentary. The open-air red, white, and blue sightseeing trolley runs a route that covers more than a dozen sites relating both to the events of April 19, 1775, and Concord's 19th-century literary legacy. You'll cover a lot of ground in just 90 minutes. Your ticket also includes admission to the Lexington historical houses; tickets are good the entire day, and you can reboard for free. Tickets $28 adults, $10 ages 5 to 17, free for children ages 4 and under.

Scottish Rite Masonic Musuem & Library. 33 Marrett Rd., Lexington; (781) 861-6559; srmmi.org. Major aspects of America's cultural and scientific history come alive at this thoroughly modern museum founded and supported by the Scottish Rite of Freemasonry. Popular past exhbits have included *Sowing the Seeds of Liberty,* which describes Lexington's role in the American Revolution. Its Made in Massachusetts exhibit includes notable local inventions from the 18th century to the present. Open Wed through Sat 10 a.m. to 4:30 p.m., Sunday noon to 4:30 p.m. Free.

concord, ma

Follow the Battle Road Trail to Concord and see the hallowed ground where the colonists experienced their first military success.

getting there

Concord is just 7 miles from Lexington. Follow MA 2A (Mass Ave) as it parallels the Battle Road Trail. Bear right at Lexington Road and follow the signs to Concord Center.

where to go

The Concord Museum. 53 Cambridge Tpke.; (978) 369-9763; concordmuseum.org. Stop here on your travels to see the Concord Museum's prized holding: the lantern of "one, if by land, and two if by sea" fame. This exceptional museum has a comprehensive collection of artifacts related to native son Henry David Thoreau, and Ralph Waldo Emerson's study, taken lock, stock, and fountain pen from his home across the street. Open Apr through May and Sept through Dec Mon through Sat 9 a.m. to 5 p.m., Sun noon to 5 p.m.; June through Aug daily 9 a.m. to 5 p.m.; Jan through Mar Mon through Sat 11 a.m. to 4 p.m., Sun 1 to 4 p.m. Admission $10 adults, $8 seniors and students, $5 children ages 6 to 17, children under age 6 are free.

Minute Man National Historical Park. North Bridge Visitor Center, 174 Liberty St.; (978) 369-6993; nps.gov/mima. Concord's parcel of the Minute Man National Historical Park encompasses the site of the Old North Bridge, where Concord's minutemen—so named because they needed to be ready at a moment's notice—met the advancing British forces and succeeded in forcing the British to retreat. Across the bridge, Daniel Chester French's *Minute Man* statue memorializes the battle. Grounds open year-round, dawn to dusk. Visitor center open daily Apr through Oct 9:30 a.m. to 5 p.m., check website for off-season hours. Free.

where to eat & stay

Wayside Inn. 72 Wayside Inn Rd., Sudbury; (978) 443-1776; wayside.org. There are few American inns with the storied history of the Wayside. Located on the historic Boston Post Road and dating from 1716, the Wayside is said to be America's oldest operating inn. The inn inspired Longfellow's *Tales of a Wayside Inn,* most known for the poem "Paul Revere's Ride" that begins, "Listen my children and you shall hear." There are 9 "bed-chambers," each has a private bathroom and is done in a historically accurate style with antique canopy beds and reproduction furniture. As you might suspect, the rooms don't have TVs—but they do have Wi-Fi. Rates include continental breakfast in the inn's post-and-frame Tap Room, which is also open to the public and serves traditional New England victuals like chicken potpie, Yankee pot roast, and apple pie. The Wayside is still a hub of colonial activity for the area. The inn has 3 museum rooms, a gristmill, and a one-room schoolhouse that are open to the public. The local fife and drum corps practices on the property on Wednesday, and there are weekend horse and carriage rides around the grounds. Restaurant open Sat 7 to 10:30 a.m., 11:30 a.m. to 2:30 p.m., and 5 to 8:30 p.m.; Sun 7 to 10:30 a.m. and noon to 7:30 p.m.; Mon through Fri 11:30 a.m. to 2:30 p.m. and 5 to 8:30 p.m. Inn: $$–$$$. Restaurant: $$.

deerfield, ma

Surrounded by the fields of the Connecticut River Valley, this typical rural 18th-century New England village has been faithfully preserved.

getting there

Pick up MA 2 West and follow for 60 miles as it alternates names between MA 2, MA 2A, and the Mohawk Trail along the way. At Greenfield, take US 5/MA 10 South and follow signs to Deerfield Village.

where to go

Historic Deerfield. 80 Old Main St.; (413) 775-7214; historic-deerfield.org. Historic Deerfield is a National Historic Landmark village and a favorite destination for history enthusiasts. This open-air living-history museum has 11 restored buildings dating from the 1730s to the 1840s that are open for guided and self-guided tours. Those with specific interests in history, antiques, or architecture may want to take advantage of Deerfield's "VIP Tours by Appointment" program. A custom itinerary led by a Master Guide will be created just for you. Make reservations two weeks in advance: (413) 775-7132. Open Apr through Dec daily 9:30 a.m. to 4:30 p.m.; Jan through Mar houses by appointment; Flynt Center open Sat and Sun 9:30 to 4:30 p.m. Admission $18 adults, $5 children ages 6 to 17.

where to eat

Champney's Restaurant & Tavern. Deerfield Inn, 81 Main St.; (413) 772-3087; champneysrestaurant.com. Since 1884, the Deerfield Inn has been at the center of town life. In keeping with the theme of Historic Deerfield, have lunch or dinner at the inn's Champney's Restaurant & Tavern, which serves seasonal, upscale pub fare. Open Sun through Fri 7:30 a.m. to 9 p.m., Fri and Sat 7:30 a.m. to 10 p.m., Sun noon to 8 p.m. $$.

day trip 32

historic trips

southern new england colonial trail:
quincy, ma; providence, ri; newport, ri

Head south from Boston along the coast to get a glimpse of two of New England's earliest colonies. Religious dissenters fleeing the intolerance of Puritan-ruled Massachusetts founded both Providence and Newport in the 1630s. Each city boasts a walkable historic district that harkens back to colonial roots with lots of examples of pre- and post-Revolutionary architecture. Along the way, stop in Quincy at the Adams National Historic Park and learn about one of the most prominent families in colonial America.

quincy, ma

New England abounds in historic house tours of all types, but the Adams National Historic Park, home to the first American father-son presidential dynasty, is one of the most significant house tours in all of New England. Don't miss it.

getting there

From Boston take I-93 South (also known as Route 128 here), then take exit 7 to merge onto MA 3 South, bear left to take exit 19 and follow signs into Quincy Center. From Cape Cod and points south, travel north on MA 3. Take exit 19 and follow signs to Quincy Center. You can also take public transportation. Take the T's Red Line train to Quincy Center; the Adams National Historical Park Visitor Center is across from the T station.

where to go

Adams National Historical Park. 1250 Hancock St.; (617) 770-1175; nps.gov/adam. Since the HBO miniseries *John Adams,* the Adams National Historical Park in Quincy is newly popular. This is the oldest surviving presidential birthplace in the country, dating from 1670. The second and sixth US presidents, John Adams and his son John Quincy Adams, were born here. You'll also tour the "Old House," the Adams family ancestral home. Among the treasures you'll see is a rare 1823 engraving of the Declaration of Independence, and you will be reminded that not only was John Adams one of its signers, he was one of the Committee of Five that helped write it. You can only see the sites of the park by guided tour. From the visitor center, you take a free trolley tour of the birth houses and then reboard the trolley to visit the Old House and the next-door Stone Library, which serves as the Adams presidential archives. The period gardens are especially pretty. Houses open mid-Apr through mid-Nov daily 9 a.m. to 5 p.m. Admission $10 adults, free children ages 16 and under.

providence, ri

Rhode Island's capital was founded in 1636 by Roger Williams, who was banished from Massachusetts by the Puritans for his religious views. He purchased land from the Narragansett Indians and named the city in gratitude for "God's merciful Providence."

getting there

It's an easy 45-minute highway drive from Quincy to Providence. Take I-93 South (there are signs all over downtown Quincy pointing you to it) for 7 miles, merge onto I-95 South and follow for 32 miles, then take exit 22A for RI 10 West and follow signs to downtown.

where to go

Benefit Street. Begin your visit with a leisurely stroll along leafy Benefit Street where you will encounter 300 years of art, architecture, and history. There are a wealth of colonial- and Victorian-era homes on both sides of the narrow street (most are privately owned), but as you walk, you certainly will get a sense of why the street is referred to as Providence's "Mile of History." Stop by the **Providence Preservation Society** (21 Meeting St.; 401-831-7440; ppsri.org) for a self-guided Benefit Street tour map.

Brown University. 45 Prospect St.; (401) 863-1000; brown.edu. Established in 1764, Brown is the third college founded in New England and the nation's seventh oldest college. Brown was a Baptist school originally named the Rhode Island College, and, unusual for the time, it was open to students of all religious persuasions. Walk through the green, a contemplative parklike space of lawn and trees surrounded by redbrick buildings. Prominent here, the first and oldest structure of the college, 4-story University Hall that was built in 1771 and originally called "the College Edifice."

First Baptist Church. 75 Main St.; (401) 454-3418; fbcia.org. This really is a first Baptist church: Roger Williams established America's first Baptist congregation here in 1638. The building itself dates from 1775, and with its Ionic columns, an ornate steeple, and the fine craftsmanship of its interior, it's a noted departure from the austere meetinghouse-style Baptist churches of the day. The church is an active Baptist congregation; guided and self-guided tours are available Mon through Fri 10 a.m. to noon and 1 to 4 p.m. Admission is $2 per person.

John Brown House Museum. 52 Power St.; (401) 273-7507; rihs.org. Atop College Hill this sumptuous 3-story mansion was built for John Brown, a merchant who made his fortune in trade with the Far East and in the slave trade in the years after the Revolutionary War. The Rhode Island Historic Society has restored the 1786 house with furnishings, textiles, wall coverings, and paint that are faithful to the period. Visits of the house are by guided tour only, but this is not your standard historic house tour. The guides are as exceedingly well versed in the history of the home and the decorative arts as they are in discussing Brown's support of the slave trade and the role of the slave trade in Rhode Island. The Rhode Island Historical Society also offers a daily 90-minute walking tour of Benefit Street. Walking tour Tues through Sat 11 a.m. Tickets $15 adult, $10 children ages 8 and under. Tour times Apr 1 to Nov 30 Tues through Fri 1:30 p.m. and 3 p.m.; Sat 10:30 a.m., noon, 1:30 p.m., and 3 p.m.; Dec 1 to Mar 31 Fri through Sat 10:30 a.m., noon, 1:30 p.m., and 3 p.m. Admission $10 adults, $8 seniors and students, $6 children ages 7 to 17.

Museum of Art, Rhode Island School of Design. 224 Benefit St.; (401) 454-6500; risd museum.org. The university museum of the Rhode Island School of Art is known as the RISD (say RIZ-dee) Museum. It's notable for its collection of 19th-century Impressionist paintings as well as its contemporary art collection, but its early American furniture collection is outstanding as well. The Pendleton House is the country's first museum wing devoted to American decorative arts. It's a 1906 replica of a Federal-style house and directly connected to RISD (access is through glass doors between the galleries).The period room settings are decorated with fine wallpaper and lush draperies that are all the better for displaying the museum's collection of American furniture, silver, and ceramics, which includes a fabulous example of a block-front, carved desk and bookcase by Newport cabinetmaker John Goddard. Open Tues through Sun 10 a.m. to 5 p.m.; closed Mon. Admission $12 adults, $10 seniors, $3 children ages 5 to 18.

Stephen Hopkins House. 15 Hopkins St.; (401) 421-0694; stephenhopkins.org. Located off Benefit Street, the earliest portion of this dark clapboard house dates from 1709, making this the oldest standing structure in Providence. It was the home of Stephen Hopkins, who served multiple times as governor and was one of Rhode Island's two signers of the

Declaration of Independence. Open May through Nov Sat and Sun 10 a.m. to 4 p.m. Admission by donation.

newport, ri

Newport was settled in 1639, and during the early colonial period Newport became a haven for followers of several different religions including Baptists, Quakers, and Jews.

A harbor city, these early settlers helped Newport make its fortune through trade, and by the 1760s Newport was the fifth busiest port in the New World. Stroll the warren of streets that make up Newport's Point neighborhood, the compact village has survived development with more than 200 homes (most are privately owned) that are more than 200 years old. Think of this itinerary as Newport without the mansions.

getting there

Follow I-195 East from Providence for 2 miles. Take exit 7 to RI 114 South and follow for 24 miles through the towns of Portsmouth and Middletown. In Newport, RI 114 South becomes Broadway, then follow signs to the Newport Visitor Center.

where to go

Brick Market Building. 127 Thames St.; (401) 841-8770; newporthistory.org. Another Peter Harrison–designed building, the Brick Market Building has evolved over many years since its construction in 1762 when it served as an open-air market and then, in later years, it became the Newport Town Hall. Today Brick Market houses the Museum of Newport History and operates as the ticket office and gift shop for the Newport Historical Society. Open daily 10 a.m. to 5 p.m. Museum admission $4 adults, $2 children.

Colony House. Washington Square; (401) 846-0813; newporthistory.org. Dating from 1739, the distinguished Georgian brick building facing Washington Square was the first seat of Rhode Island's colonial government and served as the state's primary capitol building until its replacement in Providence was completed in 1900. Worth a peek is the painting of George Washington by Rhode Island native Gilbert Stuart on the second floor. Guided site tours are offered June through Dec, daily 11 a.m. to 3 p.m.; check website for rest of year. Tours also include a visit to the Wanton-Lyman-Hazard House, 17 Broadway St., Newport's oldest house museum, dating from 1697. Tickets $15 adults, $5 children ages 12 and under.

Great Friends Meeting House. 29 Farewell St.; (401) 846-0813; newporthistory.org. Along with Baptists, Quakers (also known as the Society of Friends) were the most influential religious group in colonial Rhode Island. Built in 1699, this is the oldest house of worship in the state, and it served as the center of Quaker life for the entire New England region until

1905. The site can only be visited by guided tour. Tours also include a guided visit to the 1730 Seventh Day Baptist Meeting House. Guided tours are offered June through Dec, daily 11 a.m. to 3 p.m.; check website for rest of year. Admission $15 adults, $5 children ages 12 and under.

Redwood Library & Athenaeum. 50 Bellevue Ave.; (401) 847-0292; redwoodlibrary.org. The august Redwood Library is a private library founded in 1747. It is one of the country's oldest libraries—worthy of museum status—with an impressive collection of rare books, oil paintings, marble sculpture, and antiques. The Redwood membership has included an illustrious group of writers and thinkers: Henry Wadsworth Longfellow, Henry James, Julia Ward Howe, and Edith Wharton have made use of its collections. The library is open to the public Mon, Tues, Thurs, Fri, and Sat 9:30 a.m. to 5:30 p.m., Wed 9:30 a.m. to 8 p.m., Sun 1 to 5 p.m.

Touro Synagogue and Loeb Visitor's Center. 85 Touro St.; (401) 847-4794; touro synagogue.org. Newport's Jewish community traces back to colonial beginnings in 1658. Dedicated in 1763, this historic treasure is America's oldest synagogue and the only one that survives from colonial times. Designed by architect Peter Harrison, it's a small synagogue but is supremely elegant. Among the design elements are 12 classical pillars that represent the tribes of Israel, 5 massive hanging candelabra, and Palladian windows that flood the sanctuary with natural light. Adjacent to the synagogue, the Loeb Visitor's Center features exhibits on the story of religious freedom in the US and the history of Jews in colonial America. Open year-round; check website for days and times. The synagogue is an active congregation, so there are no tours on Saturday or on Jewish holidays. Admission $12 adults, $8 students, $10 seniors, children ages 13 and under free.

where to eat

White Horse Tavern. 26 Marlborough St.; (401) 849-3600; whitehorsenewport.com . This is the oldest tavern in America (since 1673), and it offers a nice bit of history—with the low ceilings to prove it—as a backdrop for traditional New England fare. Lunch is an especially good value with lots of pub-style sandwich, soup, and salad combinations. The dinner menu is more upmarket with dishes like grilled steak au poivre and seared scallops with lump crabmeat. Open Mon through Thurs 11 a.m. to 9 p.m., Fri and Sat 11 a.m. to 10 p.m., Sun 11 a.m. to 9 p.m. $$.

day trip 33

historic trips

northern new england colonial trail:
salem, ma; exeter, nh; portsmouth, nh

Throughout colonial America, the earliest settlements were coastal. Follow the curve of shoreline north of Boston to the great seaport cities of Salem and Portsmouth. Prosperous before the Revolution—Salem from maritime trade, Portsmouth from shipbuilding—in the years immediately following the Revolution, even more staggering fortunes were made. And since you're passing through, take a small detour inland to Exeter to visit the American Independence Museum to see documents related to the nation's founding, including two early drafts of the Constitution.

salem, ma

Although Salem was one of the richest and most important seaports in America for nearly 200 years, Salem's colonial history will forever be linked to the witchcraft hysteria of 1692 that led to the execution of 20 "witches."

getting there

From Boston take I-93 North to exit 37A for I-95/MA 128 North. Take exit 25A and follow MA 114 East into Salem. From the north take I-95 South (from Maine) or I-93 South (from New Hampshire) to MA 128 North. Take exit 25A and MA 114 East to Salem. From the west take I-90 East (the Mass Turnpike) to I-95/MA 128 North. Take exit 25A and follow 114 East to Salem.

where to go

Salem Regional Visitor Center. 2 New Liberty St.; (978) 740-1650; nps.gov/sama. Located next to the Peabody Essex Museum and the city's main parking garage, this visitor center is doubly well staffed by both National Park Service rangers and volunteers. Other reasons to stop by are the 30-minute free introductory film *Where Past Is Present,* public restrooms, and a large, tasteful (nothing tacky here) gift shop. Open daily 9 a.m. to 5 p.m.

Salem Maritime National Historic Site. 193 Derby St.; (978) 740-1650; nps.gov/sama. Along the harbor, this 9-acre site focuses on Salem's nautical traditions. By the mid-1600s Salem was a major seaport, trading dried cod and timber throughout the British Empire. During the Revolution, Salem's prominent merchant class helped the war effort the best way they knew how—by privateering. Hear these stories and more on ranger-led tours or take a self-guided walk of the park's historic buildings, wharves, and the park's centerpiece attraction, the replica 1797 Schooner *Friendship.* Visitor center open Apr through Oct daily 9 a.m. to 5 p.m.; check website for days and hours at other times of the year. Site and tours are free.

House of the Seven Gables. 115 Derby St.; (978) 744-0991; 7gables.org. For a dose of colonial American architecture, classic American literature, and spooky Salem, this tour can't be beat. Overlooking Salem Harbor, the gloomy mansion immortalized in Nathaniel Hawthorne's book of the same name dates from 1668. Hawthorne knew the house well; it was owned by his cousin Susannah Ingersoll—and some say her ghostly presence remains. The home's interior retains many of its original period features. The smaller, more modest mid-18th-century house on the property is Nathaniel Hawthorn's birthplace and is open for self-guided visits. Open Nov through June 10 a.m. to 5 p.m., July through Oct 7 a.m. to 7 p.m., closed the first two weeks of Jan. Admission $14 adults, $13 seniors, $9 children ages 5 to 12.

Peabody Essex Museum. 161 Essex St.; (978) 745-9500; pem.org. From elaborately stitched embroidery samplers to elegant mahogany tea tables, fine women's dressing gowns, musket powder horns, carved ship's figureheads, and oil paintings, the Peabody Essex Museum holds a treasure trove of art that offers a glimpse of life in colonial America. Other highlights of this world-class museum include major holdings in Asian export art and maritime art. What is not well known is that the Peabody Essex Museum is also the steward of nearly two dozen historic houses that are located on nearby Chestnut, Essex, and Federal Streets. A good one to see? The John Ward House, dating from 1684, is a terrific early colonial house example; the timber frame house has a steeply gabled roof, massive chimney, and small leaded glass windows. Check with the information desk to see which historic houses are open during your visit. House tours are included with museum admission. Open Tues through Sun and holiday Mon 10 a.m. to 5 p.m. Admission $20 adults, $18 seniors, $12 students, free for children ages 16 and under,

Salem Witch Trials Memorial. Off Liberty Street, next to Salem's Burying Point. Adjacent to Salem's oldest burying ground, this small, leafy parklike space invites contemplation. Each of the 20 victims of the witchcraft trials is remembered with a granite bench inscribed with their name and the date and the means of their execution. Open dawn to dusk.

where to shop

Ye Olde Pepper Candy Companie. 122 Derby St.; (978) 745-2744; oldpeppercandy.com. If you have a sweet tooth, pop into this old-fashioned family-owned candy shop. Established in 1806, this is one of the oldest sweet shops in the country. It specializes in handmade hard sweets like melt-in-your-mouth lemon and peppermint Gibraltars, homemade penuche fudge (made with brown sugar), and Black Jacks fresh licorice sticks made with blackstrap molasses. Open July through Oct, daily 10 a.m. to 6 p.m.; Nov through June daily 10 a.m. to 5 p.m.

where to eat

Naumkeag Ordinary. 118 Washington St., (978) 744-4968; naumkeagordinary.com. Naumkeag or "fishing place" was the Native American name for this region. The word "ordinary" referred to a colonial tavern. Right dab in the middle of Salem's historic center, Naumkeag Ordinary welcomes locals and tourists alike with a rustic reclaimed wood bar and a menu that feels friendly and familiar. The kitchen sends out shareable small plates inspired and sourced from New England: deviled eggs with chipotle and lardon and pork belly bahn mi sliders along with local cheese and charcuterie. Entrée highlights include a beautiful bacon bleu burger and a sophisticated puff pastry chicken pot pie. Open daily 11:30 a.m. to 1 a.m. $–$$.

Red's Sandwich Shop. 15 Central St.; (978) 745-3527; redssandwichshop.com. Step back in time and sample delicious greasy diner-style food like fried eggs with crispy home fries and hot turkey sandwiches that won't burn a hole in your pocket. Cash only. Open Mon through Sat 5 a.m. to 3 p.m., Sun 6 a.m. to 1 p.m. $.

Turner's Seafood. 43 Church St.; (978) 745-7665; turners-seafood.com. Located on the 2nd floor of Salem's Lyceum Hall, Turner's Seafood recaptures the creative spirit of Alexander Graham Bell and the many other mid-19th century writers and intellectuals who once spoke here. The space itself dates from 1843; Turner's took over the space in 2013 and has been an instant success. Choose between booth and table dining in the exposed brick main dining room or snacking and drinking at the high tops in the front room. There's a city-slick element here too with a boisterous raw bar and open kitchen. Order the finnan haddie—au gratin smoked haddock—it is but one of the many old-school classics on the expansive menu. The expertly fried seafood is always a good bet, and the supremely rich lobster bisque is jam-packed with lobster meat. Open Sun through Thurs 11 a.m. to 9 p.m., Fri and Sat 11 a.m. to 10 p.m. Oyster bar open daily 4 p.m. until close. $$–$$$

where to stay

The Merchant. 148 Washington St.; (978) 745-8100; themerchantsalem.com. Plugged in and stylishly elegant, this 1784 merchant fleet captain's house once hosted George Washington. After a 2016 top-to-toe renovation each guest room is unique in its size and color scheme, but each room is large and fully up-to-date with luxury expectations and modern flair. What you'll find: original wainscoting and millwork, plush beds decked out with jewel-tone fabrics, marble bathrooms with heated floors and a gas fireplace in each of the inn's 11 rooms. For history buffs, the George Washington bedroom is the one to book complete with a king bed and window seat. Rates include free parking and snacks all day. There isn't an on-site restaurant, but rates include a breakfast voucher which can be used at one of three local cafes. $$–$$$.

exeter, nh

Exeter was founded in 1638 as one of New Hampshire's four original plantation settlements. Tiny Exeter soon played an important role in colonial history when the state capital was moved here from Portsmouth during the Revolution to escape the guns of the British Navy. Today Exeter is known mostly as the home to the prestigious Phillips Exeter Academy, which dates from 1783. Stop here along the way between Salem and Portsmouth to experience the essence of a classic New England small town and to visit the American Independence Museum. It's just the sort of historical house museum that you would expect to find in the "Live Free or Die" state.

getting there

Return to MA 114 West and take I-95 North toward Salisbury/Portsmouth for 30 miles. Take exit 2 for NH 101 toward Exeter and follow for 4 miles. Take exit 11 for NH 108 to Exeter.

where to go

American Independence Museum. 1 Governor's Ln.; (603) 772-2622; independence museum.org. This museum focuses on Exeter's prosperous Gilman family and their role in the years leading up to and during the Revolutionary War. The family was politically active: John Taylor Gilman read the Declaration of Independence to the citizens of Exeter and later served as New Hampshire governor; his son Nicholas Gilman Jr. was a signer of the Constitution. The museum's treasured collections include an original Dunlap Broadside of the Declaration of Independence (it's fragile so you'll see a copy of the copy) and working drafts of the US Constitution. You can see the museum on your own, but you'll get a lot more from your visit if you take the guided tour that is offered on the hour. Of special note is the museum's annual Revolutionary War Festival, complete with period-clad revolutionaries held on the third weekend in July. Open mid-May through Oct Thurs through Sat 10 a.m. to 4 p.m., by appointment the rest of the year. Admission $6 adults, $5 children and students.

where to eat

Blue Moon Evolution. 8 Clifford St.; (603) 778-6850; bluemoonevolution.com. Visitors to Exeter will find much to like at this two-for-one spot, which at lunch features seasonal salads, hearty soups, and big-flavored sandwiches. At night, the cafe transforms into a full-service restaurant that brims with organic and farm-to-table comfort food offerings like whole grilled trout with horseradish crème fraîche and apple-butter-glazed pot roast brisket. The menu gets high marks for its vegan, vegetarian, and gluten-free choices too. Open Mon through Thurs 4 to 9 p.m., Fri and Sat 4 to 9:30 p.m. $–$$$.

portsmouth, nh

One of the most charming and historic towns in New England, Portsmouth was one of the busiest seaports in all of colonial America. Today, step back in time to see some of New England's finest examples of Georgian- and Federal-style mansions built from fortunes made in the maritime trade. Then visit Strawbery Banke, which stands at the site of Portsmouth's original settlement with a living history museum that chronicles daily life in this neighborhood from the 17th to 20th century.

getting there

You need to backtrack to I-95 to get to Portsmouth. Follow NH 101 East for 4 miles. Take the exit to I-95 North and follow 10 miles to Portsmouth.

where to go

John Paul Jones House. 43 Middle St.; (603) 436-8420; portsmouthhistory.org. "I have not yet begun to fight" is how John Paul Jones is best known to the American public. Learn the story of the Scottish-born Revolutionary War hero and the "father of the US Navy," who rented rooms in this fine clapboard house from the widow Purcell while he waited for the ship *America* to be built nearby. This is also the headquarters of the Portsmouth Historical Society, which presents ongoing and special exhibits. Open Mar through mid-Nov daily 11 a.m. to 5 p.m. Admission $6 adults, free for children ages 12 and under.

Moffatt-Ladd House. 154 Market St.; (603) 436-8221; moffattladd.org. Built in 1763, this impressive Georgian Revival house was built for merchant John Moffatt. Moffatt had his family mansion built next to the wharf and warehouses of his business. The interior features carved millwork, period wallpaper, family furniture, and mementos. The gardens are especially lovely. Particularly notable is the horse chestnut tree in the front of the house. It was planted in 1776 by William Whipple, John Moffatt's son-in-law, upon his return from Philadelphia after signing the Declaration of Independence. Open June through mid-Oct, Mon through Sat 11 a.m. to 5 p.m., Sun 1 to 5 p.m. Admission $7 adults, $2.50 children, $2 garden only.

Strawbery Banke Museum. 14 Hancock St.; (603) 433-1100; strawberybanke.org. This 10-acre living-history museum tells the stories of four centuries of New Englanders who once lived and worked in this working-class neighborhood along the Piscataqua waterfront. There are some 40 restored buildings and gardens on the site that date from colonial times to the modern day. The Sherburne House is the museum's oldest structure, dating from 1695. It depicts a ship captain's 2-story home typical of the era with a practical, raised bed kitchen garden and an orchard out the back door. Ponder colonial life at the Pitt Tavern, which dates from 1766 and is said to have been visited by George Washington, John Hancock, and the Marquise de Lafayette (although not at the same time!). You can tour at your own pace, and there are costume presenters, trades people, and site interpreters throughout the village to answer questions. Open May through Oct daily 10 a.m. to 5 p.m. Admission $17.50 adults, $10 ages 5 to 17, ages 4 and under free. Open additional days in Dec; check website for hours.

Wentworth-Gardner House. 50 Mechanic St.; (603) 436-4406; wentworthlear.org. Built in 1760 for Thomas Wentworth, the brother of John Wentworth who was New Hampshire's last British Royal governor, this mansion is considered to be an excellent example of American Georgian architecture. The interior has many fine details including heavy woodcarvings, a front-to-back center hall, and hand-painted murals. This is a house/museum twofer. Admission to the Wentworth-Gardner House also includes admission to the next-door Tobias Lear House, which dates from 1740 and represents a more modest upper-middle class home of the period. Open mid-June through mid-Oct Wed through Sun noon to 4 p.m. Admission $6 adults, $3 children.

where to eat & stay

Three Chimneys Inn. 17 Newmarket Rd., Durham; (603) 868-7800; threechimneysinn .com. High on a wooded hill overlooking the Oyster River, this handsomely restored 1649 mansion and carriage house enjoys a serene setting. The 23 individually decorated rooms have been recently refreshed and combine 21st-century modern comforts with New England colonial charm. Some rooms offer gas fireplaces, others include comfortable sitting rooms, and many have draped four-poster beds. The inn is in Durham, home to the University of New Hampshire, just minutes outside Portsmouth. All rates include an expanded continental breakfast and free Wi-Fi.

Enjoy colonial ambience at the inn's **ffrost Sawyer Tavern.** The post-and-beam room with wide plank floors, an open hearth, and the glow of candles are surroundings an 18th-century diner would recognize. Representative of the seasonal menu are dishes like potato-crusted haddock with lemon and dill sauce and venison steak over mustard spaetzle with blackberry sage sauce. Open daily; check website for times. Restaurant and inn: $$.

food & drink

day trip 34

food & drink

new england food tour:
providence, ri; boston, ma; burlington, vt

Food lovers who have yet to discover New England's dining are missing some of the most interesting and diverse cuisine in the country. This itinerary offers a culinary adventure for your appetite, from Rhode Island, where the degree programs at Johnson & Wales have made the state a breeding ground for the next generation of culinary artists, to Boston, where restaurants offer every sort of ethnic food and the highest of high-end meals, to Vermont's passion for farm-to-table cuisine. On this tour you'll experience coastal Rhode Island's seafood, visit some of Boston's hottest restaurants, and tour the farms in Vermont's fertile mountains. You'll also visit several farmers' markets, and there's a cooking class option at each destination in case you want to hone your own culinary skills.

providence, ri

Those searching for a New England gourmet escape would do well to include a visit to Providence. Ever since 1980 when Al Forno burst on the food scene with its then-pioneering wood-grilled pizza, the city has welcomed dozens of terrific restaurants, developing into a bona fide dining destination. New Rivers in Providence is widely considered one of the best restaurants in the city, so do make your "big-night" dinner reservation well in advance.

getting there

From either Boston or New York drive to Providence via I-95 and take exit 22A to downtown. From points east, take I-195 West, follow to merge with I-95 North, and continue into Providence. From the west, take US 6 East and follow until it merges with RI 10 North, and follow signs to downtown Providence.

In Providence, take a recreational cooking class at the acclaimed culinary institute, Johnson & Wales, before heading out to both the country and the sea. Take I-95 South for 9 miles to RI 4 South for 6 miles, take exit 5B to RI 102 North for 1 mile to RI 2 South for almost 2 miles and Schartner Farm in Exeter. Continue south on RI 2 for 7 miles and take RI 138 East/Kingston Road for 1 mile to Kenyon Grist Mill in West Kingston. From there, take RI 110 South for 6 miles and then US 1 North for another mile until you reach Matunuk Oyster Bar for lunch in South Kingston at Narragansett Bay. The total distance is just about 40 miles, and depending on how long you stop, it's a half-day of driving and includes enough time to enjoy a dinner in Providence.

where to shop

Kenyon Grist Mill. 21 Glen Rock Rd., West Kingston; (401) 783-4054; kenyonsgristmill .com. Real Rhode Island johnnycakes are made from flint-ground Kenyon's white cornmeal. The historic 1696 gristmill along the Queen's River still operates, and the company store sells the full line of Kenyon flours and baking mixes along with other products made in Rhode Island like pine-scented soap and coffee syrup. If the mill is operating (generally Mon through Fri) you can peek in and watch the two 5,000-pound granite grindstones in action. Narrated tours of the mill take place at seasonal events scheduled throughout the year and on request. Work off your culinary weekend indulgence with a little kayaking from **Queen's River Kayak,** located directly behind the mill (queensriverkayaks.com). Open Mon through Fri 9 a.m. to 4 p.m., Sat and Sun 11 a.m. to 4 p.m.

Schartner Farms. 1 Arnold Place, Exeter; (401) 294-2044; schartnerfarms.com. This is an especially scenic farm that attracts Rhode Islanders for low-key fun in a rural setting. In the summer you can pick-your-own strawberries and blueberries. In the fall, there is a corn maze and weekend hay rides. The farm stand is housed in an authentic barn and stocked with gourmet food and produce that is harvested straight from the fields out back. The on-site bakery specializes in pies, scones, and muffins made from their farm-grown berries. Open daily 7:30 a.m. to 7 p.m.

where to go

Cuisinart Culinary Center for Excellence. 333 Shipyard St., South Providence; (401) 598-2336; jwu.edu. The popular Chef's Choice cooking classes are designed for the recreational cook. Classes are held at Johnson & Wales state-of-the art kitchens. Recent themes have included Spanish Tapas, Spa Cuisine, and Oktoberfest Fare. Most classes last 3 hours, and afterward you get to enjoy eating what you have made. Most classes $85.

Hope Street Farmers Market. Lippett Park, 1059 Hope Street; hopestreetmarket.com. Providence's talented chefs regularly shop the local farmers and fishers at this market, and you will find that the produce, dairy, meat, and seafood from these vendors are highlighted on many menus in town. Consider taking home artisan products like Providence Granola, goat cheese from Narragansett Creamery or salami from Daniele. Saturday market day represents a nice convergence of the city's food and art scenes as the Providence Artisan Market takes place at the same time at the other end of the park. Open May through Oct, Sat 9 a.m. to 1 p.m., Wed 3 to 6 p.m.

Matunuk Oyster Bar. 692 Succotash Rd., South Kingston; (401) 783-4202; rhodyoysters .com. Located on the water, a few miles down the road from Kenyon Grist Mill, this seafood restaurant serves standards like New England clam chowder and fried whole-belly clams, but their best menu item is, predictably, oysters. This is water-to-table eating—Matunuk owns and operates its own oyster farm. Plan well and call ahead to schedule a tour of the operation located on nearby Potter Pond to see how it is done. You even get to pull on some waders. Open Sun through Thurs 11:30 a.m. to 8:30 p.m., Fri and Sat 11:30 a.m. to 9:30 p.m. $$–$$$.

where to eat

Local 121. 121 Washington St., Providence; (401) 274-2121; local121.com. Both sleek and smart, this is one of the city's most vibrant dining destinations. Local 121 uses farm-fresh and seasonal ingredients to serve fare that is both adventurous (barbecued quail on braised collards and pickled peaches) and everyday (a grass-fed beef burger with Great Hill blue cheese). Open Wed and Thurs 5 to 10 p.m.; Fri 5 to 11 p.m.; Sat 10 a.m. to 3 p.m., 5 to 11 p.m.; Sun 10 to 3 p.m., 5 to 9 p.m. $$–$$$.

New Rivers. 7 Steeple St., Providence; (401) 751-0350; newriversrestaurant.com. The dining room is spacious with an organic feel, with reclaimed wood floors and soft candlelight. Chef Beau Vestal is noted for his interpretations of American bistro food that showcase small-scale local producers with astonishing creativity. Find dishes like pigeon mascarpone agnolotti with fava beans or day boat flounder with salsify, mâche, and herb radish salad. And he has a killer charcuterie menu with more than a dozen different offerings including *merguez* with North African spice, venison and juniper sausage, and griddled tasso ham. Open Mon through Thurs 5 to 9 p.m., Fri and Sat 5 to 10 p.m. $$–$$$.

boston, ma

Boston is home to some of the most interesting and innovative cuisine in the country, from the street food in the North End and Chinatown to a host of restaurants helmed by some of the country's best-known celebrity chefs. From a culinary walking tour, chef-led cooking classes, and a weekend's worth of great restaurant picks, here are a few of Boston's top food experiences.

getting there

The drive from Providence to Boston takes exactly an hour. You can take one of several routes between the cities, but I-95 North is the easiest.

where to go

Boston Food Tours. (617) 523-6032; bostonfoodtours.com. Culinary walking tours are a great way to get an insider's take on the history, sightseeing, and food of a neighborhood. Boston Food Tours offers 2 popular culinary adventures: a North End Italian food tour and a Chinatown tour. Both tours include visits to authentic food markets and specialty stores and lots of food samples (the Chinatown tour also includes a dim sum lunch). North End tours are offered Wed through Sun, Chinatown tours on Thurs and Sat; check website for meeting place, times, and prices.

Stir. 102 Waltham St.; (617) 423-7847; stirboston.com. This is the place for those who love to eat and talk about food. Chef Barbara Lynch (Menton, No. 9 Park, B&G Oysters, etc.) and her colleagues offer an inventive schedule of food-related classes at her demonstration kitchen/cookbook store. You'll find classes devoted to a variety of wide-ranging topics from pie making to butchering to cocktails. The chef's table dinners on Friday nights (accompanied by wine) are a weekly sellout. Retail store open Mon through Sat noon to 6 p.m.; check website for class schedule.

where to shop

Boston Copley Farmers' Market. Boylston and Dartmouth Streets. Located in Copley Square, across from the Boston Public Library, this is Boston's trendiest outdoor farmers' market, where even local boldfacers (celebrities, politicians, etc.) can be spotted shopping under the white awnings stacked with organic dairy products, fresh fruit, and vegetables. Recipe for a perfect farmers' market sandwich? Garlic and basil goat cheese from Crystal Brook Farm and some sliced heirloom tomatoes from Siena Farms on an Iggy's baguette. Open mid-May through late Nov Tues and Fri 11 a.m. to 6 p.m.

where to eat

Blue Dragon. 324 A St., Boston; (617) 338-8585; ming.com/blue-dragon.htm. Opened in 2013, this foodie attraction located in Boston's happening Fort Point waterfront neighborhood allows the opportunity to sample celebrity chef-owner Ming Tsai's unrivaled "East meets West" approach to cooking. Case in point: the buttery, lemony garlic sake clams with udon noodles—reminiscent of Italian coastal cuisine. Open Mon through Fri 11:30 a.m. to 1 a.m. Sat 3 p.m. to 1 a.m. $$.

Coppa. 253 Shawmut Ave.; (617) 391-0902; coppaboston.com. Start with a pretty Prosecco cocktail and ease into a weekend of serious eating with a casual meal at this intimate, locavore enoteca. The menu features sophisticated plates made for sharing; there's a fanciful wood-fired white pizza with ramps, a sea urchin carbonara, and lots of offal. Everything goes only too well with an admirable wine list that is also admirably priced. Open Mon through Thurs noon to 10 p.m.; Fri noon to 11 p.m.; Sat 3 to 11 p.m.; Sun 3 to 10 p.m. $$.

James Hook. 15 Northern Ave.; (617) 423-5501; jameshooklobster.com. Looking for a bare-bones lobster shack next to the water in Boston? James Hook is a lobster wholesaler located at the Northern Avenue Bridge, which happens to sell one of Boston's best lobster rolls: a simple hot dog roll overflowing with whole lobster meat and just a touch of mayo. They offer clam chowder and lobster bisque, too. Seating is limited to a couple of picnic tables, but the better idea is to eat your lobster roll on the benches at the Rose Kennedy Greenway Park across Atlantic Avenue. Open Mon through Thurs 9 a.m. to 5 p.m., Fri 9 a.m. to 6 p.m., Sat 9 a.m. to 5 p.m., Sun 9 a.m. to 2 p.m. $.

Sofra. 1 Belmont St., Cambridge; (617) 661-3161; sofrabakery.com. Kilim rugs decorate the seats at local culinary goddess Ana Sortun's (she's also the chef-owner of Oleana) all-day cafe. The menu of organic Middle East cuisine is unparalleled in these parts. To wit: the sausage flatbread with cumin, olives, feta, and orange and the kohlrabi pancakes with green harissa. The Turkish breakfast—a soft-boiled egg served with cucumbers, tomato, olives, feta, and a ramekin of thick yogurt with figs and honey—is a great way to fire up your day. Nearly every week, Sofra opens its kitchens after hours for a cooking class led by the Sofra pastry chefs or the chefs from Oleana or Sarma, Sortun's other restaturants. Topics have included "fearless about phyllo" and "sweet sugar and sultry spice: wake up your baking." Open Mon 8 a.m. to 5:30 p.m., Tues through Fri 8 a.m. to 7 p.m., Sat and Sun 8 a.m. to 6 p.m. $.

Uni. 370 Commonwealth Ave.; (617) 536-7200; uni-boston.com. In Boston, Uni, Ken Oringer's high temple to sushi, stands alone. The dining room is understated and elegant; the service is impeccable. The straightforward sashimi is melt-in-your mouth good, but for real fireworks, order the sea urchin with quail egg and ostera caviar or the *foie gras* with barbecued eel and green-apple glaze. On weekends when the dinner rush dies down, late-night ramen junkies descend upon the space for gourmet bowls of richly satisfying hot broth and noodles. Tables can be difficult to land, so it's best to make a reservation as early as you can. Open Sun through Thurs 5:30 to 10:30 p.m., Fri and Sat 5:30 p.m. to 1 a.m. $$$.

where to stay

Eliot Hotel. 370 Commonwealth Ave.; (617) 267-1607; eliothotel.com. This charming boutique hotel, housed in a beautiful brownstone building and located on leafy Commonwealth Avenue, hides an interior of supreme style. Each of the 95 rooms exudes class; they are done up in soothing shades of cream, brown, and azure, with flat-screen TVs and marble baths. The hotel's top-notch service pleases its loyal clientele who appreciate the small touches like turndown service and overnight shoeshine. The Eliot is home to award-winning restaurant Uni, so this is a hotel that understands gourmet. $$$.

burlington, vt

For a small state, Vermont has more than its share of top-notch restaurants and a stunning number of food-related businesses, dairies, vineyards, and artisan-made food producers. On this food-centric tour you'll visit several farmers and sample award-winning cheese, wine, smoked meats, and chocolate. You'll stay with like-minded travelers here—home base is the Essex, Vermont's "culinary resort and spa," which is located just outside of Burlington and features several cooking classes and seminars daily.

getting there

It's a nearly 4-hour drive from Boston to Essex Junction, Vermont. From Boston, take I-93 North toward New Hampshire for 63 miles. Near Concord, New Hampshire, merge right onto I-89 North for 140 miles. Take exit 12 for VT 2A North and follow to Essex Junction.

Visit the Lake Champlain factory in the morning—you'll have a better chance at catching production. Pick up I-89 South to Route 2 West to South Burlington. From the chocolate factory to Shelburne Farms take US 7 for 3 miles. Take a left on Harbor Road and follow to the farm. Shelburne Vineyard is nearby. Continue along Harbor Road for 1.5 miles. Turn right at Shelburne Road and follow for 1 mile to the vineyard. Finish your day at Dakin Farm. It's located 8 miles away; follow VT 7 South to get there.

Along the way to or from Burlington, consider a detour at Waterbury (30 minutes outside the city) to visit the Ben & Jerry's Ice Cream Factory, Cold Hollow Cider store, and the Cabot Creamery Cheese Annex. It couldn't be easier, the stores are lined up next to each other just off exit 10 from I-89.

where to go

Burlington Farmers' Market. City Hall Park, College and St. Paul Streets (summer); University of Vermont Dudley Center, 59 Main St. (winter); (802) 310-5172; burlingtonfarmersmarket.org. At this farmers' market the sale of farmhouse cheeses, organic vegetables, honey, maple syrup, pickles, and Vermont-made crafts is sound tracked by local musicians. There are also mouthwatering displays of international street food from Nepal, Africa, China, and more. And this is one serious farmers' market—it's open even during Burlington's frigid winter. Open Sat May through Oct 8:30 a.m. to 2:30 p.m.; Nov through Apr, selected Sat, 10 a.m. to 2 p.m.

Dakin Farm Vermont. 5797 US 7, Ferrisburgh; (800) 993-2546; dakinfarm.com. Maple syrup–brined smoked and cured meats are another Vermont specialty food. Dakin Farm is particularly known for its smoked ham, maple syrup, and smoked cheddar cheese. On this factory tour you can tour the smokehouse facility and watch as the workers hand-wax the cheese. Afterward, your samples await tasting in the farm's enormous store. Open daily 8 a.m. to 6 p.m.

Lake Champlain Chocolates. 750 Pine St.; (802) 864-1807; lakechamplainchocolates .com. Watch the chocolatiers make magic as they temper, mold, and hand-decorate each piece of Lake Champlain chocolate. A guide in front of a viewing window narrates "tours" of this working factory. At the factory store, you can pick up factory seconds at excellent prices. And at the end of the tour, they give out full-size chocolate samples. Sweet! Factory tours Mon through Fri 11 a.m. to 2 p.m., on the hour. Free.

Shelburne Farms. 1611 Harbor Rd.; (802) 985-8686; shelburnefarms.org. There are lots of cheese "factory" tours in Vermont, but wouldn't you rather see the cheese being made on the farm and meet the cows who gave the milk? This 1,400-acre teaching farm on the shores of Lake Champlain is the whole Vermont package: rolling meadows dotted with grazing cows and a cluster of classic shingled barn buildings. Shelburne Farms handcrafts its artisan cheddar cheese, made exclusively from the milk of its herd of Brown Swiss cows. It takes the better part of the day to produce a single 500-pound batch of cheese. You can watch the process through the viewing window in the Farm Barn and then head over to the welcome center to taste cheese samples (cheddar gets sharper as it ages) to decide which is your favorite. Open May through Oct 9 a.m. to 5 p.m., Nov through Apr 10 a.m. to 4 p.m. Admission $8 adults, $6 seniors, $5 children ages 3 to 17.

Shelburne Vineyard. 6308 Shelburne Rd., Shelburne; (802) 985-8222; shelburnevineyard .com. Nothing goes better with Vermont cheese than wine. Lake Champlain produces a microclimate and soil conditions similar to northern France. Shelburne Vineyard produces award-winning Rieslings, Chardonnays, and a light-bodied Merlot blend. The winery features a tasting room in a beautiful barn building with a massive patio that overlooks lush lawn and rows of vines. Tours of the winery operations are available daily. Tasting room open daily 11 a.m. to 5 p.m. Cost $7 (includes a souvenir glass). Tours daily 1 to 4 p.m., on the hour.

where to stay

Essex Culinary Resort and Spa. 70 Essex Way, Essex; (802) 878-1100; essexresortspa .com. Hands-on cooking classes are this hotel's most popular amenity. This four-season resort located 10 miles from Burlington puts food front and center with an on-site Cook Academy. There are several classes offered daily and taught by master chefs in the resort's professional teaching kitchen. There are classes on everything from Basic Knife Skills and Classic Sauces to fun, specialty topics like Baking with Vermont Cheese and Sushi Rolling to advanced programs on French Haute Cuisine. They offer sessions just for kids, too. Classes usually follow a format that includes a 3- or 4-course meal with wine so you get to enjoy the results of your effort. The hotel has a tavern for casual meals, and its fine dining space, Journey, features farm-to-table cuisine where you can choose kitchen-side seating to watch the chef prepare your meal. Dishes such as rabbit gnocchi in thyme drawn butter and smoked veal breast with polenta and tomato jam are sure to impress. (The excellent wine list helps too.) The resort's 120 rooms are traditional with recently spruced-up decor. The resort's new 22,000-square-foot spa, indoor and outdoor pools, 6 tennis courts, and a stocked casting pond mean that you have plenty of activities to enjoy between thinking about your next meal. Hotel: $$$. Restaurant: $$$–$$$$.

Kitchen Table Bistro. 1840 W. Main St., Richmond; (802) 434-8686; kitchentablebistro .com. Many serious foodies have flocked to this French bistro sleeper run by New England Culinary Institue graduates (and now husband and wife) Steve and Lara Atkins. Sparkling flavors distinguish the tantalizing dishes; spicy grilled scallops with an apple and parsnip puree, and a short rib shepherd's pie are recent offerings. For dessert, choose the molten chocolate cake with Zinfandel cherry sauce and cherry and vanilla ice cream. Open Tues through Sat 5 to 8:30 p.m. $$–$$$.

day trip 35

food & drink

new england seafood trail:
chatham, ma; boston, ma;
mid-coast maine

Nothing captures the essence of New England seafood like an authentic New England clambake on a Cape Cod beach. Next, head up to Boston, the capital of seafood in New England, to seek out fish and shellfish that have always inspired the best in the city's cuisine. Then continue north to the heart of Maine to gorge on lobster. Drive along coastal US 1, where every few miles you'll spy a lobster shack at the end of a rickety pier overlooking a rocky sound.

chatham, ma

getting there

From the Sagamore Bridge follow US 6 East to exit 11. Turn left onto MA 137 and follow to MA 28 and Chatham.

where to eat

Chatham Bars Inn. 297 Shore Rd.; (508) 945-0096; chathambarsinn.com. Four nights a week, the Chatham Bars Inn puts on a beachside New England clambake, which is open to the public (do make reservations), at the hotel's Beach House Grill restaurant. Clambake preparations begin at 5 p.m., and many diners arrive early to watch the entire process unfold. A maple- and oak-wood fire is made in the hotel's sand and rock fire-pit, which is then covered with seaweed. Whole lobsters, steamers, and mussels, corn on the cob, and red potatoes are placed in the pit, covered with a tarp, and allowed to steam. There is a raw bar, several salads, grilled meats, a kids' buffet, and an assortment of New England–inspired desserts like a warm spiced-peach crumble. The Chatham Bars Inn clambakes are a culinary event—and a pricey one at that—but it is the definitive New England seafood experience. Clambakes take place mid-July through early Sept Mon through Thurs 6 p.m. $$$.

boston, ma

getting there

From the Cape take US 6 West for 30 miles, cross over the Sagamore Bridge to MA 3 and follow for 42 miles. Take exit 20B to merge onto I-93 North toward Boston. The drive is 90 miles and should take 1.5 hours.

where to eat

East Coast Grill. 1271 Cambridge St., Cambridge; (617) 714-4662 eastcoastgrill.net. Visitors always want to try New England's best lobster roll, oysters, and fried clams, but local fin fish is often given short shrift. Not at East Coast Grill. The fire-grilled flavor of the fish really comes through at this casual barbecue joint/seafooder. Entrees include dishes like a grilled spice-crusted mahimahi or grilled white pepper tuna. Open daily 5 to 11 p.m. $$.

Spectacle Island Clambake. Long Wharf; (617) 669-8552; bostonharborislands.org. Hop on the ferry and take a sunset cruise to Spectacle Island for a traditional New England clambake prepared. Dinner includes a steamed lobster, clam chowder, mussels, corn on the cob, dessert, and even beer. Spectacle Island is part of the Boston Harbor Islands and just a 15-minute boat ride from downtown. Ticket price includes both the ferry ride and meal. Memorial Day through Labor Day Thurs 6:15 to 9 p.m. Tickets $99 adults, $70 children ages 3 to 12.

Legal Sea Foods. 255 State St., Waterfront; (617) 227-3115; 26 Park Plaza, Park Square; (617) 426-4444; 100 Huntington Ave., Copley Place; (617) 266-7775; 800 Boylston St., Prudential Center; (617) 266-6800; 270 Northern Ave., Waterfront; (617) 477-2900; other locations throughout the region; legalseafoods.com. Creamy, milky clam chowder is Legal's claim to fame; its clam chowder has been served at every presidential inauguration since 1981, so it's probably good enough for the rest of us. Restaurant hours vary by location. $$–$$$.

Neptune Oyster. 63 Salem St., North End; (617) 742-3474; neptuneoyster.com. Some of Boston's best lobster rolls and raw oysters are found in the North End, the city's Italian neighborhood. It's a cozy space with a long, dark wood bar and leather banquettes. The raw bar is something to behold; with a dozen or more (always changing depending on what's fresh) varieties to choose from. And then there's the lobster roll: pure knuckle and claw meat served in a toasted roll with either mayonnaise or butter. They don't take reservations, so come when they open if you can. Open Mon through Thur 11:30 a.m. to 9:30 p.m., Fri through Sun 11:30 a.m. to 10:30 p.m. $$–$$$.

worth more time

Clam Box of Ipswich. 246 High St., Ipswich; (978) 356-9707; ipswichma.com/clambox. You will not find better clams than those from the towns along Boston's North Shore. The area's best clam shack is subject to fierce debate, but among the contenders are the fried whole-belly clams from this Ipswich institution. It's an easy detour from I-95 North. Take exit 54A to MA 133E for 6 miles. Open Wed and Thurs 11 a.m. to 7 p.m., Fri and Sat 11 a.m. to 7:30 p.m. $–$$.

mid-coast maine

getting there

To Georgetown, Maine, take I-93 North to US 1 North and follow for 14 miles to I-95. Take I-95 North for 92 miles and take exit 52 toward I-295. Follow I-295 for 18 miles and take exit 28 for US 1 North. Follow US 1 North for 13 miles. Then follow ME 127 South for 9 miles down the peninsula to Five Islands Lobster.

To Wiscasset, head back along ME 127 North for 9 miles and follow US 1 for 10 miles to Red's Eats (you won't miss it, there is always a backup).

To Rockland continue along US 1 North for 33 miles to the harbor.

where to go

Captain Jack's Lobster Tour. 1 Park Dr., Rockland; (207) 542-6852; captainjacklobster tours.com. Captain Hale will take you out on his Maine lobster boat for a 1.25-hour cruise around Rockland Harbor; all the while you'll pass lighthouses and learn everything there is to know about lobstering from dockside lobster lingo to how to bait a lobster trap. A lobster lunch on the boat is available too. Tour season runs May through Oct Mon through Sat 9 a.m. to 4:30 p.m. Tickets $30 adults, $18 children ages 12 and under.

where to eat

Five Islands Lobster. 1447 Five Islands Rd., Georgetown; (207) 371-2990; fiveislandslob-ster.com. Five Islands is a tiny fishing village outside of Bath. At Five Islands you pick your lobster from the tank and it's boiled in seawater. When it's ready, take it out to the picnic tables overlooking the picture-perfect harbor and chow down. Open May Sat and Sun 11:30 a.m. to 7 p.m.; and June through Columbus Day daily 11:30 a.m. to 7 p.m. $$.

Red's Eats. 41 Water St., Wiscasset; (207) 882-6128. You'll find the real reason to visit Maine is Red's Eats. This tiny lobster shack in the town of Wiscasset in mid-coast Maine causes a miles-long backup on US 1 heading into town. Red's serves great hunks of whole lobster meat—nearly a pound—piled into a toasted split-top buttered bun. Served on the side is either mayo and/or butter. Your choice. Open Apr through May and Sept through Oct daily 11 a.m. to 8 p.m., June through Aug 11 a.m. to 11 p.m. Cash only. $$.

day trip 36

food & drink

new hampshire & massachusetts wine trail:
lee, nh; south hampton, nh; bolton, ma; new marlborough, ma; richmond, ma

In New Hampshire, wineries along the seacoast are making surprisingly good wines from grapes, apples, and berries. After visiting them, meander over to Massachusetts and explore the rural countryside and sample carefully crafted wines from artisan vineyards. Plan this itinerary in the fall and you can take advantage of the best of the season; it's the time of year that New England's foliage comes into brilliant color, and the vineyards are busy celebrating the harvest.

lee, nh

getting there

To get to Flag Hill Winery from points south, take I-95 North and exit at NH 101 and follow 12 miles. Take NH 125 North for 4 miles. Take a right onto NH 155 to Flag Hill. From points east take the Spaulding Turnpike north and exit onto US 4 and follow for 10 miles. Follow NH 125 South for 4 miles. Take a left onto NH 155 to Flag Hill. From points north take NH 101 East to Epping. Take NH 125 North for 4 miles to NH 155 to Flag Hill.

where to go

Flag Hill Winery. 297 N. River Rd.; (603) 659-2949; flaghill.com. This charming New England winery turns out wines that wow connoisseurs. Varietals include Cayuga and Marechal Foch, as well as several wines and spirits made from apples. Flag Hill's wines are made exclusively from their estate-grown grapes. Flag Hill also offers a popular monthly seasonal wine dinner in its dining room overlooking the vines. Tasting room open Wed through Sun 11 a.m. to 5 p.m. Tours May through Oct Sat and Sun at noon. Tastings $5, tours $5.

south hampton, nh

getting there

Pick up NH 125 South and follow for 11 miles, then follow NH 107A for 5 miles to Jewell Street and the vineyard.

where to go

Jewell Towne Vineyards. 183 Whitehall Rd.; (603) 394-0600; jewelltownevineyards.com. Located along the Massachusetts–New Hampshire border (some of the wine labels say "origin 50 percent New Hampshire, 50 percent Massachusetts"!), this small winery is starting to be noticed, winning more than 100 medals in regional competitions over the years. Its Riesling is a standout. Open Mon through Fri 11 a.m. to 5 p.m., Sat and Sun 11 a.m. to 4 p.m. Tastings (up to 5) are free.

bolton, ma

getting there

Pick up I-495 South and drive 48 miles. Take exit 27 for MA 117 West and follow signs for Nashoba Valley Winery.

where to go

Nashoba Valley Winery. 100 Wattaquadock Hill Rd.; (978) 779-5521; nashobawinery .com. This destination winery/orchard/restaurant has lots to do and appeal for everyone—including the kids. In season, you can pick your own apples, peaches, and plums. On weekends, tours of the winemaking facilities include tastings of Nashoba's award-winning wines. Their fruit wines, especially their cranberry-apple and blueberry Merlot are outstanding. And oenophiles will find a lot to like about Nashoba's massive wine shop/tasting bar. But there is quiet, too; the hillside orchard setting is a lovely place to walk. Pick up gourmet picnic lunches (grilled asparagus and hummus on pita, ham and havarti on brioche) to eat at the tables of the winery porch. Or make reservations in advance for lunch, dinner, or Sunday brunch at J's at Nashoba Valley for New American cuisine in a country estate setting. Wine shop/tasting bar/orchards open daily 10 a.m. to 5 p.m., winery tours Sat and Sun 11 a.m. to 4 p.m. Tour $12 includes 6 tastings and souvenir glass.

new marlborough, ma

getting there

From MA 117 East merge onto I-495 South and drive for 12 miles. Follow I-90 (the Mass Turnpike) for 65 miles and take exit 3. Follow MA 10 South for 1 mile and pick up US 20 West for 5 miles. Follow MA 23 West for 25 miles and then MA 183 South to New Marlborough.

where to go

Les Trois Emme Vineyard & Winery. 8 Knight Rd.; (413) 528-2051; ltewinery.com. Located in the Berkshire Hills, this family-owned vineyard provides their visitors with an intimate wine-tasting experience. Les Trois Emme takes its name from the letter *M* that begins the first names of three of the owner's granddaughters. They produce a dozen or so wines; all are grape varieties including a delicious sparkling wine. Tour/tastings Apr through June and Nov through Dec, Fri through Sun noon to 5 p.m.; July through Oct Thurs through Sun noon to 5 p.m. Tastings $8 include 5 tastings paired with hors d'oeuvres.

where to eat & stay

Old Inn on the Green. 134 Huntsville-New Marlborough Rd.; (413) 229-7924; oldinn.com. Once a stagecoach stop, this 1760 inn offers quiet refuge and genuine hospitality. Guests will find antique furniture, wide plank floors and fireplaces throughout the 11-room property. The main attraction here is the food. Visitors come from far and wide to enjoy chef-owner Peter Platt's innovative American cuisine, served fireside in the winter or on the outdoor patio in the summer. Room rates include a continental breakfast buffet with fresh-baked French pastries. Hotel $$. Restaurant $$–$$$.

richmond, ma

getting there

Drive toward Great Barrington Road and follow for 1 mile. Turn onto MA 183 North/MA 23 West drive 2 miles to MA 41 North and follow for 14 miles to MA 295 West (New Canaan Road).

where to go

Furnace Brook Winery at Hilltop Orchards. 508 Canaan Rd.; (413) 698-3301; furnace brookwinery.com. With hiking, cross-country skiing, apple picking, and hayrides, there is something to do year-round at this winery/orchard just outside of Lenox. Furnace Brook produces both classic-style grape wines and fruit wines with something to suit most any taste. Their sparkling Moscato is an award winner. This is also your chance to try newly hip hard cider. Furnace Brook makes theirs from estate-grown apples aged in oak, and it's absolutely fabulous. Open Thurs through Sun. Wine tastings $5 for 5.

day trip 37

food & drink

southern new england wine tour:
north dartmouth, ma; westport, ma; little
compton, ri; portsmouth, ri; middletown, ri

This self-guided tour through the vineyards of southern New England is perfectly paced
for a long weekend. If you're day tripping through the region, you can tack this itinerary onto
almost any other trip you have planned. As you make your way among these five wineries you'll quickly learn that the region's southeastern-facing Atlantic coastline favors cool
climate white-wine production. And if you make the Stone House in Little Compton, Rhode
Island, your home base, you'll be positioned so that you don't have to spend all day in the
car and you'll avoid the crowds in Newport.

north dartmouth, ma

getting there

From Boston, take I-93 South to exit 4 to MA 24 South. Take exit 24 South to MA 140
South to I-195 West. Take exit 12 and make a left onto Old Fall River Road. From Newport,
follow MA 24 North to exit 3 for I-195 East to exit 12. Take exit 12 to Faunce Corner Road
and follow for 2 miles. Take left onto Old Fall River Road.

where to go

Running Brook Vineyard and Winery. 335 Old Fall River Rd.; (508) 985-1998; running
brookwine.com. This small local winery produces a dozen or so wines, a mix of red and

white blends along with sparkling and dessert wines. This is a laid-back winery where the tasting "room" is a wooden counter in the production facility. Tastings take place in the working winery Mon through Wed noon to 5 p.m., Thurs through Sun noon to 6 p.m. Tastings $8 for 6 to 9 samples and a souvenir glass.

westport, ma

getting there

Although just 20 minutes from each other, it's back-road driving all the way between Running Brook and Westport Rivers Winery. Take Old Fall River Road toward Energy Road. Take the second right onto Faunce Corner Road and drive for about 3 miles. The road changes its name to Old Westport Road; follow for another 3 miles. Turn left onto Fisher Road for 2 miles and then turn right onto White Oak Road. After 1 mile turn right onto Hixbridge Road.

where to go

Westport Rivers Winery. 417 Hixbridge Rd.; (508) 636-3423; westportrivers.com. This picturesque Westport winery produces a popular Riesling, elegant Champagne-style sparkling wines, and a signature Chardonnay. On Friday evening in the summer, there are performances by local musicians and local barbecue for purchase. Tastings take place in the vineyard's 19th-century farmhouse. Open Mon through Sat 11 a.m. to 5 p.m., closed Sun. Vineyard tour Sat, 1 p.m. and 3 p.m. Winery tours year-round, noon and 3 p.m. daily. Tastings $10 for 6 samples and a souvenir glass. Tours free.

little compton, ri

getting there

Carolyn's Sakonnet Vineyard is a little out of the way, but it is one of New England's largest vineyards, so don't skip it. From Westport Rivers Winery (in Wesport, Massachusetts) head west toward Cadman's Neck Road and follow for 1.5 miles. Turn right onto Main Road and a quick left onto Adamsville Road. Drive for 2.5 miles, continue to Main Street, and make a slight left onto Colebrook Road. Follow Colebrook for 2 miles, make slight right onto Peckham Road and follow for 2 miles. Turn right onto RI 77 and follow signs to Sakonnet.

where to go

Carolyn's Sakonnet Vineyards. 162 W. Main Rd.; (401) 635-8486; sakonnetwine.com. A pioneer among the New England wineries, Sakonnet has been making acclaimed wines for 35 years. Sakonnet has recently been purchased by Carolyn Rafaelian, president and founder of jewelry company Alex and Ani. Located on 115 acres of rolling farmland just 30 minutes from Newport, Sakonnet's grounds are lovely for a stroll. In the tasting room, the staff is experienced, and if you're interested, you can learn the finer points of tasting. You may want to plan your day to have lunch here. Carolyn's Cafe (open Mon through Wed 11 a.m. to 5 p.m., Thurs through Sun 11 a.m. to 7 p.m.) serves gourmet sandwiches, salads, and sophisticated nibbles that pair well with wine. Wine shop open for tastings Memorial Day through Columbus Day daily 10 a.m. to 6 p.m. Day after Columbus Day through Memorial Day open 11 a.m. to 5 p.m. Winery tours year-round, noon and 3 p.m. daily. Tastings $14 (with souvenir glass) for 7 samples. Tours free.

Goosewing Beach Preserve. South Shore Road; (401) 635-9974; nature.org. A dip in the warm ocean and time for a beach read rounds out nicely a weekend in the vineyards. Untouched and largely free from development, this quiet, pocket-size beach is worth seeking out. You have to cross a tidal creek to get there, but that's part of what makes it special. Open dawn to dusk. Parking fee during the summer (pay at South Shore Beach parking lot) $12 weekday, $15 weekend.

where to eat

Gray's Ice Cream. 116 East Rd., Tiverton; (401) 624-4500; graysicecream.com. Coming back from the beaches in Little Compton, a stop at Gray's for ice cream is a must. In business for more than 40 years, Gray's features some 30 classic New England flavors. Order a scoop of coffee; a homemade waffle cone makes it even better. Open May through Aug Mon through Thurs 6:30 a.m. to 9 p.m., Fri through Sun 6:30 a.m. to 10 p.m., rest of the year daily 6:30 a.m. to 7 p.m. $.

where to stay

Stone House. 122 Sakonnet Point Rd.; (401) 635-2222; stonehouse1854.com. In a restored 1854 Italianate seaside mansion, this romantic inn is celebrated for its luxe spa, expert service, and posh accommodations. All 13 guest rooms and suites feature a cool color palette, modern wood tones, iPod docking stations, and handmade quilts from New England–based designer Denyse Schmidt. Some rooms have gas fireplaces, and some have water views. The hotel's Prohibition speakeasy–style cellar Tap Room features upscale tavern food like seared New Bedford scallops with bacon-leek fondue and potato gratin. Rates include continental breakfast and free Wi-Fi. The hotel is just steps away from Round Pond Beach. $$$.

portsmouth, ri

getting there

Take RI 77 toward Old Main Road for 8 miles. Keep right at fork and take a sharp left and merge onto RI 24 South for 4 miles. Turn right onto RI 138 for 3.5 miles. Turn left onto Sandy Point Avenue and take the right onto Wapping Road.

where to go

Greenvale Vineyards. 582 Wapping Rd.; (401) 847-3777; greenvale.com. In a stunning location overlooking the banks of the Sakonnet River, this small, family-run, 24-acre vineyard produces a number of award-winning wines. The vineyard tour here is just that—a walk and talk among the vines. Afterward head to the converted 1863 barn for tastings. Greenvale produces only a handful of wines each year, so you'll likely try their entire lineup. The best of the lot? Greenvale's Vidal Blanc, which consistently has all the right floral notes and is a great summer wine. This winery is well known for its jazz tasting events, which are held Sat, May through Nov, from 12:30 to 3:45 p.m. and feature live jazz and tastings for $15. Wine shop open for tastings Apr through Dec Mon through Sat 10 a.m. to 5 p.m., Sun noon to 5 p.m., Jan through Mar Mon through Sat 11 a.m. to 4 p.m., Sun noon to 4 p.m. Tastings (with souvenir glass) $12 for 8.

middletown, ri

getting there

Greenvale Vineyards and Newport Vineyards are practically next to each other; it would be a shame to visit one and not the other. From Greenvale head north on Wapping Road toward Diane Avenue. Take the second left onto Bramans Lane. Turn left on RI 138 to Newport Vineyards.

where to go

Newport Vineyards. 909 E. Main Rd.; newportvineyards.com. Located just outside of Newport, Newport Vineyards produces nearly 20 wines: including red and white blends along with a few dessert wines. Tours start near the vines, and you'll hear the history of the vineyard and grape growing in southern New England. Tours end in the tasting rooms, where you'll sample five wines of your choosing (their whites are better than their reds). Store open Mon through Sat 10 a.m. to 5 p.m., Sun noon to 5 p.m. Tours daily at 1 p.m. and 3 p.m. Tour and tastings (with glass) $15

day trip 38

food & drink

litchfield hills wine tour:
brookfield, ct; new preston, ct; litchfield, ct

Connecticut might not be the first place that comes to mind when you think of wine. But after a couple of days of wine tasting on this scenic looping tour through the Litchfield Hills, you'll swear you spent the weekend in the Loire Valley and not in northwest Connecticut.

Note: All of the vineyards listed below belong to the **Connecticut Wine Trail** (ctwine .com), a trade association that includes 24 wineries throughout the state. As you drive the region's twists and turns, look for the trail's blue highway signs—they'll help you find your way.

brookfield, ct

getting there

Take exit 9 from I-84, follow CT 25 North for 3.5 miles. Take a right onto CT 133 East, and turn right onto Tower Road.

where to go

DiGrazia Vineyards. 131 Tower Rd.; (203) 775-1616; digrazia.com. Tucked into a hilltop, Digrazia Vineyards is among the more established vineyards in the Litchfield Hills. This small, family-owned winery produces 15 to 18 different wines including white and reds, but

DiGrazia's strength is its dessert wines. Among them are lovely sipping ports: a signature Blacksmith port and a not-so-common white port named White Magnolia. You'll sample wines in the cozy tasting room, and Dr. DiGrazia is often on hand to talk about his favorites. For a unique souvenir, buy a bottle of Autumn Spice and bring home a taste of New England. Informal, short tours of the production facilities are offered on weekends. Tasting room open Jan through Apr Sat and Sun 11 a.m. to 5 p.m.; May through Dec daily 11 a.m. to 5 p.m. Drop-in tours on Sat and Sun. Tasting fee $10 for 6 (no glass, though). Tours free.

new preston, ct

getting there

Follow CT 133 North for 6 miles, continue as it changes to CT 67 West and follow for 3 miles. Turn right on East Street and follow US 202 for 7 miles. Follow CT 45 North for 2 miles and follow signs to Hopkins Vineyard, for a total drive time of 20 miles and 30 minutes.

where to go

Hopkins Vineyards. 25 Hopkins Rd.; (860) 868-7954; hopkinsvineyard.com. On a wooded slope overlooking Lake Waramaug, the first grape vines at Hopkins Vineyard were planted in 1979 on land that had been a family dairy farm since 1787. All of Hopkins's 11 varieties of wine are estate cultivated. Their Chardonnay is consistently one of their best vintages. Tastings take place in the restored barn. Afterward head up to the vineyard's Hayloft Wine Bar to enjoy cheese, country pâté, and bread with even more wine, which you can purchase by the glass or bottle. Wine shop and tasting room open May through Oct Mon through Fri 10 a.m. to 5 p.m., Sat 10 a.m. to 7 p.m., Sun 11 a.m. to 6 p.m. Open daily the rest of the year too; check website for times. Tasting fee $12 for 6 samples (with souvenir glass).

where to stay

Hidden Valley Bed & Breakfast. 226 Bee Brook Rd., Washington Depot; (860) 868-9401; hiddenvalleyct.com. With its antique furniture, high-thread-count linens, and fluffy down comforters, this B&B calls to mind a fine European manor. There are just 3 guest bedrooms in this intimate home. All rates include a made-to-order gourmet breakfast; in the evening, step out to the sweeping terraces with a glass of wine to watch the sun set over the estate grounds with the Litchfield Hills in the distance.

litchfield, ct

getting there

From CT 45 North for 1.5 miles take CT 341 East and follow for 3 miles to US 202 East and drive for 7 miles to Haight-Brown Vineyard. The drive is about 12 miles and should take 20 minutes.

where to go

Haight-Brown Vineyard. 29 Chestnut Hill Rd.; (860) 567-4045; haightvineyards.com. Located just outside of Litchfield center, Haight-Brown is Connecticut's oldest winery, established in 1975. This winery boasts a particularly gorgeous tasting room with a field-stone fireplace and a custom-made bar that looks out onto beautiful views of the vineyard below. The vineyard produces 12 varieties of wine that include seasonal blends, but they are best known for their Chardonnays and Rieslings. Haight-Brown's tastings come with an option to purchase either a cheese or chocolate plate to go along with your wine, and the staff will help you make the best pairings. Tasting room open May through Nov, Mon through Thurs noon to 5 p.m., Fri and Sat noon to 6 p.m.; check website for days and hours during the rest of the year. Tasting fee includes souvenir glass: $12 for standard wines, $15 for limited release wines.

Lee's Riding Stable at Windfield Morgan Farm. 57 E. Litchfield Rd.; (860) 567-0785; windfieldmorganfarm.com. Balance your vineyard weekend with a non-wine activity. Enjoy the Litchfield Hills countryside with a trail ride. Open daily 9 a.m. to 5 p.m. Trail rides from $40 per hour.

Sunset Meadows. 599 Old Middle St., Goshen; (860) 201-4654; sunsetmeadowsvineyard. com. Drive through the hilly farmland and by lichen-covered stone walls to this intimate family winery with some 38 acres of vineyards in cultivation. An unexpected pairing—sample their cherry-forward St. Croix with some chocolate. Be sure to try their barrel-aged Root 63—it's stellar. Open Sun through Tues 11 a.m. to 5 p.m., Fri and Sat 11 a.m. to 6 p.m. Tasting fee.

day trip 39

food & drink

vermont brewery tour:
windsor, vt; bridgewater corners, vt;
burlington, vt; morrisville, vt

Just as Vermonters are all about "eating local," its residents subscribe to the tenet to "drink local." From regional companies like giant Harpoon Brewery to little microbreweries like Rock Art and Switchback, the result for beer lovers is that Vermont is home to some great breweries.

windsor, vt

Harpoon Brewery has one of the most comprehensive beer tours around and is an obligatory Vermont stop for visitors from throughout New England who are already familiar with the brand.

getting there

From points south, take I-91 North to exit 9. Turn right onto US 5 and Harpoon is on your left. From points north, take I-91 South to exit 9. Turn left on US 5 and Harpoon is on your left.

where to go

Harpoon Brewery. 336 Ruth Carney Dr.; (802) 674-5491; harpoonbrewery.com. Boston-based microbrewer Harpoon Brewery has a major production facility in Vermont. In-depth tours last 45 minutes and cover the art and science of beer making, along with unlimited samples at the end. Be sure to try Harpoon's malty Leviathan beer—it's a true beer-lover's beer, and Windsor is the production facility for it; you'll never taste it fresher! Afterward have lunch or dinner at the Harpoon Riverbend Tap & Beer Garden for soups, salads, sandwiches, and burgers. Store and Beer Garden open Sun through Wed 10 a.m. to 6 p.m., Thurs through Sat 10 a.m. to 9 p.m. Tours cost $5 and include souvenir glass and samples. Tours take place Fri through Sun; check website for times.

bridgewater corners, vt

A mainstay of Bridgewater Corners is Long Trail Brewing Company. Its outdoor deck and long hours makes it a particularly well-suited stop in the early summer evening.

getting there

Follow VT 12 North for 10 miles. Follow US 4 West for 12 miles to Bridgewater Corners.

where to eat

Long Trail Brewing Company. 5520 US 4; (802) 672-5011; longtrail.com. This is one of the most-celebrated craft microbreweries in Vermont. Long Trail Ale is considered a good everyday beer in New England, but they also make dark, seasonal, and special edition brews. You can watch the beer being made and bottled from the viewing platform over the plant, but the reason to come here is to sit out on the back deck overlooking the Ottauquechee River at the picnic tables with a sampler (if you're a first timer) or a pitcher (if you're a regular)—it's all very rustic and very Vermont. Visitor center and pub open daily 10 a.m. to 7 p.m. $–$$.

burlington, vt

Burlington is home to both well-known Magic Hat and tiny, known-only-through-word-of-mouth Switchback. Try to see them both.

getting there

Head east on US 4 East for 18 miles. Merge onto I-89 North and follow for 85 miles. Take exit 14 west and follow into Burlington.

where to go

Magic Hat Brewing Company. 5 Bartlett Bay Rd., South Burlington; (802) 658-2739; magichat.net. Quirky Magic Hat brews a small line of year-round and seasonal beers, with their flagship No. 9 being their most popular brand. Half the fun of Magic Hat's guided tour is reading the bottle labels: Wacko, Feast of Fools, Fat Angel. All tours end in the taproom, where several beers are available to sample. Guided tours Tues through Sun; check website for times. Store open Mon through Thurs 10 a.m. to 6 p.m., Fri and Sat 10 a.m. to 7 p.m., Sun noon to 5 p.m. Tours are free.

Switchback Brewing Co. 160 Flynn Ave.; (802) 651-4114; switchbackvt.com. This is a small brewery with a very fine product. Their Switchback Ale is an unfiltered red amber ale that is available only in northern New England as a draft beer. Guided tours are intimate—straight from the brewmaster himself with a chance to gaze into the brewing kettles and tanks. Tours are offered on Sat. at 1 and 2 p.m. and are by reservation only. Tasting room and retail hours Mon through Thurs 11 a.m. to 7 p.m., Thurs and Fri 11 a.m. to 8 p.m., Sat 11 a.m. to 4:30 p.m., Sun 11 a.m. to 6 p.m. Tours free.

morrisville, vt

Morrisville? Don't worry. Rock Art Brewery is just beyond Stowe Mountain Resort. You were going in this direction anyway.

getting there

Merge onto I-89 South and follow for 35 miles. Take exit 10 for VT 100 North toward Stowe and follow for 18 miles.

where to go

Rock Art Brewery. 632 Laporte Rd.; (802) 888-9400; rockartbrewery.com. Rock Art has moved and expanded its facility to be more visitor friendly. Now you can watch the brewing process at any time through large viewing windows. They produce a good number of beers here, but you can't go wrong with either their Whitetail Ale or their darker ale, Ridge Runner. Store and tasting room open Mon through Sat 9 a.m. to 6 p.m.

day trip 40

food & drink

maine brewery tour:
kennebunkport, me; portland, me;
bar harbor, me

Fresh, locally brewed, handcrafted beer. The state of Maine is home to dozens of breweries and brewpubs and is a recognized leader in the craft beer movement. For a vacation activity that is much better than a pub crawl, follow this ale trail through three of Maine's most popular destination cities.

kennebunkport, me

Any Maine brewery tour must include a visit to Kennebunkport and Federal Jack's brewpub, the "birthplace" of Shipyard. Besides, enjoying lobster and beer on the outdoor patio is the perfect way to kick off a Maine brewery tour.

getting there

From points south, follow I-95 North and take exit 19. Follow ME 109 East to Rt 1 and ME 9 East. From points north, follow I-95 South, take exit 25 and follow ME 35 East to Kennebunkport.

where to eat

Federal Jack's Brew Pub. 8 Western Ave.; (207) 967-4322; federaljacks.com. Overlooking Kennebunkport Harbor, this is where Maine's Shipyard Brewing Company began as the Kennebunkport Brewing Company way back in 1992. All seven beers at Federal Jack's are handcrafted at the downstairs brewery. Can't decide which to have? Order the 3-, 5-, or 7-beer sampler. The outdoor seating on the patio is a big draw, so it's always crowded with tourists who come for live music on weekends. Inquire about their Maine Brewing package, which includes 2 nights' accommodations, a day working in the brewery alongside the professionals, several meals, and more. Restaurant open daily 11:30 a.m. to 1 a.m. Call in advance for brewery vacations.

portland, me

Portland is the epicenter of Maine's craft beer movement with several breweries within walking distance of each other.

getting there

From ME 35 East merge onto I-95 North and follow for 19 miles. Merge onto I-295 North and follow for 6 miles into Portland.

where to go

Allagash Brewing. 50 Industrial Way; (800) 330-5385; allagash.com. Pay a visit to this small brewery, which offers an informative and fun tour of their industrial facility. Tastings are separate from tours and include generous samples of 4 beers. Be sure to taste the Allagash Tripel, a Belgian-style ale that has a sweet aftertaste and a strong alcoholic content—with nothing light beer about it. Free tours daily 11 a.m. to 6 p.m. Retail store open Mon through Sat 10 a.m. to 5 p.m.

Shipyard Brewery. 86 Newbury St.; (207) 761-0807; shipyard.com. Shipyard is Maine's mega microbrewery—they also own Sea Dog and Casco Bay Brewing Company. Drop-in tours of its Portland plant include a video presentation of the company's hand-brewed process followed by a guided walk-through of the bottling area and free beer samples. Their signature brew has always been the Export Ale, and their Blue Fin Stout Irish-style ale is classic. Try them both. Shipyard's very popular full brewery tours take place on Tues evening 5:30 to 7:30 p.m. (by reservation) and cost $10. Tasting room open Mon through Thurs 11 a.m. to 5 p.m., Fri and Sat 11 a.m. to 6 p.m., Sun 11 a.m. to 4 p.m.

where to eat

Gritty McDuff's. 396 Fore St.; (207) 772-BREW. Located in the heart of Old Port, Gritty McDuff's became Portland's first brewpub since Prohibition when it opened in 1988. It's not so surprising then that the beer works are in the basement. Gritty's is known for its brown ales, stouts, and seasonal beer. A good one to try: Gritty's Best Bitter is always on cask, and it's one of the beers that is brewed on-site (some of Gritty's beer is brewed at their other locations). The sweet potato fries topped with cheddar cheese and maple sour cream is hands down the best thing that comes out of the kitchen. Know, too, that the "seat yourself with anyone else" policy can create chaos. Open daily 11 a.m. to 1 a.m. $–$$.

Novare Res. 4 Canal Plaza; (207) 761-2437; novareresbiercafe.com. This funky subterranean gastropub has an extraordinary selection of rare beers (more than 20 taps and 500 bottles), all served in the proper glassware. Good thing the servers know their beers and can make a recommendation for the overwhelmed. There's a short but sophisticated menu of cheese and cured meats and other small things: three-cheese mushroom panini, shrimp tacos, and a Mediterranean plate. Good to know: Novare Res means, "it's a revolution." That explains a lot. Open Mon through Thurs 4 p.m. to 1 a.m., Fri and Sat 3 p.m. to 1 a.m., Sun noon to 1 a.m. $$.

bar harbor, me

A long road trip to Atlantic Brewing is a terrific reason to visit remote Bar Harbor. You may want to stay on the island forever.

getting there

Pick up I-295 North and follow for 46 miles. Merge onto I-95 North and follow for 10 miles. Take exit 113 for ME 3 East and follow for 102 miles into Bar Harbor.

where to go

Atlantic Brewing Company. 15 Knox Rd.; (207) 288-2337; atlanticbrewing.com. Located in the countryside, a few miles outside of downtown Bar Harbor, the Atlantic Brewing Company invites visitors to come for brewery tours and tastings every day. Guided tours are a quick talk near the vats; afterward you'll have the opportunity to taste most of their brews, including their popular Bar Harbor Real Ale. Consider having a late lunch at next-door Mainly Meat Barbecue, which has the full line of Atlantic Brewing Company beers on tap. Tours Memorial Day through Labor Day daily at 2, 3, and 4 p.m. Gift shop open daily 10 a.m. to 6 p.m. Tours free.

scenic & seasonal

day trip 41

scenic & seasonal

cape cod lighthouse tour:
falmouth, ma; chatham, ma; nauset
beach, ma; truro, ma; provincetown, ma

The lighthouse standing as a sentry along a rocky coast, its bright beacon shining out to sea, is one of New England's most iconic images. With almost 200 miles of coastline, Massachusetts has a particularly strong lighthouse tradition. America's first lighthouse was established in Boston in early colonial times, and a visit to Boston Harbor Light is a must for any lighthouse enthusiast.

Jutting out 65 miles into the ocean, the Cape Cod peninsula has always presented a navigational challenge for mariners. And with a history of more than 3,000 shipwrecks, the string of lighthouses along the Cape has served to warn sailors of its sometimes treacherous shores. Today 13 lighthouses remain; 7 are active lighthouses, the rest are decommissioned. This lighthouse driving tour along the coast takes in 6 of the Cape's most popular lighthouses. From Nobska Light in Falmouth to Race Point Light at the very tip of the Cape, each lighthouse is unique and has a story to tell. You can drive the entire route over one or two days or choose to visit just a few and adjust your length of stay.

falmouth, ma

getting there

From the Bourne Bridge, follow MA 28 South through two rotaries and follow signs to Falmouth.

first light, boston light

Marking the entrance to Boston Harbor, Boston Light stands tall. It's the first light-house station built in America, it was fittingly the last to be automated, and it is the only remaining continuously staffed US Coast Guard lighthouse. Little Brewster Island has been a lighthouse station since 1716; the original lighthouse was damaged during the Revolutionary War and was replaced with the current tower, which dates from 1783—still quite old! It's no wonder most visitors experience a sense of awe as the excursion boat approaches the island. Little Brewster is part of the Boston Harbor Islands National Recreational Area, and Boston Light is accessible only by guided tour boat. Boston Harbor Islands National State Park (bostonharbor islands.org) partners with the National Park Service to offer the only regularly sched-uled Boston Light tours. The 3-hour narrated tours cruise by the other lighthouses in Boston Harbor—Long Island Light and Graves Light—but the highlight is disem-barking at Little Brewster for a tour and climb (76 steps!) to the top of Boston Light. Cruises run mid-June through early Oct Fri through Sun; check website for depar-ture times. Tickets $41 adults, $37 seniors, $32 ages 3 to 11.

where to go

Nobska Light. Church Street; lighthouse.cc/nobska. Sitting high on a grassy bluff overlook-ing Woods Hole Harbor, Nobska Light is among the Cape's most photographed lighthouses; it's seen by countless visitors every day as they ferry to and from Martha's Vineyard. Built in 1876, the lighthouse was constructed of iron lined with brick and is still an active navigation aid, exhibiting a flashing white light that is visible for 17 miles out to sea. The adjacent keep-er's house serves as the home to the Coast Guard commander stationed at Wood's Hole, but the lighthouse grounds are open to the public daily. There are open houses throughout the year; most take place in the summer, check website for dates and times.

chatham, ma

getting there

Head east along a mix of highway and scenic byway to reach charming Chatham. Take MA 28 North for 13 miles then take US 6 East for 29 miles. Take exit 11 for MA 137 toward Cha-tham Center and follow for 2 miles. Turn right onto MA 28 North for 3 miles and Shore Road.

where to go

Chatham Light. Shore Road; (508) 430-0628; lighthouse.cc/chatham. At the "elbow" of the Cape, Chatham's coast is known for its shifting shoals and riptides. Established in 1808, Chatham became the Cape's second lighthouse station; the current tower dates from 1877. Chatham remains an active light station; its keeper's house is currently used as Coast Guard housing. The grounds are open to the public, and the Coast Guard offers a full schedule of open houses. If you have the opportunity to climb the tower, you can catch a glimpse of nearby Monomoy Point Light offshore; it's reached only by ferry and a long hike, making it one of Massachusetts's most inhospitable lighthouses. Chatham Light is open for tours May through Oct on the first and third Wed of the month, 1 to 3:30 p.m.

nauset beach, ma

getting there

Skirt around Chatham taking MA 28 South for 8 miles. At the traffic circle, MA 6A, US 6, and MA 28 will converge. Take US 6 East for 3 miles to Nauset Beach.

where to go

Nauset Light. Nauset Light Beach on Ocean View Drive, Eastham; (508) 255-3421; nps .gov/caco. Nauset Light dates from 1877 and is the twin to Chatham Light; it was moved to this location in 1923 to replace the Three Sisters Lights that originally stood here. With its distinctive red and white paint, this iron lighthouse is a beauty—and easily the Cape's most recognized lighthouse as it's the logo for the Cape Cod Potato Chip Company. Nauset Light is located on the Cape Cod National Seashore, making this lighthouse visit a particularly good one to combine with a day at the beach. The grounds are open daily dawn to dusk. Nauset Light is open for tours May through Oct on Sun from 1 to 4 p.m.; also on Wed in July and Aug from 4:30 to 7:30 p.m. Note that the Cape Cod National Seashore collects a parking/beach fee ($20 per car) during the summer until 4:30 p.m.

Nauset Light Beach. Ocean View Drive, Eastham; (508) 255-3421; nps.gov/caco. Part of the Cape Cod National Seashore, this broad, white-sand beach is backed by breathtaking dunes. This is also the closest beach to the park's main visitor facility, the Salt Pond Visitor Center, which offers a full slate of guided walks, talks, and children's activities and is the starting point for many of the park's walking and biking trails. Beach fee collected Memorial Day to Labor Day daily 9 a.m. to 5 p.m. Vehicle parking fee $20.

Three Sisters Lighthouses. Cable Road, Eastham; (508) 255-3421; nps.gov/caco. These stubby 22-foot towers, called the "Three Sisters," date from 1892 and once stood 150 feet from each other atop the cliffs at Nauset Beach. Made of wood, the towers succumbed to the elements, were replaced by Nauset Light, and decommissioned. The Three Sisters have been reunited in a clearing just a short walk from the Nauset Light Beach parking lot. Free National Park Service ranger–led tours of the towers are offered weekly throughout the summer. Check website for days and times.

truro, ma

getting there

From Nauset Beach to Highland Light continue along US 6 East for 13 miles.

where to go

Highland Light. Highland Light Road; (508) 487-1121; capecodlight.org. Officially this lighthouse is named Cape Cod Light, recognizing its historical importance as the region's first lighthouse. The station was established in 1797; this iron and brick lighthouse dates from 1857. In 1996 the lighthouse was relocated from its original cliff position to prevent it from falling into the sea. Its current location is 450 feet inland (and in the middle of the Highland Links Golf Course). This is the only Cape Cod lighthouse that is open for climbing daily during the summer. There is a small museum and gift shop located in the adjacent keeper's house. Open May through Oct daily 10 a.m. to 5:30 p.m., and by appointment off-season. Admission $6 adults, $5 seniors and students, free for children ages 12 and under.

provincetown, ma

getting there

From Highland Light to Race Point you'll drive another 8 miles along US 6 East.

where to go

Race Point Light. Race Point Beach; (508) 487-9930; racepointlighthouse.net. Seemingly at land's end, Race Point Light is located at the tip of Cape Cod. Until the construction of the Cape Cod Canal in 1916, this beach was in the middle of a major maritime route and witnessed many shipwrecks. The station was established in 1816, and the cast iron and brick structure dates from 1876. This is a lighthouse for the adventuresome; getting here requires that you walk across 2 miles of sandy beach from the Race Point Beach parking lot. But the views from the top are worth it. You may even see some whales. The grounds are open daily year-round. Lighthouse tours open June through Oct on the first and third Sat of the month from 10 a.m. to 2 p.m. This is also one of the few places in New England where you can experience lighthouse life. Shared accommodations in the Keeper's House ($$) or private accommodation in the Whistle House ($$$) (sleeps up to 8) are available from May through Oct.

day trip 42

scenic & seasonal

maine lighthouse tour:
york, me; cape elizabeth, me;
bath, me; boothbay harbor, me;
bristol, me; rockland, me

From York in the southern part of the state all the way to Lubec in far Down East Maine, the coast of Maine is dotted with more than 60 lighthouses. This mid-coast Maine itinerary features one of Maine's largest clusters of lighthouses, along with spectacular coastal scenery.

york, me

getting there

From I-95 take exit 7 for US 1 South. At the top of the hill, take a left on US 1A. Travel along 1A as it follows the coast and take a right onto Nubble Road.

where to go

Cape Neddick Lighthouse. 11 Soheir Park Rd.; nubblelight.org. Better known as Nubble Light, this 1870s-era lighthouse sits 200 yards offshore atop rocky Nubble Island. Nubble is not accessible to the public but can easily be seen from nearby Soheir Park, which has telescopes, benches, and a lighthouse-themed gift shop. Note the miniature brass lighthouses that ornament the top of the gallery railing, a feature that is unique to only a handful of lighthouses. Automated in 1987, Nubble exhibits a fixed red light 88 feet above sea level and remains an active aid in navigation. Combine your lighthouse visit with some beach time; Nubble is adjacent to both Short Sands and Long Sands Beaches.

cape elizabeth, me

getting there

Just south of Portland, Cape Elizabeth has two top lighthouses to visit. It's a nice mix of highway and scenic coastal road for 50 miles and should take just about an hour to drive.

From US 1 South, turn right onto I-95 North and follow for 28 miles. Take exit 36 to merge onto I-195 East toward Saco/Old Orchard Beach and follow for 2 miles.Take exit 2B to pick up US 1 North for 8 miles. Turn right onto ME 207 South and follow for 3 miles. Turn left onto ME 77 North and follow for the coast to Cape Elizabeth Light. Continue for another 3 miles to Portland Head Light.

where to go

Cape Elizabeth. Two Lights Road. Located at the southern edge of Portland Harbor, this lighthouse is known as "Two Lights." When the lighthouse station was established in 1828, it was the first of Maine's "twin" lighthouses. The current lighthouses, located just 300 yards apart, are cast iron and both date from 1874. The eastern beacon is an active navigational aid (and Maine's most powerful lighthouse beacon). The western beacon was discontinued in 1924 and since the 1970s has been privately owned. Neither the lighthouse or grounds to either lighthouse are open to the public, but good views and photo ops can be had from adjacent Two Lights State Park.

Lobster Shack at Two Lights. 225 Two Lights Rd.; (207) 799-1677; lobstershack twolights.com. Located between the Cape Elizabeth and Portland Head lighthouses, the Lobster Shack is a natural pit stop. Locals and visitors alike favor this place for dinner with a view of Casco Bay and the sound of waves crashing on the rocks to accompany the steamed lobster, lobster rolls, and fried fish that is served at picnic tables outside or in the cozy dining room. Open Mar through Oct daily 11 a.m. to 8 p.m. $$.

Portland Head Light. 1000 Shore Rd.; (207) 799-2661; portlandheadlight.com. Standing majestically on a rocky headland above crashing surf, Portland Light is one of the most popular tourist attractions in Maine. Maine's first lighthouse, this beacon has guided generations of Maine seafarers into Portland Harbor since it was built in 1791 under the authorization of George Washington. Although the tower is not open to the public, the lighthouse grounds are. The former keeper's house is now the Museum at Portland Light, which displays historic memorabilia and has a gift shop. Portland Head Light is part of Williams State Park, and the grounds are open year-round, dawn to dusk. Museum is open June through Oct daily 10 a.m. to 4 p.m.; weekends Apr through May and Nov through Dec. Grounds are free; museum admission $2 adults, $1 children ages 6 to 16.

bath, me

getting there

Continue along ME 77 North for 5 miles and cross over the Casco Bay Bridge. Merge onto I-295/US1 North and follow for 23 miles. Take exit 28 and merge onto US 1 North and follow for 10 miles.

where to go

Maine Maritime Museum. 243 Washington St.; (207) 443-1316; mainemaritimemuseum .org. See Maine lighthouses from their best vantage point—from the water. The Maine Maritime Museum offers several popular lighthouse-themed cruises. Lighthouse cruises depart from the museum's Bath pier; enjoy up-close views of as many as 10 lighthouses. Cruise fees also include 2-day admission to the Maine Maritime Museum. Cruises run mid-June through Columbus Day; check website for dates, departure times, and prices.

boothbay harbor, me

getting there

Take US 1 North for 12 miles and turn right onto ME 27 South and follow for 11 miles to the harbor.

where to go

Burnt Island Living Lighthouse Museum. Balmy Day Cruises, Pier 8; (207) 633-2284; balmydayscruises.com. Learn about life as a lighthouse keeper on this unique living history/ cruise tour experience. As you approach Burnt Island aboard the *Novelty* it's easy to imagine the isolation of lighthouse living. Meet "keeper" Joseph Muise and his family, dressed in period clothing, and learn about lighthouse living in the 1950s. The 3-hour excursion includes a short 15-minute boat ride to and from the island and allows plenty of time to check out the lighthouse and explore the island (a picnic lunch is a great idea). Burnt Island Cruise season runs July through Aug Mon and Thurs departures at 1:45 p.m. Tickets $25 adults, $15 ages 3 to 11.

bristol, me

getting there

Take ME 27 North for 11 miles. Turn right onto US 1 North and follow for 6 miles. Turn onto ME 129 South and follow for 3 miles. Make a left on ME 130 South and follow for 3 miles.

where to go

Pemaquid Point Lighthouse. Lighthouse Park, Pemaquid Point Road. Pemaquid Point is one of Maine's most recognized lighthouses—it's the lighthouse depicted on Maine's state quarter. There has been a lighthouse at this tip of land that separates Johns Bay from Muscongus Bay since 1827. The painted rubblestone lighthouse dates from 1835 and is especially admired for its stunning location overlooking surf-pounded, exposed granite bedrock. You can climb the 39 stairs to the top and experience a breathtaking view from the lantern deck of the harbor and Monhegan Island 15 miles away. Next door, check out the tiny Fisherman's Museum at Pemaquid. If you want a total lighthouse experience, consider renting the keeper's house, which is available for weekly rental (see below). Lighthouse open for climbing Memorial Day through Labor Day daily 10:30 a.m. to 5 p.m. Admission fee $2 per person.

where to stay

The Keeper's House at Pemaquid Point. New Castle Square Vacation Rentals; (207) 563-6500; mainecoastcottages.com. Ever dream of living in a lighthouse? Stay in the 1857 keeper's house next to the lighthouse at Pemaquid Point and you'll enjoy beautiful sunsets and fall asleep listening to the waves. (Remember, too, that Pemaquid is an operational lighthouse, so you'll also see the constant light of the beacon and the comings and goings of tourists visiting the lighthouse next door!) The second-floor, 1-bedroom, 1-bath apartment sleeps four, has a covered front porch to enjoy the view, and is available for weekly rentals only. But you can feel good about paying this room rate—proceeds help pay for the lighthouse's upkeep. $$.

rockland, me

getting there

This scenic 30-mile drive should take about 50 minutes. Follow ME 32 North for 14 miles. Turn right onto US 1 North and follow for 16 miles along the coast to Rockland.

where to go

Maine Lighthouse Museum. 1 Park Dr.; (207) 594-3301; mainelighthousemuseum.org. Home of the world's largest collection of lighthouse artifacts and memorabilia, this museum is a must-stop for lighthouse enthusiasts. Among the relics are foghorns, lanterns, and an outstanding collection of Fresnel lenses. There's also a special section devoted to the Coast Guard. The gift shop has everything lighthouse, from knickknacks to fine art. Open Mon through Fri 9 a.m. to 5 p.m., Sat and Sun 10 a.m. to 4 p.m. Admission $8 adults, $6 seniors, free for children age 12 and under.

Rockland Breakwater Light. Jameson Point. Walking the breakwater is not for the timid. To reach this lighthouse, it's an almost 1-mile walk across the flat expanse of granite blocks that jut into Rockland Harbor. Your reward? The chance to climb to the top of Rockland Breakwater Light for views of Penobscot Bay. Open Memorial Day weekend through Columbus Day, Sat and Sun 10 a.m. to 5 p.m. (weather dependent). A donation of $1 suggested.

where to eat

Claws. 743 Main St.; (207) 596-5600; clawsrocklandmaine.com. The harborside red lobster shack suggests boiled lobster dinners and lobster rolls, but Claws has more sophisticated chops. On this menu you'll also find hot maine lobster dip, lobster quesadillas and a lobster burger. Other pluses? They accept credit cards and serve beer and wine (both are rare in lobsterland). Open May through Sept daily, 11 a.m. to 9 p.m. $$.

day trip 43

scenic & seasonal

christmas in new england:
boston, ma; newport, ri; stowe, vt

A New England Christmas evokes images of horse-drawn sleighs, children ice-skating on a frozen pond, and snow-covered villages. From big-city Christmas shopping and seasonal performances in Boston to Newport's month-long holiday festival to the winter-wonderland village of Stowe, the holidays are a great time to visit New England. It's a Christmas scene that Currier & Ives might recognize.

The holiday season in New England begins in earnest in mid-November—just about the time that the first snowflakes fly. This itinerary begins in Boston, although you certainly could visit these cities in any order.

boston, ma

Twinkling lights, holiday music, and hot cocoa all around. Boston hosts several holiday performances and events that will entertain you and warm you with the holiday spirit.

getting there

From the west, the Massachusetts Turnpike (I-90) runs directly to the city. From the south, take I-95 North to I-93 North to downtown. From Vermont and points northwest, take I-93 South to downtown. From Maine and points northeast, take I-95 South to I-93 South to downtown.

where to go

Boston Ballet's *Nutcracker*. Opera House; (617) 695-6955; bostonballet.org. The charming tale of a young girl's magical Christmas gift is a delight for all ages. The Boston Ballet's production features dazzlingly beautiful dancing, elaborate sets, colorful costumes, and Tchaikovsky's score. The *Nutcracker* season runs from the end of Nov through Dec. Ticket prices vary.

Boston Holiday Pops. Symphony Hall; (617) 266-1492; bso.org. If attending a Christmas performance of the Boston Pops doesn't put you in a ho-ho-ho mood, then nothing will. Concerts feature holiday seasonal music such as Handel's *Messiah* and "Sleigh Ride" and an audience sing-along (with projected lyrics in case you've forgotten the words to "Rudolph"!). If you are seated at the floor tables (orchestra), you can enjoy light refreshments while watching the performance. And all concerts end with a visit by the big guy himself. The Christmas Pops season runs from the second week of Dec through the end of Dec. Ticket prices vary.

First Night Boston. Venues throughout the city; (857) 600-1590; firstnightboston.org. Bundle up! First Night is the country's oldest and largest New Year's celebration of the arts. Check out the ice sculptures in Copley Square and on Boston Common. Families will want to hang out at the Hynes Convention Center, which is the site for the Family Festival. As the day progresses, the venues become more sophisticated with all sorts of programs from improv to Irish step dance to operatic arias and zydeco performances. Everyone converges on Boylston Street for the First Night Mardi Gras–style parade, which steps off from the Hynes at 5:30 p.m. and wends its way toward Boston Common, finishing with a fireworks display at 7 p.m. All events are free.

Frog Pond. Boston Common; (617) 635-2120; bostonfrogpond.com. In the shadow of the Massachusetts State House, the cityscape setting of Boston's Frog Pond ice-skating is pure magic. Take a spin on Frog Pond's refrigerated outdoor ice to the sound of wonderful holiday skating music. Strauss anyone? There are skate rentals, a concession stand (with hot chocolate), and a large warming pavilion with lockers. Open late Nov through mid-Mar Mon 10 a.m. to 4 p.m., Tues through Thurs 10 a.m. to 9 p.m., Fri and Sat 10 a.m. to 10 p.m., Sun 10 a.m. to 9 p.m. Admission $6 adults, free ages 13 and under. Skate rentals $12 adults, $6 children.

Sturbridge Village. 1 Old Sturbridge Village Rd., Sturbridge; (508) 347-3362; osv.org. By candlelight, lamplight, and firelight, Old Sturbridge Village (see Day Trip 06 for directions) is especially enchanting at Christmas. Ride in a horse-drawn wagon or sleigh (snow permitting!), sip warm cider, and listen to holiday stories and festive carols. Both Father Christmas and Santa Claus make appearances. Dec hours are Fri through Sat 4 to 9 p.m. $22 per person.

where to stay

Fifteen Beacon. 15 Beacon St.; (617) 670-1500; xvbeacon.com. The ultimate Boston winter hotel amenity during the holiday season may just be a cozy, romantic fireplace. Boutique hotel Fifteen Beacon may have only 63 rooms, but each and every one has a gas fireplace. Draw up a chair, snuggle in—cashmere throws are provided too—and order champagne or hot chocolate from room service. Located in a historic 1903 Beaux Arts Beacon Hill building, rooms are plushly decorated with modern canopy beds, silky high-thread-count cotton Frette linens, and fresh flowers. The marble bathrooms even have heated towel racks. You may never leave. $$$–$$$$.

where to eat

Four Seasons—Teddy Bear Tea in the Bristol Lounge. 200 Boylston St.; (617) 338-4400; fourseason.com/boston. Take a break from holiday shopping. Kids are not only welcome for tea at the Four Seasons, but they have their own version during the holiday season. The Four Seasons Teddy Bear tea is a Boston holiday tradition that encourages the spirit of giving. The teddy bears that are donated during the event are distributed to local hospitals and nonprofits. The tea features teddy bear–themed treats for the kids while grown-ups can enjoy sweets and pastries that incorporate the flavors of the season: chocolate peppermint, gingerbread spice, and eggnog. Dec 1 through Dec 23, daily 3 to 4:15 p.m. $65 adults, $35 children, $25 for children who make a teddy bear donation.

newport, ri

Get a taste of Christmas 18th-century style as you stroll through Newport's historic district that entertains visitors with music, food, and holiday activities. And while the gilded mansions along Bellevue Avenue are always gorgeous, during the month of December they are even more stunning, decked out with holiday decorations, twinkling white lights, and boughs upon boughs of greenery.

getting there

From I-93 South drive for 12 miles. Take exit 4 and merge onto RI 24 South and follow for 48 miles. Exit onto RI 114 South and follow for 7 miles into Newport.

where to go

Christmas at the Newport Mansions. Bellevue Avenue; (401) 847-1000; newportmansions.org. The Newport mansions celebrate the holidays in grand style. Three of the Newport Mansions—the Breakers, Marble, and the Elms—display extravagantly decorated trees, lush arrangements of flowers and greenery, and the finest period decorations. Mid-Nov through New Year's, daily, Breakers 9 a.m. to 4 p.m., the Elms 10 a.m. to 4 p.m., Marble House 10 a.m. to 4 p.m. Breakers $24 adults, $8 children ages 6 to 17; Elms and Marble House $17.50 adults, $8 children ages 6 to 17. Check website for price of combination tickets for all three.

Christmas in Newport. Venues throughout the city; (401) 849-6454; christmasinnewport .org. For more than 40 years the city of Newport, its businesses, and residents have collaborated in presenting a month-long celebration of the holiday season. Among the events are seasonal concerts, lantern tours of the Newport historic district, and holiday open houses. The Harbor Lights Boat Parade is a particular highlight with hundreds of boats illuminating the harbor, festooned with holiday lights as they file past. Most events are free; for those events that charge admission, proceeds must benefit a charity or nonprofit. Events are scheduled daily Dec 1 through 31, check website for details.

where to stay

Francis Malbone House. 392 Thames St.; (401) 846-0392; malbone.com. Just steps away from Newport's charming shops and antique stores, this 1760 mansion has been meticulously renovated to house an intimate boutique inn. The 20 luxuriously appointed rooms are individually done with beautiful period furnishings, Frette linens, flat-screen TVs, and free Wi-Fi. Rooms have plenty of natural light; many have fireplaces and/or Jacuzzi tubs. Rates include a full gourmet breakfast that features dishes like pecan waffles with maple syrup and eggs Benedict with tarragon hollandaise. Rates also include a lavish afternoon tea that is nearly enough for dinner as well as free parking (huge in Newport!). $$$.

stowe, vt

Dreaming of a white Christmas? Vermont may just be the place. And even in the unlikely event that Mother Nature doesn't cooperate, you can be sure that the snow guns at Stowe Mountain Resort will be making snow to blanket the trails at Mount Mansfield.

Stowe is a vintage Vermont ski town with an enchanting village center filled with small shops and cozy restaurants. There's plenty of snow fun to be had in Stowe, too, whether downhill or cross-country skiing or cuddling next to your honey on a horse-drawn sleigh.

getting there

Retrace your drive and head toward Boston. From MA 24 North drive 46 miles. Pick up I-93 North and drive 78 miles. Merge onto I-89 North and drive 125 miles to exit 10 and Stowe. Follow VT 100 North for 10 miles into Stowe village. Total drive time is 270 miles and 4.5 hours.

where to go

Gentle Giants. 4000 Mountain Rd.; (802) 253-2216; gentlegiantsrides.com. A moonlit ride on a horse-drawn sleigh through the snow makes a terrific New England Christmas memory. You'll travel over a covered bridge, by a brook, and through the woods on an open horse-drawn sleigh. Horse-drawn carriage rides are offered the rest of the year, too. Open daily 11 a.m.; call for pricing.

Trapp Family Lodge Cross Country Center. 700 Trapp Hill Rd.; trappfamily.com. Experience the soft "shush" of the snow and the still of the woods on a crisp winter day. With 40 miles of groomed trails and 60 miles of backcountry trails, this is one of the largest cross-country systems on the East Coast. Open to the public, this is a full-service cross-country center offering Nordic ski and snowshoe rentals, instruction, and guided tours. Try to push yourself to get to Slayton Pasture Cabin 3 miles away—your reward is a bowl of soup and hot cocoa in front of a roaring fire.

where to shop

Laughing Moon Chocolates. 78 Main St.; (802) 253-9591; laughingmoonchocolates .com. The waft of enticing chocolate will draw you in to this little shop in Stowe village. Laughing Moon specializes in handmade chocolates, truffles, and that vacation souvenir favorite, fudge. During the holidays, from mid-Nov through Dec, watch candy canes being made by hand on Wed, Fri, Sat, and Sun at 11 a.m. You can also register in advance to have the opportunity to pull and twist your own candy cane. Open daily 9 a.m. to 6 p.m.

where to stay

Trapp Family Lodge. 700 Trapp Hill Rd.; (802) 253-8511; trappfamily.com. This world-famous resort located in a magical mountain setting is owned by the family that inspired *The Sound of Music*. This is a terrific choice for those who enjoy ski resorts as much—or more—than skiing. Choose from among 96 rooms in the Austrian-inspired lodge or one of the 100 guest chalets. Dining choices are many; the formal dining room serves continental/Austrian cuisine; the lounge offers informal fare and a nightly jazz pianist.Visit the new Bierhall for beer and holiday cheer. The deli/bakery has take-away sandwiches and a dessert menu that features linzer torte and apple strudel. The resort is located on a 2,500-acre property that supports numerous activities; hiking, cross-country skiing, and mountain biking. There is a large fitness center and both indoor and outdoor pools. $$$.

day trip 44

scenic & seasonal

the mohawk trail:
deerfield, ma; shelburne falls, ma;
north adams, ma

In the western part of Massachusetts, the Mohawk Trail (MA 2) traverses rolling farmland and woods with several scenic overlooks. Designated a historic highway in 1914, this 63-mile route from Miller's Falls on the Connecticut River to Mount Greylock at the Massachusetts–New York border roughly follows the Deerfield River and is thought to have been a foot trail of the Native Americans who lived in this region. Among the numerous attractions along the way are the Massachusetts Museum of Contemporary Art (MASS MoCA) in North Adams and Deerfield Village. Popular outdoor activities include river rafting and hiking the trails around Mount Greylock.

deerfield, ma

Located between the Deerfield and Connecticut Rivers and surrounded by low, wooded hills, Deerfield dates from 1670 and became one of New England's earliest frontier towns. As a result, there were frequent skirmishes among the English settlers, the Native Americans who lived in this region, and the French from nearby Canada. Deerfield is particularly known for having one of the state's finest historic districts with house museums located on both sides of Main Street, which is referred to as simply "the Street." The other buildings in this part of town? Most belong to the prestigious boarding school Deerfield Academy.

getting there

Deerfield is located off of I-91 at exit 24.

where to go

Historic Deerfield. 80 Old Main St.; (413) 775-7214; historic-deerfield.org. The mile-long stretch of Main Street at the heart of Deerfield is lined with dozens of 18th- and 19th-century period homes (many are private) and is one of New England's most picturesque historic districts. Along the tree-lined street you can visit 11 of these well-preserved museum houses, built between 1720 and 1850, on guided and self-guided tours. Start your visit at the **Hall Tavern,** which dates from 1760, and appropriately, houses the museum's visitor center. Here you can watch an introductory film and pick up a map and schedule of the day's activities. The **Flynt Center of New England Life** features the decorative arts with exhibits on textiles, furniture making, and silversmithing. Be sure to head up to the museum's attic where 3,000 colonial artifacts—among them engraved powder horns, Chinese export vases, and toys—are displayed in floor-to-ceiling glass cases. A visit to the 18th-century apprentice workshop at the Dwight House is a more interactive experience, with weaving, woodworking, and ceramic demonstrations taking place throughout the day. Open Apr through Dec daily 9:30 a.m. to 4:30 p.m.; Jan through Mar houses by appointment, Flynt Center open Sat and Sun 9:30 to 4:30 p.m. Admission $18 adults, $5 children ages 6 to 17.

Magic Wings Butterfly Conservatory & Gardens. 281 Greenfield Rd., South Deerfield; (413) 665-2805; magicwings.com. This is a delightful spot any time of year, a flower-filled oasis where thousands of butterflies flutter about a glass-enclosed 8,000-square foot atrium. Stroll along the flower- and shrub-lined paths and don't forget your camera—the butterflies will perch on your (patiently!) outstretched hand. In the summer, the outdoor gardens attract native species of butterflies. The next-door Monarch's Restaurant is a convenient spot that serves casual lunch and dinner fare. Open Memorial Day through Labor Day daily 9 a.m. to 6 p.m., rest of the year daily 9 a.m. to 5 p.m. Admission $16 adults, $14 seniors, $10 ages 3 to 17.

where to shop

Richardson's Candy Kitchen. 500 Greenfield Rd.; (413) 772-0443; richardsonscandy .com. A must-stop along the Mohawk Trail to pick up boxes of Dixies, handmade caramel and roasted nuts covered in milk or dark chocolate. If you come early enough in the day, you can watch the workers making the chocolate. Open daily 10 a.m. to 5 p.m.

Yankee Candle Village. 25 Greenfield Rd., South Deerfield; (413) 665-8306; yankeecandle .com. This is the flagship store of the candle company that is best known for its scented glass jar candles. Sniff out your favorite candle fragrance from among the more than 200 scents at the world's largest candle shop. The store also stocks New England gifts, toys, and collectibles. This is a popular stop for families; kids can dip their own candles and visit Santa all year-round at the Christmas Shop. This is also a common stop along the Mohawk Trail for a quick bite at the Yankee Candle bakery/cafe. Open daily 10 a.m. to 5 p.m.

where to stay

Deerfield Inn. 81 Main St.; (413) 774-5587; deerfieldinn.com. Located in the center of the Deerfield Historic District, the 1884 Deerfield Inn has 24 individual guest rooms that are each decorated in a well-chosen mix of antiques, reproductions, and floral accents—it's all very vintage New England. Modern in-room amenities include flat-screen TVs, free Wi-Fi, and earth-friendly toiletries. And all inn guests receive free passes to the museum homes of Historic Deerfield. Dining options are few in Deerfield, but the inn's restaurant, Champney's, is terrific, with much of the menu sourced locally. Champney's serves lunch and dinner daily. Breakfast and afternoon tea with cookies are included with all rates. The inn's tavern serves lunch and is the (only) place in town for a nightcap. $$.

shelburne falls, ma

This hamlet in the Berkshire foothills is a must-stop along the Mohawk Trail to stroll its famed Bridge of Flowers. Just beyond the bridge, at the base of Salmon Falls, check out the dozens of glacial potholes (the largest is 39 feet across!) carved in the granite bedrock of the Deerfield River.

getting there

From Deerfield to Shelburne Falls, continue west along the Mohawk Trail (MA 2) for 13 miles to Shelburne Falls.

where to go

Shelburne Falls Village Information Center. 75 Bridge St.; (413) 625-2544; shelburne falls.com. This is a full-service, staffed information center with maps, brochures, and Wi-Fi. Open May through Oct 10 a.m. to 4 p.m., Sun noon to 3 p.m.

Bridge of Flowers. Bridge Street off MA 2; bridgeofflowersmass.org. Ever since the late 1920s, what was once an abandoned trolley bridge across the Deerfield River has been transformed by the Shelburne Falls Women's Club into a flower-filled promenade. Walk across the 400-foot span and note the huge variety of more than 500 different plants. The bridge features a splendid progression of blooms from crocus and tulips in the spring to peonies and roses in midsummer and ends the growing season with a burst of colorful mums. Open daily Apr through Oct. Free.

> ## a favorite mohawk trail photo op
>
> *There is no more iconic image of the Mohawk Trail than the 1932 bronze statue, Hail to the Sunrise, that depicts a Mohawk Indian raising his arms to the east. Check out, too, the nearby fountain memorial with stones inscribed from more than 100 tribal nations.*

Crab Apple Whitewater Rafting. 2056 Mohawk Trail, Charlemont; (413) 625-2288; crab applewhitewater.com. Experience water with attitude on a whitewater rafting adventure along the Deerfield River. For newbies, the 3-hour scenic guided floats on Class I and II rapids are a great introductory trip. For an adrenaline-fueled run, choose the full-day trip (with barbecue lunch) through Class IV rapids. Trips run spring though fall; check website for days and departure times. Prices vary depending on season and trip.

Shelburne Trolley Museum. 14 Depot St.; sftm.org. From the Bridge of Flowers you'll see a sign directing you to this tiny museum. And although the museum's hours are limited, the volunteers who run this museum are enthusiastic. The museum's point of pride is the restored 1896 No. 10 trolley that served the Pioneer Valley for 30 years. Rides are offered on the No. 10 around the railyard, and sometimes rides are also available on the museum's antique pump car. Open late May through June and Sept through Oct Sat and Sun 11 a.m. to 5 p.m.; July and Aug Sat and Sun 11 a.m. to 5 p.m., Mon 1 to 5 p.m. Trolley rides $4 adults, $2 for children ages 6 to 12.

where to shop

Mohawk Trading Post. 874 Mohawk Trail; (413) 625-2412; mohawktradingpost.com. This Native American–owned shop is an excellent source for top-quality Native American crafts that range from inexpensive weavings to elaborate beaded birch-bark baskets. Kitschy Mohawk Trail collectibles, too. Open Wed through Mon 10 a.m. to 5:30 p.m., closed Tues.

north adams, ma

This factory town at the end of the Mohawk Trail in the far northwest corner of the state was transformed with the 1999 opening of the Massachusetts Museum of Contemporary Art, known as MASS MoCa, in the city's former mill district. Artists soon followed, lured by big warehouse spaces and low rents, and now well over 30 art galleries are clustered in the area.

getting there

There's a lot to see on this 27-mile stretch of the Mohawk Trail. From Shelburne Falls continue along MA 2 West, passing through the picturesque village center of Charlemont. Along the way, you'll skirt the edge of Mount Greylock State Park. Around the 20-mile mark, look for the viewing turnout at Whitcomb Summit (the highest point of the trail) and soon after, you'll take a hairpin turn just before you arrive in North Adams.

where to go

Massachusetts Museum of Contemporary Art. 87 Marshall St.; (413) 662-2111; mass moca.org. Housed in a sprawling 13-acre industrial complex of brick factory buildings, this is the nation's largest museum for contemporary arts exhibiting work from the most cutting-edge artists of today, both established and yet-to-be discovered. Among MASS MoCA's best-known exhibits is *Sol LeWitt: A Wall Drawing Retrospective,* which features 105 of the artist's distinctive graphic works. The museum also showcases dance, avant-garde theater, performance art, film screenings, and music. When you need a museum break, stop by Lickety Split in the museum lobby for ice cream, fresh-squeezed lemonade, sandwiches, and salads. Open July and Aug daily 10 a.m. to 6 p.m.; Sept through June Wed through Mon 11 a.m. to 5 p.m. Admission $18 adults, $16 seniors, $12 students, $8 ages 6 to 16.

Natural Bridge State Park. McCauley Road (off MA 8); (413) 663-6392; mass.gov/dcr. It's worth a detour from the Mohawk Trail to walk the 0.25-mile trail in the forest to see the natural marble stone bridge over the waterfall at Hudson Brook. Open dawn to dusk. Parking fee collected Memorial Day weekend through Columbus Day $2.

where to shop

Hudson's Art. 112 Water St.; (617) 947-8534; hudsonsart.com. Located in the MASS MoCA complex, this playful gallery showcases vintage and retro finds. Their selection of early 20th-century typewriters and cameras are particularly sought after as tablesecape décor pieces. Open Wed through Sat noon to 4 p.m.

where to eat

Gramercy Bistro. 87 Marshall St.; (413) 663-5300; gramercybistro.com. This serenely stylish restaurant adjacent to MASS MoCA is the place to eat in North Adams. The menu is eclectic; mostly American but with French and Asian influences, too, and heavily market driven based on what's available from Berkshire-area farms. Among the one-of-a-kind dishes find bass with tamarind sauce, bok choy, and rice noodles, or rabbit risotto with truffles and leafy greens. Open Mon 5 to 9 p.m., Wed through Sat 5 to 9 p.m.; Sun 11 a.m. to 2 p.m. and 5 to 9 p.m. Closed Tues. $$.

Jack's Hot Dog Stand. 12 Eagle St.; (413) 664-9006; jackshotdogstand.com. Smack in the middle of North Adams, Jack's is an old-school hot dog joint that has been around since 1917. It's a classic urban hot dog counter with just a few seats, a limited menu, and a friendly grill crew. The dogs are served on a steamed bun, the french fries are hand-cut, and it's cash only. Open Mon through Sat 10 a.m. to 7 p.m., closed Sun. $.

Public Eat + Drink. 34 Holden St.; (413) 664-4444; publiceatanddrink.com. This funky urban tavern has all the makings of a great hangout. The menu is built around comfort classics with an upscale twist—flatbread pizzas, burgers, and entrees like mac and cheese with pancetta. There are small-plate offerings and seasonal salads for light eaters and an extensive menu of New England craft beer offerings. On Monday trivia nights, this is the most happening spot in all of North Adams. Open daily 11:30 a.m. to midnight.

massachusetts' highest mountain

Mount Greylock. Mount Greylock State Reservation, 30 Rockwell Rd., Lanesboro; (413) 499-4262; mass.gov/dcr. You can't really consider a drive along the Mohawk Trail complete until you have reached Mount Greylock, the highest point in Massachusetts at 3,491 feet. On the proverbial clear day (the mountain is called "Greylock" for a reason!), you can take in a spectacular multi-state vista from the summit.

Established in 1898, 11,000-acre Mount Greylock is one of the state's largest parks with more than 50 miles of hiking trails, including an 11-mile section of the Appalachian Trail. If you are terrifically fit, the trek from the base to the top will take a full day—and it's a good idea to check in at the visitor center, pick up maps and get an update on trail conditions before you head up. Most visitors, however, will opt to drive the 9-mile auto road to the top and hike one or part of several trails that circle the summit. This is not a desolate place; there's quite a lot going on at this mountain's peak. You can climb the stairs to the top of the 70-foot Veterans War Memorial Tower. Or stop by the Arts and Crafts–style timber-and-stone Bascom Lodge (bascomlodge.net) for dining with a view. The lodge serves very good home-style breakfasts, simple lunches (chili, burgers, salads), and in the evening there is an excellent fixed-price menu. Bascom Lodge also offers dormitory-style and a few private rooms for overnight guests. Auto road open late May through Oct 31. Summit parking fee $5. Bascom Lodge open June through Oct.

where to stay

Blackinton Manor. 1391 Massachusetts Ave.; (413) 663-5795; blackinton-manor.com. The traditionally styled rooms and period details are a major attraction to this dignified 19th-century Federal-style mansion. Each of the 5 guest rooms is uniquely decorated with antiques and artwork; some have fireplaces and whirlpool tubs. Rates include a full breakfast that is served in the high-ceilinged dining room. The inn is located midway between downtown North Adams and Williamstown and is convenient to both. The outdoor pool and garden is a welcome treat at the end of the day. $$.

Porches Inn. 231 River St.; (413) 664-0400; porches.com. Next to MASS MoCA, each of the 47 guest rooms in these former mill-worker row homes has been transformed into a chic retreat with boldly artistic touches. Rooms are colorful; beadboard walls are painted in mid-range pastels to complement painted wood floors that are covered by patterned wool rugs, while fun paint-by-number artwork decorates the walls. Bathrooms feature slate floors, claw-foot tubs, and luxe bath products. The hotel has a buzzing lobby bar and an enticing outdoor heated pool and hot-tub area. Rates include free Wi-Fi and complimentary continental breakfast. $$.

day trip 45

scenic & seasonal

unspoiled southern vermont:
brattleboro, vt; grafton, vt; weston, vt;
manchester, vt

Yet more verdant hills and rural vignettes. Brattleboro is as quirky as its residents, and the town brims with works by its many local artists. Be sure to sample cheddar at the Grafton cheese factory, one of the largest in the state, and load up on Vermont products in Weston. Manchester is famous for Hildene, as the headquarters for outdoor outfitter Orvis, and for the Mount Equinox Skyline Drive.

brattleboro, vt

Located in the extreme southeast corner of the state, bordering both Massachusetts and New Hampshire, Brattleboro is often a visitor's first introduction to Vermont. Its historic downtown center with numerous coffeehouses, art galleries, fine restaurants, and a year-round art scene centered around the revitalized Latchis Theater complex and the Brattleboro Museum and Art Center at the restored Union Railroad Station is a heady mix of bohemia and Main Street USA.

getting there

The most common approach to Brattleboro is from I-91, taking exit 2 to downtown. From the east or west, Brattleboro is off VT 9, also known as the Molly Stark Trail.

where to go

Brattleboro Chamber of Commerce. 180 Main St.; (802) 254-4565; brattleborochamber .org. Find maps, brochures, and event information for the general public from the chamber's member businesses. Open Mon through Fri 9 a.m. to 5 p.m.

Brattleboro Museum and Art Center. 10 Vernon St.; (802) 257-0124; brattleboro museum.org. Located in Brattleboro's former historic train station, this non-collecting museum specializes in presenting modernist work from regional, national, and international artists. Past exhibits have featured such household names as Andy Warhol and Chris Van Allsburg. Open Sun, Mon, Wed, and Thurs 11 a.m. to 5 p.m., Fri 11 a.m. to 7 p.m., Sat 10 a.m. to 5 p.m. Closed Tues. Admission $8 adults, $6 seniors, $4 students ages 6 and over.

Vermont Canoe Touring Center. 451 Putney Rd.; (802) 257-5008; vermontcanoetouring center.com. Brattleboro is located at the confluence of the Connecticut and West Rivers; seek solitude as you paddle, fish, or look for birds and wildlife. Vermont Canoe will set you up with canoe, kayak, and even river-tube rentals. Open May through Oct daily, Mon through Fri 10 a.m. to 6 p.m., Sat and Sun 9 a.m. to 6 p.m. Cash only.

where to shop

Brattleboro Farmers' Market. VT 9 West (0.5 mile after the Creamery Covered Bridge); brattleborofarmersmarket.com. It's a festive atmosphere and a visual feast with as many as 50 vendors in open-air stalls filled with piles of beets, baskets of apples, and bunches of sunflowers. This market also sells a variety of artisan and crafts items as well as quick lunch foods from around the world including wood-fired pizza, homemade gelato, Chinese dim sum, and street food from Thailand, India, and Vietnam. Bring cash (small bills are preferred) and—if you want to fit in—don't forget your reusable shopping bag. Open May through Oct Sat 9 a.m. to 2 p.m.

Brattleboro Food Co-op. 2 Main St.; (802) 257-0236; brattleborofoodcoop.com. Spreading the green food gospel since 1975, this grocery co-op is open to the public and has grown into one of state's great food experiences. Expanded in 2011 and now located in a state-of-the-art green building, the store is a great one-stop resource for made-in-Vermont products like maple syrup, artisan cheeses from independently owned small creameries, and prepared specialty foods, all at nontourist pricing. The co-op also has a superb prepared-food department where you can pick up all the essentials for a picnic. Open Mon through Sat 7 a.m. to 9 p.m., Sun 9 a.m. to 9 p.m.

Vermont Artisan Designs. 106 Main St.; (802) 257-7044; vtart.com. The handcrafted art at this delightful two-level gallery includes jewelry, blown glass, pottery, wood bowls, and fiber arts from more than 300 Vermont artists. It can be pricier than most, but everything is either one-of-a-kind or limited edition. Open Mon through Thurs 10 a.m. to 6 p.m., Fri 10 a.m. to 8 p.m., Sat 10 a.m. to 6 p.m., Sun 10 a.m. to 5 p.m.

where to eat

Amy's Bakery Arts Cafe. 113 Main St.; (802) 251-1071. Prepare to wait in line at lunch for the sandwiches or stop by in the mid-afternoon to savor a chocolate peanut butter cookie. It's a local art-filled space, and the back room has a view of the Connecticut River and the surrounding hills—nice perks both! Open Mon through Sat 7 a.m. to 6 p.m., Sun 9 a.m. to 5 p.m. $.

Mocha Joe's. 82 Main St.; Guilford (802) 257-7794; mochajoes.com. The subterranean epicenter of Brattleboro's hipster scene, Mocha Joe's is not only an indie coffeehouse serving fine coffee and espresso; it is also an artisan coffee roaster. And as you would expect, their coffee beans have every eco-credential—fair trade, organic, and rain-forest certified. Open Mon through Thurs 7 a.m. to 8 p.m., Fri 7 a.m. to 9 p.m., Sat 7:30 a.m. to 9 p.m., Sun 7:30 a.m. to 8 p.m. $.

Peter Havens. 32 Elliot St.; (802) 257-3333; peterhavens.com. After more than two decades, Peter Havens has a new chef-owner. Native Vermonter Zach Corbin continues the tradition of classic fine dining in a relaxed setting. The French classics Brattloboro residents and visitors know and love are still here—the escargots, the filet of beef with Roquefort, the apple tarte, and new dishes too. The dining room is warm and welcoming, and there are still only 10 tables. So do reserve. Open Wed through Sat 5:30 to 9 p.m. Summer deck dining at lunch is a fresh idea for Peter Havens. From May through Sept enjoy a glass of wine and Corbin's menu of salads, soup and sandwiches. Open Wed through Sat 5:30 to 9 p.m. $$–$$$.

Top of the Hill Grill. Putney Rd.; (802) 258-9178; topofthehillgrill.com. This kitchen slings some of the best barbecue anywhere, and the atmosphere couldn't be more casual with a smokehouse/order counter and picnic table seating on the outside deck or on the screened-in porch. Settle in for some amazing barbecue plates for a belly-busting bargain; choose from hickory-smoked ribs, pulled pork, and beef brisket that come with baked beans, corn bread, and coleslaw. This barbecue joint is even safe for vegetarians—this is Vermont after all—with options like a grilled tempeh wrap and Grafton cheddar mac and cheese. Remember to get the pecan pie for dessert. Open Apr through Oct Mon through Sat 11 a.m. to 9 p.m., Sun noon to 8 p.m. $$.

where to stay

The Inn on Putney Road. 192 Putney Rd.; (802) 254-6268; vermontbandbinn.com. This is not your typical overly cute New England B&B. This 1930s-era French Provincial manor home has 6 rooms that are each individually decorated in an updated country style with a private bath, flat-screen TVs, and free Wi-Fi, all in a serene, natural setting within walking distance of downtown Brattleboro. The inn's hot tub, pub, and billiard room further up the cool factor. Rates include a 2-course gourmet breakfast and lots of good Mocha Joe's coffee.

Latchis Hotel. 50 Main St.; (802) 254-6300; latchis.com. Located in Brattleboro's historic downtown district, this 3-story Art Deco gem was once the hub of Brattleboro's nightlife. Under the auspices of the nonprofit Brattleboro Arts Initiative, the Latchis Hotel and Theatre has been totally renovated. The 30 rooms vary in size but are simply done with bird's-eye maple bedroom suites indicative of the era. Free Wi-Fi and continental breakfast enhance the "budget boutique" feel. The adjacent Latchis Theatre is a classic movie house with 4 screens; the main theater has a wonderful faded glory feel with Greek murals, chipped columns, and fancy seats. $.

grafton, vt

Grafton is one of the most attractive villages in New England, and it is all by design. In the 18th century Grafton was a thriving sheep-farming community and a popular stop for weary stagecoach passengers traveling between New York and Montreal. The town's picturesque quaintness has only been slightly altered since that time, thanks to the work of the Windham Foundation, which has worked since 1963 to revitalize the village and promote Vermont rural life. Among its cornerstone projects has been reviving the Grafton Village Cheese Company and operating the Old Tavern at Grafton.

getting there

From Brattleboro it's a 40-minute drive to Grafton. Pick up VT 30 North and follow for 15 miles and merge onto VT 35 North for 3 miles. Turn left onto Townshend Road, which changes its name to Grafton Road, and then back to Townshend Road and Grafton Road (again!) for 6 miles.

where to go

Grafton Forge. 72 School St.; (802) 843-1029. One of the Windham Foundation's latest projects, stop by the historic blacksmith shop and watch raw metal being heated and hammered, inch by inch, as it is transformed into artful ironware. Open Tues through Sun 9 a.m. to 5 p.m.

Grafton Ponds Outdoor Center. 783 Townshend Rd.; (802) 843-2400; graftonponds .com. With canoeing, cross-country skiing, tubing, mountain biking, and hiking, this center offers all the outdoor-gear-rental services you need to enjoy the great outdoors. Open daily 9 a.m. to 4 p.m.

Grafton Village Cheese Company. 533 Townshend Rd.; (802) 843-1062; graftonvillage cheese.com. Any visit to Grafton must begin at the Grafton Village Cheese Factory. Watch the cheesemaking process through the viewing windows as workers make the company's award-winning cheddar. Afterward sample cheddar to your heart's content and pick up your favorites along with gourmet specialty foods like artisan-made smoked meats and a good selection of wine for a complete repast. Open daily 10 a.m. to 6 p.m. Free admission.

where to stay & eat

The Grafton Inn. 92 Main St.; (802) 843-2231; graftoninnvermont.com. At this two-centuries-old hospitality spot located in the heart of Grafton, relax in a rocking chair on the front porch or get cozy by the fire with that book you've been meaning to read. A TV-free environment, this is a great place to relax—although each of the 45 guest rooms does come with iPod docking stations and free Wi-Fi. Rooms are individually decorated with antiques and supremely comfortable bedding. Should you choose to unwind with activities, the inn can accommodate, too, with a swimming pond and tennis courts. Seasonality and sustainability are the principals at the Old Tavern Restaurant, which serves contemporary American cuisine. The inn's bar, the Phelps Barn, oozes atmosphere; Friday features flatbread pizza and local microbrews. All rates include a full country breakfast, and the cheese (Grafton Village cheddar, of course), fruit, and crackers at check-in are a welcome treat. Hotel: $$–$$$. Restaurant: $$–$$$.

weston, vt

Surrounded by the Green Mountains, Weston's claim to fame is mostly associated with what is perhaps the state's best-known country store. The overall feel here is pure Vermont; a bandstand sits on the pretty village green while nearby two steepled churches, a country inn, and the town's renowned summer playhouse complete the scene. In fact, Weston is so picturesque, the entire village is listed on the National Register of Historic Places.

getting there

From Grafton, take VT 121 West for 10 miles, merge onto VT 11 West for 4 miles, then turn right onto VT 100 North for 5 miles into Weston.

where to go

Weston Playhouse. 703 Main St.; (802) 824-5288; westonplayhouse.org. Founded in 1935, this is Vermont's oldest professional theater. Mounting a mix of classic and new, musical and nonmusical productions, these shows are always the summer's hottest tickets in southern Vermont. The 2017 season included the Tony award–winning musical *Once*. Season runs from June through early Sept. Ticket prices begin at $35.

where to shop

Vermont Country Store. 657 Main St.; (802) 824-3184; vermontcountrystore.com. The shelves of the Vermont Country Store are filled to groaning with an amazing variety of Vermont gourmet food items, practical gizmos, oddments, and hard-to-find brands from the past—glass refrigerator jugs, cotton muumuus, garden tools, and more. For visitors of a certain age, a visit to the Vermont Country Store is like a trip down memory lane with items like Lanz nightgowns, Gee Your Hair Smells Terrific shampoo, and Rock'em Sock'em Robots. Open Memorial Day weekend through mid-Oct daily 8:30 a.m. to 7 p.m.; rest of year 9 a.m. to 6 p.m.

where to eat

Bryant House. 657 Main St.; (802) 824-6287; vermontcountrystore.com. Operated by the same family that owns the Vermont Country Store, the comfort food–heavy menu is loaded with favorites like cinnamon french toast with Vermont maple syrup for breakfast, chicken pie or a turkey and cheddar melt at lunch, and Vermont apple meat loaf for dinner. Open daily 11 a.m. to 3:30 p.m. $–$$.

where to stay

Inn at Weston. 630 Main St.; (802) 824-6789; innweston.com. Located on Grafton's village green in a gorgeous turn-of-the-century building and carriage house, the rooms at this romantic retreat are decorated with pretty wallpaper, wide-pine flooring, antique furniture, quilted feather beds, and mountains of pillows. Of the 13 rooms, 9 have fireplaces, and several also have whirlpools. The innkeeper's collection of nearly 500 orchid plants (more than 375 species, and some are rare) is a memorable inn extra. Amid white linen and candlelight, the inn's popular (it's open to the public) restaurant serves creative dishes like Vermont maple–brined pork tenderloin with herb spaetzle, accompanied by live piano music nightly. Rates include a full gourmet breakfast and afternoon tea. $$–$$$.

manchester, vt

The marble sidewalks (which are remnant slabs from the nearby quarries) are just one indication that this is a moneyed town. At the base of Mount Equinox, the Equinox hotel has been a force in Manchester since 1769, attracting then, as now, a wealthy clientele. It was from extended summer stays at the Equinox hotel as a young man that Robert Todd Lincoln first became familiar with the area and later decided to build his family estate, Hildene, here. The town is also the birthplace of Orvis, the sporting goods retailer that made its name from fly fishing. And just outside of the center of town, shopping is another kind of sport, with dozens of designer outlets to browse.

getting there

To reach Manchester from Weston, retrace your steps back to VT 100 South for 5 miles and continue to follow VT 11 West into Manchester for 15 miles, turning left on VT 7A South, which is also known as Main Street (and is always slow-going because of the outlet shopping traffic).

where to go

Manchester Chamber of Commerce. 39 Bonnet St.; (802) 363-6313; visitmanchestervt .com. This is a good source of tourism info for Manchester and the southern Vermont region with itinerary ideas, travel brochures and maps, and other up-to-the-minute info. Open Mon through Fri 9 a.m. to 5 p.m., Sat 10 a.m. to 4 p.m., Sun 11 a.m. to 3 p.m.

American Museum of Fly Fishing. 4104 Main St.; (802) 362-3300; amff.com. Next door to Orvis, this offbeat museum holds the world's largest collection of angling artifacts, including more than 1,200 rods; 400 reels; and 20,000 flies. You'll hear lots of tall fish stories here—and everything that you ever wanted to know about the sport, art, craft, and business of fly fishing. Among the well-known antique rods in the collection are those that once belonged to Winslow Homer, Ernest Hemingway, and Ted Williams. Other museum treasures include a 1789 fly that is believed to be the oldest still in existence, fly-fishing fine-art pieces, and the world's most comprehensive collection of fly-fishing books. There is a casting pond behind the building that is often used for special events and demonstrations. Open June through Oct, Tues through Sun 10 a.m. to 4 p.m.; rest of the year Tues through Sat 10 a.m. to 4 p.m. Admission $5 adults, $3 ages 5 to 14, $10 family rate.

Hildene. 1005 Hildene Rd.; (802) 362-1788; hildene.org. Explore Hildene, the 412-acre estate and home of Robert Todd Lincoln, the only son of Abraham Lincoln to survive to adulthood. Robert Lincoln graduated from Harvard, held political appointments in the Garfield and Harrison administrations, and eventually became the president and long-time chairman of the board of the Pullman Company. Hildene was the summer home of Robert and his family; you can take a self-guided tour or guided tour by reservation of the mansion, which is filled with Lincoln family memorabilia, including one of only three surviving Abe Lincoln stovepipe hats. Stroll the impressive grounds and gardens (Hildene comes from the Old English for "hill and valley") and walk through Sunbeam, the restored 1903 Pullman Palace rail car on the property. In the winter, you can cross-country ski or snowshoe on 2 miles of backcountry trails. Equipment is available for rent at the pavilion. Year-round be sure to stop by Hildene's cheesemaking operation. The post-and-beam timber-frame barn is powered by renewable energy; here you can watch the milking of the goat herd and see fresh chèvre being made. "Twinkle" and her friends make some mighty fine cheese; buy some at the Museum Store to take home. Open daily 9:30 a.m. to 4:30 p.m. Admission $20 adults, $5 ages 6 to 17, free for ages 5 and under.

Mount Equinox Skyline Drive. VT 7A, Sunderland; (802) 362-1114; equinoxmountain .com. A few miles south of Manchester, the 5-mile Skyline Drive is the longest private (it's run by an order of Catholic monks), paved toll road in the US. It's a winding road to the top with several hairpin turns to keep it interesting, but at the summit you will be rewarded with a breathtaking panorama of the Green, White, Adirondack, Taconic, and Berkshire mountain ranges. Several marked hiking trails crisscross the area; best to pick up a map at the toll house before you set out. Open May through June Mon through Wed 9 a.m. to 5 p.m., Thurs through Sun 9 a.m. to sunset; July through Oct daily 9 a.m. to sunset. Closed Nov through Apr. Vehicle and driver $15, and $5 per additional passenger (children under age 10 free).

Southern Vermont Art Center. West Road; (802) 362-1405; svac.org. Stop here on your travels to visit this community art museum/gallery located in a 400-acre estate setting. The Wilson Museum houses the center's permanent collection of over 700 works by well-known 19th- and 20th-century American artists. Be sure to browse the Yester House; the 10 separate galleries are devoted to displaying the work of local artists, and all the items are available for sale. Open May through Oct Tues through Sat 10 a.m. to 5 p.m., Sun noon to 5 p.m. Free admission.

Separate (before galleries) was marked to replace in 1pp PDF but not what to replace it with

where to shop

Manchester Designer Outlets. 97 Depot St., Manchester Center; (800) 955-7467; man chesterdesigneroutlets.com. Leave some room in your car—high-end outlet shopping has come to earthy-crunchy Vermont in a very big way. Find scores of designer and high-end specialty shops including **Vineyard Vines** (448 Depot St.; 802-362-8012) for women's resort wear, **Coach** (18 Depot St.; 802-362-1771) for statement handbags, and re-create that hotel-bed feeling at home with linens from **Yves Delorme** (4783 Main St.; 802-366-4974). Open Mon through Sat 10 a.m. to 7 p.m., Sun 10 a.m. to 6 p.m.

Northshire Bookstore. 4869 Main St., Manchester Center; (802) 362-2200; northshire .com. If (when) you've had enough outlet shopping, Northshire Bookstore is a welcome retreat. This is a classic indie bookseller that stocks a fantastic selection of carefully chosen titles. The children's book section is outstanding as well. The store occupies an old Victorian inn; you'll find lots of nooks and crannies to settle into with your finds, or you can head over to the in-store Spiral Press Cafe, which offers light and casual meals that range from organic roasted-vegetable soup to brie, ham, and apple panini, all served in a large light- and art-filled space. If it's operating, it's fun to watch the EBM (Espresso Book Machine) in the front of the store that prints self-published books under the Shire Press imprint. Open Sun through Wed 10 a.m. to 7 p.m., Thurs through Sat 10 a.m. to 9 p.m.

Orvis Company Store. 4180 Main St.; (802) 362-3750; orvis.com/manchester. Manchester can lay claim to the headquarters of Orvis, the upscale outdoor sporting goods store that was founded by Charles F. Orvis in 1856. Renowned for its fly-fishing equipment, this is the company's flagship store, selling all the necessary accessories for the upscale sporting life, including adventure-ready clothing, wicker porch furniture, and memory-foam dog beds. The store is also a tremendous resource for fly fishermen and runs courses for all levels from its Orvis Fly-Fishing School across the street, which takes advantage of fishing on the nearby Battenkill River. Open Mon through Fri 10 a.m. to 6 p.m., Sat 9 a.m. to 6 p.m., Sun 10 a.m. to 5 p.m.

where to eat

Bistro Henry. 1942 Depot St.; (802) 362-4982; bistrohenry.com. The tender braised lamb shank and scrumptious sea scallops with corn and leek risotto and ginger butter that emerge from Henry Bronson's kitchen would be enough to make you swoon. But then there are his wife Dina's desserts, including her rightfully famous flourless chocolate cake with house-made espresso ice cream. And overall decent tabs (for pricey Manchester) sweeten the deal. Open Sun through Thurs 5 to 9 p.m., Fri and Sat 5 to 9:30 p.m., closed Mon. $$–$$$.

Little Rooster Cafe. 4645 Main St.; (802) 362-3496. This cute and cozy spot serves some of the best breakfasts around: corned beef hash with 2 poached eggs and béchamel sauce or hand-cut cinnamon-swirl french toast for breakfast. Lunch offerings skew to European-style fare with homemade soups, seasonal frittatas and risottos, and sandwich classics like roast leg of lamb on focaccia. Open daily 7 a.m. to 2:30 p.m. Cash only. $–$$.

Perfect Wife Restaurant and The Other Woman Tavern. 2594 Depot St.; (802) 362-2817; perfectwife.com. Chef-owner Amy Chamberlain lives up to her restaurant's name with a menu that serves hearty contemporary American food like turkey schnitzel with lemon-sage butter sauce and mashed potatoes, and sesame-crusted yellowfin tuna with stir-fried vegetables. The upstairs tavern attracts a local crowd with live bands on weekends and a more casual menu that features dishes like beer-battered crawfish tails and a three-way (cheeseburger, crab cake, and grilled chicken) slider assortment. Restaurant open Mon through Sat 5 to 10 p.m.; tavern open Mon through Sat 5 to 10 p.m. Both closed Sun. $$–$$$.

where to stay

Equinox Resort. 3567 Main St.; (802) 362-4700; equinoxresort.com. From the moment you cross the expansive veranda and are greeted by the liveried doorman, you will be awed by the expert service and luxury that has brought a discerning clientele to this quiet southern Vermont village since the 18th century. Each of the resort's more than 200 rooms is contemporary and luxurious with every high-end amenity. There is a definite English country estate feel to the hotel: falconry, an off-road driving school, clay shooting, and guided fly-fishing trips are among the hotel's offerings. You'll revel in the resort's unparalleled fitness facilities and bliss out at the gorgeous spa—one of the best in the state. Dine at the hotel's venerable Chop House or the resort's other dining spaces; in the evening the stately Falcon Bar is the place to be with one of the largest single-malt scotch menus anywhere. $$$–$$$$.

Inn at Manchester. 3967 Main St.; (802) 362-1793; innatmanchester.com. This handsome 18-room, white clapboard inn has a bounty of pleasing comforts: from luxury pressed (!) linens and flat-screen TVs to the property's many public spaces, which include a fireplaced living room, formal gardens, and a secluded outdoor pool. A stocked guest pantry is another thoughtful detail. The inn is located on 4 country acres within walking distance of Manchester Center, so you have both room to relax along with proximity to restaurants and shopping. Rates include a made-to-order Vermont country breakfast. There's a pub on-site too. $$–$$$.

Reluctant Panther Inn. 39 West Rd.; (802) 362-2568; reluctantpanther.com. A boutique hotel retreat with 20 smartly appointed rooms that let you feel like a country squire. Each room is decorated with Italian linens, antiques, flat-screen TVs, and posh, modern bathrooms, and many have sitting areas and fireplaces. The dining room serves a seasonally changing American menu overlooking the gardens and Mount Equinox; dishes include a Boursin soufflé followed by a pine nut and fennel–crusted rack of lamb. Rates include a full gourmet breakfast. $$–$$$.

worth more time

Marlboro Music. 2582 South Rd., Marlboro; (802) 254-2394; marlboromusic.org. Classical music lovers are drawn to the renowned summer Marlboro Music Festival that takes place on the campus of Marlboro College and has been a fixture of the southern Vermont cultural scene since the 1950s. Currently under the artistic direction of renowned pianist Mitsuko Uchida, world-class master artists and gifted young, professional musicians come together to rehearse in an intensive collaboration, which culminates in 5 weekends of chamber music programs that are held from mid-July to mid-Aug.

day trip 46

scenic & seasonal

down east nature walks & scenic drives:
bar harbor, me; acadia national park

Just off the coast of Maine (and accessible by car), Mount Desert Island is a world unto itself—a panorama of mountains, coast, and pine forest. Frenchman Samuel de Champlain called this outcrop Isles des Monts Deserts, the "Island of Barren Mountains," in 1604. (It's spelled "Desert," and usually, correctly, pronounced "de-zert.") Not well known is that with a land area of 108 square miles this is the second largest island in the country after Long Island. Most of the island belongs to Acadia National Park, which attracts more than 2 million visitors a year and features unspoiled sandy beaches (bone-chilling water, though!) and miles of carriage lanes through wooded conservation land to hike and/or bike.

bar harbor, me

Nestled between the Cadillac Mountain range and Frenchman Bay, Bar Harbor is a bustling resort village that is an ideal base for Acadia National Park adventures with lots of lodging, restaurants, and shops. Like many northeast coastal towns, the wildness of Bar Harbor's landscape attracted artists of the Hudson River School during the Victorian era. The wealthy soon followed, building grand summer "cottages" along Shore Path, many of which were destroyed by the Great Fire of 1947.

getting there

Mount Desert Island is just off the coast of Maine and is connected to the mainland by the Trenton Bridge and the ME 3 causeway. After the bridge, follow ME 3 for 10 miles into Bar Harbor.

where to go

Bar Harbor Chamber of Commerce Welcome Center. 1201 Bar Harbor Rd., Trenton; (800) 345-4617; barharborinfo.com. Located on the mainland just before the Trenton Bridge, this staffed visitor center has maps and information on Bar Harbor and Acadia National Park. Open daily 8 a.m. to 6 p.m. from Memorial Day through Columbus Day; Mon through Fri 8 a.m. to 5 p.m. the rest of the year.

Abbe Museum. 26 Mount Desert St.; (207) 288-3519; abbemuseum.org. The 12,000-year history of Maine's native Wabanaki people is the focus of this small but growing museum. Regularly scheduled cultural demonstrations feature musical performances, birch-bark canoe making, basket weaving, and carving by members of Maine's tribal communities. Open late May through early Nov daily 10 a.m. to 5 p.m.; rest of the year Thurs through Sat 10 a.m. to 4 p.m. Closed Jan. Admission $8 adults, $4 ages 6 to 15.

Acadia Bike Rentals & Coastal Kayaking Tours. 48 Cottage St.; (800) 526-8615; acadia bike.com. Consider this a one-stop shopping destination for all your Acadia adventure needs. Bike rentals include maps, water bottle cage, and (thankfully) gel seats. Next-door, sister company Coastal Kayaking rents sea kayaks for paddling Frenchman Bay and the western side of the island. Choose from 2.5-hour, half-day, and full-day guided tours on the water. Whether you bike or kayak, you're sure to sleep like a baby afterward! Open daily May through Oct 9 a.m. to 8 p.m.

Bar Harbor Historical Society. 33 Ledgelawn Ave.; (207) 288-3807; barharborhistorical .org. For an introduction to Bar Harbor's history as a Victorian-era summer resort and exhibits related to the Great Fire of 1947, this museum is worth a look. Open June through Oct Mon through Sat 1 to 4 p.m. Open rest of the year by appointment. Free admission.

George B. Dorr Museum of Natural History. 105 Eden St.; (207) 288-5395; coa.edu/ dorr. This museum's exhibits center around Maine's natural history and wildlife and stress conservation and an appreciation for the natural world. The museum is located on the campus of the ecology-oriented College of the Atlantic and many of the exhibits are student driven and produced. Open Tues through Sat 10 a.m. to 5 p.m. Admission by donation.

***Lulu* Lobster Boat.** 55 West St.; (207) 963-2341; lululobsterboat.com. Climb aboard a traditional Down East lobster boat and take a 2-hour cruise through Frenchman Bay while Capt. John Nicolai explains lobsters and lobstering. Get up close to the harbor seals and porpoises; you might also see a bald eagle. Drift past Egg Rock Lighthouse and the summer mansions along the shore and hear the history of Mount Desert Island and some entertaining tall sea tales. Season runs May through Oct daily, check website and/or call for exact departure times. Fares $30 adults, $27 seniors, $17 children ages 2 to 12.

where to shop

Island Artisans. 99 Main St.; (207) 288-4214; islandartisans.com. You'll find a dazzling assortment of attractive, well-priced pottery, textiles, and sculpture at this premier gallery of local Maine artists. Special orders are taken, too. Open May through Dec; check website for hours.

where to eat

Cafe This Way. 14 1/2 Mount Desert St.; (207) 288-4483; cafethisway.com. Located away from the main Bar Harbor drag, this ambience-driven hot spot with dark walls, low lighting, and loungy seating is perpetually crowded both day and night. Breakfast is reasonable and done right from "the usual" (2 eggs, home fries, and toast) to some great offerings in the Benedict department, including the Smokey, which features smoked trout, basil, red onions, and tomatoes. The dinner menu really celebrates the restaurant's eclectic vibe. Start with an appetizer of grilled quail with goat cheese polenta and blueberry barbecue sauce. Then go for the lobster roll trio done Asian, spicy Southwest, and traditional style to compare and contrast. Open Apr through Oct, Mon through Sat 7 a.m. to 11:30 a.m. and 5:30 to 9:30 p.m.; Sun 8 a.m. to 1 p.m. and 5:30 to 9:30 p.m. $–$$.

Havana. 318 Main St.; (207) 288-2822; havanamaine.com. Cuba might be an unusual inspiration for Maine, but this fine-dining restaurant strives for the best of both worlds by offering New England cuisine with *nuevo latino* flair. It turns out to be an exciting experiment with dishes like herb-crusted halibut served in a banana leaf, and churrasco hanger steak with chimichurri sauce and potato purée. The menu is highlighted by an equally uncommon wine list, while gregarious husband-and-wife owners Michael and Deirdre are usually on hand to make sure everything works. Reservations recommended. Open May through Dec Mon through Thurs 5 to 9:30 p.m., Fri and Sat 5 to 10:30 p.m., Sun 5 to 9 p.m. Call for off-season hours. $$–$$$.

Mache Bistro. 135 Cottage St.; (207) 288-0447; machebistro.com. Chef-owner Kyle Yarborough and his wife, Marie, have brought classic French bistro food with an emphasis on the sea to Bar Harbor. The menu changes daily based on ingredients from local farms, fishermen, and fisheries. The Cabernet-poached pear with smoked blue cheese, cranberries, and arugula is an elegant starter. Perhaps you'll find pan-roasted fluke with lemon caper butter, or blue corn and cumin-dusted char with saffron cherry aioli as a main. And the blood orange olive oil and sherry pound cake soaked in sweet milk is memorable. Best of all, the prices are modest, and the atmosphere is relaxed. But Mache Bistro has just 10 tables, so reservations are an absolute must. Open Tues through Sat 5:30 to 9 p.m. $$–$$$.

McCay's Public House. 231 Main St.; (207) 288-2002; mckayspublichouse.com. Located in a charming Victorian building, this invitingly dark, upscale watering hole appeals to locals and visitors of all ages, who sit side by side to enjoy a drink and sustainable, moderately priced New American comfort food like seafood risotto, espresso-rubbed filet mignon with bourbon cream sauce, and ahi tuna over sesame noodles. Open daily 4:30 to 11 p.m. $$.

Mount Desert Island Ice Cream. 325 Main St.; (207) 801-4006; and 7 Firefly Ln.; (207) 801-4007; mdiic.com. For serious ice cream, look no further than Mount Desert Island Ice Cream. They are particularly known for their funky flavors. Fans of Thin Mints will love Girl Scouts Gone Wild, and you can't go wrong with their salt caramel or Callebaut chocolate. Open Apr through Oct daily 11 a.m. to 10 p.m. $.

where to stay

Bar Harbor Inn. 7 Newport Dr.; (207) 288-3351; barharborinn.com. At this 150-room complex, the price is right for large, comfortable (if traditional) rooms, a friendly and helpful staff, a heated outdoor pool (important in Maine), and enviable water views (from most rooms). Ask about dining at the hotel's Reading Room restaurant, which offers refined New England cuisine and harbor views. Indulgent treatments are available at the hotel's spa. All room rates include a continental breakfast. Open seasonally May through Oct. $$–$$$.

Bass Cottage Inn. 14 The Field; (207) 288-1234; basscottage.com. The Bass Cottage Inn is a benchmark for all small inns. With 10 rooms, each has an individually elegant decor with the finest linens and antiques, a fireplace, and an en suite bath with whirlpool tub, yet the overall feel of the inn is like a friendly country house—belonging to very wealthy friends. Wake up to the included 3-course gourmet breakfast; the guest pantry stocked with fresh fruit, home-baked brownies, and wine helps to keep the munchies at bay during the rest of the day. The inn's 10 Tables offers seasonal fine dining, and a 3-course prix-fixe menu. The hospitable innkeepers and a location away from the bustle of Bar Harbor, but still within walking distance to shops and restaurants, makes it tempting to extend your stay. Open seasonally May through Oct. $$$.

The Bayview. 111 Eden St.; (207) 288-5861; thebayviewbarharbor.com. Just outside of Bar Harbor, the Bayview Hotel offers uncommonly warm hospitality and 26 rooms that each have a large balcony and a jaw-dropping view of Frenchman Bay. The rooms aren't as wonderful as the views, but they'll do; they are spacious and decorated simply with dark wood bedsteads and white bedspreads. Rates include a deluxe breakfast with warm-from-the-oven muffins, fresh fruit, and a hot entree. There's a small, heated pool as well. Open seasonally May through Oct. $$–$$$.

acadia national park

Established in 1919, Acadia National Park was the first national park east of the Mississippi River. Here, the pine-covered mountain meets the shore in dramatic fashion with craggy granite outcrops battered by pounding Atlantic surf.

Whether you choose a windshield tour along the Park Loop road, a scenic family jaunt along the Ocean Path Trail, or a serious 7-mile scramble atop the ridge of Cadillac Mountain, you will be rewarded with some of the most spectacular scenery in all of New England.

getting there

Acadia National Park is located just 4 miles west of Bar Harbor.

where to go

Acadia National Park Visitors Center. nps.gov/acad. Acadia National Park's main summer visitor center, Hulls Cove, is just north of Bar Harbor on ME 3. Stop here to pay the park entrance fee. Acadia National Park can be overwhelming; the rangers are great at helping you map out a schedule of activities tailored to your interests. Be sure to watch the park's orientation film, *Acadia Always,* and pick up maps of the carriage roads and hiking trails. The park's newspaper, the *Beaver Log,* has park-wide tips, and check out, too, the day's schedule of ranger-led activities—always lots of interesting walks and talks, boat cruises, and fun children's programs. Hulls Cove open Apr through Sept 9 a.m. to 5 p.m., Oct 8:30 a.m. to 4:30 p.m. Closed Nov through Mar. The Acadia National Park Headquarters on ME 233 is daily 8 a.m. to 4:30 p.m. The park itself is open 24 hours, though some roads are closed in winter. Park permits are $25 per vehicle or $12 per individual and are good for 7 consecutive days. Fees are not collected Nov through Apr.

Bass Harbor Head Light. Lighthouse Road, off ME 102, Bass Harbor. Located at the southern tip of Mount Desert Island, Bass Harbor light was built in 1858. The lighthouse is an active station; the residence is Coast Guard housing, but the grounds are open to the public. Best dramatic photo shot of the lighthouse is from the rocks just below. Grounds open 9 a.m. to sunset.

Cadillac Mountain. At 1,530 feet, Cadillac Mountain is the tallest mountain on the East Coast. If you rise early, you can drive or hike to the summit and catch the first rays of the sun to touch the US and enjoy awesome 360-degree views of the entire island. Not an early riser? The sunsets are pretty good, too. The top of the mountain is usually closed Dec through Mar because of snow.

Carriages of Acadia. 21 Dane Farm Rd.; (877) 276-3622; carriagesofacadia.com. The 45 miles of auto-free carriage roads were funded in the early 1900s by John D. Rockefeller to preserve Acadia's tranquility. The carriage roads are used by bikers and hikers, but there is nothing like the experience of riding through the woods and over the stone bridges that span the streams along the way as they were intended—by horse-drawn carriage. Both 1- and 2-hour guided carriage rides are offered May through Oct; check website for hours and prices.

Park Loop Road. For an overview of the park, drive the 27-mile Park Loop Road, which brings you to many of the park's top features including Cadillac Mountain, Sand Beach, Thunder Hole, and Jordan Pond House. You can do this scenic drive in an hour, but it is best experienced at a leisurely pace; 3 or 4 hours would be just about right. And do plan to get out of your car to explore on foot at least some of the way. Begin at the entrance next to the Hulls Cove Visitor Center.

Sand Beach. Along Park Loop Road.Visitors flock to this small pocket of beach that's just 290 yards long. It's cold—wicked cold—but a good spot to dip your big toe, sunbathe, or do some beachcombing.

Sieur de Monts Spring. Intersection of Park Loop Road and ME 3. At the midway point of the Park Loop Road, the Sieur de Monts area has a mix of towering trees, a brook-fed natural spring, and graveled paths that make a nice spot for quiet reflection. Botanically minded visitors will want to visit the Wild Gardens of Acadia; the 1-acre garden has 300 (all labeled), native plant species. The original trailside Abbe Museum site is here too, focusing on Wabanaki Native American archeology. There is also a small nature center and restrooms.

Thunder Hole. Along Park Loop Road, south of Sand Beach. An impressive scenic landmark where pounding Atlantic waves crash into a crevasse, which makes a thundering sound from the force of the water exploding out of the cavern. The best time to catch the spectacle is 2 hours before high tide, and although there are protective railings, do be careful; people have been known to be swept out to sea.

where to eat

Abel's Lobster Pound. 13 Abel's Lane; (207) 276-5827. Located in a thick pine forest, overlooking Somes Sound, this totally bare-bones seafood joint specializes in lobster dinners and homemade pie. Sit at one of the picnic tables scattered about, crack open a claw (if it's buggy head over to the rustic dining room), and enjoy the sunset. It's an experience worth the 20-minute drive from Bar Harbor. Open July daily 5 to 9 p.m., Aug and Sept noon to 9 p.m. $$.

Jordan Pond House. Park Loop Road; (207) 276-3316; thejordanpondhouse.com. Whether hiking or driving, the absolute best Acadia National Park trip planning advice is to schedule your visit to include a stop for fresh-from-the-oven popovers with butter and strawberry jam at the 1870s Jordan Pond House restaurant. The famed popovers are also available accompanying lobster stew at lunch or dinner. Dining outside on the expansive

car free & green

*You can ride virtually anywhere on Mount Desert Island on the **Island Explorer Shuttle Bus.** There are 8 seasonal fixed routes that include stops at Bar Harbor hotels and restaurants and the island's beaches. There's also a Park Loop Road route, which in high summer season is the way to go—you can hop on and off and don't have to worry about parking. The dedicated Bicycle Express accommodates riders and their bikes, and has direct service to Eagle Lake. Bus service runs from late June through Oct. Free. Island Explorer; exploreacadia.com.*

lawn and gardens that overlook Jordan Pond with vistas of Penobscot Mountain is also part of the Jordan Pond House experience. Open mid-May to mid-Oct daily 11:30 a.m. to 9 p.m. (hours vary in the spring and fall). $$.

where to stay

Asticou Inn. 15 Peabody Dr., Northeast Harbor; (207) 276-3344; asticou.com. The Asticou Inn's 48 rooms have an unpretentious Down East Maine charm, while the nearby waters of Northeast Harbor and next-door Arcadia National Park beckon with adventure. The inn's restaurant, Peabody's @ the Atiscou, draws vacationers from throughout the island for its casual, regional fine dining. The inn's well-tended cutting gardens, the outdoor pool, and red-clay tennis court do a great job of reinforcing the low-key seaside retreat vibe. $$.

day trip 47

scenic & seasonal

fall foliage & mountain magnificence:
north conway, nh; mount washington;
bretton woods, nh; franconia, nh

The trees of the White Mountains blaze in the fall with crimson, gold, and scarlet leaves. The foliage season begins early here, usually by mid-September, and ends around mid-October. The Mount Washington Valley offers lots of leaf-peeping opportunities from a scenic drive along the Kancamagus Highway; to fall foliage train excursions; to tram, gondola, and chairlift rides at the ski resorts; and even tree canopy zip lines. But the Mount Washington Valley is truly an all-season destination, with some of New England's best skiing and a countless number of outdoor activities and diversions in the spring and summer, too.

north conway, nh

Area families know North Conway as "Story Land country," home to one of New England's most endearing, old-fashioned amusement parks. Several New England ski mountains are also in this area. The abundance of fast-food restaurants and the mall sprawl along the "strip"—NH 16—lets you know that you have arrived at the White Mountain's gateway city.

New Hampshire is the only New England state that does not impose a general sales tax, which makes shopping a significant tourist activity everywhere in the state. North Conway is a favorite shopping destination for serious bargain hunters with a large number of outlet stores.

getting there

Most visitors arrive in North Conway from NH 16 North, also known as the White Mountain Highway.

where to go

Mount Washington Valley Chamber of Commerce. 2617 White Mountain Hwy.; (603) 356-3171; mtwashingtonvalley.org. This visitor center is a good place to stop for maps, brochures, and useful coupons for shopping and attraction discounts throughout the entire region. Staff can also find last-minute accommodations. Open daily June through Columbus Day 9 a.m. to 6 p.m., rest of the year 9 a.m. to 5 p.m.

Conway Scenic Railroad. 38 Norcross Circle, Conway; (603) 356-5251; conwayscenic .com. A heritage railroad and a must for train buffs, Conway Scenic Railroad offers several daily excursions from its historic 1874 station. The 1-hour round-trip by electric locomotive that winds through gorgeous countryside along the Saco River to Conway is ideal for the little ones; older kids will enjoy a 2-hour round-trip to Bartlett. For serious train aficionados, the Notch Train excursion is a 5-hour round-trip through spectacular Crawford Notch to Fabyan's Station and offers several first-class options including seating in the Dome Car and a 3-course lunch in a restored Pullman dining car. Trains run May through Dec; check website for departure times and prices.

Cranmore Mountain Resort. 1 Skimobile Rd.; (603) 356-5543; cranmore.com. Not as big or challenging as other New England mountains, Cranmore is a terrific family ski area that has a well-deserved reputation for its children's learn-to-ski programs and affordable lift tickets. The resort's 50 trails are served by 5 lifts with 70 percent of the trails rated for the beginner or intermediate skier. Nonskiers will enjoy Cranmore's tubing park and its indoor fun center. In summer, the resort becomes a mountaintop playground with summer hill tubing, a bungee trampoline area, mountain coaster, and scenic chairlift rides.

Saco Canoe Rentals. 326 White Mountain Hwy.; (603) 447-4275; sacorental.com. This part of the Saco River averages just 3 feet in depth, perfect for canoe and kayaking adventures. Saco Canoe offers guided canoe and kayak trips. They also specialize in river-tube rentals—where you just go with the flow. Enjoying a day on the river can't get any easier! Open seasonally Mon through Fri 9 a.m. to 5 p.m., Sat 8 a.m. to 6 p.m., Sun 9 a.m. to 5 p.m.

Story Land. Junction of NH 16 and US 302, Glen; (603) 383-4186; storylandnh.com. Since 1954, generations of New Englanders have taken their kids to Story Land to experience quaint, old-fashioned amusement park fun. A single admission price includes a day of storybook-themed rides, shows, and attractions. Story Land is just the right size for kids ages 2 to 12; rides like Alice's Tea Cups and Cinderella's Pumpkin Coach appeal to little ones. Big-kid rides include Bamboo Chutes and Splash Battle. Everyone will want to take a break and watch a circus act, and be sure to let the kids blow off steam at the "spray-ground"—perfect for a hot summer day. Open May through Oct; June through Aug daily 9:30 a.m. to 6 p.m., check website for days and hours during spring and fall. Admission $34 ages 3 and over, $30 seniors, free ages 2 and under.

Weather Discovery Center. 2779 White Mountain Hwy.; (603) 356-2137; mountwash ington.org. Amateur weather prognosticators can explore the science of climate at this museum in a fun and interactive way. There's a replica of the original Mount Washington weather observation station that simulates a wind gust of 231 miles an hour—you can feel the building shake. Try your hand at forecasting the weather in front of the green screen and touch a tornado vortex. The Weather Store stocks the latest weather gadgetry. Open daily 10 a.m. to 5 p.m. Free admission.

where to shop

Settler's Green Outlet Village. 2 Common Court; (888) 667-9636; settlersgreen.com. Seriously addicted shopaholics can do some damage at this complex of more than 60 popular brand-name stores; among them Nike, Lindt Chocolate, Gap, Yankee Candle, and Carter's Childrenswear. Open Mon through Sat 9 a.m. to 9 p.m., Sun 10 a.m. to 6 p.m.

Zeb's General Store. 2675 Main St.; (603) 356-9294; zebs.com. In the heart of North Conway Village, be sure to stop by Zeb's to stock up on fun New England–made products: pine-scented soap, jars of pickled eggs, marshmallow slingshots, a moose cookie cutter. On your way out, hit up the antique penny-candy counter (it's 67 feet long!) and fill a paper bag with your favorites. Open daily 9 a.m. to 10 p.m.

where to eat

Flatbread Pizza Company. 2760 White Mountain Hwy.; (603) 356-4470; flatbreadcom pany.com. This regional pizza chain is a good bet for brilliantly inspired pizza and terrific salads. Organic ingredients and a wood-fired clay oven combine to create pies like a home-made maple-fennel sausage with sun-dried tomatoes, caramelized onions, and mozzarella flatbread that is the perfect indulgence after a day of skiing or hiking in the mountains. Open Mon through Thurs 11:30 a.m. to 9 p.m., Fri and Sat 11:30 a.m. to 9:30 p.m., Sun 11:30 a.m. to 9 p.m. $$.

May Kelly's Cottage. 3002 White Mountain Hwy.; (603) 356-7005; maykellys.com. This pub/restaurant has all the elements of a great Irish bar: Guinness on tap, tasty comfort food such as lamb stew and shepherd's pie, and a dark and cluttered coziness, all in a warm and friendly environment. Tap your feet during a *seisun,* an informal, traditional Irish music session on Sunday afternoons. Open Mon through Thurs 4 to 9 p.m., Fri and Sat noon to 10 p.m., Sun noon to 9 p.m. $$.

Muddy Moose. 2344 White Mountain Hwy.; (603) 356-7696; muddymoose.com. One of the biggest restaurants in the valley, this hopping family-friendly joint serves up enormous quantities of amazing ribs and other juicy meats. The campy decor—faux antler chandeliers, vintage snowshoe and skis on blond knotty pine walls—conjures up a backwoods lodge and just adds to the rip-roaring good time vibe. No reservations are taken, so be prepared to wait. Open daily 11:30 a.m. to 10 p.m. $$.

where to stay

Buttonwood Inn. 64 Mount Surprise Rd.; (603) 356-2625; buttonwoodinn.com. Just 2 miles away from the hubbub of North Conway, but still close to all the area attractions, this 1820s inn is located on 5 spacious acres on the slope of Mount Surprise, adjacent to the Merriman State Forest. The rockers on the front porch, Adirondack chairs overlooking the perennial gardens, and a pool and hot tub complete the country retreat illusion. Each of the 10 individually decorated rooms are light, bright, and comfortable with sturdy antique furniture, wide pine floors, and flat-screen TVs. A full gourmet breakfast (that if you are lucky might include the inn's signature pecan wild blueberry french toast) and afternoon refreshments with home-baked treats are included in the rate. $$–$$$.

Red Jacket Mountain View. 2251 White Mountain Hwy.; (603) 356-5411; redjacketresorts .com. With top-notch facilities—including Kahuna Laguna, one of New England's few indoor waterparks—the Red Jacket really knows how to deliver the goods to vacationing families. All guests have unlimited access to the water park, which features 4 slides, a zero-depth

driving the kancamagus highway

Travel the twisting 30-mile stretch along NH 112 from Lincoln to Conway and experience some of New England's most spectacular scenery. Named for the Native American leader who ruled this part of New Hampshire in the late 1600s, the "Kanc," as it is known locally, is designated as one of America's Scenic Byways. Traveling within the White Mountain National Forest, the drive climbs nearly 3,000 feet offering valley-to-mountain views at the Graham Wangan Ground Overlook. Along the way, stop at Sabbaday Falls to see the tumbling cascades and enjoy cool mountain swimming holes at Lower Falls on the Swift River. Autumn may be the drive's most spectacular time of year (when traffic slows to a crawl), but the drive is truly a year-round pleasure. Be sure to have a full gas tank and bring a well-stocked picnic basket and drinks—there are no businesses along the way, and the only stops are picnic areas and restrooms at the designated overlooks.

entry wave pool, a play-tower activity center, and a 25-person family hot tub. There is also a seasonal outdoor heated pool for a change of pace. This full-service resort is located on 40 acres overlooking the Mount Washington Valley. Its 150 rooms have been recently updated, and with lots of configurations like loft rooms, alcove rooms, and town homes, this is a particularly good choice for large families or for those vacationing with extended family. Breakfast and dinner are served at the hotel's fine dining venue, Champney's, which has a terrific view, while Palmer's serves more casual fare. $$.

mount washington

At 6,288 feet, Mount Washington is the highest peak in the northeastern US. It's part of the Presidential Range, a series of mountains that run through the White Mountain National Forest. Its craggy, granite summit can only be reached by the intrepid—whether by driving the Mount Washington Auto Road, taking the Mount Washington Cog Railway, or those willing to test themselves by enduring a fairly strenuous day hike to the top.

Mount Washington is also the self-proclaimed "home of the world's worst weather." In 1934, the Mount Washington Weather Observatory clocked the highest wind speed ever recorded by man at 231 mph. Fog is ever-present, and it is not unheard of to see snow at the summit during any month of the year.

getting there

To reach the base of Mount Washington for access to the Mount Washington Auto Road or the hiking trails from Tuckerman Ravine, take 16 North from North Conway for 20 miles.

where to go

Appalachian Club Pinkham Notch Visitors Center. 361 NH 16, Gorham; (603) 466-2721; outdoors.org. Does your sense of adventure include ascending Mount Washington? The Pinkham Notch Visitor Center, located at the base of Mount Washington, is an ideal starting point offering trip planning assistance, an outdoor gear store, cafeteria, and lodge-style accommodations at the Joe Dodge Lodge next door. Open year-round.

Mount Washington Auto Road. NH 16, Pinkham Notch; (603) 466-3988; mountwashingtonautoroad.com. With hairpin turns, no shoulder, and no guardrail, driving the 8 miles to the summit of Mount Washington is a white-knuckle experience. Your toll includes the iconic "This Car Climbed Mount Washington" bumper sticker. The faint-of-heart may want to opt for the guided van option. In the winter, guided snow coach tours are available. Toll road open May through Oct; check website for hours. Car and driver $29, each additional adult passenger $9, $7 children ages 5 to 12. Guided tour rates $36 adults, $31 seniors, $16 children ages 5 to 12.

Mount Washington State Park. US 302; (603) 466-3347; nhstateparks.com/washington .html. This 59-acre state park at the summit of Mount Washington offers amenities for all who conquer Mount Washington. On a clear day you'll be treated to spectacular views that reach beyond New Hampshire to include Vermont, Massachusetts, Maine, Quebec, and the Atlantic Ocean. There is an outdoor observation deck, a glassed-in viewing area, cafeteria, and gift shop. Also, don't miss the opportunity to check out the Mount Washington Weather Observatory Museum with exhibits that detail the stories behind the work of the scientists who monitor "the world's worst weather." Visitor center open daily mid-May through Aug 8:30 a.m. to 6 p.m.; check website for hours in Sept and Oct.

bretton woods, nh

Deep in the heart of the White Mountains, the village known as Bretton Woods is home to the Omni Mount Washington Resort and its related businesses, the Bretton Woods Mountain Resort and the Mount Washington Cog Railroad.

getting there

This is mountain country; driving routes are not very neat, so if you are coming from Mount Washington, you will need to retrace your path down NH 16 South and turn onto US 302 West, driving through spectacular Crawford Notch to the activities and dining that are centered around the Mount Washington Resort at Bretton Woods.

where to go

Bretton Woods Mountain Resort. US 302; (603) 278-1000; brettonwoods.com. This all-season family resort is another New Hampshire ski area well known for its children's learn-to-ski programs. The mountain boasts more than 400 acres of skiable terrain and plenty of slopes that are accessible from 9 lifts stationed throughout the mountain. The resort is also famed for its extensive Nordic network through the White Mountain National Forest, with more than 100 kilometers of trails. During the summer and fall, the base lodge is the starting point for the Bretton Woods Canopy Tour, a 3.5-hour adventure across and along the treetops. Whee!

Mount Washington Cog Railway. Base Road off US 302; (603) 278-5404; thecog.com. What began as "a railway to the moon" became the world's first mountain-climbing cog railroad when it was built in 1869. Today a trip on the Mount Washington Cog Railway is still a marvel, with a biodiesel engine (or coal-burning steam on the first trip of the day) chugging along the 3-mile route to the top with grades of up to 37 percent. The entire trip takes nearly 3 hours, including a 1-hour stopover at the summit. And be sure to bring a sweater or jacket; it can be cold at the top, even in summer. Season runs from May through early Dec; check website for departure times. Tickets $69 adults, $65 seniors, $39 ages 4 to 12.

where to eat

Fabyan's Station. 2329 US 302; (603) 278-2222. This family-casual restaurant and bar is located in a converted railroad station. The specialty is upscale tavern food that is just a step above pub food. Find burgers, Reubens and house-smoked ribs along with a tasty blackened snapper sandwich and veggie lasagna. Kids love to look up and watch the model railroad train circle the tracks that are just below the ceiling. Open daily 11:30 a.m. to 9 p.m. $$.

where to stay

Omni Mount Washington Resort. US 302; (603) 278-1000; mountwashingtonresort .com. No wonder this sprawling resort is a favorite for weekend getaways and family reunions. Built in 1902, this grand 200-room Victorian storybook hotel is located in a spectacular mountain setting with top-tier service and year-round diversions including a cross-country ski center, indoor and outdoor pools, golf facilities, stables, red-clay tennis courts, a 25,000-square-foot spa, and loads of drop-in activities. When you do want some privacy, the recently refurbished rooms are a welcome treat. And when it's time to reconvene at dinner, choose from the semiformal dining room or family-favorite Stickney's for casual, farm-to-table New England cuisine. In the tradition of grand mountain resort hotels, the Mount Washington still offers a MAP plan that includes breakfast and dinner—choose this option and you hardly have to leave the resort at all. The Mount Washington is a National Historic Landmark; it was the site of the Bretton Woods Monetary Conference in 1944, which established the International Monetary Fund. It's a fascinating story; find out all during the historical walking tour of the hotel that is offered every day from the lobby. $$$–$$$$.

franconia, nh

Known mostly for its natural attractions, the town of Franconia sprung up in the 1800s just north of the high mountain pass that has brought visitors to this area for centuries. Discover the geological wonders of the Flume Gorge at Franconia Notch State Park and look toward Cannon Mountain to imagine the "Old Man of the Mountain": five stone ledges that naturally formed a profile, which collapsed from erosion on May 3, 2003.

getting there

From Bretton Woods, continue on US 302 West to US 3 South and merge onto I-93 South through scenic Franconia Notch Park. It's one of the less-congested drives in the White Mountains, just 20 miles and 25 minutes. If time allows, drive back to North Conway via the Kancamagus Highway/NH 112 (see sidebar) by continuing along I-93 South to exit 32 and taking NH 112 East.

where to go

Cannon Mountain. 9 Franconia Notch; (603) 823-8800; cannonmt.com. It may not have all the amenities of some of the area's big-name resorts, but less is really more at this New Hampshire state-owned and -operated mountain offering skiers tremendous value. The mountain has 165 acres of varied terrain (mostly geared to intermediate skiers) that is serviced by 9 lifts, a ski school, and 2 base lodges. From May through October, Cannon's Aerial Tramway operates two 80-person cable cars nicknamed Ketchup and Mustard, which whisk visitors in just over 8 minutes to the 4,080-foot summit for sweeping views of the White Mountains and beyond. There are marked walking trails and a cafeteria at the top as well. At the base of the tramway be sure to check out 2 free attractions: the tiny New England Ski Museum (open Memorial Day through the end of ski season), which exhibits regional ski memorabilia and artifacts (local hero and Olympic medalist Bode Miller learned to ski at Cannon and often donates items for exhibit), and the Old Man of the Mountain Profile Plaza and Historic Site, which shows, through photographs and documents, the history of the "Old Man" image and honors the memory of New Hampshire's state symbol.

Flume Gorge at Franconia Notch State Park. US 3, Lincoln; (603) 745-8391; nhstate parks.org. Experience one of New Hampshire's most scenic natural wonders. You'll feel the mist of the waterfalls on this easy 2-mile looping walking trail along wooden walkways that takes you through the towering moss-covered granite cliffs that form a natural 800-foot gorge. Open mid-May through mid-Oct daily 9 a.m. to 5 p.m. Admission $16 adults, $13 ages 6 to 12, free for children age 5 and under.

Loon Mountain. 60 Loon Mountain Rd.; Lincoln; (603) 745-8111; loonmtn.com.This is a solidly family-oriented New England ski resort with some of the friendliest mountain staff in New England. Loon boasts 60 trails that are spread across more than 360 acres along with six terrain parks have been set-aside for free-style skiers and snowboarders. Stay at the Mountain Club at Loon, the full-service condominium complex at the mountain's base which offers roll-out-of-bed-onto-the-lifts convenience. Dining at either Seasons Restaurant or Black Diamond Bar & Grill won't break the bank. And après ski, there are massages and facials expertly administered at the on-site Viaggio Day Spa. Loon offers a host of non-ski diversions including ice skating, zip-lining, snow-shoeing, snow-tubing as well as an indoor pool and hot tub. Loon is appealing in the summer and fall too, with biking and hiking the summit trails the preferred activities.

where to eat

Gypsy Café. 117 Main St.; Lincoln; (603) 745-4395; gypsycaferestaurant.com. Gypsy Café is located in a converted house on busy Main Street, and is much bigger than it appears. It's handy for big breakfasts, lunches après ski, feeding the family and cheap cocktails. Every nook and cranny has been decorated with vibrant murals and colorful ceramics. With its globe-spanning menu, it's a causal and affordable place that is a lifesaver for the indecisive. Among the dishes are a Thai red curry duck, Argentine fajitas with chimichurri salsa and chicken souvlaki. Open Wed, Thurs and Sun 11:30 a.m. to 4 p.m., 5 to 9 p.m., Fri and Sat 11:30 a.m. to 4 p.m., 5 to 9:30 p.m., closed Mon and Tues. $$.

La Vista. 22 South Mountain Dr., Lincoln; (603) 745-7555; lavistaitalian.com. Don't be misled by the hotel setting. Located in the brand new RiverWalk Resort complex, La Vista is a homey place that serves unpretentious Italian food that is easy on the wallet. The menu is anchored by standbys like hand-rolled meatballs, and wood-fire pizza, but it is also loaded with elegant surprises such as grilled lamb lollipops with fennel cucumber salad and veal saltimbocca. Open Mon through Thurs 5 to 9 p.m.; Fri 5 to 10 p.m.; Sat 9:30 a.m. to 2 p.m., 5 to 10 p.m., Sun 9:30 a.m. to 2 p.m., 5 to 9 p.m. $$.

Polly's Pancakes. 672 NH 117, Sugar Hill; (603) 823-5575; pollyspancakeparlor.com. In business since 1938, this family-run breakfast joint is legendary for some of the best pancakes in New England. Choose from plain, buckwheat, whole wheat, cornmeal, or oatmeal buttermilk pancakes, which are made from organic grains that are ground on-site. Served alongside: a tray of real maple syrup, maple spread, and maple sugar. Nothing could be better! Open May through Oct Mon through Fri 7 a.m. to 2 p.m., Sat and Sun 7 a.m. to 3 p.m.; Nov weekends only 7 a.m. to 2 p.m. $.

Wendle's Deli. 297 Main Street; (603) 823-5141; wendles.com. A sandwich stalwart for hikers and skiers in northern New Hampshire who come to fuel up for the day. Be sure to check the chalkboard for the day's specials—if the cream of onion soup made with Vidalias, leeks, and Parmesan is offered—go for it. Tasty sandwich combos like the Robert Frost with chicken, bacon, alfalfa sprouts, and cheddar with maple syrup on whole wheat is another sure bet. In the late afternoon, Wendle's becomes a local gathering spot for coffee, Wi-Fi, and trading mountain stories. Open daily 7 a.m. to 4 p.m. Cash only. $.

where to stay

Sugar Hill Inn. 116 NH 117, Sugar Hill; (603) 823-5621; sugarhillinn.com. This seductive retreat is a quietly cosseting place with mountain views, perennial and herb gardens, an outdoor pool, and sumptuous breakfasts. Each of the inn's 16 rooms (all with private bath) look straight out of a country estate outfitted with fine linens, cloud-like down duvets and local art. The inn's world-class dining room is open to the public and serves Chef Val Fortin's splurge-worthy 4-course prix-fixe menu of contemporary New England cuisine. Be sure to reserve your table in advance. $$–$$$.

day trip 48

scenic & seasonal

trains, trains, trains:
mid-coast maine; white mountains;
essex, ct; hyannis, ma

A train-focused tour can be one of the most leisurely ways to experience New England's remarkably varied landscape. This trip includes some of New England's best railroad experiences: rumble along the rocky Maine coast, up the rugged peaks of New Hampshire's White Mountains, down the Connecticut River Valley, and through the cranberry bogs of Cape Cod.

This is an ambitious itinerary, a multistate road trip that works its way from north to south, while using as a base cities—Bath, North Conway, Essex, and Hyannis—that are described in earlier chapters. Plan to spend a day or two in each area, and this itinerary is just right for a one-week stay.

If you can, this is a terrific road trip to do during the fall when the landscape is majestically ablaze with fall colors. Just make sure you reserve your railroad tickets and hotel rooms well in advance—fall foliage season is one of New England's busiest.

mid-coast maine

The newest oldest way to enjoy mid-coast Maine is to take the Amtrak Downeaster (amtrak downeaster.com) from Boston or Portland to Brunswick, Maine. For some of the journey, the train cars speed along parallel to US 1, offering a panoramic view of fishing fleets, schooners, and lighthouses.

getting there

Bath is centered in mid-coast Maine, accessible by both I-95 and US 1.

where to go

Boothbay Railway Village. 586 Wiscasset Rd., Boothbay; (207) 633-4727; railwayvillage .org. This 10-acre outdoor museum of rural New England life has a lot to offer railroad enthusiasts. Take a steam-train ride on the 0.75-mile narrow gauge track through the re-created historic village. Or make tracks for the HO-scale layout in the replica Maine Central freight station house. Also don't miss the outstanding collection of more than 50 antique and vintage automobiles. If you are bringing your little cabooses along for the ride, watch for the very popular Day Out with Thomas events. Open late May through Oct daily 9:30 a.m. to 5 p.m. Adults $9, $5 ages 3 to 16.

white mountains

It was because of the advent of widespread train travel that this region became a resort destination in the early 1900s, allowing vacationers from East Coast cities to stay for the "summer season" and enjoy the cool mountain air.

getting there

This 92-mile, 2-hour drive offers a scenic combination of Maine's coastline and New Hampshire's mountains. Take US 1 South for 7 miles and merge onto I-295 South and follow for 18 miles. Take exit 11 for I-95 South and follow for 5 miles. Follow ME 25 West for 13 miles. Pick up ME 113 North and follow for 30 miles. Take US 302 for 8 miles to North Conway.

where to go

Cafe Lafayette Dinner Train. NH 112, North Woodstock; (603) 745-3500; nhdinnertrain .com. For a unique ride-and-dine experience, enjoy fine cuisine and beautiful scenery on a 20-mile, 2-hour ride on the tracks of the Boston and Maine Railroad as it runs along the Pemigewasset River. Rates include a 4-course prix-fixe menu that features choices like pesto scallops and tenderloin of pork Pinot Noir. The collection of refurbished coaches includes a 1952 dome car, a 1953 Canadian National cafe car, and a 1924 Pullman dining car. Season runs May through Oct; check website for departure days and prices.

Conway Scenic Railroad. 38 Norcross Circle, Conway; (603) 356-5251; conwayscenic .com. Depart from the historic 1874 train station in North Conway on one of Conway Scenic Railroad's 3 vintage train excursions. The 5-hour Crawford Notch excursion takes passengers through the jagged rock formations and evergreen forest of one of the region's most spectacular mountain passes. It's a fully narrated trip with an hour layover at Crawford

Station to walk about and enjoy the scenery. The Notch excursion offers options for open-coach and dome-car seating and has full-scale dining car service in a restored Pullman dining car. There are shorter 1- and 2-hour round-trip scenic excursions options, too. Trains run May through Dec; check website for departure times and prices.

Fabyan's Station. 2329 US 302, Bretton Woods; (603) 278-2222. This restaurant, located in the former Victorian-era train station that brought the wealthy to the White Mountains, belongs to the Omni Mount Washington Resort up the road. It is one of the few dining options on the western side of Mountain Washington. Satisfy your appetite with a burger or *poutine* (french fries with cheese curds and sauce). Lighter options include salads and soups; try the clam chowder in a bread bowl. There is an outdoor patio with foothill views in the summer. The operating model-railroad layout suspended below the ceiling is a fun diversion for kids. Open daily 11:30 a.m. to 9 p.m. $$.

Mount Washington Cog Railway. Base Station Road off US 302, Bretton Woods; (603) 278-5404; thecog.com. Take the Cog Railway to the summit of Mount Washington, New England's highest peak. Built in 1869, it is the second steepest mountain climbing train in the world; it uses its gear-like wheel to engage teeth in a center rail as it grinds its way up a 3-mile trestle track at a maximum gradient of 37 percent. The entire round-trip excursion takes 3 hours and includes an hour at the peak to enjoy the views and visit the Mount Washington Observatory. The Cog now runs on biodiesel fuel for most of its runs; rail fans may want to take the daily 9 a.m. coal-fired steam excursion. Season runs from May through early Dec; check website for departure times. Tickets $69 adults, $65seniors, $39 ages 4 to 12.

essex, ct

Visit the picture-perfect Connecticut River village of Essex and combine the adventure of a steam-train ride with a riverboat cruise.

getting there

This is the longest drive, taking nearly 5 hours and covering 250 miles. From NH 16 South pick up I-95 South and follow for 16 miles. Merge onto I-495 South and follow for 50 miles. Take exit 25B to connect to I-290 West. Continue for 21 miles to I-395 South for 60 miles and merge onto I-95 South for 10 miles before taking exit 69 and CT 9 North toward Essex.

where to go

Essex Steam Train and Riverboat. 1 Railroad Ave.; (860) 767-0103; essexsteamtrain .com. Take a combined steam train and riverboat journey through the picturesque Connecticut River Valley. The coal-fired locomotive puffs billows of smoke, and the restored vintage rail cars sway as they roll along the river through woods and fields broken only by the occasional sound of the train's whistle.

At Deep River Landing you will transfer to the steamboat *Becky Thatcher* for a narrated hour-long nature/history cruise (look for ospreys) along the Connecticut River past the wedding cake–like Goodspeed Opera House and the wildly eccentric Gillette Castle. Special train events are offered, too. Season runs May through Dec; check website for departure times. Steam train and riverboat tickets $29 adults, $19 children ages 2 to 11.

hyannis, ma

Cape Cod may not be the first place you think of when you think of train travel, but in fact, the area has a rich railroad tradition. A peninsula, the Cape has always been isolated. In the 1840s the Old Colony Railroad was built, connecting Boston to the Cape to include its entire length from Buzzards Bay to Provincetown. The opening of the Bourne and Sagamore Bridges in the 1930s marked the beginning of the end of the Cape's rail days. Today, the abandoned tracks have found new use: in 2013, weekend rail service between Boston and Hyannis aboard the Cape Flyer (capeflyer.com) was restored, a portion is used as the route for the Cape Cod Central Railroad excursion trains, and another section has become integrated into a very popular bike trail, the Cape Cod Rail Trail.

getting there

CT 9 South will take you back to I-95 North. Follow for 70 miles and take exit 19 to merge onto I-195 toward Providence/Cape Cod. Take exit 22A and merge onto MA 25 East crossing the Cape Cod Canal at the Bourne Bridge. From the Bourne rotary take US 6 East into Hyannis.

where to go

Cape Cod Central Railroad. 252 Main St.; (508) 771-3800; capetrain.com. Settle back and enjoy the view as the Cape Cod Central Railroad meanders along Cape Cod Bay by salt marshes and along the Cape Cod Canal at a gentle 12 miles per hour before the turnaround at Buzzards Bay. The 2-hour narrated scenic train is the railroad's most popular offering, but there are trips to accommodate all tastes, with elegant dinner trains, family supper trains, and a Sunday brunch train. In the fall, rolling past the cranberry bogs is a special bonus! Season runs from May through Oct, with special holiday trains. Check website for schedule and pricing.

Cape Cod Rail Trail. MA 134, South Dennis. To experience the Cape at its natural best, turn off the engine and turn up the foot power. The Cape Cod Rail Trail runs along the bed of the Old Colony and Penn Central railroads, through the woods, and along the coast from the town of Dennis to LeCount Beach in Wellfleet. The pedaling is easy; it's a mostly paved and flat ride. Give yourself at least 2 hours to complete the route (although no one says that you have to bike the entire trail!). There are bike-rental and (very importantly) several ice-cream shops along the way.

arts & culture

day trip 49

arts & culture

the berkshire hills are alive with music, dance & art:
lenox, ma; stockbridge, ma; pittsfield, ma; williamstown, ma

In western Massachusetts, the unspoiled beauty of the Berkshire Hills is a magnificent backdrop to internationally acclaimed performances of music, dance, and theater. The visual arts are well represented by several museums including the Norman Rockwell Museum in Stockbridge, the Berkshire Museum in Pittsfield, and the Clark Institute in Williamstown.

lenox, ma

Quiet, rural Lenox has always attracted a well-heeled crowd. During the Gilded Age, Lenox rivaled Newport and Bar Harbor for its grand summer country estates that were built for the families of America's wealthy industrialists.

Since the 1930s, Lenox has been famed for hosting the Tanglewood Music Festival, the summer home of the Boston Symphony Orchestra, which attracts as many as 350,000 visitors during the summer season. Lenox accommodates its concertgoers with lots of lodging choices and a thriving dining-out culture, making the town a good base for exploring the region.

getting there

Lenox is located off of the Mass Pike (I-90) at exit 2 and is nearly equidistant—around 130 miles—between both Boston and New York City.

where to go

Lenox Chamber of Commerce. 6 Walker St.; (413) 637-3646; lenox.org. Located in the Lenox town library, this staffed visitor center not only provides all the usual maps and information on attractions, but also offers same day, half-price (cash only) tickets to area events, among them Tanglewood, Jacob's Pillow, and the Williamstown Theater Festival. Open June through Aug daily 10 a.m. to 6 p.m., rest of year Wed through Sat 10 a.m. to 4 p.m. .

Frelinghuysen Morris House & Studio. 92 Hawthorne St.; (413) 637-0166; frelinghuysen .org. A very different Berkshire estate, this stucco-and-glass block home belonged to American abstract artist Suzy Frelinghuysen and her husband, the artist George L. K. Morris. Built from 1930 to 1941, this is the first modernist home to be constructed in New England. You'll explore the house on a guided tour; among the couple's furniture and their own art pieces, there's a sense of intimacy as you view their private art collection that includes works by Pablo Picasso, Georges Braque, and Henri Matisse. Open late June through Labor Day Thurs through Sun 10 a.m. to 3 p.m., day after Labor Day through Columbus Day Thurs through Sat 10 a.m. to 3 p.m. Admission $15 adults, $14 seniors, $7.50 students, free for children under age 12.

Kennedy Park. A town-owned park that has nearly 15 miles of well-maintained running and walking trails through wooded forest. Open daily, sunrise to sunset. Free.

The Mount. 2 Plunkett St.; (413) 551-5111; edithwharton.org. This turn-of-the-last-century, 50-acre country estate was designed and built by Edith Wharton; here she lived, wrote, and entertained for nearly a decade. Wharton is well known as a novelist (she won the Pulitzer Prize for *The Age of Innocence*), but what is less well known is that Wharton was an accomplished designer; her first published book, *The Decoration of Houses,* was at the forefront of interior and garden design of the time. You can choose to do a self-guided walk-through or a 45-minute guided tour that includes both the mansion and manicured grounds. The Terrace Cafe overlooks the garden, offering light dishes and refreshments from a brief, but excellent, menu. Open May through Oct daily 10 a.m. to 5 p.m., Nov through December 20 weekends 10 a.m. to 4 p.m. Admission $18 adults, $17 seniors, $13 students, free for children ages 18 and under.

Shakespeare & Company. 70 Kemble St.; (413) 637-1199; shakespeare.org. The Bard lives on in the Berkshire Hills. This highly respected, year-round professional repertory company mounts several of Shakespeare's plays during the course of its summer season, along with premieres of new, thought-provoking works. Tickets range from $20 to $85.

Tanglewood. 297 West St.; (888) 266-1200; bso.org. There really is nothing quite like sitting outside on a blanket, listening to the Boston Symphony Orchestra perform on a soft summer evening. There's a rhythm to every Tanglewood season: always plenty of great 19th-century symphonic pieces to be sure, but also concerts by popular artists, jazz greats, and works by contemporary composers. Highlights of recent seasons include the performances by singer/songwriter (and local resident) James Taylor, and John Williams's annual stint conducting Film Night, when you'll hear his scores from *Star Wars, Harry Potter,* and more. You can also see the next generation of talented musicians perform recitals and small chamber works as part of the prestigious Tanglewood Music Center. Enjoying an elaborate picnic on the lawn is a big part of the Tanglewood experience. The Boston Symphony makes it easy with lawn chair rentals and gourmet boxed dinners available for purchase. The campus also features a Cafe and Grille for sit-down dining. Ticket prices range from $12 to $104.

where to shop

Hoadley Gallery. 21 Church St.; (413) 637-2814; hoadleygallery.com. A gallery that specializes in a new generation of artists with paintings and photography as well as wearables and beautifully made home furnishings will appeal to modernists. Open daily 10 a.m. to 6 p.m.

where to eat

Alta. 34 Church St.; (413) 637-0003; altawinebar.com. This casually handsome eatery does contemporary New England cuisine with Mediterranean finesse. The menu changes depending on what's fresh and regionally available but has included the likes of roasted pork tenderloin with peppermint mashed peas and pan-seared salmon with lemon zest and roasted tomatoes. A wine list that features 24 by-the-glass choices and service that is both friendly and informed make this a favorite for the Tanglewood crowd. ***Note:*** Alta does take reservations, a must during the summer season. Open Sun through Thurs 11:30 a.m. to 3 p.m. and 5 to 9 p.m.; Fri and Sat 11:30 a.m. to 3 p.m. and 5 to 10 p.m. $$.

Betty's Pizza Shack. 26 Housatonic St.; (413) 637-8171; bettyspizza.com. Betty's has a retro California surfer vibe as it serves thin-crust pizza with inventive toppings. The Corona bucket (six Coronitas for $9) draws in the Tanglewood student musicians, but feel free to take the kids, too; Betty's is a family favorite in the area. $.

Chocolate Springs Cafe. 55 Pittsfield Rd.; (413) 637-9820; chocolatesprings.com. This isn't your ordinary chocolate shop: The artisanal confections like lavender-honey dark chocolate and whipped milk chocolate infused with rum appeal to a sophisticated sweet tooth. Serious chocoholics will want to linger in the cafe over delectable chocolate pastries and perfect cups of coffee. They make gelato, too, so you may find yourself making an excuse to visit more than once. Open Sun through Thurs 9 a.m. to 9 p.m., Fri and Sat 9 a.m. to 10 p.m. $.

Haven Cafe & Bakery. 8 Franklin St.; (413) 637-8948; havencafebakery.com. A local breakfast and lunch spot that offers comfort food made interesting, and nearly everything on the menu is local and organic. Early risers can opt for the stellar smoked salmon scramble, a buttermilk biscuit breakfast sandwich, or perhaps grilled polenta triangles and maple syrup, all served along with a bottomless (and very good) cup of coffee. It's worth planning your Berkshire itinerary to arrive in Lenox for a late lunch of a roasted steak sandwich with blue cheese and onion confit. Open Mon through Fri 7:30 a.m. to 3 p.m., Sat 8 a.m. to 3 p.m., Sun 8 a.m. to 3 p.m. $–$$.

Nudel. 37 Church St.; (413) 551-7183; nudelrestaurant.com. This chic little dinner-only restaurant is one of the hottest spots around. A simple, often-changing menu (as in every few days) of beautifully executed pastas means you won't be overwhelmed by choice, but you may be overwhelmed with flavor. You can expect appetizers like hazelnut and chicken liver pâté or the turnip tart with chèvre and truffle. Mains could be orecchiette pasta (little ears) with mussels, chiles, and saffron cream or linguine with beet greens and walnut pesto. Open Tues through Sun 5:30 to 9:30 p.m., closed Mon. $$.

where to stay

Cranwell Resort and Spa. 55 Lee Rd.; (413) 637-1364; cranwell.com. This former Gilded Age Tudor-style mansion on gorgeously landscaped grounds still retains an air of dignified luxury. Simple elegance reigns in each of the resort's 116 rooms and suites. And then there are the activities, which is when you're going to have to make some tough choices. Exfoliating body treatment at the lavish spa? Post-Tanglewood drinks in the Music Room Lounge? A round at the 18-hole championship golf course? The only easy decision may be choosing to extend your visit. $$$.

Garden Gables Inn. 135 Main St.; (413) 637-0193; gardengablesinn.com. Set back from Main Street on 5 lush acres, yet just a short walk from the buzz in Lenox, this inn will relax the weary traveler in no time. Guests can choose from 9 rooms in the main inn, 2 stand-alone suites, or 4 cottages. Each of the very comfortable rooms is different, but each has a cozy elegance with flat-screen TVs and free Wi-Fi. All rates include a breakfast buffet with cooked-to-order entrees, a guest pantry, and afternoon sherry. The grounds have a heated, Olympic-size pool, there's a dedicated spa room, and a chef-prepared, 4-course gourmet dinner is available Thurs and Sun night in the summer (and it's much anticipated by inn guests). $$$.

Yankee Inn. 461 Pittsfield Rd.; (413) 499-3700; yankeeinn.com. With room choices that include fireplace Jacuzzi suites and property amenities like both an indoor and outdoor pool, this well-priced Lenox hotel is equally able to welcome couples and families. Although fronting US 20, there are woods and a private pond in the back. The 96 rooms are basic with the better, newly built rooms in the main building. Rates include continental breakfast with made-to-order omelets. It's a good value for the money, and important for the Berkshires, it doesn't require a minimum stay in summer. $$.

stockbridge, ma

Beloved American illustrator Norman Rockwell lived in Stockbridge for the last 25 years of his life, and the town and Rockwell's neighbors became the models for many of his most popular works. Actually, Stockbridge can boast of being the home of two great American artists. Just down the road from the Norman Rockwell Museum is Chesterwood, the summer home and studio of Daniel Chester French, most known as the sculptor of the Lincoln statue at the Lincoln Memorial in Washington, DC.

getting there

From Lenox, the drive to Stockbridge is just about 10 minutes. Pick up MA 183 South for 5 miles and turn left onto MA 102 East for another mile or so into Stockbridge.

where to go

Stockbridge Information Booth. 56 Main St.; (413) 298-5200; stockbridgechamber.org. Staffed by volunteers and generally open daily June through Oct.

Berkshire Theatre Festival. 83 E. Main St.; (413) 298- 5576; berkshiretheatregroup.org. Founded in 1928, the Berkshire Theatre Festival entertains with a mix of classics, musicals, comedies, and drama with plays nightly from June through August. The Fitzpatrick Mainstage home is the very grand 1888 Stockbridge Casino; newer contemporary productions generally take place at the smaller Unicorn Theatre. Ticket prices $14 to $49.

Chesterwood. 4 Williamsville Rd.; (413) 298-3579; chesterwood.org. For more than 30 years, Daniel Chester French lived and worked at Chesterwood, his 122-acre Stockbridge summer estate. Besides the seated Lincoln statue at the Lincoln Memorial, French is known for his sculptures of the *Minute Man* statue in Concord and the *John Harvard* statue in Cambridge. You can see the residence, studio, and gardens on your own or take a guided tour. The studio is particularly fascinating, with the modeling tools, casts, and maquettes (smallscale models) French used to create his work on view. Open May through Oct daily 10 a.m. to 5 p.m. Admission $18 adults, $9 ages 13–17, free for children ages 12 and under.

Naumkeag. 5 Prospect Hill Rd.; (413) 298-3239; thetrustees.org. This 1885 estate was the family summer home of prominent New York lawyer Joseph Hodges Choate. Designed by the architectural firm McKim, Mead, and White, the 44-room shingle-style mansion is relatively modest for a Berkshire "cottage," but it holds an impressive collection of period furnishings and family treasures including 2 portraits by John Singer Sargent and a sculpture by Augustus Saint-Gaudens. The house can only be visited by guided tour, and self-guided audio tours are available for the 8 acres of designed gardens. The rose garden, a Chinese garden, and the famed Blue Steps, a series of water fountains, are particularly noteworthy.

Open late May through Columbus Day daily 10 a.m. to 5 p.m. Admission $15 adults, free for children ages 12 and under.

Norman Rockwell Museum. 9 MA 183; (413) 298-4100; nrm.org. The art of Norman Rockwell is celebrated in this museum. The museum has the largest collection—nearly 600 of Rockwell's paintings and drawings—including many of his iconic *Saturday Evening Post* covers, among them *Triple Self-Portrait* and *The Runaway*. You can also visit Rockwell's studio, which was moved here in its entirety from Stockbridge Center. Open May through Nov daily 10 a.m. to 5 p.m.; Nov through Apr Mon through Fri 10 a.m. to 4 p.m., Sat and Sun 10 a.m. to 5 p.m. Admission $18 adults, $17 seniors, $10 students, $6 ages 6 to 18.

where to eat

Once Upon a Table. 36 Main St.; (413) 298-3870; onceuponatablebistro.com. Located down an alley (ask anyone in town to point you in the right direction), this little restaurant has the easy-going sophistication of a French bistro. At lunch, linger over the escargot potpie and a simple green salad or perhaps the smoked salmon plate with wheat toast points and lentil soup. For dinner, the pan-seared chicken with cranberry-orange glaze and the herbed rack of lamb with brussels sprouts are among the highlights. Weekend breakfast is a new offering; the gingerbread waffles are a wonderful treat. Open Mon through Fri 11 a.m. to 3 p.m., 5 to 9 p.m.; Sat 10 a.m. to 3 p.m., 5 to 9 p.m., Sun 10 a.m. to 8 p.m. $$.

where to stay

Kripalu Center for Yoga and Health. 57 Interlaken Rd.; (866) 200-5203; kripalu.org. How about a true vacation retreat? De-stress as you discover yoga, surrounded by nature and fortified by organic, mostly vegetarian meals. The 80 rooms in the ecofriendly annex have a clean-line minimalist aesthetic and views of the idyllic Berkshire Hills from oversize windows; they feature private bathrooms and wireless Internet. Rates include yoga classes by excellent instructors, all your meals, and use of the facilities. And Tanglewood is next door—just follow the path at the edge of the Kripalu grounds. $$$.

Red Lion Inn. 30 Main St.; (413) 298-5545; redlioninn.com. Pints have been pulled for guests stopping at this inn since before the Revolutionary War. Then, as now, the Red Lion Inn dominates Stockbridge life, and one of the real pleasures of staying here is watching the world pass by from a rocking chair on the wide front porch. The inn offers 108 guest rooms; rooms in the Main Inn are full of antique furniture, prints, and chintz, but they have a modern sensibility with high-count sheets, TVs, and free Wi-Fi. More modern-style guest rooms are dispersed among several close-by buildings and are ideal for families (and kids will love the inn's large outdoor heated pool and hot tub). There are 3 good dining options: a formal dining room for breakfast, lunch, and dinner; the comfortable Widow Bingham's Tavern, and the Lion's Den Pub also offers live entertainment nightly. $$–$$$.

pittsfield, ma

The largest city in the Berkshires, Pittsfield has transitioned from a manufacturing center and has found success through new cultural endeavors including the restoration of the Gilded Age–era Colonial Theater, the Barrington Stage Company's refurbishment of a vaudeville stage, and the recent opening of the Beacon, an independent movie house in an abandoned department store building.

getting there

To drive from Stockbridge to Pittsfield you need to backtrack through Lenox. Head north on MA 102 West to pick up MA 183 North, driving 6 miles and turn onto Main Street (MA 7A) in Lenox. Turn left onto US 20 W/ US 7 North for 6 miles into Pittsfield.

where to go

Berkshire Museum. 39 South St.; (413) 443-7171; berkshiremuseum.org. With art, ancient history, and natural science exhibits all under one roof; there's a little bit of everything here. There are landscape paintings from the Hudson River School, an ancient Egyptian mummy, kinetic toy sculptures by Alexander Calder (made early in his career), and 20 aquarium tanks that feature tropical and local species. Open Mon through Sat 10 a.m. to 5 p.m., Sun noon to 5 p.m. Admission $13 adults, $6 ages 4 to 18.

Hancock Shaker Village. 1843 Housatonic St.; (413) 443-0188; hancockshakervillage .org. There is an austere grace to the Round Stone Barn and the 20 simple timber-frame buildings set on 250 acres of farmland. The Shakers were a religion founded by Mother Ann Lee in England on principals of pacifism, celibacy, and communal living. You can learn about Shaker life as it was lived here from the 1700s to the 1960s. Visit the barn and gardens, watch artisans demonstrate oval-box making and chair-seat weaving, and tour the Laundry and Machine Shop. Be sure to visit the 1830s-era Brick Dwelling, which was the dormitory for as many as 100 Shaker Brethren and Sisters—it houses the museum's extensive collection of Shaker furniture and objects. Open mid-Apr through Oct daily 10 a.m. to 5 p.m. Admission $20 adults, $8 ages 13 to 17, free ages 12 and under.

where to eat

Flavours. 75 North St.; (413) 443-3188; flavoursintheberkshires.com. Although it might not look like much from the outside, this dining room with its red walls and lacquered chairs is one of the best Asian restaurants in western Massachusetts. The real draw is what comes out of the kitchen—Malaysian fare featuring a fusion of Malay, Chinese, Thai, and Indian cuisines. Start with a round of dumplings—either the robust pork or the more offbeat steamed shrimp rice dumplings. The star dish on the menu may just be the beef rendang—spicy sirloin in a lemongrass, ginger, and chile sauce and is itself reason enough to come. $$.

williamstown, ma

At the far reaches of Massachusetts's northwestern border with Vermont and New York, Williamstown was named in honor of Revolutionary war hero Ephraim Williams, who donated money for the founding of a free school. The school became the state's second college, and to this day, students who attend prestigious Williams College are called "Ephs," pronounced "Eefs." This college town is packed with cultural activities from the renowned Williamstown Summer Festival to art treasures at both the Clark Institute and Williams College Museum of Art.

getting there

This drive really winds up and down through the Berkshire Hills. The route from Pittsfield to Williamstown is 20 miles along US 7 North and should take 30 minutes.

where to go

Clark Art Institute. 225 South St.; (413) 458-2303; clarkart.edu. This small gem of a museum is highly focused, created initially from the personal art collection of Singer sewing-machine heir Sterling Clark and his wife, Francine. The museum features works by American and European artists with an especially large number of more than 30 works by Pierre Auguste Renoir. Open July and Aug daily 10 a.m. to 5 p.m.; Sept through June Tues through Sun 10 a.m. to 5 p.m. Admission July through Oct, $20 adults, free for students and children ages 18 and under. Free for all Nov through May.

Williams College Museum of Art. 15 Lawrence Hall Dr.; (413) 597-2429; wcma.org. Williams College has its own art museum, which emphasizes American and modern art. The museum has a large collection of works by the post-Impressionist artists (and brothers) Charles and Maurice Prendergast and a cross-section of 20th-century American artists including Andy Warhol, Edward Hopper, and Georgia O'Keeffe. Open Thurs through Tues 10 a.m. to 5 p.m. Closed Wed. Free.

Williamstown Theater Festival. 1000 Main St.; (413) 597-3400; wtfestival.org. Founded in 1955, this Tony Award–winning summer theater festival takes place from June through July on the campus of Williams College, attracting a loyal audience of both residents and visitors. Productions range from the classics to the contemporary, musicals to comedy and drama. The Williamstown Theater Festival has always drawn some big name talent—Broadway stars and directors come to escape summer in the city; Hollywood actors come to hone their stage skills.

where to eat

Mezze Bistro & Bar. 777 Cold Spring Rd.; (413) 458-0123; mezzerestaurant.com. Considered by many to be one of the top restaurants in the region, this is the place in town for celebrity spotting during the Williams Theatre Festival. This renovated rambling 19th-century building on 3 pastoral acres is both modern and organic, featuring low-VOC painted walls, local art, and a menu of sophisticated dishes that showcase the abundance of Berkshire produce, meat, and cheese. Typical plates on the menu may feature homemade tagliatelle with vegetables from the restaurant's backdoor garden, a local farm pork loin, and a market fish choice. Urban dwellers will appreciate the French-press coffee service. Open Mon through Thurs 5 to 9 p.m., Fri through Sun 5 to 10 p.m. $$–$$$.

Tunnel City Coffee. 100 Spring St.; (413) 458-5010; tunnelcitycoffee.com. Laptop-packing patrons linger over aromatic coffee (they roast their own beans here) to go along with tasty treats: maple walnut scones, cranberry muffins, and their famous triple chocolate mousse cake. In the summer, there's outdoor cafe seating. Open daily 6 a.m. to 6 p.m. $.

where to stay

The Guest House at Field Farm. 554 Sloan Rd.; (413) 458-3135; guesthouseatfieldfarm .org. Set in a nondescript 1948 farmhouse on 300 acres of conservation land in the shadow of Mount Greylock, this 6-bedroom B&B is a modernist traveler's dream. The former owners of the home donated the property and its contents to the Trustees of Reservations (a Massachusetts conservation organization) and were avid modern-art collectors. Look for an original Eames chair, a Noguchi coffee table, and Kagan sofas. Each of the guest bedrooms is appointed with modern furnishings; handmade mattresses, down duvets, and sleek, luxurious bathrooms. Rooms do have free Wi-Fi (but no TVs). $$.

Orchards Hotel. 222 Adams Rd.; (413) 458-9611; orchardshotel.com. This small, 49-room upscale inn combines country charm with contemporary elegance. The rooms have a boutique feel with a mix of antique reproduction furniture, high thread-count linens, pillow-top mattresses, flat-screen HD-TVs, and luxurious bathrooms. Inside rooms have views of the garden courtyard and reflecting pool; outside rooms have gas fireplaces. There's a small, seasonal outdoor pool that's not quite big enough for a swim, but fine for a dip. Dine at the hotel's superb Gala Steakhouse & Bistro from a menu that focuses heavily on chargrilled meats with a wide range of cuts and sauces. $$–$$$.

day trip 50

arts & culture

new england family fun:
boston, ma; cape cod, ma;
white mountains

Whether enjoying the big-city buzz that is Boston, spending carefree beach days on Cape Cod, or enjoying action-packed outdoor adventure and theme park fun in New Hampshire's White Mountains, there are tons of awesome things for vacationing families to do in New England.

boston, ma

New England's largest city is also a great city for vacationing families, a mix of old and new with American history galore, fun children's museums, and lots of terrific dining options.

getting there

From the west, the Massachusetts Turnpike (I-90) runs directly to the city. From the south, take I-95 North to I-93 North to downtown. From Vermont and points northwest, take I-93 South to downtown. From Maine and points northeast, take I-95 South to I-93 South to downtown.

where to go

Picking the best sites in Boston for your family depends on the age of your kids and what they like to do best, but it will probably include a mix of some of the following must-see attractions.

The Boston Children's Museum. 308 Congress St., Waterfront; (617) 426-6500; boston childrensmuseum.org. Good luck trying to drag your family away from this waterfront children's museum. Here kids can just be kids and enjoy messy fun at the Art Studio, make a take-home wood project at Johnny's Workbench, and create giant soap bubbles in the Science Playground. Open Sat through Thurs 10 a.m. to 5 p.m., Fri 10 a.m. to 9 p.m. Admission $16 per person, free ages 12 months and under. Admission Fri 5 to 9 p.m. $1 per person.

Boston Duck Tours. Departures from the Museum of Science and the Prudential Center; (617) 267-3825; bostonducktours.com. Quack! Quack! Here's a tour worth getting a little wet for. Boston Duck Tours utilize amphibious World War II vehicles that take visitors on a narrated 80-minute ride through downtown Boston before a climactic splashdown into the Charles River for a short cruise. Kids are often invited to help steer the boat. Season runs Mar through Nov daily 9 a.m. to 1 hour before sunset. Tickets $39 adults, $33 students, military, and seniors, $27 children ages 3 to 11, $10.50 children ages 2 and under.

Freedom Trail. Boston Common Visitors Center. First in the nation this, oldest in the nation that—walking the Freedom Trail is a great way to introduce American history to your kids. The Freedom Trail is tremendously educational with 16 sites relating to American history on the 2.5-mile trail. But with kids, it's probably better to spend quality time on a few of the Freedom Trail sites than to do a forced march to see them all. Best bets for kids include the **Benjamin Franklin statue and site of first public school,** the **Granary Burying Ground** and the **Paul Revere House.** Want just one guaranteed kid-pleasing stop on the Freedom Trail? It's got to be the **USS *Constitution*.** She's berthed in Charlestown, and the easiest way to get there is to take the T-ferry from Long Wharf. Kids will rate a boat ride across the harbor as one of the high-water marks of their vacation, and Old Ironsides is pretty cool, too. For a change of pace, sit on the steps in front of the **Quincy Market** and watch the free jugglers and musicians that perform throughout the day at **Faneuil Hall Marketplace.**

Boston by Little Feet Tours. Faneuil Hall Marketplace, Boston; (617) 367-2345; boston-byfoot.com. For an organized tour of the Freedom Trail, this walking tour is an easy way to see the highlights without wearing out the troops and is geared specifically for kids ages 6 to 12 and their parents. Tour season May through Oct, Fri and Sat 10 a.m., Sun 2 p.m. $12.

Harvard Museum of Natural History. 26 Oxford St.; Cambridge; (617) 495-3045; hmnh .harvard.edu. It's eccentric and charming, maybe even a little dusty to preteens, but young children generally adore the Harvard Museum of Natural History, which is home to lots of kid-friendly exhibits like dinosaurs, stuffed and mounted animals, and really big shiny rocks and minerals. Open daily 9 a.m. to 5 p.m. Admission $12 adults, $10 seniors and students, $8 children ages 3 to 18.

Harvard Square. Cambridge. Kids of all ages take to the unique hodgepodge of old and new that is Harvard Square. Walk through the gates of Harvard University to Harvard Yard and tell your kids of the academic greats who have attended the country's oldest university—including some 50 Nobel Prize winners and 8 US presidents; among them both Barack Obama and George W. Bush. More likely, though, your kids will be more impressed with Harvard's famous dropouts, including Bill Gates, Matt Damon, and Mark Zuckerberg. Afterward browse the scores of shops that line Brattle and JFK Streets and people watch in Harvard Square—an interesting mix of free-spirited beatnik residents, earnest college students, tourists, and runaway kids. Stay late, and in the evening real street entertainers, musicians, mimes, and magicians take over.

Museum of Science. 1 Science Park, West End; (617) 723-2500; mos.org. You can satisfy your kids' curious minds and perhaps cultivate a scientist of the future. Or you and the kids can just have a blast. At Investigate! kids can practice thinking like a scientist by building simple machines like a scale model car and testing their results. The bicycle-riding skeleton is perennially popular at the Human Body Connection—even for kids not quite able to reach the pedals! And there are always several live animal presentations scheduled throughout the day. You can watch a movie on the 8-story-high IMAX dome screen or reach for the stars at the renovated (in 2011) Hayden Planetarium (with super comfy reclining seats!). Tickets for both are extra, but they're worth the price. Open from the day after Labor Day through July 4 Sat through Thurs 9 a.m. to 5 p.m., Fri 9 a.m. to 9 p.m.; July 5 through Labor Day open Sat through Thurs 9 a.m. to 7 p.m., Fri 9 a.m. to 9 p.m. Admission $25 adults, $21 seniors, $20 ages 3 to 11, free ages 2 and under.

New England Aquarium and New England Aquarium Whale Watch Excursions. Central Wharf, Downtown; (617) 973-5200; neaq.org. Home to sharks, moray eels, and schools of exotic fish, the aquarium's 4-story Giant Ocean Tank is a big hit with kids. See if your kids can spy Myrtle, the giant green sea turtle. She is thought to be more than 70 years old! The aquarium has a large colony of penguins that are always a delight. Tip: The very best way to enjoy the New England Aquarium is to arrive early in the day—it can get crazy crowded, especially during the summer and weekends. Thrill-seeking kids will enjoy the 3D ocean-related films that are shown at the aquarium's 6-story IMAX screen. Four-hour, naturalist-led New England whale watch cruises leave from the aquarium's dock several times daily during the summer season. Museum hours from the day after Labor Day through June are Mon through Fri 9 a.m. to 5 p.m., Sat and Sun 9 a.m. to 6 p.m. From July 1 to Labor Day open Sun through Thurs 9 a.m. to 6 p.m., Fri and Sat 9 a.m. to 7 p.m. Aquarium tickets $26.95 adults, $24.95 seniors, $18.95 children ages 3 to 11, free for children ages 2 and under. Whale Watch Excursions take place Apr through Oct; check website for exact departure times. Whale watch tickets $53 adults, $45 seniors, $33 children ages 3 to 11, $16 children ages 2 and under. Also check website for good value aquarium/whale watch and aquarium/IMAX packages.

The Public Garden. Bordered by Arlington, Beacon, Charles, and Boylston Streets, Back Bay. Since 1877, a peaceful cruise on Boston's elegant Swan Boats in the Public Garden has charmed generations of visitors. Afterward find a bench and read Robert McCloskey's *Make Way for Ducklings* to your own brood. You can buy a paperback version of the 1941 Caldecott Award book at the Swan Boat ticket booth. Then stroll the Public Garden and find your way over to the bronze *Make Way for Ducklings* statues at the corner of Charles and Beacon—they are sized just right for kids to sit on. The Public Garden is open year-round from dawn to dusk. The **Swan Boats** (617-522-1966; swanboats.com) are open mid-Apr to mid-Sept daily, spring and fall hours 10 a.m. to 4 p.m., summer (June 21 to Labor Day) 10 a.m. to 5 p.m.; $3.50 adults, $3 seniors, $2.50 children ages 2 to 15.

where to eat

Fire + Ice. 205 Berkeley St., Back Bay; (617) 482-3473; (617) 547-9007; fire-ice.com. For one all-you-can-eat price fill a bowl with your choice of meat, fish, vegetables, noodles, and sauces. Then bring your bowl to the giant open grill and watch the chef stir-fry it for you. Tortillas and rice, which go perfectly with food combinations and sauces that skew to Asian and Mexican, are brought to your table. Open Mon through Thurs 11:30 a.m. to 10 p.m., Fri and Sat 11:30 a.m. to 11 p.m., Sun 10 a.m. to 10 p.m. $$.

Full Moon. 344 Huron Ave., Cambridge; (617) 354-6699; fullmoonrestaurant.com. Eating out with little kids in Boston does not necessarily mean culinary exile. This family dining cafe not only serves a divine menu of American and European bistro classics like grilled salmon fillet with ginger-lime vinaigrette and grilled sirloin with blue cheese butter, but the restaurant also has a dedicated play space with a train table, buckets of toys, and books. The patient staff serves drinks in sippy cups, and kids'-meal favorites like cheddar quesadilla, mac and cheese, and "green eggs and ham" come with fruit and vegetables on the side. Open Mon through Fri 11:30 a.m. to 2:30 p.m., 5 to 9 p.m., Sat and Sun 9 a.m. to 2:30 p.m., 5 to 9 p.m. $$.

Jasper White's Summer Shack. 50 Dalton St., Back Bay; (617) 867-9955; summershack restaurant.com It's a fun and raucous lobster-pound atmosphere where kids can be kids and chow down on the city's best corn dogs and fried fish while you feast on lobster. Open Mon through Thurs 11:30 a.m. to 10 p.m., Fri and Sat 11:30 a.m. to 11 p.m., Sun 11:30 a.m. to 10 p.m. $$.

where to stay

Royal Sonesta. 40 Edwin Land Blvd., Cambridge; (617) 806-4200; sonesta.com/boston. Located on the banks of the Charles River near the Museum of Science, this hotel is as good as it gets if you're traveling with the family. Rooms are spacious and modern. Some rooms have views of the Charles River. With kids, a pool is a must, and the Royal Sonesta's large atrium-style indoor swimming pool with a retractable roof is pretty nifty. The hotel's popular summer family-package rate includes complimentary bicycles, afternoon ice cream, and a scenic boat ride from the Charles River Boat Company. Kids ages 12 and under eat free at the hotel's Artbar restaurant. $$$.

cape cod, ma

Legendary beaches. Divey clam shacks. Serious minigolf. Pack up the car and head to Cape Cod. New England boasts some of the world's best coastline, and it's hard to pick just one, but the 40-mile stretch of sand that is the Cape Cod National Seashore is pretty spectacular.

getting there

Pick up I-93 South and drive for 9 miles. Take exit 7 toward Cape Cod. Merge onto MA 3 and follow for 41 miles, crossing the Sagamore Bridge. Continue onto US 6 East to exit 9A and Dennisport.

where to go

Cape Cod National Seashore–Salt Pond Visitor Center at the Cape Cod National Seashore. Nauset Road and US 6, Eastham; (508) 255-3421; nps.gov/caco. Likely the most famous seascape in all of Massachusetts, the stretch of pristine beach and sea between Eastham and Provincetown not only includes 40 miles of idyllic beaches but hiking and biking trails that meander through dunes and forest. There are 6 separately named Cape Cod National Seashore beaches; all are outer ocean beaches with colder water and serious surf. Kids love it.

Cape Cod Rail Trail. The Cape Cod Rail Trail is one of New England's most well-known off-road bike paths. The 25-mile route follows the Old Colony Railroad bed from the town of Dennis and ends at the beach in Wellfleet. The path is paved, flat, and safe for new, young riders. You can start your family's adventure anywhere along the route. Bring your own bikes or you can rent—there are several bike shops located along the way. All the shops carry a full range of kids' bikes as well as trailer carts, children's tandems, and baby seats for kids not ready to pedal on their own.

The Farm Institute. 14 Aero Ave., Edgartown, Martha's Vineyard; (508) 627-7007; farm institute.org. The Farm Institute is a working farm and conservation center where kids can participate in farm chores like collecting eggs or helping with the harvest for a few hours during a day or every day for a week or more. There are also 1-day farmer workshops for parents on subjects like composting and cooking seasonal vegetables. Check online for classes, drop-in programs, and farm tour times and costs.

Pirate's Cove. 782 Main St., South Yarmouth; (508) 394-6200; piratescove.net. There are two 18-hole golf courses here, each with an over-the-top-pirate theme. It's a well-land-scaped course with lots of shade and several water features and "exploding" cannonballs in the pond. Open Apr through May and Sept through Oct 10 a.m. to 7 p.m., June through Aug 10 a.m. to 10 p.m. $10.50 adults, $9.50 children.

Wellfleet Drive-In Theater. US 6; (508) 349-7176; wellfleetdrivein.com. Make some memories this summer. Put the kids in their pajamas, pile into the minivan, and catch a family-friendly flick at the Wellfleet Drive-In. Admission $10 for adults, $7.50 seniors and children ages 4 to 11, children ages 3 and under are free.

where to eat

Kream 'N' Kone. 961 Main St., West Dennis; (508) 394-0808; kreamnkone.com. The cuisine is prototypical of a Cape Cod clam shack and ice-cream stand; fried seafood and soft-serve cones with the bonus of eating in either the spacious air-conditioned dining room or on the waterfront patio dining next to the Swan River. Open mid-Feb through June and Sept through Oct daily 11 a.m. to 9 p.m.; July and Aug Sun through Thurs 11 a.m. to 10 p.m., Fri and Sat 11 a.m. to 10:30 p.m. $$.

School House Ice Cream. 749 MA 28, Harwichport; (508) 432-7355; capecodtravel.com/schoolhouseicecream. A nostalgic ice-cream shop located in a neat-as-a-pin Cape Cod–style house. The premium ice cream is homemade—Harwichport Mud Pie is the one to get. Get a double scoop and enjoy it on the covered front porch or outside in the back garden. $.

where to stay

The Corsair and Cross Rip Ocean Resort. 41 Chase Ave., Dennisport; (508) 398-2279; corsaircrossrip.com. The perfect home base for a family Cape vacation, the spacious rooms feature kitchenettes. With an amazing location directly on Nantucket Sound, the resort's best amenity is its own private beach. Further conveniences include 2 outdoor pools, an indoor pool, and a game room. $$$.

white mountains

The White Mountains are a favorite vacation destination for active families with kid-appropriate mountain activities and several timeless theme parks for wholesome vacation fun.

getting there

From US 6 West drive 14 miles, crossing the Sagamore Bridge. Continue along US 3 for 42 miles and take exit 20B to merge onto I-93 toward Boston. Follow I-93 North for 12 miles and take exit 27 to US 1 North and follow for 14 miles. Take I-95 North and follow for 38 miles. Take exit 4 and merge onto MA 16 North and follow for 20 miles. Continue onto US 202 East for 2 miles and follow NH 16 North for 32 miles. Turn right to NH 25 East and drive 5 miles, continue on NH 153 North for 16 miles and pick up NH 16 North/White Mountain Highway for 5 miles to North Conway. The drive time is nearly 4 hours and 200 miles.

where to go

Clark's Trading Post. 110 US 3, Lincoln; (603) 745-8913; clarkstradingpost.com. Around for more than half a century, the big draw at this family-run, western-themed roadside attraction is the trained black bear performances. Other features are the 30-minute steam train ride, a Chinese acrobatic show, water-blaster bumper boats, and Segway rides through the woods. Open mid-May through Columbus Day daily, check website for times. Admission $22 adults and ages 4 and over, $20 seniors.

Franconia Notch State Park. US 3, Lincoln; (603) 745-8391; nhstateparks.org. There's quite a lot for families to do at Franconia Notch Park. Walk through the natural granite chasm across the suspended wood boardwalk and small bridges to the Flume Gorge. On the return loop the Wolf Den is just big enough for (most!) grown-ups to squeeze through, but your kids will scamper through easily. And for a bird's-eye view of the Whites, treat the family to a ride on the Cannon Mountain Aerial Tramway. Tramway open mid-May through mid-Oct daily 9 a.m. to 5 p.m. Admission $17 adults, $14 ages 6 to 12, free for children age 5 and under.

Mount Washington Cog Railway. Base Road off US 302, Bretton Woods; (603) 278-5404; thecog.com. Kids will be totally awed by a mountain-climbing train ride to the summit of Mount Washington. Season runs from May through early Dec, check website for departure times. Tickets $69 adults, $65 seniors, $39 ages 4 to 12.

Santa's Village. 528 Presidential Hwy., Jefferson; (603) 586-4445; santasvillage.com. It's Christmas every day at this family amusement park, which features 16 themed rides including a Christmas Carousel, Yule Log Flume, and the new Ho, Ho, H2O water park. Kids can visit with Santa and have their picture taken. And in the Christmas Village the stores sell ornaments, stocking stuffers, and even gingerbread cookies in high summer. Open Memorial Day weekend through Columbus Day and weekends in Nov and Dec; check website for times. Admission $32 ages 4 and older, $29 seniors.

Story Land. Junction of NH 16 and US 302, Glen; (603) 383-4186; storylandnh.com. Story Land is a charmingly low-key theme park with fairy-tale rides geared to families with young children ages 2 to 12. Open May through Oct and June through Aug daily 9 a.m. to 6 p.m.; check website for days and hours for spring and fall. Admission $34 ages 3 and over, $30 seniors, free ages 2 and under.

festivals & celebrations

january

Stowe Winter Carnival. Stowe, VT; stowewintercarnival.com. In Vermont, they know how to embrace winter. Held the last two weeks of January, this winter carnival features a snow sculpture competition, live music, a kids' expo, a snowgolf tournament, and ski races.

february

Beanpot Hockey Tournament. Boston, MA; beanpothockey.com. Local bragging rights are at stake at this annual four-team hockey tournament that features Harvard, Boston College, Boston University, and Northeastern University. Held the first two Mondays in February.

Chinese New Year. Boston, MA; (617) 350-6303; chintatownmainstreet.org. Firecrackers announce the Chinese Lunar New Year as a colorful parade of lions and dragons, dancers and drummers make their way through Boston's Chinatown. Afterward fill up on dumplings and noodles at one of Chinatown's many restaurants.

Newport Winter Festival. Newport, RI; newportwinterfestival.com. Newport has the antidote to cabin fever—two weeks of more than 150 events (many are free) that include a Chili Cook-off, ice-sculpting competition, musical entertainment, children's fair, and more.

march

Boston Flower and Garden Show. Boston, MA; thebostonflowershow.com. The sight of the extraordinary display gardens at this annual flower show herald spring for winter-weary New Englanders.

St. Patrick's Day Parade. Boston, MA; southbostonparade.org. Boston is the most Irish state in America with nearly a quarter of the state's population of Irish descent, which makes the annual St. Patrick's Day Parade (typically on the Sunday after St. Patrick's Day) through Southie a very big deal.

april

Boston Marathon. Boston, MA; baa.org. Taking place on Patriots' Day, the third Monday of April (and a Massachusetts state holiday), the Boston Marathon is an annual world-class athletic race and a great spectator event. Stake out a spot anywhere along the 26-mile course from the town of Hopkinton to the finish line in Copley Square and cheer on the runners.

Nantucket Daffodil Festival. Nantucket, MA; (508) 228-1700; nantucketchamber.org. The vision of millions of daffodils in bloom along roadsides throughout the island will take your breath away. The festival takes place the last full weekend in April and events include an antique car parade, daffy dog parade, a kids' parade, daffodil flower show, and tailgate picnic event.

Patriots' Day Events. Boston, Lexington, and Concord, MA; battleroad.org. The reenactment of the Battle of Lexington is just one of many events scheduled on Patriots' Day (third Mon of Apr) to commemorate Paul Revere's infamous midnight ride and the first skirmishes of the Revolutionary War.

Vermont Maple Festival. St. Albans, VT; vtmaplefestival.org. A celebration of Vermont's sugaring heritage on the last weekend of April with maple sugarhouse tours and demonstrations, a fiddler's variety show, arts and crafts, a parade, and of course, pancake breakfasts.

may

Boston Calling. Boston, MA; (no phone); bostoncalling.com. Boston Calling is one of the city's newest annual events: a three-day multi-stage music festival that takes place at the Harvard Athletic Complex during the last weekend in May. The wide variety of national headliners includes rock, hip-hop and indie acts (expect lots of blistering guitar solos).

Brimfield Antique and Collectibles Show. Brimfield, MA; brimfieldshow.com. The largest outdoor antique show in New England is held in the fields along a 1-mile stretch of US 20 in Brimfield and features thousands of dealers of every interest and taste. The show takes place over Tuesday through Sunday in early to mid-May with additional shows in mid-July and early September.

Lilac Sunday. Boston, MA; (617) 524-1718; arboretum.harvard.edu. The Arnold Arboretum's annual Lilac Sunday coincides nicely with Mother's Day. Stroll the paths and take in the heady scent of lilacs in full bloom, watch Morris English country dancing, and go on a guided tour. This is also the one day of the year that the arboretum allows picnicking on the grounds, so bring a blanket and your favorite provisions.

Moose Mainea. Moosehead Lake Region, ME; (207) 695-2702; mooseheadlake.org. In Maine, they celebrate the moose with a month-long festival from mid-May to mid-June. A canoe race down the Moose River, a craft fair, Kids' Day, and a moose-calling contest are all part of the fun.

Nantucket Wine Festival. Nantucket, MA; (617) 527-9473; nantucketwinefestival.com. What started in 1996 as a one-day island wine-tasting event has grown to a five-day celebration that has become one of the country's premier destination culinary festivals. This mid-May event showcases some of the world's most renowned wine and spirit producers along with the talents of Nantucket's acclaimed chefs.

WaterFire. Providence, RI; (401) 273-1155; waterfire.org. Providence's signature event, WaterFire's 100 bonfires along the riverfront illuminate the heart of downtown Providence. WaterFire events take place from May through October.

june

Boston Pride March. Boston, MA; (617) 262-9405; bostonpride.org. New England's largest gay-pride event takes place over nine days in early June, culminating in a parade and festival at Boston City Hall Plaza.

International Festival of Arts and Ideas. New Haven, CT; (888) 278-4332; artidea.org. In mid-June these nearly two weeks of contemporary and unique programming (much of it free), feature concerts, poetry readings, films, lectures, and musical performances at venues throughout the city and on historic New Haven Green. Past headliners of the festival include Salman Rushdie, Little Richard, and Yo-Yo Ma and the Silk Road Ensemble.

Jimmy Fund Scooper Bowl. Boston, MA; (617) 632-5008; jimmyfund.org. In early June, Boston kicks off the summer season with a three-day ice-cream festival. Your Scooper Bowl ticket purchase supports research at the Dana Faber Cancer Institute, and of course, all-you-can-eat ice cream is also a very good thing.

Motorcycle Week. Laconia, NH; laconiamcweek.com. Held each year since 1923, this is the oldest motorcycle rally in the country with a full week of partying in mid-June. There are rides through the streets, music, and food as well as several charity and benefit events.

Nantucket Film Festival. Nantucket, MA; (508) 325-6274; nantucketfilmfestival.org. The Nantucket Film Festival looks at what's new in American and international features and short films. In 2013, the five-day festival (over the last weekend in June) featured nearly 75 screenings and included such special events as the All-Star Comedy Roundtable, presided over by Ben Stiller (his parents, actors Jerry Stiller and Anne Meara, are longtime Nantucket summer residents), who brings his friends; Seth Meyers and Mike Myers in 2013; and Jim Carrey and Chris Rock in 2012.

North End Feasts and Processions. Boston, MA; northendboston.com. It's a party in the street nearly every weekend from June through August in Boston's North End. Italian patron saints are honored by a solemn procession, followed by days-long celebrations of live music and Italian street food.

Portsmouth Market Square Day. Portsmouth, NH; proportsmouth.org. On the second Saturday of June, downtown Portsmouth becomes a vehicle-free and pedestrian-friendly zone, and the city becomes a giant block party celebrating the arts with live entertainment and booths featuring local crafts and food.

Rockport Chamber Music Festival. Rockport, MA. Since 1981, the Rockport Chamber Music Festival has presented the very best in classical music soloists and ensembles including Marc-Andre Hamelin, the Borromeo String Quartet, and piano duo Anderson and Roe. Concerts take place at the state-of-the-art Shalin Liu Performance Center, which features a stage with a 2-story window wall and magnificent views of Rockport Harbor and the Atlantic Ocean as the backdrop.

Sea Music Festival. Mystic, CT; (860) 572-0711; mysticseaport.org. Experience traditional songs of the sea as well as storytelling aboard the historic ships of Mystic Seaport. The event is usually held on the second weekend of June. The chantey sings are a highlight— old ditties (sometimes colorful!) sung by sailors to the rhythm of their work on the vessels.

Tanglewood Music Festival. Lenox, MA; (617) 227-1528; tanglewood.org. The Berkshire Hills are the summer home of the Boston Symphony Orchestra. Musical programming includes plenty of Mozart, Beethoven and Brahms and often features world-class guest soloists like Joshua Bell, Itzhak Perlman, and Leon Fleisher. Late June, July, and August.

Yale-Harvard Regatta. New London, CT. Also in early June, spectators bring blankets and beer to the banks of the Thames River to witness one of the oldest collegiate crew rivalries in the country.

july

Barnstable County Fair. East Falmouth, MA; (508) 563-3200; barnstablecountyfair.org. A mid-July Cape Cod tradition for more than 160 years with locals vying for best pie and best canned vegetables along with livestock exhibits. There's a midway, monster trucks, and headline entertainment each night.

Bath Heritage Days. Bath, ME; bathheritagedays.com. During the first weekend in July, enjoy four days of family fun that include a boat parade, antique cars, musical entertainment, and old-fashioned midway rides. Don't miss the fireman's muster.

Boston Harborfest. Boston, MA; (617) 227-1528; bostonharborfest.com. The summer festival gets into high gear with Boston's annual six-day-long Fourth of July celebration with more than 200 events scheduled throughout the city including historical reenactments, street performances, and the Boston Chowderfest on City Hall Plaza.

Boston Pops Fireworks Spectacular. Boston, MA; july4th.org. The city caps off the Fourth of July in grand style with a free concert by the Boston Pops along the Esplanade; it includes Tchaikovsky's 1812 Overture, canons, and fireworks.

Greater Hartford Jazz Festival. Hartford, CT; hartfordjazz.com. For more than 20 years, Bushnell Park has staged a mid-July weekend of free music with some of the greatest names in jazz.

Lowell Folk Festival. Lowell, MA; (978) 970-5000; lowellfolkfestival.org. Held the last full weekend in July, this is the largest free folk festival in the country. Whatever your musical taste—rockabilly, blues, or jazz—there is something for everyone. Culinary offerings are wide-ranging and better than your usual festival fare with treats from Cambodia, Armenia, Thailand, and more.

Maine Lobster Festival. Rockland, ME; (207) 596-0376; mainelobsterfestival.com. People from all over the country, and increasingly from around the world, descend on tiny Rockland in early August to enjoy 20,000 pounds of steamed lobster, along with clams, mussel, corn, and blueberry pie. Other festival highlights include a road race, a lobster crate race (contestants try to run across a string of 50 lobster crates floating across Rockport Harbor without falling into the water!), a codfish carry for kids, a parade, and the crowning of the Maine Sea Goddess to preside over all.

Newport Folk Festival. Newport, RI; newportfolkfest.net. The granddaddy of all folk festivals, where Bob Dylan and Joan Baez were first introduced to national audiences in the 1960s. Held the last weekend in July, in recent years the festival headliners have included the Allman Brothers Band, the Decemberists, Elvis Costello, and Emmy Lou Harris.

Stoweflake Hot Air Balloon Festival. Stowe, VT; stoweflake.com. Second weekend in July. Up, up, and away! Against the backdrop of Mount Mansfield and picturesque Stowe valley, this festival features more than 25 spectacular hot air balloons, lots of live music, family entertainment, food, and a beer and wine garden. Balloon rides and tethered rides are available too.

Vermont Cheesemakers Festival. Shelburne, VT; (800) 884-6287; vtcheesefest.com. Held annually at picturesque Shelburne Farms on the third Sunday in July, this festival showcases some of Vermont's best cheesemakers and artisan food producers. Watch cheesemaking and cooking demonstrations, meet the cheesemakers, and sample cheeses and other Vermont-made goodies.

Yarmouth Clam Festival. Yarmouth, ME; clamfestival.com. Attracting nearly 100,000 fairgoers on the third weekend of July who come to feast on fried clams, clam chowder, and clam cakes. There's a clam parade, a firefighter's muster competition, and evening fireworks. Highlight of the weekend is the clam-shucking contest with both professional and amateur categories.

august

Feast of the Blessed Sacrament. New Bedford, MA; (508) 992-6911; portuguesefeast .com. Billed as the oldest and largest Portuguese festival in the world, this four-day event takes place on the first weekend in August. Expect a host of authentic activities—performances by traditional Portuguese bands and folk dancers, handcrafted wares, and a parade. Feast on linguica sausage sandwiches and skewers of barbecue beef washed down with Madeira.

Machias Wild Blueberry Festival. Machias, ME; machiasblueberry.com. Way up north, in Down East Maine, the tiny town of Machias celebrates the blueberry harvest on the third weekend in August with a Friday evening fish fry, a Saturday morning blueberry pancake breakfast, a crafts fair, and musical entertainment throughout the weekend. The fair highlight has to be cheering on the contestants in the blueberry pie–eating contest.

Newport Jazz Festival. Newport, RI; newportjazzfest.net. Held at Fort Adams State Park, this two-day musical festival celebrates the sounds of jazz with a lineup that typically includes big names like Wynton Marsalis and up-and-comers like Esperanza Spalding.

Provincetown Carnival Week. Provincetown, MA; ptown.org. This prideful event includes a week of parties and events that precedes a zany Mardi Gras–style parade down Commercial Street that draws as many as 80,000 spectators. Usually held the third weekend of August.

Woods Hole Film Festival. Woods Hole, (508) 495-3456; woodsholefilfestival.org. One of the region's best summer destination festivals featuring dozens of films from around the world during its eight-day run during the first week of August. Year-round, the festival sponsors a monthly dinner and a movie series with screenings of films like *Landfill Harmonic* and *A Man Called Ove*.

september

The Eastern States Exposition. West Springfield, MA; thebige.com. Known as the Big E, this is the region's largest agricultural fair taking place over 17 days (and three weekends) beginning the first Friday after Labor Day. Each of the six New England states showcases their attractions and products along the Avenue of States.

New Hampshire Scottish Games. Lincoln, NH; nhscot.org. Scottish heritage rules the third weekend in September with the largest gathering of the clans in New England. There is bagpiping, traditional Celtic games such as the hammer throw, and entertainment that includes Highland dance and sheep dog trials.

Topsfield Fair. Topsfield, MA; topsfieldfair.org. Dating back to 1818 and said to be the country's oldest agricultural fair, this event takes place over 11 days in late September through early October and entertains with oxen pulls, amusement rides, and all the fried dough you can eat.

What the Fluff Festival. Sommerville, MA; flufffestival.com. A wonderfully wild and wacky festival that celebrates Fluff, the spreadable marshmallow cream that was invented in Sommerville in 1917 by Archibald Query. Highlights include Fluff jousting and a Fluff lick-off.

october

Fryeburg Fair. Fryeburg, ME; fryeburgfair.com. Maine's largest agricultural fair takes place here for one week in early October. There are prize livestock exhibits, pie-eating and woodsmen events including log rolling, cross-cut and axe throwing competitions.

Haunted Happenings. Salem, MA; hauntedhappenings.org. Every October Salem hosts a full schedule of more than 100 Halloween events; with ghost tours, costume balls, children's activities, and special presentations and extended hours at the city's many attractions. It all climaxes with a Halloween parade and fireworks.

Head of the Charles Regatta. Boston, MA; hocr.org. Party down by the banks of the river Charles with hundreds of thousands of college students and cheer on your favorite crew team. It all takes place on the third weekend in October, with more than 50 races that attract college and club crew teams from throughout the country and around the world.

New Hampshire Pumpkin Festival. Laconia, New Hampshire; nhpumpkinfestival.com. Welcome fall at this celebration of all things pumpkin: pumpkin race, pumpkin bowling, a costumed pumpkin parade and pumpkin foods of all kinds. The festival's centerpiece attraction is the pumpkin tower made up of more than 15,000 carved illuminated jack-o-lanterns.

Wellfleet Oyster Festival. Wellfleet, MA; wellfleetoysterfest.org. Oysters are well worth celebrating, and Wellfleet pulls out all the stops with a craft fair, local foods, live music, activities for the kids, and an oyster-shucking contest.

november

America's Hometown Thanksgiving Celebration. Plymouth, MA; usathanksgiving.com. Plymouth does a "Grand Parade" on the Saturday before Thanksgiving along with a full weekend of concerts and family activities along Plymouth Harbor.

december

Boston's Official Christmas Tree and Menorah Lightings. Boston, MA; cityofboston .gov. Herald the holiday season with light—lots of lights. The Boston Common is the setting for both Boston's official Christmas Tree and Chanukah Menorah. The Christmas tree lighting takes place in early December; the menorah lighting takes place on the first night of Chanukah. Musical performances accompany each celebration.

Bright Night Providence. Providence, RI; (401) 621-6123; brightnight.org. Bright Night Providence is an artist-run New Year's Eve Party at venues throughout the city. Highlights include strolling clowns, musicians, and the ever-popular Big Nazo Band. At midnight fireworks lights up the sky behind the State House.

Christmas in Newport. Newport, RI; christmasinnewport.org. Celebrate the holidays with a month-long calendar of seasonal events that harken back to simpler times. Highlights include a blessing of the fleet, free holiday concerts, and historic home open houses.

First Night Boston. Boston, MA; (617) 632-5008; firstnight.org. First Night Boston is the country's oldest and largest New Year's celebration of the arts. Highlights include the ice sculptures in Copley Square and the Boston Common and the Grand Procession, followed by the family fireworks at 7 p.m. The celebration culminates at midnight with a second fireworks display over Boston Harbor.

Nantucket Stroll Weekend. Nantucket, MA; (508) 228-1700; nantucketchamber.org. For the month of December, Nantucket celebrates "Nantucket Noel" where the island is transformed into a Victorian holiday wonderland. The highlight of the month is Nantucket Stroll, which takes place the second weekend after Thanksgiving. A town crier rings in the arrival of Santa by Coast Guard vessel, and a parade of musicians and costumed carolers serenading visitors add to the festive atmosphere. In Town Square, there's a European-style Christmas Market offering artisan crafts and seasonal food specialties.

index

A

Abacus Gallery, 245
Abba, 89
Abbe Museum, 348
Abbot's Lobster in the
    Rough, 171
Abel's Lobster Pound, 352
Abenaki Tower, 224
Abrash Galleries, 177
Acadia Bike Rentals &
    Coastal Kayaking
    Tours, 348
Acadia National Park, 351
Acadia National Park
    Visitors Center, 351
Adams National Historical
    Park, 64, 274
Addison Art Gallery, 88
AHA! night, 69
A & J King Artisan
    Bakers, 52
Ale House Inn, 220
Alex and Ani, 139
Alex and Ani City
    Center, 126
Al Forno, 130
Alisson's, 241
Allagash Brewing, 313
Allen, Ethan, 199
Alta, 370
American Flatbread, 187
American Independence
    Museum, 281

American Museum of Fly
    Fishing, 343
American Seasons, 120
America's Hometown
    Thanksgiving
    Celebration, 390
Amy's Bakery Arts
    Cafe, 339
Anchor In, 83
Angela Adams, 235
Annalee's Outlet
    Store, 226
Antico Forno, 20
Antonio's, 69
Appalachian Club Pinkham
    Notch Visitors
    Center, 358
Aquitaine Boston, 20
Armsby Abbey, 73
Arnold's Lobster & Clam
    Bar, 103
Artistry on the Green, 39
Art's Dune Tours, 107
Ash Street Inn, 215
Asticou Inn, 353
Atlantic Brewing
    Company, 314
Atlantic Inn, The, 146
@ the Corner, 179
Atticus Bookstore
    Cafe, 155
Audrain Auto
    Museum, 137

B

Back Bay, 17
Ballard's, 145
Bandaloop, 241
Bar Bouchee, 166
Bar Harbor Chamber of
    Commerce Welcome
    Center, 348
Bar Harbor Historical
    Society, 348
Bar Harbor Inn, 350
Bar Harbor, ME, 314, 347
Barnacle Billy's, 245
Barn Bowl & Bistro, 113
Barnstable County
    Fair, 387
Bartlett's Farms, 119
Bass Cottage Inn, 350
Bass Harbor Head
    Light, 351
Bass Rocks Ocean
    Inn, 57
Bath Heritage Days, 387
Bath, ME, 253, 322
Battle Green, 38, 269
Bay State Cruise, 106
Bayview, The, 350
Beachcomber, The, 105
Beachmere Inn, 246
Beacon Hill, 18
Beacon Hill Chocolates, 18
Beale Street
    Barbecue, 253

Beanpot Hockey
   Tournament, 384
Bear in Boots
   Gastropub, 99
Beauport Hotel, 58
Bedford Farms Ice
   Cream, 43
Beechwood Hotel, 74
Beehive, 20
Bee & Thistle Inn, 170
Belfry Inne & Bistro, The,
   97, 98
Benefit Street, 126, 274
Benjamin Franklin and
   Boston Latin, 10
Ben & Jerry's Ice
   Cream, 195
Berkshire Museum, 374
Berkshire Theatre
   Festival, 372
Berry Manor Inn, The, 255
Bethel Inn Resort, 262
Bethel, ME, 261
Bethel Outdoor
   Adventure, 261
Beth's Bakery & Cafe, 98
Betty's Pizza Shack, 370
Billings Farm &
   Museum, 207
Birch Tree Bread, 74
Birdwatchers General
   Store, The, 89
Bistro Henry, 345
Bite, The, 113
Black Dog Tavern,
   The, 114
Black Eyed Sally's, 162
Black-Eyed Susan's, 120
Black Ink, 30
Blackinton Manor, 336
Black Rose, The, 24

Blackstone's of Beacon
   Hill, 18
Black Trumpet Bistro, 219
Block Island Chamber of
   Commerce, 145
Block Island Express, 143
Block Island Ferry, 143
Block Island, RI, 143
Blue, 60
Blue Dragon, 290
Blue Hound Cookery &
   Taproom, 168
Blue Moon Evolution, 282
Blue Stone, The, 197
Bob's Clam Hut, 248
Bob Slate Stationer, 31
Bolton, MA, 299
Boothbay Harbor, ME, 322
Boothbay Railway
   Village, 364
Boott Cotton Mills
   Museum, 45
Boston by Little Feet
   Tours, 378
Boston Calling, 385
Boston Children's Museum,
   The, 4, 378
Boston Common, 8
Boston Copley Farmers'
   Market, 289
Boston Duck Tours, 378
Boston Flower and Garden
   Show, 384
Boston Food Tours, 289
Boston Harbor
   Cruises, 106
Boston Harborfest, 387
Boston Harbor Islands
   National Park, 5
Boston Holiday Pops, 326
Boston Light, 317

Boston, MA, 3, 266, 289,
   295, 325, 377
Boston Marathon, 384
Boston Massacre,
   The, 10
Boston Pops Fireworks
   Spectacular, 387
Boston Pride March, 386
Boston Public Library, 5
Boston Public Market, 19
Boston's Official Christmas
   Tree and Menorah
   Lightings, 390
Boston Symphony Hall, 6
Boulevard Diner, 74
Brattleboro Chamber of
   Commerce, 338
Brattleboro Farmers'
   Market, 338
Brattleboro Food
   Co-op, 338
Brattleboro Museum and
   Art Center, 338
Brattleboro, VT, 337
Breakers, The, 136
Bretton Woods Mountain
   Resort, 359
Bretton Woods, NH, 359
Brew'd Awakening
   Coffeehaus, 47
Brewster by the Sea, 87
Brewster Fish House,
   The, 86
Brewster, MA, 84
Brewster Store, The, 86
Brick Market Building, 276
Bridge of Flowers, 332
Bridgewater Corners,
   VT, 310
Bright Night
   Providence, 300

Brimfield Antique and
Collectibles Show,
76, 385
Bristol, ME, 323
Brookfield, CT, 306
Brown University,
126, 274
Bryant House, 342
B.T.'s Smokehouse, 76
Buckman Tavern, 39, 270
Bull McCabe's, 24
Bunker Hill Monument, 11
Burlington Farmers'
Market, 292
Burlington, VT, 185,
291, 310
Burnt Island Living
Lighthouse
Museum, 322
Buttonwood Inn, 357

C

Cabot Cheese Annex, 197
Cadillac Mountain, 351
Cafe Chew, 98
Cafe Lafayette Dinner
Train, 364
Cafe Miranda, 255
Cafe Prego, 245
Cafe Sicillia, 56
Cafe Sushi, 32
Cafe This Way, 349
Cambridge Artist
Cooperative, 31
Cambridge, MA, 27, 268
Camden Chamber of
Commerce, 256
Camden Harbour Inn, 257
Camden Hills State
Park, 256
Camden, ME, 256

Camille's, 131
canal boat tours, 46
Cannon Mountain, 361
Cape Ann Chamber of
Commerce, 54
Cape Ann Museum, 54
Cape Cod Baseball
League, 93
Cape Cod Central
Railroad, 366
Cape Cod, MA, 381
Cape Cod Museum of
Natural History,
The, 84
Cape Cod National
Seashore, 108
Cape Cod National
Seashore Province
Lands Visitor
Center, 107
Cape Cod Potato Chip
Factory, 81
Cape Cod Rail Trail, The,
87, 366, 381
Cape Cod Visitor
Center, 81
Cape Elizabeth
(lighthouse), 321
Cape Elizabeth, ME, 321
Cape Neddick
Lighthouse, 320
Captain Daniel Packer
Inne Restaurant and
Pub, 172
Captain Fairfield Inn, 242
Captain Jack's Lobster
Tour, 296
Captain Parker's Pub, 93
Cap't Cass, 89
Carolyn's Sakonnet
Vineyards, 303

Carriages of Acadia, 351
Casco Bay Lines, 234
Caseus, 155
Castle Hill and Resort, 141
Castle Hill on the Crane
Estate, 58
Castle in the Clouds, 229
Cava, 219
Champney's Restaurant &
Tavern, 272
Chapoquoit Grill, 99
Charles Hotel, The, 34
Charlesmark Hotel, The, 23
CharlieCard, 14
CharlieTicket, 14
Chateau-sur-Mer, 136
Chatham Bars Inn, 92, 294
Chatham Candy Manor, 91
Chatham Inn at 359
Main, 92
Chatham Light, 91, 318
Chatham, MA, 90,
294, 317
Chatham Squire, 92
Chester-Hadlyme
Ferry, 168
Chesterwood, 372
Chez Pascal, 131
Children's Museum &
Theatre of Maine, 234
Chinese New Year, 384
Chocolate Springs
Cafe, 370
Cho Sun, 261
Christmas at the Newport
Mansions, 327
Christmas in Newport,
328, 391
Christmas Tree Shops, 89
Christopher Dodge
House, 132

Church Street
    Marketplace, 186
Cisco Brewers, 118
Claire Murray, 86
Clam Box of Ipswich,
    59, 296
Clam Shack, 241
Clark Art Institute, 375
Clark's Trading Post, 383
Classic Cruises of
    Newport, 137
Claws, 324
Cliff Walk, 137
Coach, 344
Cobblestone
    Restaurant, 69
Cobblestones, 47
Cold Hollow Cider Mill, 197
Colony Hotel, 242
Colony House, The,
    137, 276
Concord Book Shop., 43
Concord Cheese Shop, 43
Concord, MA, 41, 271
Concord Museum, The,
    41, 271
Concord's Colonial Inn, 44
Concord Visitor Center, 41
Congdon's Doughnuts, 243
Connecticut River
    Museum, 167
Connecticut Science
    Center, 160
Connecticut Wine Trail, 306
Conway Scenic Railroad,
    355, 364
Cooke's Seafood, 90
Copley Place, 17
Coppa, 290
Copper Wok, 114
Corner Store, 92

Corsair and Cross Rip
    Ocean Resort,
    The, 382
Coskata-Coatue Wildlife
    Refuge, 119
Cottage Grove, 103
Courtyard by Marriott
    Burlington Harbor, 188
Cozy Inn and
    Cottages, 229
Crab Apple Whitewater
    Rafting, 333
Craigie on Main, 32
cranberries, 66
Crane Beach, 59
Cranmore Mountain
    Resort, 355
Cranwell Resort and
    Spa, 371
Crepes Choupette, 156
Crescent Beach, 145
Crowne Point Inn &
    Spa, 109
Cry Innocent: The People
    vs. Bridget Bishop, 51
Currier Museum of Art, 214
Cyndi's Dockside, 260

D
Dakin Farm Vermont, 292
Danforth Inn, 237
Danforth Pewter Workshop
    & Store, 193
Darius Hotel, 146
David's KPT, 241
Daytrip Society, 240
Dean Hotel, 132
Deerfield, MA, 272, 330
Delmonico Hatter, 155
DiGrazia Vineyards, 306
Dolphin Fleet, 107

Doretta Tavern and Raw
    Bar, 20
Dottie's Diner, 177
Downtown New Haven
    Visitor Information
    Center, 152
Doyle's Café, 24
Druid, 24
Duckfat, 236
Duckworth's Bistro, 56
Dunne's Ice Cream, 248

E
East Coast Grill, 295
Eastern States Exposition,
    The, 389
Eastham, MA, 101
Easton's Beach, 137
Eataly Boston, 21
Echo Lake Aquarium and
    Science Center, 186
Ecotarium, The, 73
Edgewater Gallery, 194
Edward Gorey House, 93
Eliot Hotel, 291
Eli's, 146
Elizabeth Park, 160
Elms, The, 136
Envoy, 25
Equinox Resort, 345
Eric Sloane Museum, 180
Essex, CT, 167, 365
Essex Culinary Resort and
    Spa, 293
Essex Steam Train and
    Riverboat, 167, 365
Essex, The, 293
Eventide Oyster
    Company, 236
Exeter, NH, 281

F

Fabyan's Station, 360, 365
Falmouth, MA, 98, 316
Faneuil Hall, 10
Faneuil Hall
    Marketplace, 19
Farmaesthetics, 139
Farmhouse Tap & Grill, 187
Farm Institute, The,
    112, 381
Farnsworth Art
    Museum, 254
Fat Cat, 64
Feast of the Blessed
    Sacrament, 388
Federal Hill, 127
Federal Jack's Brew
    Pub, 312
Fenway Park, 6
ffrost Sawyer Tavern, 283
F. H. Gillingham &
    Sons, 207
Fifteen Beacon, 327
Finz Seafood & Grill, 53
Fire + Ice, 380
First Baptist Church,
    127, 275
First Night Boston,
    326, 391
Fisherman's Catch, 244
Five Islands Lobster, 296
Flag Hill Winery, 299
Flatbread Pizza
    Company, 356
Flat of the Hill, 18
Flavours, 374
Florence Griswold
    Museum, 169
Flo's Clam Shack, 139
Flo's Steamed Hot
    Dogs, 248

Flour Bakery + Cafe, 21
Fluke Wine Bar and
    Kitchen, 140
Flume Gorge at Franconia
    Notch State Park, 361
Flying Horses
    Carousel, 112
Flying Saucer Pizza, 53
Flynt Center of New
    England Life, 331
Fog Island Cafe, 120
Four Seasons–Teddy Bear
    Tea in the Bristol
    Lounge, 327
Foxwoods Resort
    Casino, 173
Franciscan Guest
    House, 242
Francis Malbone
    House, 328
Franconia, NH, 360
Franconia Notch State
    Park, 383
Frankie and Johnny's, 248
Franklin Cafe Cape Ann, 56
Franklin Park Zoo, The, 7
Frank Pepe
    Napoletana, 156
Freedom Cruise Line, 116
Freedom Trail, 8, 267, 378
Freeport, ME, 250
Freeport shopping
    outlets, 252
Frelinghuysen Morris
    House & Studio, 369
French Cable Station
    Museum, 88
Fresh, 17
Friendly Toast, The, 220
Frog Hollow Vermont State
    Craft Center, 186

Frog Pond, 326
Fryeburg Fair, 390
Full Moon, 380
Fun Spot, 228
Furnace Brook Winery at
    Hilltop Orchards, 301

G

Gallery 53, 55
Garden Gables Inn, 371
Gazebo Inn, 246
Gentle Giants, 329
George B. Dorr Museum of
    Natural History, 348
George's Diner, 226
Georgetown Pottery, 252
Gertrude Jekyll
    Garden, 175
Gifford's, 181
Gilbert's Chowder
    House, 236
Gilded, 141
Gillette Castle State
    Park, 168
Giordano's, 114
Glass Onion, 99
Glebe House Museum, 175
Gloucester Fisherman's
    Memorial, The, 55
Gloucester, MA, 54
Golden Eagle Resort, 201
Goldenrod, 248
Good, 18
Good Harbor Beach, 55
Good News Cafe, 178
Goose Hummock, 89
Goosewing Beach
    Preserve, 304
Gourmet Dumpling
    House, 21

Governor Prence Inn,
The, 90
Grafton Forge, 340
Grafton Inn, The, 341
Grafton Notch State
Park, 261
Grafton Ponds Outdoor
Center, 340
Grafton Village Cheese
Company, 341
Grafton, VT, 340
Gramercy Bistro, 334
Granary Burying Ground, 9
Granary Gallery, 113
Gray's Ice Cream, 304
Greater Boston Convention
and Visitors Bureau,
The, 4
Greater Hartford Jazz
Festival, 387
Greater Hartford Welcome
Center, 158
Greater Manchester
Chamber of
Commerce, 213
Greater York Region
Chamber of
Commerce Visitors
Center, 246
Great Friends Meeting
House, 276
Green Animals Topiary
Gardens, 142
Green Briar Nature Center
and Jam Kitchen, 95
Green Harbor, 94
Green Mountain Coffee
Cafe & Visitor
Center, 197
Green Mountain Inn, 202
Greenvale Vineyards, 305

Greydon House, 121
Griswold Inn, The, 168
Gritty McDuff's, 313
Grolier Poetry
Bookshop, 31
Guapo's Tortilla Shack, 87
Guest House at Field Farm,
The, 376
Gunstock, 228
Gypsy Café, 361

H

Haight-Brown Vineyard,
178, 308
Hall Tavern, 331
Hammonasset Beach State
Park, 166
Hampton Beach, 221
Hancock-Clarke House,
39, 270
Hancock Shaker
Village, 374
Hanger B, 92
Harbor Sweets, 52
Harpoon Brewery, 309
Harraseeket Inn, 252
Harraseeket Lunch &
Lobster Co., 252
Harriet Beecher Stowe
Center, 160
Hartford, CT, 158
Hartford Marriott, 163
Hartstone Inn, 257
Hart's Turkey Farm
Restaurant, 226
Harvard art museums, 29
Harvard Coop, 31
Harvard Museum of Natural
History, 29, 378
Harvard Square, 29, 379
Harvard University, 29, 268

Harvest, 32
Haunted Happenings, 390
Havana, 349
Haven Cafe & Bakery, 370
Hawthorne Hotel, 53
Hawthorne Inn, 45
Haymarket, 12
H.B. Provisions, 241
Head of the Charles
Regatta, 390
Hen of the Wood, 188, 197
Heritage Garden Museums
& Gardens, 97
Hidden Valley Bed &
Breakfast, 307
Highland Light, 319
Hildene, 343
Hilton Mystic, 172
Historic Deerfield, 272, 331
Hoadley Gallery, 370
Hob Knob, 115
Hole in One Donut
Shop, 103
Home Kitchen Cafe, 255
Homeport, 186
Homestyle, 129
Hood Museum, 203
Hooked, 214
Hope Street Farmers
Market, 288
Hopkins Vineyards, 307
Hotel Commonwealth, 23
Hotel Kendall, 34
Hotel Manisses, 147
Hotel Portsmouth, 220
Hotel Providence, 133
Hotel Veritas, 35
Hotel Vermont, 188
Hotel Viking, 141
Housatonic River
Walk, 180

House of the Seven
    Gables, 51, 279
Hudson's Art, 334
Hughes Bosca at the Side
    Street Gallery, 56
Hyannis, MA, 80, 366
Hyannis Mall, The, 82
Hy-Line Cruises, 116
Hy-Line ferry, Hyannis–Oak
    Bluffs, 110

I

Ice Cream Place, 146
Impudent Oyster, 92
Inn at Castle Hill, The, 60
Inn at Hastings Park, 40
Inn at Kent Falls, 181
Inn at Manchester, 346
Inn at Montpelier, 199
Inn at Shelburne
    Farms, 192
Inn at St. Botolph,
    The, 25
Inn at Weston, 342
Inner Harbor Ferry, 8
Inn on Putney Road, 339
Inn on the Green, 194
Inn on the Sound, 100
Institute of Contemporary
    Art, 12
International Festival of Arts
    and Ideas, 386
International Tennis Hall of
    Fame, 138
Intown Trolley, 240
Ipswich, MA, 58
Ipswich Visitor Center, 58
Isabella Stewart Gardner
    Museum, The, 12
Island Alpaca, 112
Island Artisans, 349

Island Explorer Shuttle
    Bus, 353
Ithaki, 59
Ivoryton Playhouse, 167

J

Jack's Hot Dog Stand, 335
Jaho Coffee & Tea, 53
Jalapeños, 56
James Hook, 290
Jasper White's Summer
    Shack, 380
Jetties Beach, 118
Jewell Towne
    Vineyards, 299
Jimmy Fund Scooper
    Bowl, 386
J.J. Foley's Café, 24
John Brown House
    Museum, 127, 275
John Carver Inn, The, 67
John F. Kennedy Hyannis
    Museum, 81
John F. Kennedy Library
    and Museum, 13
John Nesta Gallery, 55
Johnny Cupcakes, 17
John Paul Jones House,
    218, 282
John's Cafe, 178
Jordan Pond House, 352
Jo's American Bistro, 140
Joseph Sylvia State
    Beach, 112
J. P. Gifford Market &
    Catering, 181
J. Press, 155
Julian's Providence, 131

K

Kaede Bed & Breakfast, 60

Kancamagus Highway,
    The, 357
Katama Beach, 112
Kedron Valley Inn, 208
Keeper's House at
    Pemaquid Point, 323
Keepsake Quilting, 226
Keltic Kitchen, 82
Kennebunk &
    Kennebunkport
    Chamber of
    Commerce, 240
Kennebunkport Inn, 242
Kennebunkport, ME, 312
Kennebunk's beaches, 240
Kennebunks, ME,
    The, 238
Kennedy Park, 369
Kent, CT, 180
Kent Falls State Park, 180
Kenyon Grist Mill, 287
Killington Resort, 209
Killington, VT, 209
King Arthur Flour Baker's
    Store, 205
King's Chapel, 9
King's Chapel Burying
    Ground, 9
Kitchen Cravings, 229
Kitchen Little, 172
Kitchen Table Bistro, 293
Kittery, ME, 246
Kream 'N' Kone, 382
Kripalu Center for Yoga
    and Health, 373

L

La Brioche, 198
L. A. Burdick, 32
Lake Champlain
    Chocolates, 292

Lake Champlain Regional Chamber of Commerce, 186
Lala's Hungarian Pastry, 214
Langham, The, 25
Lang House, 188
Laughing Moon Chocolates, 329
La Vista, 362
Lee, NH, 298
Lee's Riding Stable at Windfield Morgan Farm, 308
Legal Sea Foods, 21, 295
Lenny & Joe's Fish Tale, 166
Lenox Chamber of Commerce, 369
Lenox, MA, 368
Les Trois Emme Vineyard & Winery, 300
Leunig's Bistro & Cafe, 187
Lexie's Joint, 220
Lexington Battle Green reenactment, 38
Lexington Historical Society, 38, 269
Lexington, MA, 36, 269
Lexington Visitor Center, 38
Lexx, 40
Liberty Ride, 270
Life Alive Organic Cafe, 47
Lilac Sunday, 385
Litchfield, CT, 178, 308
Litchfield Hills Visitor's Booth, 178
Litchfield Inn, 180
Litchfield Law School, 179
Little Compton, RI, 303
Little Donkey, 32

Little Inn on Pleasant Bay, A, 90
Little Rooster Cafe, 345
L. L. Bean, 252
L. L. Bean Outdoor Discovery Schools, 250
Lobster Hut, The, 66
Lobster Pot, 108
Lobster Shack at Two Lights, 321
Local 121, 288
Loeb Visitor's Center, 138, 277
Longfellow House– Washington Headquarters National Historic Site, 30, 269
Long Grain, 257
Long Trail Brewing Company, 310
Loon Mountain, 361
Louis' Lunch, 156
Lowell Folk Festival, 47, 388
Lowell, MA, 45
Lowell National Historical Park, 46
Lucky Hank's, 114
Lulu Lobster Boat, 348

M

Mache Bistro, 349
Machias Wild Blueberry Festival, 389
Mac's Shack, 105
Made Inn Vermont, 188
Madison Beach Hotel, 166
Madison, CT, 164
Magic Hat Brewing Company, 186, 310

Magic Wings Butterfly Conservatory & Gardens, 331
Maine Island Kayak, 234
Maine Lighthouse Museum, 255, 324
Maine Lobster Festival, 388
Maine Maritime Museum, 322
Maine, mid-coast, 296, 363
Maine Wildlife Park, 258
Main Street Antiques Center, 177
Main Streets Market & Cafe, 44
Maison Villatte, 100
Manchester Chamber of Commerce, 343
Manchester Designer Outlets, 344
Manchester, NH, 213
Manchester, VT, 342
Maps of Antiquity, 91
Marble House, 136
Marconi Beach, 104
Marginal Way, The, 244
Mark Twain House & Museum, 160
Marlboro Music, 346
Marsh-Billings-Rockefeller National Historical Park, 207
Martha's Vineyard Chamber of Commerce, 112
Martha's Vineyard, MA, 110
Mashantucket Pequot Museum, 173
Massachusetts Historical Society, 267

Massachusetts Museum
of Contemporary Art
(MASS MoCA), 334
Massachusetts State
House, 9
Matunuk Oyster Bar, 288
Mayflower II, 65
May Kelly's Cottage, 356
McCarthy's
Restaurant, 201
McCay's Public House, 350
Merchant, The, 281
Meredith Marina, 225
Meredith, NH, 225
Mezze Bistro & Bar, 376
Middlebury, VT, 193
Middletown, RI, 305
Migis Lodge, 263
Mill at Simon Pearce, 206
Mill Falls Marketplace, 226
Mills Falls at the Lake, 227
Millyard Museum, 214
Milly & Grace, 119
Minute Man National
Historical Park, 39, 41,
269, 271
Mirbeau Inn & Spa, 67
Mise en Place, 224
MIT Museum, The, 30
Miyake, 236
Miya's Sushi, 156
Moby Dick Brewing
Company, 69
Mocha Joe's, 339
Modern Pastry, 21
Moffatt-Ladd House, 282
Mohawk Trading Post, 333
Mohawk Trail, 333
Mohegan Bluffs, 145
Mohegan Cafe &
Brewery, 146

Mohegan Sun, 174
Monomoy National Wildlife
Refuge, 91
Montpelier, VT, 198
Montshire Museum of
Science, 205
Moona, 33
Mooring Seafood Kitchen
and Bar, The, 140
Moose Mainea, 385
Morning Glory Café, 169
Morning Glory Farm, 113
Morrisville, VT, 311
Motorcycle Week, 386
Mountain Creamery, 208
Mount Auburn
Cemetery, 30
Mount Desert Island Ice
Cream, 350
Mount Equinox Skyline
Drive, 344
Mount Greylock, 335
Mount, The, 369
Mount Washington, 358
Mount Washington Auto
Road, 358
Mount Washington Cog
Railway, 359, 365, 383
Mount Washington State
Park, 359
Mount Washington
Valley Chamber of
Commerce, 355
Mr. Bartley's Burger, 33
M/S Mount Washington
Cruises, 228
Muddy Moose, 357
Munroe Tavern, 39, 270
Murray's Toggery
Shop, 119

Museum of African
American History, 13
Museum of Art, Rhode
Island School of
Design, 127, 275
Museum of Fine Arts,
13, 267
Museum of Russian Icons,
The, 76
Museum of Science,
14, 379
Museums of Old York, 247
Mystic and Shoreline
Information
Center, 170
Mystic Aquarium & Institute
for Exploration, 170
Mystic, CT, 170
Mystic Pizza, 172
Mystic Seaport, 171

N

Nahcotta, 219
Naked Oyster, 82
Nantucket Bookworks, 120
Nantucket Culinary
Center, 120
Nantucket Daffodil
Festival, 385
Nantucket Film
Festival, 386
Nantucket Inn, 121
Nantucket Looms, 120
Nantucket, MA, 116
Nantucket Stroll
Weekend, 391
Nantucket Visitors Center
and Information
Bureau, 116
Nantucket Wine
Festival, 385

Napi's, 108
Nashoba Valley
    Winery, 299
National Hotel, 147
Natural Bridge State
    Park, 334
Naumkeag, 372
Naumkeag Ordinary, 280
Nauset Beach, 88
Nauset Beach, MA, 318
Nauset Light, 103, 318
Nauset Light Beach,
    103, 318
Neillio's Gourmet
    Kitchen, 40
Neptune Oyster, 22, 295
Nesting, 43
New Bedford, MA, 68
New Bedford Visitor
    Information Center, 68
New Bedford Whaling
    Museum, 68
New Bedford Whaling
    National Park, 69
Newbury Comics, 17
Newbury Street, 17
New England Aquarium,
    15, 379
New England Aquarium
    Whale Watch
    Excursions, 15, 379
New England Culinary
    Institute on Main, 198
New England Holocaust
    Memorial, 15
New England Quilt
    Museum, 46
New Hampshire Boat
    Museum, 224
New Hampshire Pumpkin
    Festival, 390

New Hampshire Scottish
    Games, 389
New Haven, CT, 151
New Haven Green, 152
New Haven Hotel, 157
New Marlborough,
    MA, 300
Newport Beach Hotel and
    Suites, The, 141
Newport Folk Festival, 388
Newport International Polo
    Series, 142
Newport Jazz Festival, 389
Newport mansions, 136
Newport, RI, 134, 276, 327
Newport Visitor Information
    Center, 134
Newport Winter
    Festival, 384
New Preston, CT, 307
New Rivers, 288
New York City, 154
Nickerson State Park, 86
Nicks on Broadway, 131
Nobnocket Inn, 115
Nobska Light, 98, 317
Nor'East Beer Garden, 109
Norman Rockwell
    Museum, 373
North, 132
North Adams, MA, 333
North Conway, NH, 354
North Dartmouth, MA, 302
North End Feasts and
    Processions, 386
North Lighthouse, 145
North Market, 19
Northshire Bookstore, 344
Norwich Inn, 205
Norwich, VT, 203
Novare Res, 314

Nudel, 371

O

Oar, The, 146
Ocean's Edge, 87
Offshore Ale Company, 114
Ogunquit Beach, 244
Ogunquit Chamber of
    Commerce Visitor
    Center, 244
Ogunquit, ME, 244
Ogunquit Museum of
    American Art, 245
Ogunquit Playhouse, 245
Old Corner Bookstore, 10
Olde Mistick Village, 171
Old Inn on the Green, 300
Old Lyme, CT, 169
Old Manse, The, 42
Old North Church, 11
Old Silver Beach, 99
Old South Meeting
    House, 10
Old State House, 10, 161
Old Sturbridge Village, 75
Old Sturbridge Village Inn &
    Reeder Lodges, 76
Old Tavern at Grafton, 341
Oleana, 33
Omni Mount Washington
    Resort, 360
Omni New Haven Hotel at
    Yale, 157
Omni Parker House, 25
Once Upon a Table, 373
Orange Peel Bakery, 113
Oran Mor, 121
Orchard House, 42
Orchards Hotel, 376
Orleans, MA, 88
Orleans Waterfront Inn, 90

Orvis Company Store, 344
Osteria La Civetta, 100
Other Woman Tavern, 345
Otto Pizza, 236
Out of Town News, 29

P

Pain D'Avignon, 82
Pantry & Hearth, 177
Parker River National
    Wildlife Refuge, 61
parking, 19
Park Loop Road, 352
Parkside, 132
Park Street Church, 9
Patrick J. Mogan Cultural
    Center, 46
Patriots' Day Events, 385
Paul Revere House, 11
Pawtucket Red Sox, 133
PB Boulangerie &
    Bistro, 105
Peabody Essex Museum,
    51, 279
Penny Cluse Cafe, 187
Peqout Hotel, 115
Perfect Wife
    Restaurant, 345
Pemaquid Point
    Lighthouse, 323
Perro Salado, 140
Persephone's Kitchen, 146
Peter Havens, 339
Picco, 22
Pickwick's Mercantile, 219
Pier 6, 22
Pilgrim Monument, 107
Pilgrim Sands on Long
    Beach, 68
Pirate's Cove, 382
Pittsfield, MA, 374

Pizzeria Brick, 70
Plate, 201
Pleasant Street Tea
    Company, 56
Plimoth Plantation, 65
Plymouth, MA, 65
Plymouth Rock, 66
Plymouth to Provincetown
    Express Ferry, 106
Plymouth Visitor
    Information Center, 65
Poland Spring, ME, 258
Poland Spring Preservation
    Park, 260
Poland Spring Resort, 260
Polly's Pancakes, 362
Pomegranate Inn, 237
Pomir Grill, 74
Popham Beach State
    Park, 253
Popovers on the
    Square, 220
Porches Inn, 336
Portland Architectural
    Salvage, 235
Portland Convention and
    Visitors Bureau, 234
Portland Harbor Hotel, 237
Portland Head Light,
    234, 321
Portland, ME, 233, 313
Portland Museum of
    Art, 235
Portland Regency
    Hotel, 237
Portsmouth Chamber of
    Commerce, 218
Portsmouth Harbor
    Cruises, 218
Portsmouth Market Square
    Day, 386

Portsmouth, NH, 216, 282
Portsmouth, RI, 305
Primo, 255
Prince & the Pauper, 208
Providence Athenaeum
    Library, 128
Providence Biltmore Hotel,
    The, 133
Providence Children's
    Museum, The, 128
Providence Place, 129
Providence Preservation
    Society, 274
Providence, RI, 125,
    274, 286
Providence Warwick
    Convention &
    Visitors Bureau
    Visitor Information
    Center, 126
Provincetown Carnival
    Week, 389
Provincetown Chamber
    of Commerce Visitor
    Center, 107
Provincetown cruises, 106
Provincetown Hotel at
    Gabriel's, 109
Provincetown, MA,
    105, 319
Provincetown
    Museum, 107
Prudential Center
    Skywalk, 15
Prudential Center, The
    Shops at the, 18
P-town Pedicabs, 107
Public Eat + Drink, 335
Public Garden, The,
    16, 380
Punjabi Dhaba, 33

Puritan & Company, 31

Q

Quarry, The, 64
Quechee Gorge State
    Park, 206
Quechee, VT, 206
Queen's River Kayak, 287
Quincy, MA, 62, 273
Quincy Market
    Colonnade, 19

R

Race Point Beach, 107
Race Point Light, 319
Rachel Carson National
    Wildlife Refuge, 243
Radisson Hotel
    Manchester, 215
Rami's, 22
Red Arrow Diner, 214
Red Jacket Mountain
    View, 357
Red Lion Inn, 373
Red's Eats, 297
Red's Sandwich Shop, 280
Redwood Library &
    Athenaeum, 138, 277
Reluctant Panther Inn, 346
Renaissance
    Providence, 133
Republic Cafe, 215
Resails, 139
Residence Inn Hartford-
    Downtown, 163
Revolution Kitchen, 187
Rhode Island School of
    Design Bookstore, 129
Rhode Island State House,
    The, 126

Richardson's Candy
    Kitchen, 331
Richmond, MA, 301
RISD Works, 129
Riverrun Bookstore, 219
Robert Frost Interpretive
    Trail, 193
Robert's Main Grill, 249
Rock Art Brewery, 311
Rockfish, 115
Rockland Breakwater
    Light, 324
Rockland, ME, 254, 323
Rockport Chamber Music
    Festival, 387
Rocky Neck Art Colony,
    The, 55
Rodman's Hollow, 145
Roger Williams Park, 128
Roost Cafe & Bistro, 245
Rosemary & Thyme, 140
Royal Sonesta, 380
Running Brook Vineyard
    and Winery, 302
Russell House Tavern, 34
Rye Tavern, 67

S

Sabbathday Lake Shaker
    Village & Musuem, 260
Saco Canoe Rentals, 355
Salem, MA, 49, 278
Salem Maritime National
    Historic Site, 279
Salem Regional Visitor
    Center, 279
Salem Waterfront Hotel &
    Suites, 53
Salem witch trials, 52
Salem Witch Trials
    Memorial, 52, 280

Salt House Inn, 109
Salt Kitchen + Rum Bar, 60
Salt Pond Visitor Center,
    Cape Cod National
    Seashore, 103, 381
Salute, 162
Samoset Resort, 256
Sand Beach, 352
Sandwich Glass
    Museum, 97
Sandwich, MA, 95
Santa's Village, 383
Schartner Farms, 287
School House Ice
    Cream, 382
Schooner *Argia*, 171
Scottish Rite Masonic
    Musuem &
    Library, 270
Sea Breeze Inn, 147
Sea Coast Inn, 83
Sea Lion Motel &
    Cottages, 58
Sea Mist Thimble Islands
    Cruise, 152
Sea Music Festival, 387
Seashore Trolley
    Museum, 240
Sebago Lake, ME, 262
Sebago Lakes Region
    Chamber of
    Commerce, 262
Sebago Lake State
    Park, 262
Sebasco Harbor
    Resort, 254
Serenella, 17
Settler's Green Outlet
    Village, 356
Seven Stars, 132

Seven Suns Coffee & Tea, 224

Shakespeare & Company, 369

Shelburne Falls, MA, 332

Shelburne Falls Village Information Center, 332

Shelburne Farms, 190, 292

Shelburne Museum, 192

Shelburne Trolley Museum, 333

Shelburne Vineyard, 292

Shelburne, VT, 190

Shipwreck and Cargo, 235

Shipyard Brewery, 313

Shops at the Prudential Center, The, 18

Shops at Yale, The, 155

Short & Main, 57

Shreve, Crump & Low, 18

Sieur de Monts Spring, 352

Simmons Homestead Inn, 83

Simon Pearce, 18, 206

Simply Khmer, 48

Singing Beach, 53

1640 Hart House, 60

Skaket Beach, 88

Skappo Italian Wine Bar, 156

Skinny Pancake, 199

Slate Stationer, 31

Sleepy Hollow Cemetery, 42

Slice of Life Cafe, 115

Sofra, 290

Sole Proprietor, 74

Something Natural, 121

Songo River Queen II, 262

South Bridge Boathouse, 42

Southern Vermont Art Center, 344

South Hampton, NH, 299

South Market, 19

Spanky's Clam Shack, 82

Spectacle Island Clambake, 295

Spirit of Ethan Allen III Lake Champlain Cruises, 186

Squam Lakes Natural Science Center, 227

Stage Neck Inn, 249

State Capitol (CT), 161

Steamboat Inn, 172

Steamship Authority, 116

Steamship Authority ferry, Woods Hole–Vineyard Haven, 110

Stephanie's on Newbury, 22

Stephen Hopkins House, 275

Stir, 289

Stockbridge Information Booth, 372

Stockbridge, MA, 372

Stoddard's, 22

Stone House, 304

Stonewall Kitchen, 247

Storm Cafe, 194

Story Land, 355, 383

Stowe Area Association, 200

Stoweflake Hot Air Balloon Festival, 388

Stowe Mountain Resort, 200

Stowe Recreation Path, 200

Stowe, VT, 199, 328

Stowe Winter Carnival, 384

St. Patrick's Day Parade, 384

Strawbery Banke Museum, 218, 283

Study at Yale, 157

Sturbridge, MA, 75

Sturbridge Village, 326

Sugar Hill Inn, 362

Sugar Magnolias, 57

Sundae School, 90

Sunday River, 261

Sunset Meadows, 308

Surfside Beach, 118

Surfside Smokehouse, 67

Swan Boats, 380

Sweet Lady Jane, 186

Switchback Brewing Co., 311

T

Taj, The, 25

Tanglewood, 369

Tanglewood Music Festival, 387

Tapping Reeve House, 179

Tatte, 34

Thames Glassblowing Studio & Gallery, 139

Thomas E. Lannon, The, 55

Thos. Moser Cabinetmakers, 252

Three Chimneys Inn, 283

Three Penny Taproom, 199

Three Sisters Lighthouses, 318

Thunder Hole, 352

Top of the Hill Grill, 339
Top of the Hub, 23
Topsfield Fair, 389
Toscanini's, 34
Touro Synagogue,
    138, 277
Tower Hill Botanical
    Garden, 75
Town Docks, 226
Townshend, The, 64
Trapp Family Lodge,
    202, 329
Trapp Family Lodge Cross
    Country Center, 329
Trattoria Delia, 188
Trattoria La Festa, 201
Trinity Church, 16
Trumbull Kitchen, 162
Truro, MA, 319
Tunnel City Coffee, 376
Turner's Seafood, 280
Two Fat Cats Bakery, 236

U
U-Burger, 23
Umiak Outdoor
    Outfitters, 201
Uni, 290
Union Oyster House, 23
USS *Albacore*, 218
USS *Constitution*, 12
UVM Morgan Horse
    Farm, 193

V
Vaillancourt Folk Art
    Studios, 77
Venda Ravioli, 130
Veranda House, 122
Vermont Artisan
    Designs, 338

Vermont Canoe Touring
    Center, 338
Vermont Cheesemakers
    Festival, 388
Vermont Country
    Store, 342
Vermont Maple
    Festival, 385
Vermont Museum, 198
Vermont Ski Museum, 200
Vermont Soap, 192
Vermont State House, 198
Vermont Teddy Bear
    Company, 192
Vermont Wildflower
    Farm, 194
Via Lago, 40
Victoria Mansion, 235
Viking Fleet, 143
Vineyard Vines, 344

W
Wadsworth Atheneum of
    Art, 162
Walden Pond, 42
Warren Tavern, 268
Waterbury, VT, 195
WaterFire, 129, 386
Waterplace Park and
    Riverwalk, 128
Wauwinet, The, 122
Wayside Inn, 271
Weather Discovery
    Center, 356
Webb-Deane-Stevens
    Museum, 161
Weekend, 89
Weirs Beach, NH, 227
Wellfleet Bay Wildlife
    Sanctuary, 104

Wellfleet Drive-In Theater,
    105, 382
Wellfleet, MA, 104
Wellfleet Oyster
    Festival, 390
Wells Beach, 243
Wells Chamber of
    Commerce, 243
Wells, ME, 243
Wendle's Deli, 362
Wentworth by the Sea, 221
Wentworth-Gardner
    House, 283
Wesleyan Grove National
    Historic District, 112
West Concord Five &
    Ten, 43
West India Goods
    Store, 52
Weston Playhouse, 341
Weston, VT, 341
Westport, MA, 303
Westport Rivers
    Winery, 303
West Street Grill, 179
Whaler's Inn, 173
What the Fluff Festival, 389
Whistler House Museum of
    Art, 46
White Flower Farm, 179
White Horse Tavern, 277
White Mountains, 364, 382
Wild Meadow Canoes &
    Kayaks, 225
Willard Street Inn, 189
Williams College Museum
    of Art, 375
Williamstown, MA, 375
Williamstown Theater
    Festival, 375

Windjammer Cruises,
The, 256
Windsor, VT, 309
Wingaersheek Beach, 55
Winnetu, 115
Winnipesaukee Scenic
Railroad, 229
Wolfeboro Chamber of
Commerce Information
Center, 224
Wolfeboro Inn, 225
Wolfeboro, NH, 222
Wolfetrap Grill and Raw
Bar, 225
Wolf Hollow, 59
Woodbury Antiques
Dealers
Association, 177
Woodbury, CT, 175
Woodbury Pewter, 177
Woods Hill Table, 44
Woods Hole Film
Festival, 389
Wood's Hole Science
Aquarium, 99

Woodstock Farmers'
Market, 208
Woodstock Inn &
Resort, 209
Woodstock, VT, 207
Woodstock Welcome
Center, 207
Woody's, 162
Worcester Art Museum,
The, 73
Worcester Historical
Museum, 73
Worcester, MA, 71
World's Only Curious
George Store, 31
Worthy Kitchen, 208
Wright Museum, 224

Y

Yale Center for British
Art, 153
Yale-Harvard Regatta, 387
Yale Peabody Museum of
Natural History, 152
Yale Repertory
Theater, 153

Yale University, 153
Yale University Art
Gallery, 154
Yankee Candle Village, 331
Yankee Ingenuity, 91
Yankee Inn, 371
Yarmouth, 93
Yarmouth Clam
Festival, 388
Ye Olde Pepper Candy
Companie, 280
York, ME, 320
York's beaches, 247
Yorks, ME, The, 246
York's Wild Kingdom, 247
Yves Delorme, 344

Z

Zeb's General Store, 356
Zinc, 157